Public Intellectuals in South Africa

Public Intellectuals in South Africa

Critical Voices from the Past

Edited by
Chris Broodryk

WITS UNIVERSITY PRESS

Published in South Africa by:
Wits University Press
1 Jan Smuts Avenue
Johannesburg 2001

www.witspress.co.za

Compilation © Chris Broodryk 2021
Chapters © Individual contributors 2021
Published edition © Wits University Press 2021

First published 2021

http://dx.doi.org.10.18772/22021076895

978-1-77614-689-5 (Paperback)
978-1-77614-690-1 (Hardback)
978-1-77614-691-8 (Web PDF)
978-1-77614-692-5 (EPUB)

All rights reserved. No part of this publication may be reproduced, stored in a retrieval system, or transmitted in any form or by any means, electronic, mechanical, photocopying, recording or otherwise, without the written permission of the publisher, except in accordance with the provisions of the Copyright Act, Act 98 of 1978.

Project manager: Alison Lockhart
Copyeditor: Alison Lockhart
Proofreader: Sally Hines
Indexer: Sanet le Roux
Cover design: Hybrid Creative
Typeset in 10 point Minion Pro

CONTENTS

ACKNOWLEDGEMENTS		vii
INTRODUCTION	The Prismatic Nature of Public Intellectualism — *Chris Broodryk*	1
CHAPTER 1	Recalibrating the Deep History of Intellectual Thought in the KwaZulu-Natal Region — *Carolyn Hamilton*	21
CHAPTER 2	Elijah Makiwane and Early Black South African Public Intellectualism — *Luvuyo Mthimkhulu Dondolo*	44
CHAPTER 3	Black Art Criticism in *The Bantu World* during the 1930s — *Pfunzo Sidogi*	68
CHAPTER 4	In Conversation with the Nation: *Sowetan*'s Maverick Editor Aggrey Klaaste — *Lesley Cowling*	86
CHAPTER 5	William Pretorius and the Public Intellectualism of the Film Critic — *Chris Broodryk*	108
CHAPTER 6	Cultural Policy and the Arts: Mewa Ramgobin and Public Dialogue — *Keyan G. Tomaselli*	129
CHAPTER 7	'*Kaalgat* Critique': The Public Intellectualism of Koos Roets as Afrikaans Satirist — *Anna-Marié Jansen van Vuuren*	158
CHAPTER 8	The Public Intellectualism of Artivist Mandisi Sindo — *Katlego Chale*	179
CHAPTER 9	The Janus-Faced Public Intellectual: Dr Thomas Duncan Greenlees at the Institute for Imbecile Children, 1895–1907 — *Rory du Plessis*	200
CONTRIBUTORS		223
INDEX		227

ACKNOWLEDGEMENTS

This edited volume was funded with assistance from the Andrew W. Mellon Foundation's grant for 'The Public Intellectual in Times of Wicked Problems', a research project hosted by the office of the Dean in the Faculty of Humanities, University of Pretoria.

I would like to thank the following individuals: Professor Vasu Reddy, Dean of Humanities, and Professor Maxi Schoeman, University of Pretoria, for supporting this volume; Heather Thuynsma, Communications Manager, Faculty of Humanities, University of Pretoria, for her skilful logistical support; Bianka Thom, University of Pretoria, for her editorial support; Roshan Cader, Wits University Press, for her guidance, support and patience throughout the development of the volume and the publication process; and the anonymous peer reviewers for their valuable feedback and insights.

The Archive & Public Culture Research Initiative (http://www.apc.uct.ac.za/), University of Cape Town, hosted a colloquium titled 'Public Life: Past, Present and Future' on 7 August 2020, during which this publication and its contributors were put into conversation with the edited volume *Babel Unbound: Rage, Reason and Rethinking Public Life* (Wits University Press, 2020). This colloquium helped to streamline and crystallise several ideas in selected contributions in this book. I would like to thank the colloquium organisers Carolyn Hamilton and Lesley Cowling for their generosity.

Chapter Five, 'William Pretorius and the Public Intellectualism of the Film Critic', was partly developed through funding from the University of Pretoria's Research and Development Programme.

Chris Broodryk
Pretoria
2021

Introduction: The Prismatic Nature of Public Intellectualism

Chris Broodryk

Public Intellectuals in South Africa: Critical Voices from the Past is aimed at scholars and researchers whose academic interests and activities link with the ideas and practices of public intellectualism. The book is intended to engage with those whose work in academia is politically committed, whose research on and in the various aspects of the humanities in South Africa is dedicated to speaking truth to power, and who help to give voice and presence to those figures who have been (and possibly remain) marginalised and even silenced in South African history.

This volume ranges in scope from public intellectualism in journalism to the idea of the public intellectual in mental health, to the ways in which the practice of art and the critical response to it are in themselves acts of public intellectualism. The aim of the volume is to provide incisive and insightful discussion and analysis of instances and practices of public intellectualism.

The ideas and arguments in this volume provide original research on key movements and figures in different histories of public intellectualism in South Africa. Each chapter offers a particular inflection on and demonstration of the public intellectual and their activities in South Africa as located in acts of journalism, storytelling, the arts and the larger context of the humanities. Taking the different historical contexts into account, the historical figures discussed in each chapter can be considered politically progressive.

For the most part, this volume follows the historical approach of Mcebisi Ndletyana's *African Intellectuals in 19th and Early 20th Century South Africa*, which highlights how 'material collected from oral tradition or orature tends be to complex'.[1] Equally complex, of course, was how African intellectuals straddled African and Western worlds. In Ndletyana's account, 'early African intellectuals were a product of the missionary enterprise and the British civilising mission'.[2] One of Ndletyana's contributions to his edited volume focuses on Tiyo Soga (1829–1871), whose ideas were influential in both Black Consciousness and black theology.[3] Soga is also referenced in Chapter Two of this volume by Luvuyo Mthimkhulu Dondolo.

Njabulo S. Ndebele wrote in the foreword to Megan Jones and Jacob Dlamini's *Categories of Persons: Rethinking Ourselves and Others*: 'The space of expanding and interacting identities might just be the space for a future politics, one founded on and comfortable with the creative uncertainties of the interaction of multiple identities. The more varied the interactions, the more robust will be the politics founded on them.'[4] It is our hope that this volume will inform constructive conversations around these identities and the 'robust politics' that follow from these discursive engagements.

SPEAKING OF DEMOCRACY: PUBLIC INTELLECTUALISM AS AN INTERPRETIVE PRISM AND ACTIVIST PRINCIPLE

In her book on South African writer J.M. Coetzee, Jane Poyner lists the influence of Greek thinkers (Aristotle, Socrates), as well as later thinkers outside the Western tradition (Edward Said, Arundhati Roy, Wole Soyinka) on the idea of (public) intellectualism. In South Africa, the acts of writing and of intellectualism 'under the conditions of colonialism and then apartheid ... have been profoundly politicized' to the extent that speaking out against those in power might have led to punishment and prohibition.[5] Increasingly, the idea of the public intellectual has come to identify an individual who verbally or in writing speaks out against oppression, censorship and other mechanisms that serve to silence marginalised groups and individuals. These intellectuals take upon themselves an investment in democracy, where democracy is seen as a politically productive counter-position to authoritarianism and totalitarianism (consider, for instance, Pankaj Mishra's book *The Age of Anger: A History of the Present* and its critique of India's Modi regime).[6] As A.C. Grayling reminds us, 'subverted democracy ... is no democracy', where 'government is operated in the interests of only one part of the populace'.[7]

In this current volume, the idea of the public intellectual is used as an interpretive prism for specific individuals, their public and the parameters of their context, and also of selected written and visual texts. In some contexts, though, the idea of the public intellectual is also meant to evoke an activist principle in which the political commitment of the intellectual is emphasised.

DEFINING PUBLIC INTELLECTUALISM

Poyner argues: 'The intellectual, as Coetzee suggests, in supporting his or her own position with reasoned and rationed argument, is ready to accept the reasoned and rationed criticism of fellow intellectuals (and others), indeed, sees this as his or her social function: to criticize and be criticized while, importantly, imparting expertise or knowledge with the purpose of effecting change.'[8]

In defining and discussing the notion of public intellectualism, the ur-text is Edward Said's renowned *Representations of the Intellectual*.[9] For Said, individuals such as James Baldwin informed his own work; Said found himself gripped by 'a spirit of opposition' activated in resistance to the political oppression of marginalised and minority groups.[10] Evoking Michel Foucault, Said maintains that the labour of the intellectual involves 'a sense of the dramatic and the insurgent', often linked to 'reviving forgotten (or abandoned) histories' and making 'connections that were denied, to cite alternative courses for action.'[11] 'Each intellectual,' explains Said, following American sociologist Alvin Gouldner, 'the book editor and the author, the military strategist and the international lawyer, speaks and deals in a language that has become specialized and usable by other members of the same field, specialized experts addressing other specialized experts in a *lingua franca* largely unintelligible to unspecialized people.'[12] Said insists that the intellectual has a specific public role not determined by their class: 'The intellectual is an individual endowed with a faculty for representing, embodying, articulating a message, a view, an attitude, philosophy or opinion to, as well as for, a public.'[13] This role is linked with a specific representational medium, such as writing, teaching or radio appearances.[14] Indeed, every intellectual 'has an audience and a constituency'.[15]

Taking our cue from Said, in this book we ask: what are 'the image, the signature, the actual intervention and performance' of specific intellectuals?[16] The intellectual pursues justice and fairness, and must find a way to have the concepts crystallise from the abstract to the context-specific application, 'actual situations where the gap between the profession of equality and justice, on the one hand, and the rather less edifying reality, on the other, is very great.'[17] This intellectual 'stands between loneliness and alignment' and must choose to position themselves with either the powerful or the 'the forgotten and ignored.'[18] The problem of loyalty is a perpetual presence in the intellectual's labour.[19] Some Afrikaans-speaking South Africans positioned themselves as the victims of brutal British colonialism, only to set up their own oppressive policies, enforced through the violence of apartheid.[20] During periods of crisis, it often happens that intellectuals 'fall into modes of vindication and righteousness that blind them to the evil done in the name of their own ethnic or national community'.[21] The intellectual faces the additional challenge of negotiating 'the impingements of modern professionalization' by embracing and encouraging amateurism, 'an activity fuelled by care and affection rather than by profit and selfish, narrow specialization'.[22] To be an amateur is to be 'a dabbler, a devotee caught in an awkward spot between the generative passion of creation … and the casual promiscuity of the consumer'.[23]

For Thomas Sowell, an intellectual is an individual who occupies 'an *occupational* category' and who deal primarily with ideas ('the dealer in ideas'), such as academics and writers.[24] Sometimes, intellectuals themselves are not positioned as public intellectuals, but the impact of their work might be far-ranging in stimulating other writers, creators and thinkers to use specific platforms to convey certain ideas to the general public.[25] As the chapters in this volume demonstrate, the public intellectual disseminates their ideas to the general public, that is, beyond their own professional networks of peers. Sowell's concern is that such an engagement between the intellectual and their public might lack intellectual rigour.[26]

Experts are clear examples 'of people whose knowledge is concentrated within a narrow band out of the vast spectrum of human concerns'.[27] Unlike the expert who is known for and consulted within a limited area of specialisation, the amateur may be more politically productive. Andy Merrifield contends that the contemporary cult of professionalism can be, as Said suggested, 'countered by courageous intellectual *amateurism*'.[28] This amateurism is characterised by 'a readiness to withstand comfortable and lucrative conformity', thereby upholding 'a vision of reality that's more expansive and eclectic, that isn't hampered by the conservatism of narrow expertise, preoccupied as that is with defending one's scholarly turf'.[29]

Said's intellectual must be politically active and they cannot turn away from the moment principled thought becomes principled action and, in so doing, remain in 'the responsible mainstream'.[30] Such passivity undermines the intellectual's drive to 'actively represent the truth to the best of [their] ability'.[31] It is in the spirit of locating the truth, as it were, that literary critic Michiko Kakutani, Pulitzer-Prize-winning former chief books editor of the *New York Times*, used her voice to articulate an incisive critique of the rise of Donald Trump against the backdrop of Russian election meddling and the alt-right. Kakutani reminds the reader that 'the migration of postmodern ideas from academic to the political mainstream is a reminder of how the culture wars – as the vociferous debates over race, religion, gender, and school curricula were called during the 1980s and 1990s – have mutated in unexpected ways'.[32] These culture wars returned with a vengeance to divide and bring into (often violent) conflict those Americans who considered themselves politically progressive and those who were conservative.[33] While much of this newly radical political division was attributed to fake news, the presence of fake news itself had 'helped drum up public support for the Spanish-American War, and Julius Caesar spun his conquest of Gaul as a preventive action'.[34] In her book, Kakutani demonstrates public intellectualism as speaking truth to power, challenging the narratives that hold the American president in position. In her own way, then, Kakutani demonstrates the positive capacities of Merrifield's amateur: she is not a professional or expert political analyst, yet she is highly articulate in communicating her insights, concerns and recommendations to her readership. She is a 'public intellectual' – that is, an individual of some intellectual pedigree who critically reflects on issues of the day.[35]

In the introduction to her book *General Intellects: Twenty-One Thinkers for the Twenty-First Century*, McKenzie Wark asks: 'Where are the *public intellectuals* like we used to have back in the good old days? Whenever one talks about the figure of the public intellectual, one is supposed to be talking about their decline.'[36] Wark prefers general intellects to public intellectuals. In addressing the perception of the decline of the public intellectual, she suggests that the often obfuscatory vocabulary of intellectuals – when it is not just a soundbite delivered by an expert – is at least partially invalid.[37] By general intellects, Wark refers to 'people who are mostly employed as academics, and mostly pretty successful at that, but who try through their work to address more general problems about the state of the world today'. Wark differentiates between two meanings of general intellects: firstly, these individuals think, speak and write in work that is commodified; secondly, these same individuals explore ways to resist this very commodification. 'They try to address a general *situation*, one that many people find themselves in today' and they attempt this intervention 'intelligently, by applying their training and competence and originality'.[38]

In the chapters that follow, the various authors address how the public intellectuals they have identified for study were trained, what their competences are and were as intellectuals or as artists, creators and political commentators and activists, and how the voices of these individuals remain original. These public intellectuals are located in the broad interlinked domains of journalism, the arts and humanities.

SOME KINDS OF PUBLIC INTELLECTUALISM IN SOUTH AFRICA

Public intellectualism can also bring local and international concerns into conversation with one another. Cape-Town-based academic Adam Haupt, for instance, addresses the extreme polarisation between the political right and left in an opinion piece comparing Economic Freedom Fighters (EFF) leader Julius Malema to United States President Trump. Criticising both political leaders for their negative attitudes to the media and journalists in particular and foregrounding Malema's politically regressive myopia, Haupt writes that these leaders 'invoke racist binaries that make true dialogue about decolonisation difficult'; for Malema, specifically, 'any critical voice is automatically the white racist enemy'.[39]

Years before newspapers ran headlines about Malema or Trump, the public intellectual Ruth Schechter was profoundly influenced by Olive Schreiner, an 'admirer of Lenin and the Russian Revolution of 1917'.[40] Schechter's presence would become 'central to the intellectual life of Cape Town', where her and her husband Benjamin's ideas 'shone out in this conservative (white-controlled) society'.[41] Schechter's article 'The Colour Line in South Africa' was published in *The Nation* in 1928. In this piece of writing she criticised the ways in which white South Africans exploited and restricted other populations' political and economic participation in their own country.[42]

Criticism of how those in the corridors and conference rooms of power in various ways exploited those individuals outside of these spaces and processes would continue to feature in more recent auto-intellectual writing. Sisonke Msimang's autobiographical account *Always Another Country: A Memoir of Exile and Home* constitutes another kind of public intellectualism. Here, the author explores her Africanness while challenging the South African, African National Congress (ANC) government. Msimang's work positions the individual – and her own considerable individual agency – as inseparable from larger political events and their aftermaths. She describes herself as 'an African feminist, a meddlesome social justice type', adding that she writes 'for the sisterhood', as the South African media needs more women's voices.[43] Significantly, Msimang says she writes 'because Africans and women and humans who have been considered less than others have always had stories and imaginations to come take us out of the impossibility of the situations in which we have found ourselves stranded'.[44] She says she also writes because South Africa was liberated, but is not free: 'What else can I do but write when I know life is not just breath, but it is also voice?'[45]

Many dissident voices in South Africa's histories were silenced as they articulated a response to the apartheid government's discriminatory policies. One such historical figure was Stephen Bantu Biko (1946–1977), whose book *I Write What I Like* became a major foundational work about the South African Black Consciousness movement of the 1970s.[46] Biko addressed black South Africans at political rallies and raised his concerns about apartheid with international politicians. He was an organic intellectual in the Gramscian sense and an intellectual in the way Ngũgĩ wa

Thiong'o broadly conceives of the intellectual as an individual who uses ideas and language to inform and educate.[47] Biko's philosophical trajectories are the subject of Mabogo Percy More's book *Biko: Philosophy, Identity and Liberation*. More notes that Biko's '"true humanity" symbolised the synthetical moment of the dialectical progression towards antiracism'.[48]

Many South African public intellectuals such as Biko have a set of tangible, collective concerns at the heart of their political activism. These intellectuals have played an important historical role in shaping the ANC. Solomon Plaatje (1876–1932), whom Peter Rule identifies as a 'public educator',[49] is the subject of Brian Willan's 2018 monograph *Sol Plaatje: A Life of Solomon Tshekisho Plaatje, 1876–1932*.[50] A journalist, translator, writer and teacher, Plaatje's life was 'driven by his response to change' and he was present during significant historical events in South Africa.[51] He adapted Shakespeare in Setswana and his adaptation of *Julius Caesar* constituted 'a wholly different conception of the nature and purpose of translation'.[52] Plaatje's full-length novel *Mhudi* was the first book 'to have been written by a black South African' and the only English-language novel Plaatje had published.[53] In *Mhudi*, Plaatje addresses the notion that tribal savagery ruled Barolong society until the civilising force of colonialism reigned it in; or what Willan calls 'the familiar trope of the conventional imperial romance'.[54] A similar demythologisation informs Carolyn Hamilton's chapter on oral intellectual practice and tradition in the early KwaZulu-Natal region (Chapter One), Dondolo's comments on Christian missionary education in South Africa (Chapter Two) and Pfunzo Sidogi's introductory survey of public intellectualism in arts criticism in *The Bantu World* (Chapter Three).

Two other public intellectuals who need to be mentioned here for their political commitment, and also because they exemplify public intellectuals who have remained somewhat under-recognised and hidden from contemporary public view, are Harry Gwala and Benjamin Kies. Harry (Mphephethwa) Themba Gwala (1920–1995) was a teacher and trade unionist, 'a member of both the national executive of the ANC and the central committee of the South African Communist Party' and was appointed 'chairman of the ANC's Midlands region' in the early 1990s, where he was known as 'Munt'omdala or The Lion of the Midlands'.[55] He served prison time on Robben Island, 'which was often referred to as "our university"', where he 'became known for his Marxist-Leninist teachings, particularly among the youth'.[56] In an interview with Yvonne Muthien, Gwala quickly undercuts two key ideas: that there is an honorable entity that goes by the title 'KwaZulu/Natal homeland' ('they are reservoirs of cheap labour') and that apartheid has created autonomous territories ('these are bantustans in the true sense of the word').[57] Upon his death, the *New York Times* identified Gwala as 'among the most vociferous opponents of tribalism in South Africa's most violently divided province, KwaZulu/Natal'.[58]

In his University of Cape Town Summer School lecture of 16 and 17 January 2020, 'Ben Kies: His Contribution to New Social and Political Thought in South Africa', Emeritus Professor Crain Soudien celebrates Benjamin Kies (1917–1979), who played a 'founding role in the New Era Fellowship (NEF) in 1937' and played an 'instrumental role in the establishment of the Anti-Coloured Affairs Department (Anti-CAD) movement and the Non-European Unity Movement (NEUM) in the 1940s'.[59] Kies's political position was one of non-collaboration and non-racialism. In 1953 Kies delivered his pivotal lecture, 'The Contribution of the Non-European Peoples to Civilisation'. The focus of Kies's lecture, as Soudien describes it, was an 'incredible provocation against the idea of Western civilisation; he also dismissed the idea that Europe had "proprietary rights" to the idea of civilisation; that they were the originators or inheritors of it'. Here, Kies 'reveals the depth of the implication of Western civilization in the development of nineteenth-century capitalist imperialism and its foundations in ideas of race'.[60] Kies played a vital role in progressive publications, such as the Teachers League of South Africa's *Education Journal* and *The Torch*.[61] Corinne Sandwith locates Kies in a 'younger generation of petit-bourgeois intellectuals and activists schooled in the left-wing traditions of groups like the (Trotskyist) Workers' Party of South Africa and the New Era Fellowship' who were invested in the struggle for liberation. In this context, Kies was 'a gifted young intellectual who spearheaded many of the attacks on the conservative old-guard'.[62]

THE UNIVERSITY AS A SITE OF AND FOR INTELLECTUAL LABOUR

While this volume casts a predominantly historical perspective on its subjects, it is worth discussing the extent to which the contemporary university alternately impedes and facilitates intellectual labour towards public intellectualism. Part of both the value and the sustained crisis of the humanities has to do with the difficulty in determining and measuring the impact of the arts and humanities (excluding for the moment the social sciences). It is therefore not surprising that 'current debates over the value of the arts and humanities take place mostly in rhetorical, political, and economic terms, with educators and policymakers trading broadsides about the supposed value or waste that follows from engaging them'.[63] Does the utility of these interlinked domains reside in how easily an artist or academic can link their work to a flavour-of-the-year research theme (the Fourth Industrial Revolution, Wellness,

Sustainable Development Goals)? Or does the artist or academic demonstrate their usefulness by an externally awarded prize, professional recognition or an increase in citations?

It is difficult to reconcile the sustained emphasis on how academics must break free from the so-called ivory towers of academia by way of public intellectualism, for instance, with the statistics-driven, quantified nature of the contemporary university. What is the impact of an act of public intellectualism? How are citations of arts and humanities scholars' writings for the general public collated and counted towards a performance management agreement in which a line manager has some institutional guideline about the stretch targets that such public intellectualism must accomplish? As Keyan Tomaselli puts it: 'Academia ... is the only industry that deliberately encourages overproduction, irrespective of markets, outlets or consumers (readers, libraries or retailers). The research has been done, the writing completed, and the papers submitted.'[64] How do acts of public intellectualism play into this overproduction? Such is the neo-liberal model of the university's recently revitalised emphasis on entrepreneurialism, 'a figure neo-liberalism wants to extend across the board to everyone, artists included'.[65] In this context, there is very little meaningful difference between the wage-earner and the entrepreneur.[66]

One needs only to read the work of Martha Nussbaum (*Not for Profit: Why Democracy Needs the Humanities*) and Stefan Collini (*What Are Universities For?* and *Speaking of Universities*) to obtain a sense of how integral the arts and humanities are to academia.[67] At the same time, it becomes clear that the arts and humanities often are compromised within a university context, in which value is measured as receipts of third-stream income, and whether, for instance, a lecturer had met or exceeded their 'targets' in decolonising their curriculum. Behind this dynamic lies a larger question of how university faculties and the institutions themselves perceive success and are perceived by others as successful.

How, for instance, does all the above impact positively or negatively on the university's world ranking? This educational system has repercussions for the present and future practice of public intellectualism. As Merrifield describes it: 'The downgrading of purely intellectual or politically critical research is one perpetual shortcoming in a strange looping argument that suggests to improve education you need to fix targets to show improvement: but when you do this you find an education system geared to achieving targets and nothing else.'[68]

Within the systemic narrow-mindedness of many contemporary universities – and of course this is a generalisation, albeit a generalisation of a salient pattern – 'academics are pressed by their administrative masters to produce their own repertoire of unambiguous soundbites ... We find a scholar's intellectual profile whittled down to a half-dozen expertise keywords, a peculiar branding peddled by all universities and "Centres of Excellence".[69] This notion of public intellectualism is far removed from the ideal of it, since in this context, 'expertise frustrates genuine interdisciplinarity and inquisitive learning, muffles curiosity. It crushes imaginative flair, ignores the pure joy of not knowing what you're doing, of zigzagging and fumbling around a subject until you master it.' The amateur occupies a position of self-enrichment; such amateurism pursues an imagination of subversion, or a subversive imagination.[70] The public intellectual is often an amateur in the sense that Merrifield describes and operates within (and despite) the confines of professionalism.

It is of course possible to flourish under contemporary conditions as an intellectual at a university, to at least partially negate the confines of professionalism in favour of the amateur's sustained curiosity and investment in the world. In *Stopping the Spies: Constructing and Resisting the Surveillance State in South Africa*, Jane Duncan addresses a global concern – debilitating and invasive surveillance technologies – in the context of the Global South, writing that 'less principled members of the security apparatus [could] abuse the state's surveillance capabilities to advantage the ruling group in the ruling party and disadvantage their perceived detractors'.[71] She notes with concern how little public controversy the negative uses of surveillance technologies have elicited since it is possible to politicise surveillance in South Africa.[72] For Duncan, apartheid-era intelligence practices have persisted in post-apartheid democratic South Africa.[73] She raised similar concerns outside of her book in the public sphere in online publications such as *Daily Maverick* and traditional media presences such as the *Sunday Times*. Her public intellectualism is linked to her academic position at the University of Johannesburg.

CHAPTER PREVIEW

In each chapter of this book a particular kind of intellectualism is identified in the practice of an individual public intellectual, as is a specific public to whom this intellectualism (orally, textually or in performance) is directed. Each chapter provides a context in which both its 'public' and its 'intellectualism' are located. Here, the phrase 'public intellectual' often serves as a descriptor of an individual's particular potencies for promoting critical thinking and social change; it is not an indicator of any fixed positionality overdetermined by a specific professional or social role.

The first two chapters of this volume consider various latent and overt tensions in early South African black public intellectualism. These tensions, such as between oral and written traditions, or between Christian civilising missions and African traditions, came to characterise much of early public intellectualism. Reflecting on these tensions in contextualising key historical figures and processes is part of what Sidogi calls the 'opening up [of] unexplored histories' in Chapter Three. These opening chapters provide critical voices from the past, whose political concerns have been under-represented or whose political concerns have remained relevant in post-apartheid South Africa.

In Chapter One, Hamilton explores the orality of black public intellectualism in the early KwaZulu-Natal region. She details how intellectualism in this context had long preceded – and did not result from – colonialism. In providing a historical overview of the contributions made by Magema Fuze, John Dube and other figures in early black public intellectualism, Hamilton offers an important historical perspective on black public intellectualism that resonates with contemporary South African public intellectual discourse, specifically with what Bhekizizwe Peterson has termed the 'Black Humanities'. Hamilton offers the following provocation at the outset of her chapter: 'It is indeed possible to watch ideas travel across oral forms, from oral forms into written ones, and into ones with the oral and written inextricably entangled. To accomplish this, the pervasive distinction between literate, modern, hybrid and synthesising intellectuals and illiterate, authentic tribal informants relaying handed-down tradition requires robust interrogation.'

In Chapter Two, Dondolo focuses on Elijah Makiwane (1850–1928). He uses the phrase 'from the barrel of a gun to the barrel of a pen' to encapsulate Makiwane's mode of response to the tensions existing between the European colonial project and indigenous African traditions. Among other causes, Makiwane championed the use of indigenous languages in self-expression and political expression. He was 'an African clergyman and a pioneer journalist whose career spanned 40 years, between 1877 and 1917'; during this time, the ordained reverend 'instilled the African intellectual culture among African people after rejecting westernised identity and missionary perspectives'.[74] Dondolo provides an overview of Makiwane's contribution to black public intellectualism and explores Makiwane's Christian education and his activities as a journalist to demonstrate the ways in which Makiwane's politically progressive ideas were ahead of their time.

Journalism has come under fire from various men in power across the global political spectrum, from Trump's statement that journalists are the enemy of the people to EFF commander-in-chief Malema's descriptions of journalists as pawns of white monopoly capital. As Maria Ressa puts it, journalists are the proverbial canaries in the coal mine in a time of rampant disinformation and conspiracy theories; by joining forces with academic and civil society, journalists and others committed to truth telling can resist the waves of emotion-baiting fake news.[75] Before the battle against fake news amassed more and more print and digital space, it was in popular journalism that emerging and established intellectuals often pursued those interests that resonated with their communities. In Chapters Three and Four, critical voices from the past in journalism take centre stage. Foregrounding art criticism and nation-building respectively, both these chapters demonstrate the value of and need for journalism to flourish without fear of censorship or threats of harm.

In Chapter Three, Sidogi provides an expansive and nuanced critical overview of what he calls formative black public intellectualism on black art during the first half of the twentieth century. He focuses specifically on such art criticism in *The Bantu World* newspaper between 1932 and 1945. Sidogi writes that 'public intellectualism introduced here was certainly different from, but not lesser than, the professional art criticism – professional insofar as someone could have a career as an art critic – found in Europe and America at the time'. *The Bantu World*, which at one point featured the writing of black journalists such as Herbert Dhlomo, was the precursor to the newspapers *The World* and the still-in-print *Sowetan*. As Lesley Cowling demonstrates, the latter would become the print platform for Aggrey Klaaste's hopeful nation-building project.

In Chapter Four, Cowling explores the ways in which the popular newspaper journalist and editor Aggrey Klaaste (1940–2004) constructed, promoted and negotiated the idea of nation-building in the *Sowetan* in working towards and beyond the 'new' South Africa following 1994. As Cowling wrote elsewhere: '*Sowetan* launched a community-oriented programme centred on the theme of nation-building; he refocused the newspaper around this philosophy'.[76] Using selected excerpts of Klaaste's popular newspaper column, Cowling highlights the meaningful public role he played in engaging his readers in preparing for a democratic future based on black dignity and accomplishment. Arguing for a constructive nation-building project was no mean feat, as Cowling explains: 'Nation-building represented a significant shift from the radical activism of the Sowetan's newsroom, inherited from its predecessor paper, *The World*, which had aligned itself with the Black Consciousness struggles of the 1970s.'

Chapters Five and Seven link public intellectualism and film in two ways: firstly, Chris Broodryk positions film criticism as a form of public intellectualism and, secondly, Anna-Marié Jansen van Vuuren positions an Afrikaans film-maker within public intellectualism. Tomaselli's chapter about the politics of cultural policy is nestled between these film-centric chapters. His reflections on policy and television, for instance, offer a conceptual kinship to the other two chapters. These three chapters locate their publics and their intellectualisms primarily in the 1980s and 1990s.

In Chapter Five, Broodryk discusses South African film criticism as public intellectualism. He focuses on the film criticism of William Pretorius (1941–2007), whose politically inflected discussions of South African cinema and popular culture constituted an enduring voice, which opposed censorship, market-driven film-making and the political-aesthetic narrow-mindedness of most Afrikaans films of the 1980s and 1990s. Beyond his film criticism, in his writing on art and performance and in his personal reflections available online, Pretorius emerges as a politically committed critic who used his education, and print and online platforms, to promote a vision of a revitalised Afrikaans cinema.

In Chapter Six, Tomaselli traces the contribution of political activist Mewa Ramgobin (1932–2016) as part of a larger discussion about the history and post-millennium concerns and politics of South African cultural policy. Tomaselli argues for the 'need for an informed historical memory and awareness of the importance of cultural theory in political struggle and cultural policy formation', which follow 'different thematic trajectories depending on the disciplines of the respective scholars'. Charting a course through media representations of South Africa in selected television advertisements, Tomaselli suggests that 'cultural policy best practice must engage in a public critical dialogue on names, naming, monuments, artefacts and statues. These should be considered symbolic and material resources open to dis-articulation from crude meanings and re-articulated via creative dialectical engagement into new reconciliatory images and social practices.'

In Chapter Seven, Jansen van Vuuren demonstrates that Afrikaans director and cinematographer Koos Roets's feature film satires, specifically *Die Groen Faktor* (The Green Factor), constituted a public symbolic good. (In Chapter Five, William Pretorius lauds *Die Groen Faktor* as socially progressive satire, while criticising the ostensibly more progressive *Broer Matie* (My Brother My Mate)). Jansen van Vuuren critically analyses Roets's Afrikaans-language comedy feature films to make the case for his legacy as a South African film director worthy of serious consideration by demonstrating the political potency of Roets's contribution to Afrikaans cultural discourse, both during and shortly after apartheid. While he is most often acknowledged as a renowned cinematographer, Jansen van Vuuren duly positions Roets as a film director whose use of satire and 'lowbrow' gender comedy addressed issues pertinent to the political tumult of 1980s' South Africa.

Moving from visual art to performing art, Katlego Chale demonstrates in Chapter Eight that Cape Town-based theatre maker and activist Mandisi Sindo is a prominent public intellectual, whose art is located in community activism. 'As the founder and artistic director of Theatre4Change, a non-profit organisation based in Khayelitsha that provides arts activities and mentorship, Sindo is interested in finding new ways to use art and theatre to prompt positive social change', such as being artistic director of 'the only shack theatre in the history of South Africa'.[77] Chale argues that Sindo, given his activist concerns and his use of theatre to promote social aims, is best positioned as an artivist. As Chale locates Sindo's creative work within the parameters of artivism, he positions artivism as a form of public intellectualism. This chapter focuses on a contemporary subject, Sindo, whose work in theatre continues to gain acclaim. Chale sees Sindo – in many ways an exemplary amateur – as continuing the work of the public intellectual that Said outlined.

The ninth and final chapter addresses another kind of performance altogether: the performance of the public self in a mental health context. Rory du Plessis offers a thought-provoking portrait of Dr Thomas Duncan Greenlees (1858–1929) at the Grahamstown Lunatic Asylum and the Institute for Imbecile Children. Du Plessis discusses the ways in which Greenlees embodies contradiction, evident in the ways his professional (private) and public personas differed. In his public intellectualism Greenlees aimed at demystifying mental health and improving charity for the mentally ill. In his professional capacity, however, Greenlees went so far as to actively encourage the termination of children with intellectual disabilities. In focusing on Greenlees, Du Plessis offers a description of Janus-faced public intellectualism in a historical mental health context that has, to date, been under-researched and under-reported. Here, Du Plessis compels the reader to acknowledge the duality of the public intellectual and the ethics of public intellectualism, especially but not exclusively in mental health contexts. Greenlees's voice was critical of specific approaches to mental health, yet it promoted the destigmatisation of mental health only in the public sphere.

A VERY BRIEF CODA ON CONTEMPORARY SOUTH AFRICAN POLITICS

The ANC government, led by President Cyril Ramaphosa following Jacob Zuma's resignation in 2018, remains marked by the massacre at Marikana in 2012, when 34 miners were gunned down by police. Ramaphosa himself was implicated in the massacre; as non-executive chair of mining company Lonmin at the time, Ramaphosa had used strong language in email correspondence advising a response to the brewing conflict at the mine.[78]

In addition to the events at Marikana, the South African government has been criticised in some quarters for the economic toll resulting from the national state of disaster and heavy national lockdown in response to the Covid-19 pandemic. The rampant corruption and nepotism that the ANC government became vilified for persisted and even intensified during South Africa's strict national lockdown. Beyond the detrimental effects of these epochal events, South Africa remains a country ravaged by gender-based violence.

The Covid-19 pandemic of 2020 further exposed the worn nerve-endings of racial and class discrepancies that scar South Africa almost 25 years after the end of apartheid. The country's universities have become one of the primary sites where these discrepancies, here crystallised in tertiary education curricula and the idea of 'the canon', have been and continue to be contested. These contestations are sometimes collectively referred to as Fallism (see Chapter Six in this volume, in which Tomaselli addresses Fallism and its dissatisfactions). In a contribution to *Critical Arts* Ndebele grapples with decolonisation and its discontents.[79] Addressing whiteness, memory and the idea of 'being "black" in a "white" world', Ndebele asks: 'What did the "blacks" of South Africa have to become once they had been conquered?'[80] The many answers to this question are infused by notions of surrendering and servitude. Ndebele cautions: 'Those who have been victims of a single story can so easily impose the single story on others as a weapon of explaining them away, avoiding the responsibility to know them. In the public space, to free the human form from the historical distortions of race, South Africans need to continue to affirm their idealism.'[81] This volume serves the multiplicity of voices to have emerged in and through various South African publics in response to injustices and in the pursuit of sociopolitical reflection and tangible change.

NOTES

[1] Mcebisi Ndletyana, ed., *African Intellectuals in 19th and 20th Century South Africa* (Cape Town: HSRC Press, 2008), xi.
[2] Ndletyana, *African Intellectuals*, 5.
[3] Ndletyana, *African Intellectuals*, 17.
[4] Njabulo S. Ndebele, 'Foreword', in *Categories of Persons: Rethinking Ourselves and Others*, ed. Megan Jones and Jacob Dlamini (Johannesburg: Picador Africa, 2013), xii.
[5] Jane Poyner, 'Introduction', in *J.M. Coetzee and the Idea of the Public Intellectual*, ed. Jane Poyner (Athens: Ohio University Press, 2006), 8.
[6] Pankaj Mishra, *The Age of Anger: A History of the Present* (New York: Farrar, Straus and Giroux, 2017).
[7] A.C. Grayling, *Democracy and Its Crisis* (London: Oneworld Publications, 2018), 202.
[8] Poyner, 'Introduction', 2.
[9] Edward Said, *Representations of the Intellectual* (New York: Vintage Books, 1996).
[10] Said, *Representations of the Intellectual*, xvii.

11 Said, *Representations of the Intellectual*, xviii, 22.
12 Said, *Representations of the Intellectual*, 9.
13 Said, *Representations of the Intellectual*, 11.
14 Said, *Representations of the Intellectual*, 13.
15 Said, *Representations of the Intellectual*, 83.
16 Said, *Representations of the Intellectual*, 83
17 Said, *Representations of the Intellectual*, 94.
18 Said, *Representations of the Intellectual*, 22, 32–33.
19 Said, *Representations of the Intellectual*, 40–41.
20 Said, *Representations of the Intellectual*, 45.
21 Said, *Representations of the Intellectual*, 45.
22 Said, *Representations of the Intellectual*, 82.
23 A.O. Scott, *Better Living through Criticism: How to Think about Art, Pleasure, Beauty, and Truth* (London: Penguin, 2017), 149.
24 Thomas Sowell, *Intellectuals and Society* (New York: Basic Books, 2009), 2, 3.
25 Sowell, *Intellectuals and Society*, 4.
26 Sowell, *Intellectuals and Society*, 10.
27 Sowell, *Intellectuals and Society*, 22.
28 Andy Merrifield, *The Amateur: The Pleasures of Doing What You Love* (London: Verso, 2018), 15; emphasis added. Merrifield draws on Said's writing on intellectual amateurism.
29 Merrifield, *The Amateur*, 15. Interestingly, Merrifield identifies Hannah Arendt and Henri Lefebvre as amateurs (173, 184).
30 Said, *Representations of the Intellectual*, 100.
31 Said, *Representations of the Intellectual*, 121.
32 Michiko Kakutani, *The Death of Truth: Notes on Falsehood in the Age of Trump* (New York: Tim Duggan Books, 2018), 49.
33 Kakutani, *The Death of Truth*, 50–51.
34 Kakutani, *The Death of Truth*, 123.
35 Sowell, *Intellectuals and Society*, 284.
36 McKenzie Wark, *General Intellects: Twenty-One Thinkers for the Twenty-First Century* (London: Verso, 2016), 1.
37 Wark, *General Intellects*, 2.
38 Wark, *General Intellects*, 2–3.
39 Adam Haupt, 'Malema and the Like Are No Different to Trump', *Mail & Guardian*, 22 January 2019, accessed 30 January 2019, https://mg.co.za/article/2019-01-22-malema-and-the-likes-are-no-different-to-trump
40 Baruch Hirson, *The Cape Town Intellectuals: Ruth Schechter and Her Circle, 1907–1934* (Johannesburg: Wits University Press, 2001), 4.
41 Hirson, *Cape Town Intellectuals*, 5.
42 Hirson, *Cape Town Intellectuals*, 184.
43 Sisonke Msimang, *Always Another Country: A Memoir of Exile and Home* (Johannesburg: Johnathan Ball, 2018), 293.
44 Msimang, *Always Another Country*, 295.
45 Msimang, *Always Another Country*, 296.
46 Steve Biko, *I Write What I Like: A Selection of His Writings*, ed. Aelred Stubbs (Johannesburg: Picador Africa, 2017).
47 Ngũgĩ wa Thiong'o, 'For Peace, Justice, and Culture: The Intellectual in the Twenty-First Century', *Profession* (2006): 33–39.

48 Mabogo Percy More, *Biko: Philosophy, Identity and Liberation* (Cape Town: HSRC Press, 2017).
49 Peter Rule, 'Remembering Sol Plaatje as South Africa's Original Public Educator', *The Conversation*, 5 October 2016, accessed 30 August 2020, https://theconversation.com/remembering-sol-plaatje-as-south-africas-original-public-educator-65979
50 Brian Willan, *Sol Plaatje: A Life of Solomon Tshekisho Plaatje, 1876–1932* (Johannesburg: Jacana Media, 2018).
51 Willan, *Sol Plaatje*, xx–xxi.
52 Willan, *Sol Plaatje*, 515.
53 Willan, *Sol Plaatje*, 525, 543.
54 Willan *Sol Plaatje*, 529.
55 'Harry Gwala, Natal's (Other) Warlord', *The Economist* 325, no. 7783 (1992): 44; 'Harry Themba Gwala', *South African History Online*, 3 September 2019, accessed 15 December 2020, https://www.sahistory.org.za/people/harry-themba-gwala
56 'Harry Gwala, Natal's (Other) Warlord'.
57 Yvonne Muthien and Harry Gwala, 'Spear of the Midlands', *Indicator SA* 8, no. 2 (1991): 21.
58 Associated Press, 'Harry Gwala, 74, a Zulu Ally of Mandela Who Fought Zulus', *New York Times*, 21 June 1995, accessed 25 July 2020, https://www.nytimes.com/1995/06/21/obituaries/harry-gwala-74-a-zulu-ally-of-mandela-who-fought-zulus.html
59 Carla Bernardo, 'Ben Kies: The Cape Radical', *UCT News*, 22 January 2020, accessed 25 July 2020, https://www.news.uct.ac.za/article/-2020-01-22-ben-kies-the-cape-radical
60 Zimitri Erasmus, 'Rearranging the Furniture of History: Non-Racialism as Anticolonial Praxis', *Critical Philosophy of Race* 5, no. 2 (2017): 215.
61 'Benjamin Magson Kies', *South African History Online*, 4 August 2020, accessed 15 December 2020, https://www.sahistory.org.za/people/benjamin-magson-kies
62 Corinne Sandwith, 'Contesting a "Cult(ure) of Respectability": Anti-Colonial Resistance in the Western Cape, 1935–1950', *Current Writing* 16, no. 1 (2004): 48.
63 Louis Tay, James O. Pawelski and Melissa G. Keith, 'The Role of the Arts and Humanities in Human Flourishing: A Conceptual Model', *Journal of Positive Psychology* 13, no. 3 (2018): 222.
64 Keyan G. Tomaselli, 'Perverse Incentives and the Political Economy of South African Academic Journal Publishing', *South African Journal of Science* 114, no. 11–12 (2018): 2.
65 Maurizio Lazzarato, 'The Misfortunes of the "Artistic Critique" and of Cultural Employment', trans. Mary O'Neill, in *Critique of Creativity: Precarity, Subjectivity and Resistance in the 'Creative Industries'*, ed. Gerald Raunig, Gene Ray and Ulf Wuggenig (London: MayFlyBooks, 2011), 47, accessed 25 May 2019, http://mayflybooks.org/wp-content/uploads/2011/05/9781906948146CritiqueOfCreativity.pdf#page=59
66 Lazzarato, 'The Misfortunes', 49.
67 Martha Nussbaum, *Not for Profit: Why Democracy Needs the Humanities* (Princeton: Princeton University Press, 2010); Stefan Collini, *What Are Universities For?* (London: Penguin, 2012); Stefan Collini, *Speaking of Universities* (London: Verso, 2017).
68 Merrifield, *The Amateur*, 51.
69 Merrifield, *The Amateur*, 148.
70 Merrifield, *The Amateur*, 170, 183.
71 Jane Duncan, *Stopping the Spies: Constructing and Resisting the Surveillance State in South Africa* (Johannesburg: Wits University Press, 2018), 12–13.
72 Duncan, *Stopping the Spies*, 14, 217.
73 Duncan, *Stopping the Spies*, 223.

74 'Elijah Makiwane', *The Journalist*, 21 April 2015, accessed 30 June 2020, http://www.thejournalist.org.za/pioneers/elijah-makiwane/
75 Maria Ressa, 'When Journalists Are under Attack, Democracy Is under Attack', *Daily Maverick*, 30 September 2019, accessed 2 October 2019, https://www.dailymaverick.co.za/article/2019-09-30-when-journalists-are-under-attack-democracy-is-under-attack/
76 Lesley Cowling, 'Shaped by Their Histories', *Good Governance Africa: Africa in Fact* 53 (2020), accessed 12 August 2020, https://gga.org/shaped-by-their-histories/
77 Kate-Lyn Moore, 'Art and the Township', *UCT News*, 20 June 2017, accessed 30 June 2020, https://www.news.uct.ac.za/article/-2017-06-20-art-and-the-township; Mike Loewe, 'Vibrant Shack Theatre Project', *Dispatch Live*, 28 September 2017, accessed 15 December 2020, https://www.dispatchlive.co.za/lifestyle/2017-09-28-vibrant-shack-theatre-project/
78 Tom Head, 'Marikana: What Was Cyril Ramaphosa's Role?' *The South African*, 16 August 2018, accessed 14 December 2020, https://www.thesouthafrican.com/news/marikana-what-did-cyril-ramaphosa-do/
79 Njabulo S. Ndebele, 'They Are Burning Memory', *Critical Arts* 31, no. 1 (2017): 102–109.
80 Ndebele, 'They Are Burning Memory', 103.
81 Ndebele, 'They Are Burning Memory', 109.

REFERENCES

Associated Press. 'Harry Gwala, 74, a Zulu Ally of Mandela Who Fought Zulus'. *New York Times*, 21 June 1995. Accessed 25 July 2020. https://www.nytimes.com/1995/06/21/obituaries/harry-gwala-74-a-zulu-ally-of-mandela-who-fought-zulus.html

'Benjamin Magson Kies'. *South African History Online*, 4 August 2020. Accessed 15 December 2020. https://www.sahistory.org.za/people/benjamin-magson-kies

Bernardo, Carla. 'Ben Kies: The Cape Radical'. *UCT News*, 22 January 2020. Accessed 25 July 2020. https://www.news.uct.ac.za/article/-2020-01-22-ben-kies-the-cape-radical

Biko, Steve. *I Write What I Like: A Selection of His Writings*. Edited by Aelred Stubbs. Johannesburg: Picador Africa, 2017.

Collini, Stefan. *Speaking of Universities*. London: Verso, 2017.

Collini, Stefan. *What Are Universities For?* London: Penguin, 2012.

Cowling, Lesley. 'Shaped by Their Histories'. *Good Governance Africa: Africa in Fact* 53 (2020). Accessed 12 August 2020. https://gga.org/shaped-by-their-histories/

Duncan, Jane. *Stopping the Spies: Constructing and Resisting the Surveillance State in South Africa*. Johannesburg: Wits University Press, 2018.

'Elijah Makiwane'. *The Journalist*, 21 April 2015. Accessed 30 June 2020. http://www.thejournalist.org.za/pioneers/elijah-makiwane/

Erasmus, Zimitri. 'Rearranging the Furniture of History: Non-Racialism as Anticolonial Praxis'. *Critical Philosophy of Race* 5, no. 2 (2017): 198–222.

Grayling, A.C. *Democracy and Its Crisis*. London: Oneworld Publications, 2018.

'Harry Gwala, Natal's (Other) Warlord'. *The Economist* 325, no. 7783 (1992): 44.

'Harry Themba Gwala'. *South African History Online*, 3 September 2019. Accessed 15 December 2020. https://www.sahistory.org.za/people/harry-themba-gwala

Haupt, Adam. 'Malema and the Like Are No Different to Trump'. *Mail & Guardian*, 22 January 2019. Accessed 30 January 2019. https://mg.co.za/article/2019-01-22-malema-and-the-likes-are-no-different-to-trump

Head, Tom. 'Marikana: What Was Cyril Ramaphosa's Role?' *The South African*, 16 August 2018. Accessed 14 December 2020. https://www.thesouthafrican.com/news/marikana-what-did-cyril-ramaphosa-do/

Hirson, Baruch. *The Cape Town Intellectuals: Ruth Schechter and Her Circle, 1907–1934*. Johannesburg: Wits University Press, 2001.

Kakutani, Michiko. *The Death of Truth: Notes on Falsehood in the Age of Trump*. New York: Tim Duggan Books, 2018.

Lazzarato, Maurizio. 'The Misfortunes of the "Artistic Critique" and of Cultural Employment'. Translated by Mary O'Neill. In *Critique of Creativity: Precarity, Subjectivity and Resistance in the 'Creative Industries'*, edited by Gerald Raunig, Gene Ray and Ulf Wuggenig, 41–56. London: MayFlyBooks, 2011. Accessed 25 May 2019. http://mayflybooks.org/wp-content/uploads/2011/05/9781906948146CritiqueOfCreativity.pdf#page=59

Loewe, Mike. 'Vibrant Shack Theatre Project'. *Dispatch Live*, 28 September 2017. Accessed 15 December 2020. https://www.dispatchlive.co.za/lifestyle/2017-09-28-vibrant-shack-theatre-project/

Merrifield, Andy. *The Amateur: The Pleasures of Doing What You Love*. London: Verso, 2018.

Mishra, Pankaj. *The Age of Anger: A History of the Present*. New York: Farrar, Straus and Giroux 2017.

Moore, Kate-Lyn. 'Art and the Township'. *UCT News*, 20 June 2017. Accessed 30 June 2020. https://www.news.uct.ac.za/article/-2017-06-20-art-and-the-township

More, Mabogo Percy. *Biko: Philosophy, Identity and Liberation*. Cape Town: HSRC Press, 2017.

Msimang, Sisonke. *Always Another Country: A Memoir of Exile and Home*. Johannesburg: Johnathan Ball, 2018.

Muthien, Yvonne and Harry Gwala. 'Spear of the Midlands'. *Indicator SA* 8, no. 2 (1991): 21–23.

Ndebele, Njabulo S. 'Foreword'. In *Categories of Persons: Rethinking Ourselves and Others*, edited by Megan Jones and Jacob Dlamini, ix–xii. Johannesburg: Picador Africa, 2013.

Ndebele, Njabulo S. 'They Are Burning Memory'. *Critical Arts* 31, no. 1 (2017): 102–109.

Ndletyana, Mcebisi, ed. *African Intellectuals in 19th and 20th Century South Africa*. Cape Town: HSRC Press, 2008.

Ngũgĩ wa Thiong'o. 'For Peace, Justice, and Culture: The Intellectual in the Twenty-First Century'. *Profession* (2006): 33–39.

Nussbaum, Martha, ed. *Not for Profit: Why Democracy Needs the Humanities*. Princeton: Princeton University Press, 2010.

Poyner, Jane. 'Introduction'. In *J.M. Coetzee and the Idea of the Public Intellectual*, edited by Jane Poyner, 1–20. Athens: Ohio University Press, 2006.

Ressa, Maria. 'When Journalists Are under Attack, Democracy Is under Attack'. *Daily Maverick*, 30 September 2019. Accessed 2 October 2019. https://www.dailymaverick.co.za/article/2019-09-30-when-journalists-are-under-attack-democracy-is-under-attack/

Rule, Peter. 'Remembering Sol Plaatje as South Africa's Original Public Educator'. *The Conversation*, 5 October 2016. Accessed 30 August 2020. https://theconversation.com/remembering-sol-plaatje-as-south-africas-original-public-educator-65979

Said, Edward. *Representations of the Intellectual*. New York: Vintage Books, 1996.

Sandwith, Corinne. 'Contesting a "Cult(ure) of Respectability": Anti-Colonial Resistance in the Western Cape, 1935–1950'. *Current Writing* 16, no. 1 (2004): 33–60.

Scott, A.O. *Better Living through Criticism: How to Think about Art, Pleasure, Beauty, and Truth*. London: Penguin, 2017.

Sowell, Thomas. *Intellectuals and Society*. New York: Basic Books, 2009.
Tay, Louis, James O. Pawelski and Melissa G. Keith. 'The Role of the Arts and Humanities in Human Flourishing: A Conceptual Model'. *Journal of Positive Psychology* 13, no. 3 (2018): 215–225.
Tomaselli, Keyan G. 'Perverse Incentives and the Political Economy of South African Academic Journal Publishing'. *South African Journal of Science* 114, no. 11–12 (2018): 1–6.
Wark, McKenzie. *General Intellects: Twenty-One Thinkers for the Twenty-First Century*. London: Verso, 2016.
Willan, Brian. *Sol Plaatje: A Life of Solomon Tshekisho Plaatje, 1876–1932*. Johannesburg: Jacana Media, 2018.

CHAPTER

1

Recalibrating the Deep History of Intellectual Thought in the KwaZulu-Natal Region

Carolyn Hamilton

In the literature that deals with public intellectual activity in South Africa there is a tacit understanding that one of its defining features is sustained reading and writing.[1] The literature shares this feature with European understandings of public intellectual activity and has not, to my knowledge, actively considered the possibility of intellectual life in settings without writing. There is further implicit agreement that 'public' in the phrase 'public intellectual' refers to the public of the 'public sphere', one of the social imaginaries of a modern democracy. It is the public called into being by the wide circulation of printed texts, the public that must read, consider and debate its options and make political choices then realised through the ballot box.[2]

In South Africa these assumptions about public intellectualism combine with deeply entrenched ideas about pre-colonial societies as practising timeless tribal culture and relaying oral traditions, the combination thereby precluding any exploration of pre-colonial intellectual currents and activities. These combined assumptions foreclose any investigation of how intellectual engagements in oral forms sought to persuade people and to shape political futures, both deep within the eras before colonialism and persisting into the colonial era. They obscure how such modes of debate and discussion overlapped and intersected with early literate forms of public intellectual activity.

This chapter challenges the assumptions that position thinkers of the nineteenth and early twentieth centuries, who expressed their ideas orally and who did not write, as atavistic relayers of oral tradition, and their literate counterparts – often their very own kin – as modern thinkers engaged in public intellectual life. Members of both seemingly distinct categories, I argue, were deeply cognisant of the immense changes of their times and both attempted to reconcile the past with the present. People in both categories were critically concerned with the navigation of change and the nature of the brokering of the past into the present that each saw as necessary to navigate that change. This involved drawing on banks of inherited knowledge, reconciling the old with the new, testing ideas and deliberating in multiple settings.

The chapter shows that deliberative activity of this kind was also a feature of life *before* colonialism. Such activity shows up in the historical record wherever significant change had to be navigated. For too long, colonialism and literacy have been allowed to constitute the effective beginning of South African history, with any earlier cognitive activity consigned to 'tradition'. Where what went before is historicised at all, it is, at best, only ever a background chapter to the rest of history, or situated in the field of archaeology, which draws heavily on ethnographies from later eras to interpret its findings.[3] However, it is more than possible to begin to undertake research into political praxis in the eras before colonialism and to follow currents of political thought changing in response to changing circumstances within the pre-colonial world and across the pre-colonial/colonial divide. It is indeed possible to watch ideas travel across oral forms, from oral forms into written ones, and into ones with the oral and written inextricably entangled. To accomplish this, the pervasive distinction between literate, modern, hybrid and synthesising intellectuals and illiterate, authentic tribal informants relaying handed-down tradition requires robust interrogation.

In the rest of this chapter I attempt such an interrogation in relation to one region of southern Africa – KwaZulu-Natal – where sufficient research already exists to make it possible to pursue these issues across the pre-colonial/colonial temporal boundary. Furthermore, the era immediately before colonialism saw the rapid rise of new power in this area, the kingdom under Shaka (*c.*1816–28). Shaka's reign was short-lived and ended with a palace coup that saw a dramatic shift of power away from his closest allies, to supporters of the new incumbent, his brother, Dingane. These changes and realignments in the late independent era required political and intellectual agility, which has left discernible traces in the historical record that allow us to research how change was navigated in the late independent period and across the pre-colonial/colonial divide.

My interrogation proceeds in four steps. First, I consider the now substantial scholarly work on two prominent intellectuals, Magema Magwaza Fuze and John Langalibalele Dube. Their writings in isiZulu in the late nineteenth and early twentieth centuries made use of existing, and presumably long-standing, concepts – about, among other things, the nature of rule, government and nation, as well as gender roles – to discuss how things were in the past, as well as to discuss present changes and to imagine new futures. My aim is to highlight the extent to which their use of such concepts was rooted in earlier, pre-colonial currents of political thought and in inherited conceptual language that they were able to invoke, or where necessary, to refurbish to meet new needs.

Second, I consider a range of other places where such discussions were going on, also in isiZulu, about the same and related topics, but which happened orally and were written down by people other than those doing the speaking. The point of this is to register the existence of a wide and rich discursive environment in which isiZulu speakers were deliberating about the key questions of the day and, like the literate intellectuals, were exploring a variety of ways of brokering the past into the present, but doing so orally. These points are not well established in the relevant literature.

Third, I set out an argument for recognising that what these speakers offered was not relayed, formulaic oral tradition, but thoughtful disquisitions on the past. These sometimes engaged with the past in its own right, but in many instances, the past was drawn on for the intellectual resources and insights it offered for navigating contemporary changes and envisaging the future.

The final step in my argument is to show that both the written and oral political discourses, and the intellectual activity that they involved, which drew thoughtfully on the past, were not new features in the region in the late nineteenth century. There are clear indications of similar debates and forms of brokering of the past into the present in the eras before colonialism, especially in circumstances of dramatic political changes.

THE WRITINGS OF THE MODERN INTELLECTUALS

There is now considerable scholarly work on early black intellectuals writing in both isiZulu and English, which offers rich insights into the multiple ways in which they navigated the enormous changes that came with colonialism.

Hlonipha Mokoena's study of Magema Fuze offers a detailed examination of the thinking and writing of one of the earliest writerly intellectuals of the region.[4]

From the late 1860s Fuze played an increasingly important role in the complex intersecting spheres of royal Zulu, local chiefly and colonial politics.[5] This entailed missions to the Zulu king, writing and printing political commentary, involvement in the trials of Zulu leaders and even joining King Dinuzulu in exile on the island of Saint Helena in 1896. While Fuze was distinctively a product of a mission education, he operated in close proximity to Zulu royalty over a long period and during his sojourn on Saint Helena he developed a cosmopolitan and pan-African consciousness. Central to his work across some 50 years was an extended engagement with questions of sovereignty, the rights, responsibilities and reach of king- and chiefship, and how their forms in previous eras would be reconfigured under colonialism.[6]

Diverse political and intellectual networks shaped his thought and writing, much of it expressed in isiZulu, in letters, articles in the British and local press (*Macmillan's Magazine, Ipepa lo Hlanga, Inkanyiso* and *Ilanga lase Natal*) and in his 1922 book on the history and origins of the black inhabitants of the region, *Abantu Abamnyama Lapa Bavela Ngakona*.[7] Mokoena argues that the picture of his thinking and writing that emerges is of a bricoleur, combining strands of thought drawn from diverse places – Christian, indigenous, Darwinian, scientific – and employing a collage of ideas and arguments, in which the history of the region loomed large.[8] Not only did he have much to say about the nature of the Zulu kingship and questions of sovereignty, he also tackled numerous other aspects of what has been termed 'custom', including its misappropriations under colonialism, and did so in a manner that fostered a knowledge and appreciation of the past.[9] As Mokoena puts it, the Christianised educated elite, or *amakholwa*, were paradoxically 'champions of modernity's enlightenment, while at the same time rejecting its colonial form'. Her argument is that the rejection took the form of a reach into the past: 'Fuze's notion of history as discourse was based on the assumption that reviving the past was the first step in the construction of Africanist knowledge.'[10]

By the 1890s a new generation of young literate intellectuals was making their presence felt in Natal, including John Langalibalele Dube, who was to become a leading figure. Dube is probably best known as the founding president of the African National Congress, but arguably his greatest legacy lies in the dynamism he brought into African intellectual life. He was responsible for the establishment of Ohlange, which was to become the leading school for Africans in the region, and in 1903 he began publishing the newspaper *Ilanga lase Natal*, which engaged with the pressing debates of the day about, among other things, citizenship, discrimination and government policies. Heather Hughes's biography of Dube tracks his life and work in detail.[11]

Dube was the author of a number of historical texts, ranging from his 1890 pamphlet published in English in the United States, 'A Talk upon My Native Land' (which included discussion of the rise of Shaka and the massacre of the Qadi people under Shaka's successor, Dingane), to what is most often referred to as the first novel in isiZulu, set in the reign of Shaka, *Insila kaShaka*, published in 1930. He was a writer of letters to prominent people, including the Zulu king, and to newspapers, such as *Inkanyiso* and the *Missionary Review of the World*. He also solicited letters and opinion for his newspaper. As editor of *Ilanga*, he would have had a significant say in what was reported in the paper – such as the trials of the rebels involved in the anti-poll tax uprising of 1906 and the subsequent trial of the then Zulu king, Dinuzulu.

More squarely still than Fuze, Dube was a thoroughly modern figure, but he too operated across the full spectrum of Natal politics. It was a field shaped by the concerns of not only the educated intelligentsia whose interests Dube promoted, but also Zulu royals, local chiefs (including *kholwa* chiefs), missionaries, governors and native administrators, large- and small-scale farmers and many others. As in Fuze's work, historical consciousness was a locus of his critique of the particular form that colonial modernity took. Like Fuze, Dube was active in navigating the enormous changes of the time, engaging with pressing questions, and brokering the past into the present. The bricolage and cobbling from multiple sources that a scholar like Mokoena sees as a distinctive feature of Fuze's 1922 book, were also present in Dube's writing. We can see him reaching in many places into the world of so-called tradition and, indeed, late in life, in 1936, he even became a founding member of the rather arcane Zulu Society, which focused on preserving Zulu heritage and customs.

Fuze and Dube had plenty of reasons to reflect on and discuss the nature of the Zulu kingship and the nature of colonial government. The early decades of the twentieth century saw the rise of a form of nationalism centred on the Zulu kingship. Such nationalist impulses affected the various ways in which thinkers and writers like Fuze and Dube interacted with the Zulu royal house and engaged with the long history of the region.[12] That new nationalism, and its critique of imperial and later Union rule, is central to understanding how intellectuals at this time thought about a large range of questions concerning nation, rule, government, domination, governmental and civil responsibilities, hegemony and, indeed, history itself. Support for the Zulu royal house was far from automatic for people like Fuze and Dube, whose families had previously suffered under royal Zulu rule and who had been forced to accommodate themselves to colonial Natal politics.

While much scholarly attention has focused on *kholwa* thinking and writing as being concerned with ideas of modernity and progress, close examination of Fuze's and Dube's writings reveal their depth of interest in how to think about, and value, the pre-*kholwa* past – the world described variously in the twentieth century as traditional and tribal – as well as the role and nature of the Zulu kingship and identities and connections inherited from the distant past.[13]

Fuze and Dube are the best known and most studied of the early generations of isiZulu-speaking literate intellectuals. Research is increasingly introducing us to other writers. Of course, these writers were also prominent speakers whose words were often recorded, with varying degrees of faithfulness, by other writers. They were continually in spoken debate and discussion in a wide variety of settings, from the most ostensibly modern to what seemed to be atavistically tribal.

DISCOURSING ORALLY

There were numerous other situations at this time where the kinds of issues engaged with by the literate intellectuals were taken up by people who only discoursed orally. In certain instances their words were recorded in writing, with spoken isiZulu sometimes translated by either home-language isiZulu or home-language English translators and then written down by either home-language English or home-language isiZulu recorders, with all of these variations affecting how the spoken words entered the record.

These instances include, for example, documents from the 1880s, and published in 1978 in a compilation edited by Colin Webb and John Wright.[14] Positioned as recording the words of the Zulu king, Cetshwayo kaMpande, they were presented at the time as forms of dictation, recorded while he was a prisoner in exile, first at the Castle in Cape Town and later living in civil custody on the Cape farm, Oude Molen. The first document, described as a 'narrative ... taken down from the lips of Cetywayo, by Captain Poole ... [that] contains nothing that has not been received direct from Cetywayo', was published in English in *Macmillan's Magazine* in February 1880.[15] It was generated over a number of weeks while Cetshwayo was in the Castle, with translation by W.K. Longcast, who had been a British military interpreter in the Anglo-Zulu War. At the time, Cetshwayo was in the custody of Captain J. Ruscombe Poole, who appears to have been the facilitator, and possibly a co-author of a kind, of the publication. It offers a survey of the course of Zulu history and of the events leading to the war of 1879. The second document is a letter from the king to Sir Hercules Robinson, governor of the Cape Colony, written in

1881, giving King Cetshwayo's version of the war and subsequent events. It was part of a corpus of correspondence with a wide group of influential people and government in the Cape and in Britain that was generated by the king and his amanuensis, R.C.A. Samuelson, the son of a missionary, who was fluent in isiZulu and appointed as his interpreter after Longcast. The third document consisted of statements about the law and customs of the Zulu kingdom 'elicited from Cetshwayo under interrogation' by the Cape Government Commission at Oude Molen over two days in 1881 in a question and answer format. Samuelson was responsible for the translation, which was recorded by an unnamed minute-taker. The minutes were then read back to Samuelson, and then through him to Cetshwayo, and then amended. As published in 1978 the three texts comprise some 48 pages.

These texts were substantially mediated by their particular circumstances of recording as well as by the orientations, concerns and abilities of the translators and recorders.[16] They were also the product of what the king chose to place on record, how he engaged with the key questions of the day, the kinds of political thought he drew on, and the ways in which he brokered the past in the present. It is hardly a surprise that matters of kingship, sovereignty and the nature of rule were uppermost in his mind.

The period with which I am concerned saw many other instances of speaking in isiZulu – by Zulu royals, prominent officials, chiefs, people appearing in courts and before commissions, as well as statements made to magistrates and input rendered to experts of various stripes who were out and about collecting information. These were then set down in writing, sometimes in isiZulu and sometimes in English, by other people and many were presented as being accurate recordings. Increasingly, we know more and more about the circumstances under which these various records that purport to render spoken speech came into being.

Spoken discussions that referenced the past that were never recorded, but went on in daily life, would have happened in situations too countless to list, but a sense of the range and extent of this may be productive to keep in mind. The long-ago past would have been drawn on not only in addressing ancestors at grave sites, significant ritual settings and in fireside storytelling. This was time of rapid urbanisation and it would also have been referenced in libations in the new beerhalls and in conversations at trade union and church meetings in the growing town of Durban. Many undocumented discussions of political import would have taken place in chiefly courts and meetings of many kinds, as well as on journeys to colonial courts, in commentary on contested outcomes of justice processes, and in response to proclamations and changes in governmental policy. Some of these discussions would have taken place under circumstances that the participants considered, in one way or another, significant – that is, more than mere conversation. When we begin to think like this about all the places that political issues were being discussed, carefully picked over and debated, where past ways of doing things were being reviewed and change was being interrogated, we begin to grasp something of the extent of the richly discursive environment in which isiZulu speakers were participating in the late nineteenth and early twentieth centuries.

One of the places where this was happening was in the many conversations that a range of people were having, mostly in isiZulu, with the colonial official James Stuart, the recorded notes of which are widely described as a vast body of recorded oral tradition.

ORAL TRADITION AND THE STATING OF THEIR OWN VIEWS

Between 1897 and 1921 the Natal administrator James Stuart held discussions with some 200 people he regarded as well informed on what he thought of as Zulu history and custom. He was especially interested in the nature of rule in the time of Shaka, which he considered a useful model for colonial governance, and he steered many of the conversations onto this subject.[17] Stuart was a fluent isiZulu speaker and he took detailed notes of the conversations. In certain instances, he was concerned to record the particular narrative flow and the exact words in isiZulu of his interlocutors. Indeed, his corpus of notes is considered to be one of the richest bodies of what is often described as 'oral tradition' in southern Africa. As oral traditions recorded from what are seen by scholars as authentic tribal informants, these accounts are typically treated as narratives handed down across generations, more or less faithfully.[18]

However, close reading of the recorded texts and research into the contexts, lives and networks of these informants, of the kind that has been done by scholars who have worked on Fuze and Dube, throws light on their intellectual processes, political concerns and their praxis in a manner that invites radical reassessment of them as 'informants' and relayers of oral tradition. In this chapter I discuss in detail one of Stuart's interlocutors, Ndlovu kaThimuni, in order to demonstrate this point.[19]

In two sessions across some 11 days in 1902 and 1903 Stuart held sustained discussions with Ndlovu kaThimuni. Ndlovu was a prominent figure in Natal chiefly politics.[20] He was a grandson of Mudli kaNkwelo kaNdaba, who had been actively involved in the accession of his kinsman, Shaka, to the Zulu chieftaincy and had later been killed by Shaka.[21] According to Ndlovu, his father, Thimuni, had been forced by Shaka's assassin and successor, King Dingane, to leave the Zulu country and settle to the south in what was to become the colony of Natal.[22] Relations with the main Zulu royal house were tense in this period. Over the ensuing decades boundary disputes with neighbouring chiefs and white land encroachments forced Thimuni and his followers into an ever-smaller area, subjecting them to a colonial magistrate's authority and increasingly onerous forms of colonial taxation and labour demands. By the time Ndlovu met with Stuart, his family had some 50 years of experience in colonial Natal politics.[23]

Stuart first met with Ndlovu on Friday, 7 November 1902, probably at Stuart's place of work as assistant magistrate in Durban.[24] Stuart recorded that Ndlovu 'called on me today with another, being referred to me by my old friend, Mkando'.[25] The formulation 'called on me', with its tones of Victorian social nicety, indicates that the connection was initiated by Ndlovu, without prior arrangement but with a certain formality. In what Stuart indicates was a conversation of about 45 minutes, the men touched on aspects of the reigns of Shaka, Dingane and Mpande, and a host of other things. They then arranged to meet the next day at Stuart's home. Ndlovu accordingly arrived with a small entourage and stayed the night. Stuart's induna, Ndukwana kaMbengwana, was present.[26] Significantly, the Saturday conversation was not so much about the past as the present. It was dominated by a three-and-a-half-hour conversation 'on the native question in its general aspect'.[27] In the course of the conversation, Ndukwana intervened often, registering and discussing multiple contemporary problems, as did Ndlovu, whom Stuart recorded as noting:

> Everyone would hail with delight the holding of native public meetings in Pietermaritzburg from time to time. That is what is truly needed ... he was of the opinion the last generation had failed in not educating native children. He considers that *kolwas* and others are corrupted by new-comers from England and elsewhere who know nothing of the native. It is not mere education that alienates the young men etc.[28]

A reader familiar with the wider corpus of Stuart papers, and with the particular policies that Stuart was advocating at this time for native administration in Natal, can immediately confirm what the first-time reader probably senses, that this statement is as much a reflection of Stuart's thinking as anything that Ndlovu had to say. Stuart was an advocate of regular consultations and is many times on record commenting on the general lack of knowledge on native customs relevant to indigenous governance among the new generation of native administrators.

What Ndlovu and the men with him actually had to say on that Saturday afternoon cannot be recovered from these notes, at least not at face value, since they are the product of what Stuart chose to note down. What the notes do attest to upfront is that both parties, Stuart and Ndukwana, and their visitors, were deeply interested in and concerned about contemporary issues, and were choosing to meet and to discuss them. They were also deliberating, with ideas, opinions and, as the notes make clear, historical references, going backwards and forwards.

On the Sunday, Ndlovu began by saying that he had reflected on Stuart's remarks of the previous day about Africans being allowed their own parliament and managing their own affairs according to their own laws and customs. Stuart captured his words thus:

> He said the present state of affairs has turned them into mice ... if such a policy of allowing them to manage their own affairs were conceded, the people would be able to bear any burden, however great it might be, seeing they would then have a full knowledge of what they were doing ... Men should not continue to be *izigubu* (dummies), and not be allowed to *state their own views (pendula)*. Natives have become *izamuku* (mutes); we cannot make ourselves heard.[29]

Ndlovu had no hesitancy in asserting his criticisms: '*Umteto u isiqwaga*', which Stuart glossed in his notes as 'the law is a tyrant (no respecter of persons)'. The comments that follow, in a mix of English and isiZulu in Stuart's notes, probably reflect Ndlovu's sentiments: 'A law is passed by the European and it is forcibly applied straight away. There ought to be councils among the natives for no man can *make laws* alone.'[30] After close perusal of the many pages of notes of the conversations in which Ndlovu and his companions were involved, it is hard to imagine that any of the participants in the conversation could have been in doubt that the forays into the past were undertaken in order to explore their significance for contemporary governance.

When he was again on a visit to Durban, Ndlovu chose to resume the conversation with Stuart, this time on New Year's Day of 1903.[31] Stuart, Ndukwana and Ndlovu met again on 11 January, this time with Ndlovu's brother Mhuyi kaThimuni present, and again in March.

The first point I wish to draw attention to is that these conversations were not seen by the participating parties as recording sessions of established historical narratives (although as I shall show, there were quite separate occasions when the recording of narratives was the purpose.) While these conversations sometimes involved digressions and moments of engaging with the past with no obvious purpose, they were, for the most part, discussion occasions in their own right.[32] The engagements referenced the past in numerous ways, illuminating points, supporting lines of thought and critically considering alternatives in the present and for the future. The deliberate way in which Ndlovu approached Stuart and pursued the discussion across multiple encounters, along with chosen associates, is indicative of his praxis in entering into a dialogic space and seeking thereby to engage with and act upon the changing world in which he was operating, a praxis that was later to take a still more dramatic turn with his involvement in the 1906 rebellion.

My second point is that even when Ndlovu offered lengthy accounts of events in the past, he did not do so simply as a relayer of an established, stable story or tradition, but actively crafted his own account, drawing on multiple sources to establish the points he wished to make. Ndlovu indicated that one of his sources of information was his father, Thimuni kaMudli.[33] On the face of it, it would seem that Ndlovu as the son of Thimuni, who was himself the son of Mudli, was relaying what his grandfather told his father, who then told him. But Stuart also interviewed a brother of Ndlovu's, Mhuyi kaThimuni. The accounts offered by the brothers differ significantly, with Ndlovu offering far greater historical detail, and with the two accounts diverging on important issues. It is possible that Mhuyi, who had much less contact with his father than Ndlovu did, heard less, was less interested in the past and failed to remember family history or – and none of these points are mutually exclusive – that Ndlovu was making use of a larger variety of historical resources.

Comparison of the accounts offered by Ndlovu and Mhuyi reveals that they diverged to a degree and in a form that went beyond what might be attributed to lack of interest, poor memory or faulty transmission in a chain of testimony. The essential difference concerned the critical question of Shaka's status as son of Senzangakhona. Ndlovu stated that Shaka was illegitimate. Mhuyi said he was not and each account contained narrative details supporting its claim. One crucial differentiating factor was that Ndlovu noted to Stuart that he also owed much of his knowledge of Shaka to Sipika, a man of Senzangakhona's Mnkangala *ibutho*, who was actively involved in the events leading up to death of Senzangakhona and the accession of Shaka.[34] All this suggests strongly that Ndlovu was not only more exposed than Mhuyi to what Thimuni had to say, but that he also actively took up details provided by at least one other person than his father, namely, Sipika, braiding the accounts together for himself.

If we now turn to a consideration of what we know about Thimuni kaMudli, we discover that he too did not simply participate in a generational relay of tradition. To establish this point, we must diverge for a moment from our discussion of Ndlovu and Thimuni, to introduce someone in Ndlovu's network. In his discussions with Stuart and Ndukwana, Ndlovu offered to send to them Jantshi kaNongila, whom he recommended for his skills as a praise poet.[35] Within a month Jantshi was ensconced at Stuart's home for a set of conversations spread over about ten days. The notes indicate that Ndukwana participated in these conversations too and that again an active exchange of information ensued. The notes make it clear that Ndukwana and Jantshi argued over a variety of historical details.[36]

I have elsewhere discussed at length how Jantshi garnered the information he drew on in his discussions with Stuart and Ndukwana, concluding that he relied heavily on what his father, Nongila, an intelligence specialist under successive Zulu kings and an expert in marshalling information, told him. Jantshi claimed Ndlovu's father, Thimuni, also derived his knowledge of history from Nongila and, indeed, Jantshi's and Ndlovu's accounts overlap in significant ways.[37] The point of this digression into what Jantshi had to say is that it brings into view the networks of information, discussion flows and processes of the accrual of information that not only Ndlovu and Jantshi were engaged in, but also those of their fathers Nongila and Thimuni. Significantly, in Nongila and Thimuni's time, politics was scarcely less turbulent than in 1902–03. Nongila and Thimuni were themselves navigating rapid political change. They both fled the Zulu kingdom into what became the colony of Natal, with all the adjustments that entailed.[38] Through all of this, histories mattered politically and were assiduously reconsidered and revised. In these earlier eras history was as much a part of political discourse as it was revealed to be when Ndlovu, his followers, Ndukwana and Stuart sat down together.

What emerges from this line of investigation is a picture of a complex series of syntheses across time, drawn on thoughtfully by Ndlovu. We can track the processes of Ndlovu's take-up of ideas, including historical information. Here my substantive point is that when we give Ndlovu's accounts as much attention as we give those of writers like Fuze or Dube, we find similar processes of historical crafting, the bringing together of information and arguments from various sources, and the signs of animated intellectual activity.

In the case of Fuze, the intellectual biographer is on relatively familiar research ground, even if she must, as Mokoena does, do much that is innovative to overturn racialised habits of thinking about who is and who is not an intellectual, to enable us to hear what Fuze has to say, as well as to track little-known networks, foreground the contents of vernacular accounts, explore the nature of their forms and the manners of their mediation. Any attempt to track the intellectual biography of someone like Ndlovu must similarly overturn habits of thinking that position him as a tribal informant, reconstruct the circumstances of the making of records concerning him, as well as of the resources that he drew on, read for the signs of his thinking embedded in the notes of others, and foreground his words and concepts wherever they can be found in the record.

But the matter does not rest there, as there is another habit of thinking that requires critical review and that is the idea that the literate intellectuals were political thinkers with a wide range of connections while the so-called informants were insular tribesmen. The factors and experiences that shaped Ndlovu's thinking speak to the scope and range of the networks of ideas that Ndlovu was involved with. In 1903 when Ndlovu was talking to Stuart, these were far from self-contained Natal networks of rural tribal informants. For one thing, Ndlovu was well travelled. Not only had he traversed the region between what is today Maputo and the Kimberley diamond fields, but like Fuze, he was to end up on Saint Helena.[39] This was a result of the central role he played in the 1906 rebellion against the poll tax, the so-called Bambatha Rebellion. This turned him into a central figure in Natal politics. Ndlovu featured prominently in the highly publicised trial that followed the rebellion. The court record reveals much about Ndlovu's abilities to operate publicly in this showcase trial and to present his version of the events of the uprising in the face of a prosecution bent on depicting him as bloodthirsty, barbaric and devious. Ndlovu emerged as a 'canny leader of undoubted ability'.[40] He was at the centre of a complex network of communication and strategising among the rebels, in contact with the Zulu royal house prior to the trial, and afterwards with an even wider network of people in strategising the post-rebellion situation. These networks included many of the writerly intellectuals I have been referring to.

The trial was of pressing concern for people like Fuze and Dube, who were themselves advising King Dinuzulu at the time. It was actively discussed in the black and white press. It is hard to imagine that prominent figures like Dube and Ndlovu, whose home bases were in close proximity to each other, did not actually know each other and never talked in person. If they did not, they most certainly knew a great deal about each other and the kind of thinking and activity that the other was engaged in. Their networks were far from sealed off from each other. Both were involved in local chiefly matters, Ndlovu as a chief himself and Dube in the chiefly politics of the Qadi, with which the Dube family was historically connected.[41] From the time of King Dinuzulu's return from exile in 1898, both Ndlovu and Dube were involved with the Zulu royal house. At the time of the trial, and again at the time of Ndlovu's own return from exile that was the result of the 1906 trial, there can be no doubt that *both* Ndlovu and Dube were thinking deeply about the order of things in the past and how it was changing. And, in the course of these reflections, both engaged in consideration of the past, notably the reign of Shaka.

The lives of the supposedly authentic tribal informants were thus intertwined with those of their *kholwa* neighbours and kin – both immediate and distant – in Natal, as well as with a variety of other literate political allies. There is much more evidence that can be elucidated about these parties' shared concerns about the matters of nation, rule, government, domination, governmental and civil responsibilities and hegemony, and their thinking about the significance of what those things were like in the past and in the present. These were, after all, the pressing questions of the day, for the apparently tribal informants as much as the *kholwa* literates.

Stuart again interviewed Ndlovu in 1919 across three days, this time clearly making a specific effort to record his spoken words verbatim in isiZulu. It seems that Stuart's purpose on this occasion was to get Ndlovu to cover in detail many of the stories about Shaka first raised under very different circumstances in 1902 and 1903. The reason he took down Ndlovu's words with such precision in 1919 was because he planned to use them in an isiZulu-language school reader.[42] The discussion of contemporary political developments that characterised the earlier discussions is nowhere present in this later set of notes. By 1919 both Stuart and Ndlovu were all too aware that the kinds of consultative processes that in 1902–03 they had agreed were desirable were not to be.

Ndlovu kaThimuni, Mhuyi kaThimuni, Jantshi kaNongila, Ndukwana kaMbengwana and many others were involved in the special efforts (and sometimes chance encounters) that resulted in them talking to Stuart in isiZulu, under circumstances very much of Stuart's making but, as we are able to see in certain instances, in circumstances that involved dynamics that exceeded Stuart's agendas.[43] Of course, many other people in the region were also both talking and writing in isiZulu on a wide range of topics, including the long past.

THINKING THE PAST IN THE PRESENT WITH AN EYE TO THE FUTURE

In all sorts of ways the concerns of a significant component of the writings by the literate intellectuals overlapped with the focuses of the Stuart notes, shaped as the notes were by the congruence of interest of Stuart and many of his interlocutors in indigenous governance, practices of rule and the reign of Shaka. They also overlapped with other subjects that feature more incidentally in the Stuart corpus.

We can see that the writers were interested not merely in the modern present – and the agenda of progress and change – but were actively assessing the meaning and possibilities of the past in their present. There can be no doubt that the oral discoursers too were profoundly aware of the need to navigate a changing world. The Stuart notes abound in explicit statements on this. Unlike the interest the Stuart notes have attracted for the detail that they offer on the reigns of Shaka and Dingane, they have not been much explored for what they have to say about political thought, discursive activity and the navigation of change, though where they have, much is revealed.[44]

How researchers read the texts of the writerly intellectuals has often been a result of notions about the writerly intellectuals as acculturated and having imbibed questionable ideas of European thinkers about topics like Bantu migrations and racial origins.[45] These ideas are then regarded as having been cobbled together with fragments of oral traditions only poorly known because of *kholwa* distance from tribal situations and history. The results are judged to be either 'imperfect historical sources' with 'faults of style and errors of fact', such as Fuze's *Abantu Abamnyama*, or positioned as literary works of fiction, like Dube's *Insila kaShaka*.[46] Many of the written works on historical subjects are read as Zulu, or African, nationalist tracts of comparatively little historical substance.

Narrators like Stuart's interlocutors are regarded as not doing synthesising intellectual work in order to make sense of the world they live in, but as relaying a more or less uncontaminated oral tradition from bygone years. This impression persists in the face of a growing body of work that reveals them to be as adept in mobilising history to resource their thinking and to navigate change at the time of recording as their literate counterparts. We can see much the same kind of bricolage and cobbling that Mokoena sees in Fuze's writing, and that characterises the writing of Dube, at work in the recorded words of someone like Ndlovu kaThimuni, who has long been regarded as offering pure and authentic oral tradition. More importantly, a growing body of research indicates that historical discourse was continually being reworked in the generations that preceded Stuart's interlocutors to cope with complex and rapidly changing political circumstances.

What these accounts, written and oral, share is an understanding and treatment of history as something to be deliberated over, as manifestly a subject of debate. Much overt discussion of this kind took place in the pages of Dube's newspaper, *Ilanga*. Mokoena shows us that debate was actively solicited by Fuze when he wrote columns and letters for newspapers, and when he responded to his argumentative readers.[47] Much spoken word that was recorded as historical evidence was delivered in situations where conflicts of interpretation were understood by the participants as the very condition of the offering of historical knowledge, nowhere more so than in the contested settings of courtrooms and before commissions. And, as I have shown from this brief engagement with the encounters that resulted in the corpus of notes made by Stuart recording the words of Ndlovu kaThimuni, history as contested, debated and debatable, and subject to assessment and revision, was present in both the content and form of the discussions at Stuart's home in Durban.

* * *

In the late nineteenth and early twentieth centuries intellectual activity was not the preserve of literates. People like Ndlovu kaThimuni were just as engaged in navigating thoughtfully the changes of the time as were the writerly intellectuals. Like them, Ndlovu drew on the past to address the concerns of the present. Like them, he braided together strands of information in ways that helped in making sense of the past and that enabled thinking about the future. He paid attention to the ideas of others, exerting his critical faculties at every turn, mobilising networks and drawing on banks of knowledge to make important decisions and defend disputed actions. He was concerned to place the past on record and was active in brokering the past into the present. These were all things that the literate intellectuals of his time were doing. There are abundant signs in Ndlovu's accounts and in his own practice that 'the oral past', as Mokoena terms it, was full of resources and strategies for how to navigate change.

In focusing on the intellectual activity of Ndlovu, this chapter draws attention to currents of political thought with roots in the eras before colonialism. These currents were not timeless products, but thought in motion in response to political change. It also highlights another kind of legacy about being a public figure and speaking out on the questions of the day and not being, as Ndlovu put it, a 'nobody' or 'izamuka (mutes)'. Ndlovu clearly appreciated the value of debate and advocated for gatherings for public discussion and debate. He chose to engage with and confront colonial thinking.

A further implication of the arguments made in this chapter concerns the nature of the archive that these writings and recorded notes collectively make up. Mokoena makes the point that Fuze and the readers of his columns regularly argued about the meaning of isiZulu words and sought to develop both a linguistically correct secular vocabulary and a religious one.[48] Discussions about the meanings of words are also to be found throughout the conversations recorded by Stuart. In all the texts concerned – the writings by Fuze and Dube, and their many respondents and fellow literate intellectuals, and in the hundreds of pages of Stuart notes, in Cetshwayo's various statements, and in many instances that I have not had the space here to mention – words were set up to do work in sentences. The kinds of work they did was historically contingent but, in all cases, a more or less shared inherited vocabulary was being used by all of these writers and speakers to navigate change, to say things about the past, the present and the future. How the words did their work was not merely contingent, but also informed by legacies of thought about the nature of rule and power and many other things – indeed, the very order of things. There is a vast amount of recorded text in isiZulu that says these things, coming from multiple positions, generated under a wide variety of circumstances. The archive that this chapter delineates is a register of the navigation of change. The inherited concepts that were available in the period when the archive was laid down were not, of course, frozen time travellers into the period. They were concepts with long histories of being put to work in past discourses, with changing inflections across time. Collectively, they constitute a complex and colossal archive awaiting exploration.

The burden of my argument here is that inherited concepts were in motion in the thinking of Ndlovu as much as they were in that of Fuze and Dube, and furthermore they were also in motion in the thinking and articulations, in turn, of Thimuni kaMudli, something we glimpse through what Ndlovu, Mhuyi and Jantshi have to say about Thimuni and his knowledge of the past. We can only imagine what the case regarding concepts in motion would have been for Thimuni's father, Mudli, who oversaw the accession of Shaka within the small Zulu chiefdom and who participated in the massive changes in the political landscape that accompanied the rapid expansion of the Zulu king's control over the wider KwaZulu-Natal region.

Researchers who might be interested in what nation, rule, government, domination, governmental and civil responsibilities and hegemony might have meant and how they might have operated in Shakan or earlier times, not to mention kingship, the role of women, the nature of expertise and a million other questions, have access to a vast array of texts produced under a variety of circumstances at the end of the nineteenth century and in the early decades of the twentieth century, all concerned with these questions, with what they meant in the past, what they meant at the time, and what they might mean in the future, with much of all this expressed in isiZulu. Some texts may well offer us important details about historical events, central places and important figures. But, arguably just as significantly, the texts offer us a well-populated field of conceptual usage at a particular time, by a large range of people, in a variety of formats and mediums, with all kinds of registers of communication, modes of address, pressures and allures of cultural translation and brokerage, and conventions of rendering into text.

Just as I have argued that the written texts are as much of an archive as the recorded oral ones, so too have I sought to show that the recorded oral texts are likewise evidence of thoughtful syntheses and acts of brokerage. In the face of this extended archive it is no longer possible, if it ever was, to rely on the ethnographies of the same period for insight into the conceptual world of that time of isiZulu speakers, and to assume people in previous eras had much the same 'world view'. Scholars can no longer valorise the brokerage and syntheses of ethnographers at the expense of paying attention to the brokerage and syntheses that we can see in these texts. To make these points is not to wish simply to supplant the ethnographic texts with these ones. Rather, it is to recognise that each of these kinds of text – ethnographic as much as the literary or recorded oral – is a particular production worth investigating *as a production*.

History produced by black intellectuals, typically operating in urban settings, was consigned out of the field of historiography as literature and politics, while the oral productions of history by black thinkers, typically in rural settings, were positioned as sources. This double manoeuvre not only denied historical authority to both of these forms of history production, but also favoured the narratives of the rural informant as historically more authentic than the writings of the urban intellectual, thereby lancing both forms of historical production of their discursive potency. This chapter offers a historical perspective on the pressures on academies today to grapple with the limits of the existing disciplines and the weight of what Bhekizizwe Peterson has termed the 'Black Humanities', developed over the last century by intellectuals and thinkers outside those disciplines.

NOTES

This chapter is based on an online curation '*Umlando, Ukuqamba* and the Stating of Their Own Views', originally prepared for the Five Hundred Year Archive project (https://fhya.org/). I am grateful to participants in the Archive & Public Culture Research Development workshop for their helpful comments on an early version.

[1] Peter Vale, Lawrence Hamilton and Estelle Prinsloo, eds, *Intellectual Traditions in South Africa: Ideas, Individuals and Institutions* (Pietermaritzburg: University of KwaZulu-Natal Press, 2014); Mcebisi Ndletyana, ed., *African Intellectuals in 19th and Early 20th Century South Africa* (Cape Town: HSRC Press, 2008); William Gumede and Leslie Dikeni, eds, *The Poverty of Ideas: South African Democracy and the Retreat of Intellectuals* (Johannesburg: Jacana Media, 2009); Jane Poyner, ed., *J.M. Coetzee and the Idea of the Public Intellectual* (Athens: Ohio University Press, 2006). See also the two-part symposium on 'Exceeding Public Spheres', *Social Dynamics* 35, no. 2 (2009) and 36, no. 1 (2010), produced under the auspices of the Constitution of Public Intellectual Life Project, Wits University.

[2] Carolyn Hamilton and Lesley Cowling, 'Rethinking Public Engagement', in *Babel Unbound: Rage, Reason and Rethinking Public Life*, ed. Lesley Cowling and Carolyn Hamilton (Johannesburg: Wits University Press, 2020), 21–39.

[3] Historical studies are not entirely absent, but they are very much the minority.

[4] Hlonipha Mokoena, *Magema Fuze: The Making of a Kholwa Intellectual* (Pietermaritzburg: University of KwaZulu-Natal Press, 2011). See also Vukile Khumalo, 'The Class of 1856

and the Politics of Cultural Production(s) in the Emergence of Ekukhanyeni, 1855-1910', in *The Eye of the Storm: Bishop John William Colenso and the Crisis of Biblical Inspiration*, ed. Jonathan A. Draper (Pietermaritzburg: Cluster Publications, 2003), 207-241.

5 Jeff Guy, *The View across the River: Harriette Colenso and the Zulu Struggle against Imperialism* (Charlottesville: University of Virginia Press, 2002), 43.

6 In this chapter I follow the English language convention that uses a title and then the name proper (typically, 'Queen Elizabeth' and 'Elizabeth'), which formally implies a singularity that requires no further qualification – hence, 'King Cetshwayo' and 'Cetshwayo'. Of course, the English term 'king' imposes on indigenous forms of rulership the concepts and thinking of Europe and may well efface or obscure distinctive features of indigenous rulership. The matter of the correct title for King Shaka's father, Senzangkhona, presents further difficulties, as in his lifetime he was subject to the overlordship of Dingiswayo, king of the Mthethwa. These are all matters for critical reflection in their own right.

7 Magema Fuze, *Abantu Abamnyama Lapa Bavela Ngakona* (Pietermaritzburg: City Printing Works, 1922).

8 Mokoena, *Fuze*, 154, 160, 164.

9 Mokoena, *Fuze*, 166-167.

10 Mokoena, *Fuze*, 160.

11 Heather Hughes, *The First President: A Life of John Dube* (Johannesburg: Jacana Media, 2011).

12 Shula Marks, 'The Ambiguities of Dependence: John L. Dube of Natal', *Journal of Southern African Studies* 1, no. 2 (1975): 162-180; Nicholas Cope, 'The Zulu Petit Bourgeoisie and Zulu Nationalism in the 1920s: Origins of Inkatha', *Journal of Southern African Studies* 16, no. 3 (September 1990): 431-451; Paul la Hausse de Lalouvière, *Restless Identities: Signatures of Nationalism, Zulu Ethnicity and History in the Lives of Petros Lamula (c.1881-1948) and Lymon Maling (1889-c.1936)* (Pietermaritzburg: University of Natal Press, 2000); Benedict Carton, John Laband and Jabulani Sithole, eds, *Zulu Identities: Being Zulu, Past and Present* (Pietermaritzburg: University of KwaZulu-Natal Press, 2009).

13 Mokoena notes that the terms in which the *amakholwa* expressed their political aspirations, whether in public arenas or published books, were almost always borrowed from the political vocabulary of the colonial order. It seems to me that her point has obvious application to their writings in English. I am less certain about how this happened in their Zulu texts. See Mokoena, *Fuze*, 21.

14 This was not the first recording of King Cetshwayo's words. Many documents claimed to report on his speech, including Fuze's published account of his 1877 visit to Cetshwayo, which included details of conversations he had with the Zulu king. Magema Fuze, 'A Visit to King Ketshwayo', *MacMillan's Magazine* (March 1878): 421-432.

15 Colin de B. Webb and John B. Wright, eds, *A Zulu King Speaks: Statements Made by Cetshwayo kaMpande on the History and Customs of His People* (Pietermaritzburg: University of Natal Press, 1978), 1.

16 Webb and Wright mention the processes involved in transforming the king's statements into written documents, noting that many 'errors' crept in, and recording their editorial decision to reproduce the documents with any defects uncorrected. Webb and Wright, *A Zulu King Speaks*, xxxi.

17 Carolyn Hamilton, *Terrific Majesty: The Powers of Shaka and the Limits of Historical Invention* (Cape Town: David Philip, 1998), Chapter 4.

18 For a recent instance pertinent to this region, see Elizabeth A. Eldredge, *The Creation of the Zulu Kingdom, 1815–1828: War, Shaka, and the Consolidation of Power* (New York: Cambridge University Press, 2014), 13, 21, 23.

19 In his notes Stuart used a form of the orthography of the day in rendering Ndlovu's name as 'Ndhlovu'. As I have no indication of how Ndlovu would have elected to render his name during his life, I follow the convention of a default to modern orthography for the name of the person, rather than defaulting to the colonial recorder's choice. However, when I refer to the 'title' of the 1986 published text of the Ndlovu conversation, I reproduce without alteration the published title's elected orthography: 'Ndhlovu ka Timuni'.

20 In the period discussed in this chapter, literate black intellectuals were adopting the convention of a first name and surname. Where there is evidence of such choices, I have followed standard practice of giving full names on first mention in full (as in 'Magema Magwaza Fuze'), thereafter referring to these authors by their surnames (as in 'Fuze'). I have refrained from imposing this convention on the recordings of the statements of people who did not in their lifetimes make use of a surname. Instead, I employ the formal 'Ndlovu kaThimuni' (indicating that Ndlovu was a son of Thimuni's) on first mention and use 'Ndlovu' thereafter. However, this feels inappropriately familiar, even casual. I am not satisfied that this form of naming establishes, authorially, the sense of equivalence between the written and oral disquisitions that I am positing. The use of *izithakazelo*, or address names, would confer a status that offers a formality similar to the use of the surname for authors in English. However, it proves confusing when the account features numerous people with the same *izithakazelo*.

21 Stuart noted that Ndukwana kaMbengwana, also present when the conversation happened, described Ndlovu's branch of the royal family as the left-hand or *ikohlo*, side of the royal house, a status that would exclude them from the royal succession. 'Ndhlovu ka Timuni', in Colin de B. Webb and John B. Wright, eds, *The James Stuart Archive of Recorded Oral Evidence Relating to the History of the Zulu and Neighbouring Peoples, Volume 3* (Pietermaritzburg: University of Natal Press; Durban: Killie Campbell Africana Library, 1982), 198. In the discussion that follows I mostly reference the published account, edited by Webb and Wright. However, I worked with copies of the original handwritten text in hand, constantly consulting the latter to grasp as fully as possible how the original notes have been altered through the editing and publication process. I paid close attention also to how text recorded in isiZulu was translated by the editors.

22 Ndlovu noted that his father was forced to leave the Zulu kingdom during the reign of King Dingane and for a while lived practically independently of the Zulu royal house in Natal, though he did not dare to hold royal rituals for fear of reprisal from the Zulu royal house ('Ndhlovu ka Timuni', Webb and Wright, *James Stuart Archive 3*, 207). However, Thembinkosi Madlala references a 1973 file from the Chief Minister's Office, Ulundi (NlI1I3(44)7), to support a claim that Thimuni crossed into Natal later, after the Battle of Ndondakusuka in 1856, having supported the unsuccessful Mbuyazi in his attempt to succeed King Mpande (himself the successor to Dingane). Thembinkosi N. Madlala, 'The Role of Prince Thimuni kaMudli kaJama in Zulu History with Special Reference to the Activities of his Sons, Ndlovu and Chakijana, and their Descendants, 1842–1980' (Master's thesis, University of Zululand, 1997), 1–2.

23 Madlala, 'The Role of Prince Thimuni kaMudli kaJama', Chapter 3.

24   I take it that the first encounter was at Stuart's workplace because Stuart refers in his notes to the fact that his induna, Ndukwana kaMbengwana, was not present at this first meeting, noting that the latter was obliged to remain at home as Stuart was in the process of moving house, an activity in which Ndukwana, as Stuart's induna, would have played an important role. 'Ndhlovu ka Timuni', Webb and Wright, *James Stuart Archive 3*, 198.

25   The reference is probably to Mkando kaDhlova, a man of the Luthuli clan, also from the Maphumulo district, whom Stuart met with, and recorded the notes of the conversation, across some 26 days in July and August 1902. Webb and Wright, *James Stuart Archive 3*, 145–189.

26   'Ndhlovu ka Timuni', Webb and Wright, *James Stuart Archive 3*, 199–200, 205. 'Induna' is from isiZulu: singular noun: *induna*, pl. *izinduna*, a term used for an appointed official with authority. For a detailed account of who Ndukwana was and his relationship with Stuart, see John B. Wright, 'Ndukwana kaMbengwana as an Interlocutor on the History of the Zulu Kingdom, 1897–1903', *History in Africa* 38 (2011): 343–368.

27   'Ndhlovu ka Timuni', Webb and Wright, *James Stuart Archive 3*, 200.

28   'Ndhlovu ka Timuni', Webb and Wright, *James Stuart Archive 3*, 201. Italics in this and other quoted text from the published version of the conversations indicates that the word was rendered in isiZulu in the original handwritten notes of the conversation.

29   'Ndhlovu ka Timuni', Webb and Wright, *James Stuart Archive 3*, 207. The phrase 'state their own views' is the editors' translation of '*pendula*'). The translation of *izigubu* and *izamuka* were Stuart's.

30   'Ndhlovu ka Timuni', Webb and Wright, *James Stuart Archive 3*, 207.

31   'Ndhlovu ka Timuni', Webb and Wright, *James Stuart Archive 3*, 212.

32   'Ndhlovu ka Timuni', Webb and Wright, *James Stuart Archive 3*, 200 and 213. See also 206.

33   'Ndhlovu ka Timuni', Webb and Wright, *James Stuart Archive 3*, 200. Also see Stuart's comments about how Ndukwana developed his understanding of history. Webb and Wright, *James Stuart Archive 3*, 206.

34   *Ibutho*: singular noun: *ibutho*, pl. *amabutho*, a term used for an age-based 'regiment'.

35   'Ndhlovu ka Timuni', Webb and Wright, *James Stuart Archive 3*, 200.

36   See 'Jantshi ka Nongila', in Colin de B. Webb and John B. Wright, eds, *The James Stuart Archive of Recorded Oral Evidence Relating to the History of the Zulu and Neighbouring Peoples, Volume 1* (Pietermaritzburg: University of Natal Press; Durban: Killie Campbell Africana Library, 1976), 190, 194, 197.

37   See Hamilton, *Terrific Majesty*, 62–64, 68. At the time of writing I do not have any further genealogical information about Nongila.

38   'Jantshi ka Nongila', Webb and Wright, *James Stuart Archive 1*, 174; Madlala, 'The Role of Prince Thimuni kaMudli kaJama'.

39   'Ndhlovu ka Timuni', Webb and Wright, *James Stuart Archive 3*, 207.

40   Jeff Guy, *The Maphumulo Uprising: War, Law and Ritual in the Zulu Rebellion* (Pietermaritzburg: University of KwaZulu-Natal Press, 2005), 45–47.

41   Guy, *The Maphumulo Uprising*, 134–135. The imbrication of Madikane Cele in *kholwa* affairs and in the world of chiefly politics offers a further example of the kinds of entanglements typical of this time. See Heather Hughes, 'Politics and Society in Inanda, Natal: The Qadi under Chief Mqhawe, c.1840–1906' (PhD diss., University of London, 1996) and Heather Hughes and Mwelela Cele, 'Regionalism and the Archival Record: The Case of the Qadi in the Colony of Natal', *International Journal of Regional and Local History* 8, no. 2 (2013): 79–93.

42   James Stuart, *u Baxoxele: Incwadi Yezindaba za Bantu ba kwa Zulu, na ba seNatala* (London: Longman, 1924), 59–80; John B. Wright, 'Socwatsha kaPhaphu, James Stuart, and Their Conversations on the Past, 1897–1922', *Kronos* 41 (2015): 142–165.
43   See John B. Wright, 'Thununu kaNonjiya Gcabashe Visits James Stuart in the Big Smoke to Talk about History', *Natalia* 49 (2019): 1–12.
44   See Hlonipha Mokoena, '"The Black House", or How the Zulus Became Jews'. *Journal of Southern African Studies* 44, no. 3 (2018): 401–411; Hamilton, *Terrific Majesty*, 62–71 and more recently Carolyn Hamilton and John Wright, 'Moving Beyond Ethnic Framing: Political Differentiation in the Chiefdoms of the KwaZulu-Natal Region before 1830', *Journal of Southern African Studies*, 43, no. 4 (2017): 663–679.
45   See discussion in Mokoena, *Fuze*, 49–54.
46   Mokoena, *Fuze*, 49–50.
47   Mokoena, *Fuze*, 42, 199.
48   Mokoena, *Fuze*, 217–235.

REFERENCES

Carton, Benedict, John Laband and Jabulani Sithole, eds. *Zulu Identities: Being Zulu, Past and Present*. Pietermaritzburg: University of KwaZulu-Natal Press, 2009.
Cope, Nicholas. 'The Zulu Petit Bourgeoisie and Zulu Nationalism in the 1920s: Origins of Inkatha'. *Journal of Southern African Studies* 16, no. 3 (September 1990): 431–451.
Eldredge, Elizabeth A. *The Creation of the Zulu Kingdom, 1815–1828: War, Shaka, and the Consolidation of Power*. New York: Cambridge University Press, 2014.
Fuze, Magema M. *Abantu Abamnyama Lapha Bavela Ngakhona*. Pietermaritzburg: City Printing Works, 1922.
Fuze, Magema M. 'A Visit to King Ketshwayo'. *Macmillan's Magazine* (March 1878): 421–432.
Gumede, William and Leslie Dikeni, eds. *The Poverty of Ideas: South African Democracy and the Retreat of Intellectuals*. Johannesburg: Jacana Media, 2009.
Guy, Jeff. *The Maphumulo Uprising: War, Law and Ritual in the Zulu Rebellion*. Pietermaritzburg: University of KwaZulu-Natal Press, 2005.
Guy, Jeff. *The View across the River: Harriette Colenso and the Zulu Struggle against Imperialism*. Charlottesville: University of Virginia Press, 2002.
Hamilton, Carolyn. *Terrific Majesty: The Powers of Shaka and the Limits of Historical Invention*. Cape Town: David Philip, 1998.
Hamilton, Carolyn and Lesley Cowling. 'Rethinking Public Engagement'. In *Babel Unbound: Rage, Reason and Rethinking Public Life*, edited by Lesley Cowling and Carolyn Hamilton, 21–39. Johannesburg: Wits University Press, 2020.
Hamilton, Carolyn and John Wright. 'Moving Beyond Ethnic Framing: Political Differentiation in the Chiefdoms of the KwaZulu-Natal Region before 1830'. *Journal of Southern African Studies* 43, no. 4 (2017): 663–679.
Hughes, Heather. *The First President: A Life of John Dube*. Johannesburg: Jacana Media, 2011.
Hughes, Heather. 'Politics and Society in Inanda, Natal: The Qadi under Chief Mqhawe, c.1840–1906'. PhD diss., University of London, 1996.
Hughes, Heather and Mwelela Cele. 'Regionalism and the Archival Record: The Case of the Qadi in the Colony of Natal'. *International Journal of Regional and Local History* 8, no. 2 (2013): 79–93.

Khumalo, Vukile. 'The Class of 1856 and the Politics of Cultural Production(s) in the Emergence of Ekukhanyeni, 1855–1910'. In *The Eye of the Storm: Bishop John William Colenso and the Crisis of Biblical Inspiration*, edited by Jonathan A. Draper, 207–241. Pietermaritzburg: Cluster Publications, 2003.

La Hausse de Lalouvière, Paul. *Restless Identities: Signatures of Nationalism, Zulu Ethnicity and History in the Lives of Petros Lamula (c.1881–1948) and Lymon Maling (1889–c.1936)*. Pietermaritzburg: University of Natal Press, 2000.

Madlala, Thembinkosi N. 'The Role of Prince Thimuni kaMudli kaJama in Zulu History with Special Reference to the Activities of his Sons, Ndlovu and Chakijana, and their Descendants, 1842–1980'. Master's thesis, University of Zululand, 1997.

Marks, Shula. 'The Ambiguities of Dependence: John L. Dube of Natal'. *Journal of Southern African Studies* 1, no. 2 (1975): 162–180.

Mokoena, Hlonipha. '"The Black House", or How the Zulus Became Jews'. *Journal of Southern African Studies* 44, no. 3 (2018): 401–411.

Mokoena, Hlonipha. *Magema Fuze: The Making of a Kholwa Intellectual*. Pietermaritzburg: University of KwaZulu-Natal Press, 2011.

Ndletyana, Mcebisi, ed. *African Intellectuals in 19th and Early 20th Century South Africa*. Cape Town: HSRC Press, 2008.

Poyner, Jane, ed. *J.M. Coetzee and the Idea of the Public Intellectual*. Athens: Ohio University Press, 2006.

Stuart, James. *u Baxoxele: Incwadi Yezindaba za Bantu ba kwa Zulu, na ba seNatala*. London: Longman, 1924.

Vale, Peter, Lawrence Hamilton and Estelle Prinsloo, eds. *Intellectual Traditions in South Africa: Ideas, Individuals and Institutions*. Pietermaritzburg: University of KwaZulu-Natal Press, 2014.

Webb, Colin de B. and John B. Wright, eds. *The James Stuart Archive of Recorded Oral Evidence Relating to the History of the Zulu and Neighbouring Peoples, Volume 1*. Pietermaritzburg: University of Natal Press; Durban: Killie Campbell Africana Library, 1976.

Webb, Colin de B. and John B. Wright, eds. *The James Stuart Archive of Recorded Oral Evidence Relating to the History of the Zulu and Neighbouring Peoples, Volume 3*. Pietermaritzburg: University of Natal Press; Durban: Killie Campbell Africana Library, 1982.

Webb, Colin de B. and John B. Wright, eds. *A Zulu King Speaks: Statements Made by Cetshwayo kaMpande on the History and Customs of His People*. Pietermaritzburg: University of Natal Press, 1978.

Wright, John B. 'Ndukwana kaMbengwana as an Interlocutor on the History of the Zulu Kingdom, 1897–1903'. *History in Africa* 38 (2011): 343–368.

Wright, John B. 'Socwatsha kaPhaphu, James Stuart, and Their Conversations on the Past, 1897–1922'. *Kronos* 41 (2015): 142–165.

Wright, John B. 'Thununu kaNonjiya Gcabashe Visits James Stuart in the Big Smoke to Talk about History'. *Natalia* 49 (2019): 1–12.

CHAPTER

2

Elijah Makiwane and Early Black South African Public Intellectualism

Luvuyo Mthimkhulu Dondolo

This chapter explores the life and work of Reverend Elijah Makiwane (1850–1928). He was born in Sheshegu, Alice, in the Cape Colony (what is now the Eastern Cape), one of three children. In 1858 his parents became part of the Wesleyan Methodist Society. He attended elementary school in Ncerha village, under the guidance of a Wesleyan teacher, Joseph Mjila. Subsequently, he went on to study at Nxukhwebe (Healdtown) High School in Fort Beaufort. In 1865, at the age of 15, he enrolled at Lovedale College. The college introduced him to studies in literature, philosophy, languages and divinity, which were of a superior quality as there was no material difference between the college's curriculum and the theological curriculum offered in Scotland.

Mweli Skota maintains that Makiwane gradually mastered his lessons until he became the second of his theological class (after Pambani Mzimba) to qualify for the ministry of the Free Church.[1] Lovedale offered him an enabling environment that shaped him into the man he became. In 1871, the Lovedale Education Board awarded him a special meritorious award called the Certificate of Honourable Mention, which acknowledged his good work and positive influence on others.

During the ten years he spent at Lovedale, Makiwane became an intern in positions that were prominent among the school elite. In March 1867, in his second year of study, he was appointed as an assistant teacher to teach junior classes. Between 1875 and 1877, he was appointed to teach first-year Theology students. In November 1872 when the telegraph office opened, he was in charge of its operations for a year. In 1875, he qualified and was licensed as a minister of the Free Church of Scotland.

Makiwane was a pioneer of modern journalism among black people in South Africa and a prominent contributor to public discourse. He is known for his quest for education and knowledge production, his engagement with race consciousness and his championing of cultural, political and spiritual identities. However, Makiwane and many others who formed the early African intellectual movement are often left out of the array of South African histories and the post-apartheid memorial complexes. The African National Congress (ANC) historiography eliminates many early histories and instead focuses on the more recent past and aspects of history from the second half of the twentieth century, framed by the Mandela mythology. This period, often called the 'Mandelasation' of the South African liberation struggle against apartheid, does not engage with the intricacies and complexities of the twentieth century and results in a kind of 'cultural homogenisation order from above which has been the rule in many countries all over the world'.[2] The post-apartheid memorial complexes present a monolithic and hegemonic master historical narrative that suppresses historical specificity. However, in forging any nation state, particularly after a traumatic past, history matters in the process of constructing a nation and nation-building. This ensures a holistic presentation and interpretation of the past. It can thus be argued that South Africa needs to look beyond the master narrative peddled in the present and move towards a more comprehensive and 'historically inclusive discourse'.[3]

While there is considerable scholarship on early African intellectuals in South Africa, including work by Ntongela Masilela, Bhekizizwe Peterson, Mcebisi Ndletyana, André Odendaal, Hlonipha Mokoena, Jeff Opland, Wandile Kuse, Pamela Maseko and Mbukeni Harbert Mnguni, Makiwane has not been given the attention he deserves.[4] The purpose of this chapter, therefore, is to highlight Makiwane's contribution to the early African intellectual movement and to present-day South African constitutional liberal politics. It provides an overview of Makiwane's life and work within the context of colonialism and the early African intellectual tradition and makes an argument for remembering his legacy in the South Africa of today.

HISTORICAL CONTEXT: COLONIALISM, TRANSCULTURATION AND TRANSITION

Africans responded in different ways to the colonial enterprise, Christianity and Europeans' 'civilising' agenda. These responses included violent resistance during the wars of land dispossession. However, after they were finally defeated, the response changed from the gun to the pen and constitutional liberal politics as 'they needed to adapt to western-style constitutional politics. "Take paper and ink [and] fire with your pen" Isaac Wauchope exhorted.'[5] The struggle between African values and Western modernity is one of the major issues that African writers, including Makiwane, dealt with. Makiwane refused to be an observer on the sidelines; he refused to 'only write footnotes or a glossary when the event is over.'[6]

Some African post-colonial writers, such as Ngũgĩ wa Thiong'o, criticise the loss of African values that occurred during colonisation and the continued influence of Western modernity in post-colonial Africa. He argues that Western values had the effect of 'a cultural bomb, that aimed to annihilate a people's belief in their names, in their languages, in their environment, in their heritage of struggle, in their unity, in their capacities and ultimately in themselves'.[7] Some African writers, under the influence of Western values and Christianity, distanced themselves from their African past and cultural heritage because it did not fit with the 'modernity' narrative and with what they conceptualised as progress.

The concept of transculturation is mostly associated with the work of the Cuban scholar Fernando Ortiz Fernández, although the theory has developed its own history in different contexts. It describes the process of imposed definitions by a dominant or colonial power over the indigenous people of a particular area. The theory and the definition of transculturation presented by different scholars at various times and in various contexts helps to give meaning and impetus to the use of the term in the context of early African intellectuals in South Africa. It is a multidimensional process, conversations in both directions between the Western and African worlds. The process of cultural destruction followed by reconstruction on entirely new terms was part of the historical conditions that produced and shaped the early African intellectual movement. For instance, Mary Louise Pratt defines transculturation as the process in which subordinated or marginalised groups selected or invent from materials transmitted to them by a dominant or metropolitan culture.[8] It is also these factors that made the early African intellectuals play a major role in the struggle against colonialism and influenced the aspirations of the struggle against apartheid – constitutional democracy, rule of law and human rights.

In the South African context, transculturation at the time of the early African intelligentsia cannot be presented in any form without acknowledging Tiyo Soga, an iconic figure in the movement. It was in the midst of wars of land dispossession and conquest that Christian Western education and the modernity project were introduced. This historical moment produced individuals like Soga through a process of transculturation. The early African intellectuals were a product of the missionaries' 'civilising' enterprise of the indigenous people. Their education and ideas were a result of sociocultural and intellectual conversations between the two worlds, African and Western, which produced them.

Early African intellectuals became agents of the discourse of 'enlightenment' and these were framed by human perfectibility and projected through the mission project, constituting the grounds on which autonomy and social emancipation would be sought. The early African intellectual heritage generally demonstrates the nineteenth century's ideas within the context of colonialism and racial discrimination. This is evident in the writings of Tiyo Soga, Jonas Ntsiko, Samuel E.K. Mqhayi, Mpilo Walter Benson Rubusana, William Wellington Gqoba and John Tengo Jabavu, to mention a few.

TRANSCULTURATION OF THE EARLY AFRICAN INTELLIGENTSIA

The documentary *Early African Intellectuals*, commissioned by the Amathole District Municipality Heritage Unit and produced by Mzi Gova, traces the early African intellectual movement in the Eastern Cape and beyond during the nineteenth and twentieth centuries. It starts with an *imbongi* (praise singer), who highlights the role played by early African intellectuals. The documentary highlights that 'it is here in the land of Phalo, of Rharhabe, where Christianity, modernity and Western education were introduced, here at the foot of Amathole Mountain that the early African intellectuals emerged'.[9]

David Attwell suggests that the first transculturation in South Africa occurred during what John Comaroff and Jean Comaroff called the country's 'long history of symbolic struggle', a history in which the consciousness of coloniser and colonised arose – as well as those falling somewhere in between – and has been fashioned and refashioned through generations of interaction, from the most mundane to the most violent.[10]

While I do not intend to discuss modernity broadly, it is important to highlight how modernity relates to the early African intellectual movement. In the South African context, the modernity complex illustrates ethnic and race-based advancement and human development framed by discrimination, industrialisation and colonialism. Attwell prefaces his definition of modernity by stating that if a simple philosophical definition was available, it might be that modernity is the current governing concept of what it means to be a subject of history. He says that modernity 'refers not only to technology and the emergence of an administered and industrialised society, but also to that fluid powerful system of ideas that we inherit from the bourgeois revolutions of Europe in the late eighteenth century – ideas such as autonomy, personhood, rights and citizenship'.[11]

This definition may not be comprehensive, but it helps to ground my discussion of the African intellectual heritage as informed by the early African intellectual discourse and transculturation of 'enlightenment' within the broader human developmental discourse. The heritage of black literature and African intellectuals largely demonstrates the way in which nineteenth-century ideas were taken up by black writers and thinkers within their own context. The ideas of the bourgeois revolutions of Europe in the late eighteenth century can be seen in the black liberal constitutional politics of struggle against colonial rule and apartheid in the late nineteenth and early twentieth century.

As Odendaal puts it, the indigenous people of colonial South Africa were educated so as to be equipped to fit into Western society and they were eager to advance within the life of the colony.[12] Their mission education taught them to speak in the language of Christianity, to understand the nuances of Western constitutional politics and, in a cultural sense, to employ the protocols of civilisation, which the missionaries had emphasised in their education.

FROM THE BARREL OF A GUN TO THE BARREL OF A PEN

The notions of transculturation and the transition from the gun to the pen are two sides of the same colonial project. The colonial history of the Cape Colony (1806–1910), particularly the Amathole region, reveals the intensity of colonial invasion. The Amathole region was the crucible of wars of land dispossession and resistance and had a large number of forts that are still evident in the present heritage landscape: 'There are few places in the world where the complicated concept of a "frontier" can be better shown than in the Eastern Cape. In no area in southern Africa and possibly the world, is there such a density of military and mission sites. Memorials to the more modern struggle victims have been added to the military and mission sites.'[13]

Wars and resistance during the colonial period were about more than a struggle for land. They were also about the introduction of a particular cultural identity and way of life through which indigenous people were indoctrinated into a particular world view and value system. Christian education was an agent of change used by European settlers as part of their 'civilising' mission. Over the years, many locals went through the missionary education system, which resulted in the emergence of an educated group. For Ndletyana, these early intellectuals, based in the Cape

> owe their rise to the cumulative impact of missionary activities, as well as British colonialism. Missionaries first arrived among the Xhosa in September 1799. The pioneer of this evangelical mission was Johannes van der Kamp (known among locals as *Nyengana*, one who comes secretly) from the London Missionary Society (LMS). The LMS seemed to be the evident agent(s) of the birth of intellectual culture in the western configuration in the Cape Colony.[14]

The intellectual culture started before Van der Kamp's time, but 'he and a few others were instrumental in spreading the message. (Fifty years later, eleven missionary societies, with a total of no fewer than 150 personnel, had established themselves on South African soil. The most prominent of the station being Lovedale, founded in 1820, in Alice).'[15]

Missionaries used the concepts of education and literature to 'civilise' Africans. In other words, missionary schools were not just centres of learning, but were part of the colonial enterprise. The Christian education system introduced texts of whiteness and aimed to emphasise white supremacy, but it also resulted in a new phase of resistance to colonialism. The educated Africans used their Christian education, which was meant to 'civilise' and assimilate them into a culture and a prescribed way of life, to lodge their struggle for human rights and constitutional democracy.

Soga's work, particularly, from 1865 until his death, positioned him as an iconic figure in the African intellectual movement. His work focused on Christianity in South Africa among the Africans and his ideas about race consciousness and pan-Africanism were pioneering. Furthermore, his seminal work in the conservation and documentation of Xhosa history, culture and heritage gave him an appeal across different interest groups in his community.

Subsequent contributions by the next generation in the early days of the African studies and isiXhosa literature scholarship marked the emergence of literary studies by Gqoba, Makiwane and Mqhayi, among others, which built on the foundation laid by Soga in the 1860s for the 'Regeneration of Africa', which was later outlined by Pixley ka Isaka Seme in his speech at Columbia University in 1906.[16] This generation of writers wrote in isiXhosa, rather than in the colonial master's language, English. This had political, social and historical meaning in its Africanist consciousness and the challenge it issued to the supremacy of English. These writers' use of isiXhosa in knowledge production demonstrates a historical enterprise in the process of constructing and accepting modernity on their own terms. It symbolises their struggle with cultural and ideological dominance, a struggle against colonial hegemony and symbolism – the use of their own language was a political act.

This new discourse formed the foundation for public scholarship among the educated. They started having debates in public forums and newspapers. Issues for debate included, among others, constitutional democracy politics, the Cape Province franchise, Western 'civilisation', African culture, history, current affairs and discriminatory legislations like the Natives Land Act of 1913.

As a consequence of the missionaries' agenda, all early African intellectuals were Christians and some had completely turned their backs on their African identities. There were others who still believed in the Westernised/Christian world view, but concurrently held onto elements of African world views and history. These included individuals such as Gqoba, Makiwane, Rubusana, Mqhayi and Ntsiko, among others.

The gradual intrusion by missionaries and their influence divided the locals into the believers or *amagqomboka* (Christianised/modern Africans) and non-believers or *amaqaba* (un-Christianised/'uneducated' locals). The latter were the protectors and defenders of their culture, traditions and history. They viewed this progression as an assimilation of the locals into a Western world view, which for them signalled a struggle for spiritual and cultural identities. The differences between *amagqomboka* and *amaqaba* were not about the conflict between the educated and Christianised and the 'uneducated' and anti-Christian. Rather, the conflict was centred more on the divide and rule strategy employed by the settler administration, a familiar tactic to consolidate colonial control. It had calamitous consequences: 'The response of the chiefs and of the bulk of AmaXhosa, was a prolonged resistance to Christianity which took many forms, including returning to nativism. In its pure form, nativism is the rejection of assimilation and the restoration of aspects of traditional African religion and tribal life. Nativism on the Eastern Frontier had a strong anti-missionary strain, reached a peak with the Cattle Killing in 1856–7.'[17]

The concept of nativism – the travelling theory of nativism as presented above and in the broader colonial context – has its politics in the racialised connotations of juxtaposing settlers against indigenous people. Nativism can also be understood within Sir Henry Maine's theory of nativism, as Mahmood Mamdani historicised it. In this framework, Europe had always been presented as modern and advanced while the indigenous inhabitants were backward. Anything Western was the barometer for the level of 'civilisation' of a local.[18]

The concept of nativism as used in the context of Gcalekaland in the Eastern Cape represents resistance and an active refusal of Western gazes and a determination to retain an indigenous anti-colonial outlook. The settler-native complex with its colonial juxtaposing images can also be comprehended within the context of space, self-definition, imposed definition and power relations. Donovan Williams' depiction of the situation in Gcalekaland was also evident at Mgwali Mission.[19] The conflicts were not only between *amaqaba* and *amagqobhoka*, but also among *amagqobhoka* themselves. The case of a group of youths who circumcised themselves, a practice seen as uncivilised, in the Mgwali Mission Station – the missionaries' (Christian and Western) holy ground – shows Soga's personal dilemma as a result of the established missionary tradition and Western culture, within a broader context of the ambiguities of transculturation. Soga was the victim of the colonial and Christian establishment. His reactions to the incident of the youths, *abakwetha* (a Xhosa rite to manhood), and his description of Tutura as a place 'where midnight darkness covers the people' make this clear.[20] The action by the young boys was a sign of resistance against cultural conquest – a struggle of cultures and symbolism. This demonstrates a quest for identity and also emphasises that the loss of identity is as important as the loss of land through colonial dispossession.

REV. ELIJAH MAKIWANE: A VISIONARY

As a representative of the early African intellectuals' movement following after Soga, Makiwane was an active participant in transculturation and the new discourse in South Africa. His imprint in the footprints of the early African intellectuals' movement can be understood and presented within a particular space and time. His African feminist position was ahead of his time and his use of isiXhosa marked a pivotal point in upholding the integrity of the culture and the very identity of amaXhosa.

An early architect of gender studies scholarship

Makiwane firmly believed in and promoted women's education. He popularised the belief that African man needed wives 'who have imbibed the same ideas of progress which we suppose a young man has to receive'.[21] Makiwane did not just promote this idea; he also practised it in his family and all his daughters distinguished themselves in different fields in their adult lives.

A newspaper editor

Transculturation gave birth to modern journalism in South Africa, particularly from 1837 onwards. Modern journalism culture and ethics were evident in Makiwane's vision of the *Isigidimi samaXhosa* (the Xhosa Express, which later became known as the Christian Express) newspaper as its assistant editor (1870-75). *Isigidimi* started as a supplement in the so-called *Kaffir Express*, a precursor of the *South African Outlook*, which was a missionary journal in South Africa, and was published in both English and isiXhosa. In his first editorial, titled 'To Our Readers', in its first publication in 1870, Makiwane stated: 'The period when newspapers begin to live in the history of any people is an important era ... And were *The Kaffir Express* to become an established fact, it might be the double means of educating and informing, of carrying ideas and stimulating the desire to be able to read.'[22] Makiwane's vision and declaration exemplify profound journalism standards and practices even before Africans assumed full control of the newspaper. He envisaged a newspaper that was not sectarian, but instead addressed the interests and challenges of Africans across different belief groups.

This editorial also addresses the issues important to the indigenous people, an 'imagined community',[23] and their engagement with Western tools to redefine themselves while demanding full citizenry in a racialised colonial society. After 1878, journalism culture became more established with the increasing number of African writers and editors. In South Africa, as in most colonies, the Bible and missionary newspapers and magazines became a common vehicle for the modernity project. The first isiXhosa translation of the New Testament of the Christian scriptures was published in 1846, followed by the Old Testament in 1857.

The history of early newspapers in the Cape Colony can be presented through two taxonomies. The first is the missionary newspapers and magazines. The literature culture was inextricably linked with the Christian missionary project. Archibald Campbell Jordan (1975) indicated that in order to be able to 'preach the Word' missionaries had not only to learn the languages of the people, but also to reproduce these languages in writing. The dawn of literacy was associated with the Glasgow Missionary Society, whose representatives wrote in isiXhosa at a small mission station on the banks of the Tyhume River (Eastern Cape) in 1821. The first man ever to write a book in isiXhosa was John Bennie, one of the three Glasgow missionaries who founded Lovedale.[24]

The first missionary publishing project was launched in 1824, with the production of a small spelling book published at the Chumie (Thyume) Mission Press. The first newspaper, *Umshumayeli Wendaba* (the Publisher of News), began its operations in July 1837. It only lasted for four years, but during this period, the newspaper had produced fifteen editions, four per year, produced quarterly. This marked the start of modern journalism culture among the locals. Two years later, a number of other missionary newspapers surfaced. These included *Isibuto Samavo* – a collection of stories – in 1843, *Ikwezi* (the Morning Star) in 1844, *Isithunywa Senyanga* (the Monthly Messenger) in 1850, *Indaba* (The News) in 1861 and *Isigidimi samaXhosa* in 1870. Odendaal argues that from 1862 to 1865, *Indaba* became a vehicle for the first literate generation of Africans to articulate their aspirations and ideas in a public forum in their own language.[25] Since it was part of the scope of the missionary newspapers, Soga welcomed its appearance and encouraged indigenous people to use *Indaba* as a repository to preserve their history.

During the early days of isiXhosa literature, writers like Soga and Gqoba used the local newspapers to publish their literary work in the form of poems, short stories and essays and historical accounts. It can be argued that the period in which Soga and Gqoba's writings were published in newspapers marks the beginning of the progression of South African modernity and literary culture. Lovedale Press, established in 1830 by the London Missionary Society, became the primary production house for literature in isiXhosa.

The other historical strand of modern journalism was the alternative African independent newspapers. This, too, can be divided into two, the black liberal newspaper *Imvo Zabantsundu* (Native People's Opinion) under Jabavu and the Africanist newspaper *Izwi Labantu* (The Voice of the People) under Rubusana. The first newspaper that broke the tradition of missionary newspapers and magazines was *Imvo Zabantsundu*, in 1884, followed by *Izwi Labantu* in 1897. These two newspapers and the last of the missionary newspapers dynasty, *Isigidimi*, continued into the twentieth century, providing a space for the proliferation of isiXhosa literature and scholarship. These were to be followed by many others in what were then Natal and the Transvaal.

At the age of 20, Makiwane was introduced to journalism at Lovedale when he began working as an assistant editor of *Isigidimi samaXhosa* under James Stewart, its founding editor as well as the editor of the *Kaffir Express*. The *Kaffir Express* and *Isigidimi* grew steadily year by year. In 1873, they 'became separate newspapers, both doubling in length, and in 1874 Makiwane began to edit *Isigidimi*, though under supervision. The demand for the paper from the African readers increased to the extent that *Isigidimi* was published bi-monthly from mid-1879.'[26] In 1876, Makiwane was the first African to assume full editorial responsibility of *Isigidimi*. The control of *Isigidimi* by Africans enabled it to give space to critical voices on a range of matters relating to the South African journey to becoming a modern country.

Isigidimi presented opposing views on Western/Christian enterprises and the African world view and thinking. As Odendaal contends:

> In a letter filled with Africanist overtones in January 1871, 'Kokela' idealised the African societies of the past and lamented the radical change that had taken place in them since the advent of the missionaries. Kokela's approach met with a scathing response from other correspondents, who believed in the advantages of acculturation and the superiority of western civilisation. 'Fundani Makowetu' (be learned, my countrymen) ... countered that 'to be under the English is more advantageous'. He felt that African independence retarded progress.[27]

Kokela's concerns about the missionaries' Eurocentrism – their teaching English, Roman and Greek history at the expense of African history – would today be recognised as valid concerns about epistemic justice. This public discourse juxtaposed the two worlds. This did not only demonstrate the divergent views of 'Western civilisation' and education in the Cape Colony, but also the level of misunderstanding about the contribution of the African continent to human progress and civilisation by individuals such as 'Fundani Makowetu'. For Ntongela Masilela this public discourse began a process he dabbed as the 'secularisation of the theologically shackled African imagination or imaginary'.[28] The colonially imprisoned African imagination – anchored in a colonial consciousness and history – was profoundly political.

The newspapers also reflected public scholarship covering a range of topics, such as blackness. The debate between Magema Fuze and Philip Xulu in *Inkanyiso*, 6 September and 4 October 1890, on the politics of colour and terms such as *abantu abantsundu* (brown people) and *abantu abamnyama* (black people) and their preference is one such example. The discussion was philosophical while also reflecting linguistic politics. According to Mokoena, Fuze 'in response to a letter from Xulu from Escourt presented a very contentious argument that black people should prefer to be called brown. What is significant is that Fuze's preference for the term "*abantu abantsundu*" elicited a response from Xulu, which in turn provoked Fuze to replay and repeat his explanation.'[29]

This debate among the early African intellectuals is a long and peculiar history. Jabavu's naming of his newspaper – *Imvo Zabantsundu* (Native People's Opinion) in 1884 as against *Zabamnyama* (black people) can be understood in this context. The naming reflects his preference. The contestation over these terms permeated different historical periods in South Africa and continues today.

Isigidimi was predominantly aimed at the Xhosa Christian community. It appeared as a regular monthly paper in 1879 and fortnightly in 1884 until it stopped completely in December 1888. Makiwane headed the newsroom for eight years and became the first known African editor of a mission journal in southern Africa. In 1881, he was succeeded by Jabavu and he went on to become a founding member of a number of prominent African educational and political organisations.

Isigidimi had more than 20 correspondents, representing about 30 rural and urban areas in the colonies of the Cape and Natal. Some of its contributors and editors were the African elite who were conscious of the politics of that time and advocates of its readers' opinions. Makiwane was a pioneer newspaper editor and while he maintained that Africans should only use the English language and their mission education to advance themselves, English was not to determine their identity.

An Africanist scholar and a proponent of vernacular language

As was the case with many of his peers, Makiwane was a multidimensional figure: church minister, newspaper editor, schoolteacher, politician and Africanist feminist. These early African intellectuals played an important role in the formation of the Lovedale Literary Society and the Native Educational Association in 1879. In July 1884, he was elected to the presidency of the Association. This was an important structure for the development of South African literature scholarship and modernity. It later proved to be important for generations of early African intellectuals and the broader development of the early African intellectual movement as well as the development of Lovedale's students.

As the president of the Native Educational Association, Makiwane was genuinely concerned about the Western-African complex. He was a proponent of the use of African languages and was against the privileging of English in the advancement of South African modernity. For him, this privileging of English was used to affirm the supremacy of English cultures over African cultures, languages and being. As a result of his political and social consciousness, he promoted the equal treatment of languages.

For Makiwane, 'an indigenous African literature renaissance was overdue'.[30] He and others laid the foundation for 'an indigenous African literature renaissance' based on vernacular languages as a way of recasting themselves and also contesting the colonial images of 'otherness' through use of their languages.

To borrow from Chinua Achebe, some early African public intellectuals, including Makiwane, were 'writing back to the west' as an attempt to 'reshape the dialogue between the colonised and the coloniser'.[31] The use of vernacular languages became a vehicle to discuss politics of identity and recognition and challenge white supremacy. Indigenous languages were seen as a path to understanding the colonised, their world view, their knowledge production and their art of communication.

Languages are critical links between the past, the present and the future. They inform us about culture, history and the thoughts and feelings of the people who speak them. Ousseina Alidou and Alamin Mazrui argue:

> Language has featured quite prominently in this quest for Africa-centered knowledge ... Two contesting positions have emerged in this connection ... There is first, the 'pragmatist' school of thought which contends that imperial languages like English can be refashioned to carry the weight of African thought. This linguistic reformation ... would not only be the more pragmatic option, but also one that is in accord with the interests of national unity. On the other hand, the 'nationalists' argue that language determines people's worldview in a culturally circumscribed manner. The only path of thought, therefore, is through Africa's own indigenous languages.[32]

The early Cape writers of isiXhosa literature subscribed to the latter school of thought as most of their writings were in isiXhosa. The decision to write in isiXhosa has historically been influenced by a number of reasons that cut across generations and contexts, and in a way created a narrative of themselves, which presented a space for intergenerational discourse. The politics of language in isiXhosa literature scholarship became a historical framing of the development of the isiXhosa literature culture in the Cape.

By using their own language, the early modern isiXhosa literature authors wanted to express their world as informed by their language and social forces, as Jordan suggests.[33] These authors refused to be linguistically and culturally assimilated. For them, language and expression were about cultural and identity struggles, as well as authenticity. As in the case of the Nigerian liberation struggle and the dream of the Republic of Biafra, as argued by Achebe, their dream was of a new nation.[34]

Makiwane also worried about the cultural assimilation of Africans into Western culture. Although he supported the social progress of his fellow Africans through European enterprises, he believed that it should not be at the expense of African values and norms. Makiwane used Western education to affirm Africanness and challenge the superior status given to imperial language and the text of whiteness. This was an unintended outcome of the Christian education system and civilising enterprise.

Masilela argues that Makiwane expanded the essay form beyond the achievements of Soga and Gqoba.[35] The extraordinary essays Makiwane wrote in the 1880s, which appeared in *Imvo Zabantsundu*, were a prelude of what Selope Thema and others of the New Africa Regeneration Movement were to write 50 years later.

For Africans to overcome the construct of whiteness that had a negative impact in all spheres of their lives, they needed self-consciousness to fight until they had what Steve Biko called 'an open society'. The latter broadly refers to a democratic state, equal rights and democratic values of one man, one vote. An 'open society' is not race-based. The concept of an 'open society' was the antithesis of the racially based colonial and apartheid state configuration and was essential to the creation of a new nation state and the deeper question of nationhood. In an edited selection of Steve Biko's writings – *I Write What I Like* – by Aelred Stubbs, in a cross-examination in his trial, Biko stated: 'The attitude is a simple one, an open society, one man, one vote, no reference to colour.'[36]

The South African Student Organisation (SASO) and the Black Consciousness Movement (BCM), of which Biko was a leader, believed in a vision of a future South Africa based on the concept of an 'open society'. Biko can be understood as setting the philosophical, political and democratic values of socio-economic and historical justice. The principle of one man, one vote found its expression in ANC politics in what Neville Alexander refers to as the 'minimum demands' of the ANC in the 1950s.[37]

In historicising the notion of one man, one vote, it is important to consider the liberal politics of the Cape Colony and Natal in the 1800s and early 1900s. This can be understood through the politics of that time and the role and contribution of the (early) African public intellectuals – who viewed themselves as equal citizens to their white counterparts – with the belief that the colour of one's skin did not determine one's status and privileges being at the centre of liberal politics. The latter layered the foundation for the position of twentieth-century black political organisations and the creation of a democratic South Africa. The use of indigenous languages in the struggles of yesteryear is still relevant today.

Makiwane, the politician

Makiwane was actively involved in the creation of the Cape Colony and its political geography. He was a member of both the South African Natives Congress (SANC), formed in 1898, and the Bantu Union, formed in 1919. The SANC was the precursor of the South African National Natives Congress (SANNC), re-launched in 1912. Apart from Meshach Pelem, the SANC executive included W.B.M. Rubusana,

Charles Madosi, S.E.K. Mqhayi, Nathaniel Umhala and Makiwane himself. They attended meetings held in response to the South African draft constitution, as they were concerned with the provisions of the Act that aimed to remove the rights of educated Africans. The opinion was expressed that if these provisions became law it would lead to alienation between blacks and whites, which is exactly what happened as the construction of modern South Africa unfolded. The delegates forwarded a petition to the British House of Commons, undersigned by Makiwane, stating their opposition to the construction of a racialised configuration of modern South Africa.

Like W.E.B. Du Bois's international Pan-African Congress, the political movements that Makiwane was a member of were reformist in outlook, more concerned with the interests and privileges of the black middle class, such as the right to vote in the Cape and Natal, than with the complete dismantling of the colonial and racist regime.

Makiwane, the church minister and teacher

In 1875 the Free Church of Scotland qualified Makiwane as a minister, which allowed him to practise as a clergyman. In 1877 he was assigned to a local congregation in Krwakrwa, Tyhume, in Alice. He was then dispatched to Macfarlan Mission to oversee its operations. He found ways within the congregation to express his independence, which consequently earned him respect as he became one of the most valued ministers in the 'Kaffrarian' Presbytery. As a minister at Macfarlan, he was in charge of both the African and the European members of the congregation, which was unusual as the two were previously separated by their church ministers.

According to Skota, Makiwane did splendid work for the church, amidst great difficulties.[38] As somebody who spoke his mind, he fought for equal working conditions and equal treatment of black and white ministers in the Presbyterian Church. His comments about the disturbing racist tendencies in the case of Pambani Mzimba also mirrored his firm stance.[39] Makiwane faced challenges from his friend and fellow minister Mzimba's supporters, some of whom attacked Makiwane's family and congregation.

Makiwane was introduced to the teaching profession while still at Lovedale Mission School, in his role as an assistant teacher. After his ordination as a minister of the church, he taught first-year theological students at Lovedale until he was sent to Macfarlan Mission. His early introduction to the profession sharpened his teaching skills. According to Skota, Makiwane's students always attained the highest marks, indicative of his extraordinary dedication to teaching.[40] The Excellence

Certificate he obtained in 1871 for his exceptional conduct would likely have had a positive influence on his theological students who wanted to emulate him as exceptional achievers.

William Govan Bennie, who had been one of Makiwane's students, declared: 'Kubo bonke ababese Lovedale ngaloo mihla thina bantwana sasithanda ngokukodwa u Elijah Makiwane no John Knox Bokwe. Kodwa ngasemva kwalo lonke olu vuyo lubuntwanara ngobomi kwakufihlakele ingqondo enzulu nebukhali, ecacileyo ukucinga, nengajikwa lula kwindlela elungileyo' (In those days, we as Lovedale students loved Elijah Makiwane and John Knox Bokwe. However, behind joy and love, the former harboured high intellect, a deep thinker that was not easily convinced).[41]

THE LEGACY OF MAKIWANE, THE PUBLIC INTELLECTUAL

Makiwane's articulations in public forums and his published newspaper articles, including his popular piece in the first edition of *Isigidimi samaXhosa* in 1870, illustrate his public intellectualism. This permeated through to isiXhosa modern literature and culture and the translation of some religious texts into isiXhosa.

Robert Shepherd recalled Makiwane's intellect capabilities:

> *Bonke ubomi bakhe ubengumthandi weencwadi nendoda yengqondo. Ubuchule bakhe ezifundweni bufike bazibonakalisa kwiQumru lo Guqulo lweZibhalo, nakwezinye iincwadi, ngokukodwa inguqulo nezilungelelaniso ezenzelwe amaKrestu awayesanda ngokwanda. Umsebenzi awuphetheyo umbonakalise engumntu ozikhathazayo ngawo nonganeliyo kwakwenzileyo nokuthi ungabi naziphene. Umsebenzi wakhe njengendoda yengqondo ufika ubalasele kwiinkundla zetyalike, nakwintetho abesakuzibhala kumaphephandaba esiNtu.*[42]

Throughout his life, he loved books and was a man of mental power. His capabilities shined when he served in a committee that translated Christian books and other books as the numbers of converted Christians were growing. Through this work he appeared as someone who loved his work – but not certified with what he has done – and a perfectionist. His work excelled in Christianity and the pieces he published in various newspapers of vernacular language.

Makiwane's legacy can be observed in at least three dimensions. Firstly, he made a lasting impression while he was alive and shaped the direction that the next generation of the early African intellectual movement would take. Makiwane influenced their work in divergent ways. One such intellectual was Selope Thema, a young intellectual from the Northern Transvaal, presently known as Limpopo Province. Thema may have heard or read about Makiwane and was fascinated when he saw him for the first time. Makiwane and James Stuart were in Thema's village on missionary engagements to spread Christianity in that region.

According to Masilela, Thema's meeting Makiwane made a lasting impact on his life: 'What needs to be noted is that the historical reflections of Elijah Makiwane and his actual political practice in modernity had an electrifying influence on the succeeding generations of New African intellectuals: Selope Thema, after hearing a sermon by Makiwane in the 1900s near the Limpopo River walked over 800 miles to Lovedale.'[43] When Makiwane prayed in isiXhosa and Thema heard through the interpretation of Mokele Raphela that he was praying for the men and women, boys and girls who were still in 'darkness', he was thrilled and his imagination was stirred. Masilela argues that of all the intellectuals within the New African Movement, Thema was the most unapologetic in his conviction that traditional societies were steeped in 'backwardness' and darkness that should be left behind by the new emergent African who bought into the idea of modernity as 'civilisation', education, Christianity and 'enlightenment'. The New African, who identified with modernity, was to be Thema's great theme in the 1920s in his articles in *Umteteli wa Bantu*.

Makiwane's deep legacy can similarly be observed through Mqhayi, who was a student of Makiwane's. The next generation of African intellectuals after Makiwane were inspired by him. Makiwane's impact on Mqhayi shaped him into the icon he became. Makiwane, who was a schoolmaster at the school where Mqhayi studied, being an author and literary figure himself, took a personal interest in the young Mqhayi and mentored him. Makiwane was not only a teacher to Mqhayi, but also a father figure, owing to his personal interest in the educational advancement of the young Mqhayi. In turn, Mqhayi influenced others, such as Nelson Mandela. Mqhayi's perception of white men, whom he regarded as his benefactors, altered the young Mandela's views while he was at Healdtown missionary school. Equally, Mqhayi inspired Robert Mangaliso Sobukwe's love for (isiXhosa) literature – further amplified when the latter was teaching in the Department of African Languages at the University of the Witwatersrand from 1954 to 1960 – and his Africanist outlook. Generations after Makiwane continue to benefit from his deep scholarly, humanistic, political and Africanist thinking and his spiritual views. He left 'an image and logic that nothing will remove'.[44]

Secondly, Makiwane's rejection of the promotion of European languages over vernacular languages in education was strongly underpinned by his African identity and his struggle for recognition. What Makiwane stood for with regard to the use of vernacular languages in the late nineteenth and early twentieth centuries, and championed by generations after him, is still as relevant in the present as it was during his lifetime:

> Language is a means of organising and conceptualising reality, but it is also a bank for the memory generated by human interaction within a natural social environment. Suppressing and diminishing the language of the colonised also meant marginalising the memory they carried and elevating to a desirable universality the memory carried by the language of the conqueror. This included elevation of that language's conceptualisation of the world, including that of self and otherness.[45]

Makiwane provided an intellectual response to the language and cultural assimilation question and contributed to the progression of the concept of African nationalism. He challenged the power of the colonial language – English – and cultural hegemony, and most importantly, he recognised the danger in the colonising of people's minds. Colonialism was about conquest, the destruction of the local order and imposing the colonisers' world view. As Ngũgĩ posits:

> Its most important area of domination was the mental universe of the colonised ... For colonialism this involved two aspects of the same process: the destruction or the deliberate undervaluing of a people's culture, their art, dance, religion, history, geography, education, orature and literature, and the conscious elevation of the language of the coloniser. The domination of a people's language by the languages of colonising nations was crucial to the domination of the mental universe of the colonised.[46]

The need to 'decolonise the mind' has been part of the cultural struggle since colonial times. The promotion of former colonial languages in South Africa did not only form part of the European memorial and cultural geography that still exists, but it also formed racialised modern South Africa, as the array of education language policies passed between 1909 and 1974 illustrates. These policies privileged English and Dutch – and later Afrikaans – over African languages.

Thirdly, Makiwane's legacy can also be witnessed through his church, the Presbyterian Church. His contribution to the process of building and consolidating the congregation among the indigenous people and how he handled congregation issues, including inter-racial challenges within the Free Church of Scotland that have been carried over to the present generation, are living testimonies of his legacy.

BRINGING MAKIWANE INTO THE PRESENT

Early African intellectuals cannot be understood or remembered in a one-dimensional manner as the founders of the modern South African struggle against apartheid and the post-apartheid constitutional democracy because that limits their meaning and does not go beneath the surfaces of South African history and politics. Makiwane's educational journey, professional work and world view are evident in his passion about education, knowledge production and in his search for cultural, political and spiritual identities in the dynamic society and contradictory spaces in which he found himself.

Meshach Pelem argued that important historical events must be safeguarded and passed from one generation to the next. For him, heritage and remembrance are crucial for any nation's identity, knowledge production and history:

> *Yinyaniso engenakuphikwa mntu, le yokuba amanyange azo zonke izizwe kudala avumelanayo, angqinelana, ngento yokuba kufanelekile, kulungile, ukuba iziganeko ezibalulekileyo entlalweni nasebalini lesizwe zilondolozwe zigcinwe, kumana kubaliselwana, kukhunjuzwa ngazo kwizizukulwana ngezizukulwana. ... Ukukhumbula ukulondoloza, nokugcina amaxesha okwenzeka kweziganeko ezinkulu nezibalulekileyo kwintlalo yesizwe, kungafaniswa noluhlu olude olungaphele ndawo lwemibeko – imiphako, izivivane, amaziko omlilo abasiweyo, nezibane ezilunyekiweyo kwimimango ngemimango, namaqhina, ecaleni kweendlela ezihamba ngayo izizwe kulo mhlaba sibekwe kuwo; kusenzelwa ukuba izizukulwana ngazinye, ngokulandelelana kwazo, zibe namava ezizukulwana ezizanduleleyo.*[47]

This is the undisputed truth that ancestors of all nations have a common feature that historic significant events and moments should be safeguarded for future generations. Remembering, preservation and conserving of epoch-making historical moments in a nation is of historical and symbolical value. All this is done for the present and future generations to know about the previous generation.

This suggests that all forms of memorials must be used to commemorate this history. T.B. Soga, the descendant of Tiyo Soga, with reference to the concept and significance of *isivivane* (memorial) among amaXhosa, reasoned:

> *Izivivane yabe iyinkolo enzulu kwaXhosa kuba bonke abahambi abagqitha ngalendlela bebemana bephosa amatye xa bedlulayo ndaweni ithile, besithi,*

ngelabo, bacela ukuba iminyanya yooyisemkhulu ibakhangele, ibanike amandla namendu kwanamathamsanqa kolu hambo ... Makucace kumntu wonke osukuba elesa le ncwadi ngalo mcimbi wezivivane, iindumba zamatye afunjwe emacaleni endlela ngolu ukunqula iminyanya namashologu akwaXhosa.[48]

Memorials are important in amaXhosa community as they have deep socio-cultural, spiritual and historical meanings. These memorials, which are made up of a collection of heaps of stones along the road (*isivisane*) for communicating and revering with the dead and living ancestors of amaXhosa have provenance and aesthetic value.

The legacy of Makiwane and the early African intellectual movement is immeasurable and has continued to inform later generations. They paved the way for the New African Movement that thrived in the twentieth century and led to the flourishing of indigenous churches in South Africa, as well as laying the foundations for African nationalism, Africanist thinking and liberal politics. If past epoch-making events and heritage are important for the present and future generations, the question is why the governing ANC leaves out aspects of history and heritage that relate to the distant past and merely focuses on the recent past. It is more than history and heritage that is at stake; it is the thinkable future and its ways of knowing.

NOTES

[1] T.D. Mweli Skota, *The African Early Register: Being an Illustrated National Biographical Dictionary (Who's Who) of Black Folks in Africa* (Johannesburg: The Orange Press, 1932), 35.

[2] Mai Palmberg, *National Identity and Democracy in Africa* (Cape Town: Human Sciences Research Council and Mayibuye Centre of the University of the Western Cape, 1999), 8.

[3] Goran Therborn, cited in Neville Alexander, 'Approaches to the National Question in South Africa', *Transformation* 1 (1986): 70.

[4] Ntongela Masilela, *The Cultural Modernity of H.I.E. Dhlomo* (Trenton, NJ: Africa World Press, 2007); Ntongela Masilela, *The Historical Figures of the New African Movement: Volume One* (Trenton, NJ: Africa World Press, 2014); Ntongela Masilela, *A South African Looks at the African Diaspora: Essays and Interviews* (Trenton, NJ: Africa World Press, 2016); Bhekizizwe Peterson, *Monarchs, Missionaries and African Intellectuals: African Theater and the Unmasking of Colonial Marginality* (Trenton, NJ: Africa World Press, 2000); Mcebisi Ndletyana, ed., *African Intellectuals in 19th and 20th Century South Africa* (Cape Town: HSRC Press, 2008); André Odendaal, *The Founders: The Origins of the ANC and the Struggle for Democracy in South Africa* (Johannesburg: Jacana Media, 2012); Jeff Opland, *Abantu Besizwe: Historical and Biographical Writings 1902–1944* (Johannesburg: Wits University Press, 2009); Hlonipha Mokoena, *Magema Fuze: The Making of a Kholwa Intellectual* (Pietermaritzburg: University of KwaZulu-Natal Press, 2011); Jeff Opland, Wandile Kuse and Pamela Maseko, trans. and eds, *William*

Wellington Gqoba: Isizwe Esinembali, Xhosa Histories and Poetry (1873–1888), publications of the Opland Collection of Xhosa Literature, Vol. 1 (Pietermaritzburg: University of KwaZulu-Natal Press, 2015); Mbukeni Harbert Mnguni, ed., *New African Intellectuals and New African Political Thought in the Twentieth Century* (New York: Waxmann, 2015).

5   Odendaal, *The Founders*, x.
6   Chinua Achebe, *There Was a Country: A Personal History of Biafra* (London: Penguin Books, 2012), 55.
7   Ngũgĩ wa Thiong'o, *Decolonising the Mind: The Politics of Language in African Literature* (Nairobi: James Currey, 2005), 25.
8   Mary Louise Pratt, *Imperial Eyes: Traveling Writing and Transculturation* (New York: Routledge, 1995).
9   Mzi Gova, *Early African Intellectuals* (East London: Amathole District Municipality, 2013). King Phalo, the son of Tshiwo, of Tshawe, was the last king/*inkumkhani* of the independent Xhosa nation. He had sons by the name of Gcaleka and Rharhabe. King Phalo gave land to Rharhabe on the west of the Ngciba River (the Great Kei River). Gcaleka remained in the east of the Great Kei River, with his territory forming the Transkei area.
10 David Attwell, *Rewriting Modernity: Studies in Black South African Literary History* (Pietermaritzburg: University of KwaZulu-Natal Press, 2005), 30; John Comaroff and Jean Comaroff, *Ethnography and the Historical Imagination* (Boulder: Westview Press, 1992).
11 Attwell, *Rewriting Modernity*, 3.
12 Odendaal, *The Founders*, 13.
13 Amathole District Municipality, *Amathole Heritage Initiative*, brochure (East London: Amathole District Municipality, c.2004).
14 Ndletyana, *African Intellectuals*, 1.
15 Ndletyana, *African Intellectuals*, 1.
16 This idea also permeated Selope Thema's 'New African Movement', Anton Lembede's Africa-centred thinking and African nationalism, Edward Blyden's concept of 'African personality' (later with Kwame Nkrumah's signature), Léopold Sédar Senghor and Kenneth Kaunda's 'African humanism' and Robert Sobukwe's 'Africa reborn, Africa rejuvenated'.
17 Donovan Williams, *Umfundisi: A Biography of Tiyo Soga 1829–1871* (Alice: Lovedale Press, 1978), 83.
18 Mahmood Mamndani, *Define and Rule: Native as Political Identity* (Johannesburg: Wits University Press, 2013), 6.
19 Williams, *Umfundisi*, 84.
20 Williams, *Umfundisi*, 86.
21 'Elijah Makiwane', *The Journalist*, 21 April 2015, accessed 24 November 2020, https://www.thejournalist.org.za/pioneers/elijah-makiwane
22 Elijah Makiwane, '*The Kaffir Express*', *Isigidimi samaXhosa*, 1 October 1870.
23 Benedict Anderson, *Imagined Communities: Reflections of the Origin and Spread of Nationalism* (New York: Verso, 1983).
24 Archibald Currie Jordan, *Towards an African Literature: The Emergence of Literary Form in Xhosa* (Berkeley: University of California Press, 1975), 35.
25 Odendaal, *The Founders*, 28–29.

26 Odendaal, *The Founders*, 37.
27 Odendaal, *The Founders*, 36–37.
28 Ntongela Masilela, 'South African Language Literatures', 2009, accessed 24 November 2020, http://pzacad.pitzer.edu/NAM/general/essays/language-literatures.pdf
29 Mokoena, *Fuze*, 210.
30 Achebe, *There Was a Country*, 53.
31 Achebe, *There Was a Country*, 55.
32 Mazrui in Palmberg, *National Identity*, 102.
33 Jordan, *Towards an African Literature*, viii.
34 Achebe, *There Was a Country*.
35 Ntongela Masilela, 'Xhosa Intellectuals of the 1880s (1871–97): Elijah Makiwane (1850–1928)', accessed 3 December 2020, http://pzacad.pitzer.edu/NAM/xhosaren/writers/makiwane.shtml
36 Steve Biko, *I Write What I Like: A Selection of His Writings*, ed. Aelred Stubbs (Johannesburg: Picador Africa, 2004), 138.
37 Neville Alexander, *Thoughts on the New South Africa* (Johannesburg: Jacana Media, 2013), 8.
38 Skota, *The African Early Register*, 35.
39 Livingstone Ntibane Mzimba, the authoritative biographer of Pambani Mzimba presents a detailed sequence of events that led to Pambani Mzimba's case and his leaving the Free Church of Scotland in his *Ibali Lobomi Nomsebenzi Womfi Umfundisi Pambani Jeremiah Mzimba* (Alice: Lovedale Institution Press, 1923). A particular sore point surfaced when Mzimba returned from Scotland – where he had been a delegate to the General Assembly of the denomination – having raised a substantial amount of money, with plans to build a respectable church building. The authorities regarded his architectural designs as too magnificent for Africans. There were then even moves to constrain indigenous church leaders in their efforts to raise money abroad. Mweli Skota says: 'On his return certain arrangements were made, but it is said, the Rev. Lennox did not agree with him in his plans. Unfortunately a dispute arose which ended up in the Supreme Court at Cape Town. After this dispute Rev. Mzimba broke away from the Free Church and started his own. He found the African Presbyterian Church. He had a large following which recognised him … His work increased until he had branches all over South Africa.' Skota, *The African Early Register*, 75.
40 Skota, *The African Early Register*, 35.
41 Robert H.W. Shepherd, *Abazibaluleyo Nokubhaliweyo Ngesintu* (Alice: Lovedale Press, 1964), 71.
42 Shepherd, *Abazibaluleyo Nokubhaliweyo Ngesintu*, 70–71.
43 Ntongela Masilela, 'New Negro Modernity and New African Modernity' (paper presented at The Black Atlantic: Literatures, Histories, Cultures forum, Zurich, January 2003), accessed 24 November 2020, http://pzacad.pitzer.edu/NAM/general/modernity.pdf; 'New African Movement, 1900-60', accessed 24 November 2020, http://pzacad.pitzer.edu/NAM/newafrre/writers/thema.shtml
44 Achebe, *There Was a Country*, 107.
45 Sifiso Ndlovu, *The Soweto Uprisings: Counter-Memories of June 1976* (Johannesburg: Picador Africa, 2017), xix.
46 Ngũgĩ, *Decolonising the Mind*, 16.
47 Cited in William Govan Bennie, *Imibengo* (Alice: Lovedale Press, 1960), 174–175.
48 Tiyo. B. Soga, *Intlalo ka Xhosa* (Alice: Lovedale Press, 1989), 122.

REFERENCES

Achebe, Chinua. *There Was a Country: A Personal History of Biafra*. London: Penguin Books, 2012.
Alexander, Neville. 'Approaches to the National Question in South Africa'. *Transformation* 1 (1986): 63–95.
Alexander, Neville. *Thoughts on the New South Africa*. Johannesburg: Jacana Media, 2013.
Amathole District Municipality. *Amathole Heritage Initiative* (brochure). East London: Amathole District Municipality, c.2004.
Anderson, Benedict. *Imagined Communities: Reflections of the Origin and Spread of Nationalism*. New York, Verso, 1983.
Attwell, David. *Rewriting Modernity: Studies in Black South African Literary History*. Pietermaritzburg: University of KwaZulu Natal Press, 2005.
Bennie, William Govan. *Imibengo*. Alice: Lovedale Press, 1960.
Biko, Steve. *I Write What I Like: A Selection of His Writings*. Edited by Aelred Stubbs. Johannesburg: Picador Africa, 2004.
Comaroff, John and Jean Comaroff. *Ethnography and the Historical Imagination*. Boulder: Westview Press, 1992.
Gova, Mzi. *Early African Intellectuals*. East London: Amathole District Municipality, 2013.
Jordan, Archibald Currie. *Towards an African Literature: The Emergence of Literary Form in Xhosa*. Berkeley: University of California Press, 1975.
Makiwane, Elijah. 'The Kaffir Express'. *Isigidimi samaXhosa*, 1 October 1870.
Mamdani, Mahmood. *Define and Rule: Native as Political Identity*. Johannesburg: Wits University Press, 2013.
Masilela, Ntongela. *The Cultural Modernity of H.I.E. Dhlomo*. Trenton, NJ: Africa World Press, 2007.
Masilela, Ntongela. *The Historical Figures of the New African Movement: Volume One*. Trenton, NJ: Africa World Press, 2014.
Masilela, Ntongela. 'New Negro Modernity and New African Modernity'. Paper presented at The Black Atlantic: Literatures, Histories, Cultures forum, Zurich, January 2003. Accessed 24 November 2020. http://pzacad.pitzer.edu/NAM/general/modernity.pdf
Masilela, Ntongela. 'South African Language Literatures'. 2009. Accessed 24 November 2020. http://pzacad.pitzer.edu/NAM/general/essays/language-literatures.pdf
Masilela, Ntongela. *A South African Looks at the African Diaspora: Essays and Interviews*. Trenton, NJ: Africa World Press, 2016.
Masilela, Ntongela. 'Xhosa Intellectuals of the 1880s (1871–97): Elijah Makiwane (1850–1928)'. Accessed 3 December 2020. http://pzacad.pitzer.edu/NAM/xhosaren/writers/makiwane.shtml
Mnguni, Mbukeni Harbert, ed. *New African Intellectuals and New African Political Thought in the Twentieth Century*. New York: Waxmann, 2015.
Mokoena, Hlonipha. *Magema Fuze: The Making of a Kholwa Intellectual*. Pietermaritzburg: University of KwaZulu-Natal Press, 2011.
Mzimba, Livingstone Ntibane. *Ibali Lobomi Nomsebenzi Womfi Umfundisi Pambani Jeremiah Mzimba*. Alice: Lovedale Institution Press, 1923.
Ndletyana, Mcebisi, ed. *African Intellectuals in 19th and 20th Century South Africa*. Cape Town: HSRC Press, 2008.
Ndlovu, Sifiso. *The Soweto Uprisings: Counter-Memories of June 1976*. Johannesburg: Picador Africa, 2017.

Ngũgĩ wa Thiong'o. *Decolonising the Mind: The Politics of Language in African Literature*. Nairobi: James Currey, 2005.

Odendaal, André. *The Founders: The Origins of the ANC and the Struggle for Democracy in South Africa*. Johannesburg: Jacana Media, 2012.

Opland Jeff. *Abantu Besizwe: Historical and Biographical Writings 1902–1944*. Johannesburg: Wits University Press, 2009.

Opland Jeff, Wandile Kuse and Pamela Maseko, trans. and eds. *William Wellington Gqoba: Isizwe Esinembali, Xhosa Histories and Poetry (1873–1888)*. Publications of the Opland Collection of Xhosa Literature, Vol. 1. Pietermaritzburg: University of KwaZulu-Natal Press, 2015.

Palmberg, Mai. *National Identity and Democracy in Africa*. Cape Town: Human Sciences Research Council and Mayibuye Centre of the University of the Western Cape, 1999.

Peterson, Bhekizizwe. *Monarchs, Missionaries and African Intellectuals: African Theater and the Unmasking of Colonial Marginality*. Trenton, NJ: Africa World Press, 2000.

Pratt, Mary Louise. *Imperial Eyes: Traveling Writing and Transculturation*. New York: Routledge, 1995.

Shepherd Robert. H.W. *Abazibaluleyo Nokubhaliweyo Ngesintu*. Alice: Lovedale Press, 1964.

Soga, Tiyo B. *Intlalo ka Xhosa*. Alice: Lovedale Press, 1989.

Skota, T.D. Mweli. *The African Early Register: Being an Illustrated National Biographical Dictionary (Who's Who) of Black Folks in Africa*. Johannesburg: The Orange Press, 1932.

Williams, Donovan. *Umfundisi: A Biography of Tiyo Soga 1829–1871*. Alice: Lovedale Press, 1978.

CHAPTER
3

Black Art Criticism in *The Bantu World* during the 1930s

Pfunzo Sidogi

David Nthubu Koloane was among the most accomplished black artists, curators and scholars of the twentieth century. Besides countless accolades from around the world, his contribution to South African art was immortalised when he was awarded two honorary doctoral degrees by the Vaal University of Technology in 2008 and Rhodes University in 2015. In his now iconic article 'Art Criticism for Whom?', Koloane argued that art criticism in South Africa was 'virtually non-existent' outside the white art establishment.[1] While Koloane's assertion was part of a larger political argument, his justifiable conclusion, which was echoed by other prominent scholars, has resulted in the history of black art criticism in South Africa being grossly under-researched.[2] Contrary to this prevailing opinion, art criticism by black intellectuals has a rich heritage that extends back to the early twentieth century during the founding of black-run publications such as *Ilanga lase Natal* (established in the 1900s), *Umteteli wa Bantu* (1920s) and *The Bantu World* (1930s). These periodicals, written by black journalists, debated the nature and purpose of black art, while also appraising the creative exploits of the formative black modern artists.

In this chapter I chronicle the early manifestations of black art criticism printed in *The Bantu World* newspaper during the 1930s. In this introductory survey of the history of black art criticism in South Africa, I show how art criticism existed as a public practice among the emergent black middle class. This public discourse was facilitated by and catalogued in the leading black newspapers of the early twentieth century.

Steve Biko suggests that the ideal in any work of critical thinking is always to begin by asking the right questions.[3] When it comes to the question of criticism on the art made by black artists during the twentieth century, existing discourses have unwittingly arrived at conclusions – logical as they may have been – that were predicated on a faulty set of assumptions to begin with. Many of the pragmatic deductions regarding the history and nature of twentieth-century art criticism dealing with black art in South Africa measured it against the prevailing norms of Western art criticism. This rubric was hugely problematic on two significant fronts. First, the material, educational and overall milieu that cultivated black art in South Africa was vastly different from the situation in America and Europe throughout the twentieth century. Second, the institutionalised discrimination based on race meant that black art in South Africa could not be produced, appreciated, consumed or critiqued on the same terms as art made by white artists, both within the country and abroad. It was therefore unwise to judge black art or black art criticism without first recognising that Western art criticism existed in a context paradigmatically different from the situation in South Africa. In their analysis of art criticism in Africa, Everlyn Nicodemus and Kristian Romare contend: 'The injustice and the brutal conditions experienced by black artists make everything which could look like glossing over unacceptable.'[4] Alas, the history of black art criticism has been 'glossed over' to the point that its presumed non-existence is accepted as truth.

UNDERSTANDING THE CONTEXT

There is an urgency to revisit some of the claims made about twentieth-century art criticism produced by black writers who reflected on black creativity. The history of black art criticism has been largely ignored because of erroneous assumptions, on the one hand, and the dearth of purposeful scholarly engagement with this history, on the other. For some time, I too participated – in my role as an art history teacher – in perpetuating the assumption that black people did not theorise and philosophise their artistic practices, partly because I could not find art historical literature that spoke to this forgotten past. This chapter is my own attempt to unmask the history of black intellectualism on art, so that I can cure myself of the narrow discourses I was exposed to regarding the 'histories' of art in South Africa. As Lize van Robbroeck argues, it is instructive to talk of 'histories' of art in South Africa because to fully appreciate the complexity, diversity and multiplicity of art practices that have emerged and continue to emerge from the country, we need to move away from the canonical conception of a singular, monolithic and universal 'history' of South African art.[5] This is particularly important because of the country's segregated and apartheid past, in which a definite and fully inclusive 'South African art' was never allowed to develop and flourish.

Therefore, in order to acknowledge the existence of black public intellectualism about black art, we must first appreciate the contextual polarities between black art and white art during the twentieth century. The inequalities in art education, unfair representation in galleries and museums, unequal treatment in the marketplace and unbalanced historicisation practices cannot be ignored. Second, we must dispel the 'popular' versus 'serious' art criticism binary. This schema is inappropriate for studying the history of black art criticism in South Africa because it essentially wipes away decades of public discourse on black art that do not fit neatly into the category of 'serious' art criticism.

What then was the nature and texture of black art criticism and black public intellectualism about black art during the early twentieth century? To answer this, I review carefully selected articles, opinion pieces and letters published in *The Bantu World* newspaper during the 1930s. Established in April 1932, *The Bantu World* was the foremost black-operated weekly newspaper of its era and although it was not the first nor only black newspaper to exclusively publish articles about black artists and their art, its peculiar history and its national footprint make it the natural gateway to peel open this overlooked history.[6]

Before analysing the dynamics of black art criticism by black writers, it is necessary to first explore the complexities of the black press during the early twentieth century. Historian Tim Couzens considers the very notion of a black press as a 'fairly arbitrary' designation because newspapers that were viewed as white publications, such as *The Rand Daily Mail*, for example, had a widespread black readership and black newspapers and magazines were mostly controlled by white business interests.[7] However, as Couzens rationalises, it is those black newspapers and magazines exclusively produced for black audiences that are part of this black press. Although the beginnings of a black press can be traced back to 1836,[8] the establishment of *The Bantu World* in 1932 was probably the most defining moment in the development of a nation-wide black newspaper that engaged with a black audience across South Africa.[9] *The Bantu World* newspaper was the flagship publication of the Bantu Press holding company, which was initially owned by powerful and wealthy white capitalists and the emergent educated black elites.[10] Among other factors, *The Bantu World* was more successful than the other black newspapers that emerged before or during its existence because of the white commercial interests that injected vast capital into the paper and the lucrative advertising revenue generated from South African industry.[11] Ironically, by 1936, exactly 100 years after the publication of the first black journal, the Bantu Press company, a wholly white-owned consortium at that stage, had taken over control of the other prominent but financially ailing publications such as *Imvo Zabantsundu*, *Ilanga lase Natal*, *Ikwezi le Afrika* and *Mochochonono*.[12] While the politics of the era and the unequal business playing field contributed to the demise of black ownership of the black press, Les Switzer and Donna Switzer maintain that 'white chain ownership and corporate control transformed the black press into a mass medium of communication.'[13] Put differently, the backing *The Bantu World* newspaper received from white capital brought with it an opportunity for the massification of black intellectualism on matters related to culture, which no other black newspaper had managed to achieve before or after its establishment.

While the ownership of the black press remained in white hands, the content production was the preserve of black editors and journalists. However, the fact that these black journalists were employed by and, to a large extent, had to answer to white bosses is a fact of history that cannot be glossed over. Thus, any reading of the intellectual culture that emerged out of *The Bantu World* or any other white-owned black publications post-1936 needs to take into account this racialised power dynamic. One of the harsh realities of this black worker-white boss relationship was that black journalists were significantly underpaid compared to white journalists who did similar work. Herbert I.E. Dhlomo bemoaned the fact that black journalists performed significantly more tasks than journalists in white papers, but received lower remuneration: 'The African journalist in most cases is underpaid, over-worked, is hampered with irritating restrictions, and is not free to speak out loud and bold. Our journalists must be and are bilingual – they must write in English and Vernacular every week. They are reporters, sub-editors, Editors, proof-readers all in one. *They are expected to write on every topical subject under the sun for there is no division of work.*'[14]

Besides having to write about everything, including art, we must appreciate that in addition to the fact that the journalists and editors were inhibited by the white management of the newspapers they worked for, they also had to guard against the minefield of state laws that were repressive of dissident and anarchist voices, especially black ones. Many black editors and writers were forced to adopt pseudonyms as a precaution 'when stating unpopular or in some way awkward opinions.'[15] While the use of pseudonyms is a global phenomenon, it was especially acute in the black press in South Africa throughout the twentieth century. Thus, a vibrant culture of critical journalism about the arts, while present, was unable to fully mature because authors had to remain veiled, especially if their ideas were too radical. Surely, it was highly unlikely that a virtuoso critical voice such as Clement Greenberg in America or Peter Fuller in England would emerge and be free to evaluate, appraise and critique, not just the creativity of black artists, but of white artists as well.

TOWARDS BLACK INTELLECTUALISM OF TWENTIETH-CENTURY BLACK ART

In one of his first editorials as the chief editor of *The Bantu World*, Richard Selope Thema positioned the arts as one of the paper's seven focus areas, noting that *The Bantu World* would actively 'foster the growth of Bantu arts and crafts, literature and music'.[16] To this end, the full-time employed and freelance black journalists were obliged to engage with black creativity in their reporting. As Alan Cobley recounts, Selope Thema 'commissioned critiques of "New African" literature, music, art and sport from an emerging cohort of young African intellectuals with which he surrounded himself at the paper'.[17] From its earliest issues, *The Bantu World* gave the arts, specifically the performance arts of music and theatre, favourable mention in its pages. It was common to find animated and at times highly discursive reviews of the drama/theatre and music productions created by black artists based in Johannesburg and the other urban centres of South Africa.[18] For example, a 1933 front-page story praised the Bantu Dramatic Society after they staged *She Stoops to Conquer* at the Bantu Men's Social Centre in Johannesburg.[19] However, what was most revealing about this piece was the expert colloquial language used to describe the acting prowess of the performers. Among other astute remarks, the journalist notes that the performers were 'in many ways perfect in stage deportment, gesture and movement'.[20] Furthermore, this positive review of the show was vetted by inserting other critical appraisals from white newspapers *The Star* and *The Rand Daily Mail*. This rigorous and triangulated reporting of black creativity was, in part, meant to prove that the quality of these black productions was comparable to white artistic exploits. But more significantly, such reviews underscored the mantra of advancing black aesthetics through journalism, which was a core function of *The Bantu World*, as expressed by Selope Thema.

Articles dealing with music and drama/theatre published in *The Bantu World* during the 1930s were clearly greater in number than those referencing the visual arts. While all forms of creative expression were negatively affected by the bigoted colonial environment of twentieth-century South Africa, the impact on the visual arts was far more acute. The lack of educational opportunities for black artists, coupled with even less exhibition opportunities within the fledgling white-owned gallery system, meant that there were almost no outlets for black artists to showcase their talent. One of the few platforms where black art could be showcased was the Bantu World Trade Exhibition, first organised in 1933, which was aimed at providing white industry with direct access to the growing buying power of the black working class, but also afforded black creatives the opportunity to showcase their work to both white and black audiences. In the late 1940s initiatives such as the artist John Mohl's 'Artists under the Sun' exhibitions in Sophiatown gave black artists the space to exhibit their work to black audiences by circumventing the white-owned 'expensive commercial galleries'.[21] Such events gave black journalists front-row glimpses of art created by the most talented black artists in South Africa. The manner in which this art was intellectualised was crucial for the advancement of black creativity.

Less than six months after the first issue of *The Bantu World*, Jameson G. Coka, an authoritative intellectual figure at the time and a regular contributor to the newspaper, wrote one of the most perceptive and compelling valuations of the purpose of black-on-black criticism in *The Bantu World* and more broadly within black society. Coka's counsel was a kind of template for how any criticism of black endeavours, especially the highly theoretical and philosophical kind, needed to be handled:

> Why should criticism be the goal of our teachers, preachers, writers, leaders and ordinary men and women? Is it an inherent tendency in the Bantu or is it lack of thinking? Whatever the cause is, the growing spirit of reckless criticism must be checked ... There is constructive criticism, which has for its object, the interest and welfare of the party enlisted. But very few among the Bantu criticise with this laudable objective in view. They invariably criticise in order to stultify and hinder progress.[22]

Coka's pronouncements in this piece were profound for several reasons. First, we must consider the timing of its publication. Printed in August 1932, a few months after the christening of the newspaper in April, it seems that Coka was pre-empting and warding off a kind of negative journalism and public discourse that he feared would be counter to the goals of *The Bantu World*, which sought to facilitate black progress. Second, it is clear from Coka's concern that a culture of criticism was already burgeoning. In the printed press, academic circles, churches and beer/dance halls, black people were engaged in critical reflection of the cultural happenings of the day. What we can definitively deduce from this is that art criticism surely existed within this culture, albeit not in the form of the normative discursive essay printed in books, journals or newspapers. Based on Coka's tone, we can further speculate that this community-based and public criticism, although mostly unrecorded, seemed to have a regressive and pejorative tendency. Third, Coka cautions against a criticism based on comparison, especially comparisons with white endeavours. For Coka, it was folly to be overly critical of black exploits because the situation in which black people operated already advantaged what was perceived as white excellence. He concluded: 'It is through this over-critical attitude we assume that we are so far behind other races. If a thing is wrong why not do a better one or suggest means for its improvement? How can one criticise without being fully conversant with both sides of the question?'[23] Thus, black endeavours – and more so black creativity – needed to be evaluated using a different set of criteria and with an understanding of the context in which it existed. Lastly, Coka's idea of the function of criticism in society positioned the critic as a servant of the people, their mouthpiece in all matters, including the arts. Directly above Coka's article was an image of a craftsman/carpenter at his workshop in Klipspruit, an area outside of Johannesburg where black people had been forced to live since 1905. The caption says: 'He [the craftsman] will succeed if he gets the support of the race.'[24] Coka's article was essentially a plea on behalf of black creative practitioners and entrepreneurs for black writers to support and advance their output through their intellectualism.

EXAMPLES OF EARLY BLACK ART CRITICISM IN *THE BANTU WORLD*

In order to put to rest the erroneous idea that black intellectualism about black art did not exist, it is worth examining selected samples of art criticism content published in *The Bantu World* during the 1930s in some detail. First, I would like to spotlight the role the public played in generating intellectual critique of black creativity and how the newspaper facilitated this. Public opinion, and not just the thoughts of the educated virtuoso, was integral in formulating the theoretical infrastructure of art discourses for the urban-based black proletariat. Acknowledging this public voice is critical for dispelling the 'popular' versus 'serious' art criticism divide. In 1932 an advertisement appeared announcing an exhibition organised by the Native Commission to be held on 3 October.[25] The notice included a competition for essays on 'Bantu Arts and Crafts', offering prize money of £1 for the best essay. Although there is no evidence in later issues of the newspaper that anyone actually submitted an essay or who the winner was, this advertisement nevertheless proves that *The Bantu World* encouraged and nurtured public discourse related to the visual arts. While the nature and type of arts and craft exhibited at this show are uncertain, and the fact that fine art education for black people at the time was minimal, the newspaper nonetheless believed that public debate about black creativity was necessary, viable and publishable.[26] The newspaper's black readership was encouraged to contribute content related to art through opinion pieces and letters to the editor.

One of the most captivating letters to the editor was published in 1935. The letter was submitted by 'Sweet Pea', who was responding to an earlier article that had been written by 'The Monarch', which critiqued the kind of artworks and pictures found on the walls of black peoples' homes. In her retort, 'Sweet Pea' argues:

> As women, we believe that variety is the very spice of life; with this in mind we like to have variety in everything we do. It is quite true one seldom finds a *muntu* ['person' in isiZulu] picture in a European home and in some Bantu homes one does find a picture of the Devil tempting a sick *muntu* to Hell, hanging beside many European pictures. But that is only because we believe so much that without variety everything seems dull and monotonous. Even when we make cakes we also have a variety of ingredients in order to make a good cake. Had this not been the case, in every Bantu home you visited, you would find photos of people all round the walls of the room. Some in twos or threes or fours. One or two standing in deep attention or at ease, beside a chair or table with a vase on it, or sitting stiffly in a chair. What monotony! If, on the other hand, Bantu men took more interest in art, so that they could learn to paint really healthy and instructive scenes out of native life, we wouldn't bother our dear husbands, brothers etc., by decorating our homes with pictures that cause such disturbance to their minds.[27]

There are several significant issues here that warrant reflection. The first and most obvious, but perhaps most important, is the fact that the article was written by a woman. The female voice, black and white, has played a significant role in shaping the key discourses on South African art.[28] Among black people, *The Bantu World* was the first periodical to accord women some form of agency in the male-dominated publishing world.[29] In this letter we see one of the earliest examples of how black women were deeply concerned with the kind of visual culture that was germinating from black artists at the time. While black women were not accorded the necessary opportunities and platforms to advance as professional artists or journalists during this period, they nevertheless had strong convictions and opinions about art. 'Sweet Pea' shows an advanced awareness of the complexities and contradictions of finding European pictures in black homes, but argues that a plurality of visual themes is indispensable to a well-curated home. Her closing statement, which chastises black male artists for not creating 'healthy and instructive scenes out of native life' speaks of the yearning that existed among black audiences at the time for images of black life in all its diversity.

Black women had considerable sway over the kinds of representations that populated urban black homes. 'Sweet Pea' is not just an astute visual intellectual, but also performs the role of curating her home, something that was probably commonplace among the growing number of urbanised black families at the time. Thus, female aesthetic tastes were key influencers of the consumption trends of upper-class black families in the urban areas.

Also, this article reminds us of the obvious fact that black people collected and appreciated art during the early to mid-twentieth century. Although the structure of the economy and appalling wages limited the disposable income of urban-based black families, collecting art for home use was still a necessity. Finally, I must stress that the practice of pseudonyms was pervasive during this period, as noted earlier in this chapter. While it was common for male writers to take on female aliases, it is unlikely that 'Sweet Pea' was male.

Further evidence of the public's role in the intellectual evaluation of black art came in the form of an advert from the Bantu Crafts League, which was based in Grahamstown. In 1935 the league wrote to *The Bantu World* seeking to notify its readers of the organisation's activities:

> We draw the attention of readers to our league *which gives free advice and criticism* on all matters relating to Bantu literature, Bantu music, *the Glyphic arts of modelling and carving*. Art needlework, Weaving, Tapestry and Embroidery. Basketry, *Designing, Painting (life painting, land and seascape sketching)*. There is no joining fee and members may have their works sold within the Union or forwarded to Europe for sale and exhibitions. We do this for the advancement of Bantu arts and crafts.[30]

From this we can see the developmental function of arts criticism in how the league sought to advance the creativity of black people. Put differently, there was an awareness that the progress of black art was prefaced on the existence of an enabling critical culture, which Coka had also championed.[31] But more decisively, this advertisement further accentuates the organised 'public' participation ethos of critiquing and appraising black art, which was facilitated by the newspaper.

Besides such rare inserts by the public, *The Bantu World* also published long-form discursive essays on black art that easily fit into the rubric of 'serious' art criticism. One of the earliest of such articles, whose author was sadly unidentified, was published in 1934 and, although it was billed as a music-related piece, much of it made reference to fine art and the arts broadly:

> Political ideas about the differences between Africans and Europeans have entered the field of art. Europeans think that Africans who do exactly what whites do are 'spoiled.' Art never 'spoiled' a race ... Art is a reality, an absolute. National and individual artistic creations and idioms are but blurred pictures and visions of the universal reality – true art. If the African studies exotic art, he does so to get better visions in his search for the reality. It is all progress. It is natural. But white South Africans have reverted to the old doctrine that progress is 'unnatural'.[32]

The profundity of this argument is captivating. While the author touches on the tension between a globalised and nationalised black aesthetic, he/she was essentially speaking to the apparent mimicking of European arts by African practitioners during the early twentieth century. White intellectuals assumed that black artists were blindly appropriating Western modalities and artistic strategies in ways that rendered their art 'spoiled' and 'unnatural'. The author pushes back against these audacious claims, highlighting that black artists were instead engaged in creating a universal aesthetic, even though they were using Western styles and materials to achieve this vision of reality. The author went on to argue:

> Many budding African artists are discouraged by the assertion that if they 'copy' their European teachers, it will kill their spark of genius. How can genius be destroyed by knowledge? Academies of art do not make or unmake genius. They cannot give talent to those who haven't nor deprive the gifted of their powers. Genius is not the product of education nor of intelligence. If it were, professors and graduands would all be geniuses, which they are not.[33]

The article's argument about natural abilities, or at least the South African art world's perception of natural talent, had far-reaching implications for the reception and intellectual appreciation of black art at the time. Perhaps what is most striking when following the article's line of reasoning is that it was advocating for notions such as DNA and heritability as being major determinants of artistic giftedness, several decades before this fact was proven scientifically. As recently as

2018, Robert Plomin, a foremost scholar of genetics research in psychology, published a book based on over 40 years of rigorous scientific investigation, aptly titled *Blueprint: How DNA Makes Us Who We Are*. Plomin demonstrates that nature, and not nurture (environment), has the single greatest influence on our differences in abilities as human beings. His research reveals that 50 per cent of an individual's 'general intelligence (e.g., reasoning)' is inherited, 60 per cent of 'school achievement' is also determined by one's DNA and 40 per cent of someone's 'personality' is passed on through genes.[34]

But beyond this, the author of this article argues for the advancement of African creativity in all its forms by nourishing its raw imaginative promise through academic training – complementing natural talent with purposeful nurture. More significantly, the writer also tries to complicate the arts versus crafts distinction, which had relegated black/African art, not produced under a Westernised framework, to the lesser category of craft. The author concludes the article by highlighting that appropriation and borrowing from other creative cultures, especially those from the West 'is the only way open to African artists and thinkers. They can produce typically and genuinely African idioms and patterns, not by shunning modern exotic ideas and influences, but by transforming and reorganising what they learn, and stamping it with their individuality.'[35]

At the other end of this debate were black intellectuals who believed that the natural ability of the black artists was best served by being left to its own devices, far away from any Westernised education or tutelage. The author, 'Editress', actually Rolfes Robert R. Dhlomo, of *The Bantu World* newspaper,[36] had written about this in his review of the second Bantu Trade Development Exhibition held from 24 to 31 May 1934, which had a dedicated stand for 'African arts and crafts'.[37] In his exhibition review 'Editress' refers to the arts and craft exhibit as 'most interesting'. It is worth noting the definitional parameters that the writer presents in this article, which distinguish art and craft from an Africanist viewpoint. He argues that craft consists of creative undertakings that are essentially 'taught', whereas:

> The arts are the things which have been handed down from generation to generation in such things as wood carving and pottery. This we may call Primitive African Art and we do want our people to realise that it is a gift of God given to us generations ago, which should be kept and guarded with loving care. People from all parts of the world are intensely interested in our primitive art and will remain interested so long as original African art is not spoilt by becoming too Europeanized.[38]

The first and most pressing point of interest here is the characterisation of African creativity as 'primitive art'. Here Dhlomo was simply appropriating the colonial lexicon of the day, which had relegated African art to a primitive temporality. It is clear that Dhlomo did not believe that African art was primitive, but he adopts this designation in order to subvert it. Dhlomo is emphatic that art in Africa in that historical moment was constituted of what Europeans had termed 'traditional' and 'rural' wood carving and pottery. These mostly village-based forms of art were, in Dhlomo's eyes, paradigmatic of genius and authentic African creativity.[39] By reframing these so-called 'traditional' African art practices, Dhlomo was intentionally inserting African forms of art into the centre of the artistic and aesthetic canon.

The tension between the complementary but decidedly polar epistemologies presented in Dhlomo's piece and the previous article published only a few months earlier was centred on the production dynamics and stylistic essences of black art during the early twentieth century when black creativity was being integrated into the Westernised capitalist art market. On the one end were the New African Movement globalists, who diagnosed the training, production and consumption ecosystem offered by the Western art machine that had come to Africa via colonial contact as a historical opportunity to 'articulate new forms of artistic representation' of a renewed Africa.[40] These 'new forms' were to be generated not through isolation, but rather by transposing, transplanting, adapting and translating idioms from around the world into hybridised and Africanised artistic forms. On the other end of the spectrum were the Africanists and Afrocentrics (exemplified by Dhlomo) who believed that classical African artistic practices needed to be preserved and safeguarded from external – particularly Western – influences. As Dhlomo stressed, vintage African art was produced through innate talent that was spiritually endowed. Therefore, the true African artist did not need any 'foreign' training. Even though both texts do not refer to specific artworks or artists to support their opinions, there is a sense they were pre-empting and prophesying how black art of that era and beyond would be debated and thought of in the future, some decades before white intellectuals and historians began articulating these tensions.

Another exhibition review was written by 'Poncho', who wrote an extended account of a show held on 6 August 1934 at Pokwani, close to Middelburg in the former Eastern Transvaal (now Mpumalanga Province), which was organised by the Native Commissioner's office of Pokwani. While Poncho's article does not provide an assessment of the 'large variety of exhibits', which were rather ambiguously described as 'Native art handcrafts', it was nevertheless an important recording of an exhibition not held in one of the major urban centres of South Africa at the time.[41] Attended by over 1 750 people (1 500 black and 250 white), the exhibition was also a competition of sorts: an extremely generous 150 prizes were distributed to the over 600 entries. While the exhibition encouraged the artists to sell their work, Poncho notes that 'a great majority refused to part with their treasures'.[42] Why did they refuse? Was it because the money offered was too little? Or was it because the artists did not view their creative products as commodities of exchange? Whatever their motivations may have been, this anecdote is evidence of the uneasiness that existed between the capitalist art market, which these black artists were being introduced to through such showcases, and the attachment these artists had to 'their treasures', an attachment that transcended economic imperatives.

* * *

While the early years of art criticism in *The Bantu World* engaged with the meta-discourses about the nature and role of black art, individual artists were sparingly and slowly indexed into the reporting. One of the first occasions an individual visual artist was mentioned by name was when the newspaper announced Ernest Mancoba's six-month residency in Pretoria, where he was scheduled to produce work for the 1936 Empire Exhibition.[43] In the very short commentary, Mancoba is celebrated as a self-taught 'African sculptor whose amazing wood carvings have excited the artistic population of Cape Town' and have been 'praised by prominent critics'. Mancoba had indeed obtained some renown, having already completed commissions and participated in exhibitions prior to his inclusion in the Empire Exhibition. The article highlighted that Mancoba's creative 'dream is to present the soul of his people to the world through his little wooden statues'. It seems that the Empire Exhibition of 1936 had a defining influence on profiling the black artist as a virtuoso, as many of the artists who showcased their work at that event gained considerable recognition afterwards, in both the white and the black press.

Unfortunately, the war years (1939–45) brought with them a major lull in the reporting and criticism of the visual arts in *The Bantu World*. Many of the exhibition opportunities where black art could be appreciated and appraised were seriously compromised because of the war and the South African government's significant investment in it. In 1948 a further blow was dealt to the development of black art criticism as a professional practice when the National Party, a conservative Afrikaner nationalist political organisation led by D.F. Malan, won the national elections and proceeded to institute the programme of apartheid, which deepened race-based segregation in all facets of South African life, including the arts and its criticism.

Black art criticism during the early twentieth century mimicked the broader racially inspired sociopolitical storms of colonial and later apartheid South Africa and because of this complicated context, the nature of formative black scholarship on black artists during the early to mid-twentieth century was distinguishable from traditional Western art criticism on several fronts. Firstly, black art criticism was not generated by or linked to a master voice, as was Euro-American criticism. Second, art criticism in black society existed as a public practice, which was facilitated by entities like *The Bantu World*. Third, black art criticism during the 1930s was still in its formative phase and should therefore not be measured by the same rules used to evaluate Euro-American art writing from the same period.

The public intellectualism introduced here was certainly different from but not lesser than the professional art criticism – professional insofar as someone could have a career as an art critic at that time – found in Europe and America. The fact that art criticism among black people operated in different modes should not diminish its socio-educational value nor its level of theoretical complexity. The selected newspaper articles cited here reveal the scholarly complexity and seriousness with which various black writers thought about black art during the twentieth century. This chapter is an introductory attempt at opening up this field of unexplored histories. There is clearly a need and scope for further longitudinal investigations and focused case studies into the subtleties of twentieth-century black art criticism published in both the black and the white press.

NOTES

[1] David N. Koloane, 'Art Criticism for Whom?', in *Art Criticism and Africa*, ed. Katy Deepwell (London: Saffron Books, 1998), 69.
[2] Raimi Gbadamosi alerted me to the fact that Koloane was reminding the majority-white audience during the Art Criticism and Africa Conference in London in 1996, where he initially made this remark, that professional art criticism in the South African context had, throughout the twentieth century, only served to advance white artists and their art. Gbadamosi gave me this counsel after I delivered a paper on the history of black art criticism in South Africa at the Black Portraiture[s] V: Memory and the Archive, Past, Present, Future Conference at New York University, 17–19 October 2019.
[3] Steve Biko, *I Write What I Like: A Selection of His Writings*, ed. Aelred Stubbs (London: Heinemann, 1987).
[4] Everlyn Nicodemus and Kristian Romare, 'Africa, Art Criticism and the Big Commentary', *Third Text* 11, no. 41 (1997): 65.
[5] Lize van Robbroeck, 'Unsettling the Canon: Some Thoughts on the Design of *Visual Century: South African Art in Context*', *Third Text Africa* 3, no. 1 (2013): 27–29.
[6] In 1928 *Umteteli wa Bantu* introduced the painter Moses Tladi as a self-taught 'genius' whose work showed 'unusual merit'. Tim Couzens, *The New African: A Study of the Life and Work of H.I.E. Dhlomo* (Johannesburg: Ravan Press, 1985), 249. Also see Les

Switzer, '*Bantu World* and the Origins of a Captive African Commercial Press in South Africa', *Journal of Southern African Studies* 14, no. 3 (1988): 351–370 and Bhekizizwe Peterson, '*The Bantu World* and the World of the Book: Reading, Writing, and "Enlightenment"', in *Africa's Hidden Histories: Everyday Literacy and Making the Self*, ed. Karin Barker (Bloomington: Indiana University Press, 2006), 236–257.

[7] Tim Couzens, 'History of the Black Press in South Africa 1836–1960' (paper presented at the University of the Witwatersrand Institute for Advanced Social Research, Johannesburg, 1984), 1.

[8] Les Switzer and Donna Switzer, *The Black Press in South Africa and Lesotho: A Descriptive Bibliographic Guide to African, Coloured and Indian Newspapers, Newsletters and Magazines 1836–1976* (Boston: G.K. Hall & Co., 1979).

[9] Peterson, '*The Bantu World*'.

[10] More than 50 per cent of the initial ownership of the Bantu Press was held by black partners, among them Richard V. Selope Thema. However, in 1933 the Argus Printing and Publishing Company, working alongside Charles Maggs Investments, took majority shareholding by providing much-needed capital investment into the paper, which reduced and practically rescinded the black ownership of the newspaper. Switzer and Switzer, *The Black Press*, 7.

[11] Another fully black-owned and -managed newspaper, *African Leader* (also established in 1932), which was funded by George Hashe, a black entrepreneur, and edited by T.D. Mweli Skota, was in circulation for a few years before its collapse. Couzens, 'History of the Black Press', 27.

[12] Couzens, 'History of the Black Press', 25.

[13] Switzer and Switzer, *The Black Press*, 8.

[14] Cited in Couzens, *The New African*, 275; emphasis added.

[15] Tim Couzens, 'Pseudonyms in Black South African Writing, 1920–1950', *Research in African Literatures* 6, no. 2 (1975): 226.

[16] Richard V. Selope Thema, 'Editorial', *The Bantu World*, 9 April 1932, 4. Selope Thema was a towering figure throughout the first half of the twentieth century. He was part of the African National Congress during its formation in 1912 and became a prominent political representative of the black franchise. As one of the leaders of the New African Movement, he used his political and cultural influence to advance the interests of the small, but highly influential, black middle class at the time. Championing black art through journalism was central to this mission. Richard V. Selope Thema, *From Cattle Herding to Editor's Chair: A Forgotten Founder of the ANC*, ed. Alan Cobley (Cape Town: Kwela Books, 2018).

[17] Alan Cobley, 'Introduction', in *From Cattle Herding to Editor's Chair: A Forgotten Founder of the ANC*, by Richard V. Selope Thema (Cape Town: Kwela Books, 2018), 35.

[18] An article titled 'Bantu Jazz Band' celebrated the exploits of a popular jazz band, which was formed in 1929. The article confirmed that the band 'makes sufficient money to enable the members to live decently'. 'Bantu Jazz Band', *The Bantu Wold*, 30 April 1932, 9.

[19] The Bantu Dramatic Society had presented its first show in April 1933. In a review of that show, the writer makes an impassioned case for the value of drama as 'a social art', further suggesting that 'drama is more effective than the pulpit' in communicating meaning. 'Bantu Dramatic Society Stages Its First Show', *The Bantu World*, 15 April 1933, 1.

[20] 'Bantu Dramatic Society Surprises Its Audience', *The Bantu World*, 6 May 1933, 1.

[21] Elizabeth Rankin, 'Black Artists, White Patrons: The Cross-Cultural Art Market in Urban South Africa', *Africa Insight* 20, no. 1 (1990): 26.

22 Jameson G. Coka, 'The Bantu Would Soon Advance if All Minded Their Own Business', *The Bantu World*, 6 August 1932, 9.
23 Coka, 'The Bantu Would Soon Advance', 9.
24 'The Bantu Carpenter', *The Bantu World*, 6 August 1932, 9.
25 'Bantu Crafts Attract Notice', *The Bantu World*, 27 August 1932, 9.
26 One of the areas overlooked in discourses on art education for black creatives during the twentieth century are commercial workspaces. For example, in August 1932 an article highlighted the need for printers who can access employment in native printing offices ('Printers in Demand', *The Bantu World*, 20 August 1932, 2). Because of their 'commercial' skills, these printers were referred to as craftsmen. While historians have traced the emergence of a printmaking tradition among black artists to Polly Street and Rorke's Drift, if we look into the commercial printing industries, we find that printmaking among black craftsman, although not necessarily artistic, has a much longer history. See Philippa Hobbs and Elizabeth Rankin, *Printmaking in a Transforming South Africa* (Cape Town: David Philip, 1997).
27 Sweet Pea, 'European Pictures in Bantu Homes', *The Bantu World*, 26 October 1935, 12.
28 Without doubt, the field defining publication on South African art in the twentieth century was written by a white female scholar, Esmé Berman. See Esmé Berman, *Art and Artists of South Africa: An Illustrated Biographical Dictionary and Historical Survey of Painters and Graphic Artists since 1875* (Cape Town: A.A. Balkema, 1970).
29 Lynn M. Thomas, 'The Modern Girl and Racial Respectability in 1930s South Africa', *Journal of African History* 47, no. 3 (2006): 465.
30 'League for Bantu Crafts', *The Bantu World*, 5 October 1935, 8; emphasis added.
31 Coka, 'The Bantu Would Soon Advance', 9.
32 'Study of European Music Helps Africans to Understand Their Own', *The Bantu World*, 2 December 1934, 9.
33 'Study of European Music', 9.
34 Robert Plomin, *Blueprint: How DNA Makes Us Who We Are* (London: Allen Lane, 2018), 6.
35 'Study of European Music', 9.
36 R.R.R. Dhlomo was the younger brother of H.I.E. Dhlomo. Like his older brother, he was an accomplished novelist and journalist who is credited with authoring the first fictional book written by a black South African in English (*An African Tragedy*, 1928). R.R.R. Dhlomo served as editor of both *The Bantu World* and *Ilanga lase Natal* newspapers.
37 Editress [R.R.R. Dhlomo], 'Primitive African Art', *The Bantu World*, 2 June 1934.
38 By 'too Europeanised' Dhlomo was of course referring to the overexposure of the African artist to Western tutelage. While Dhlomo was 'grateful to the missionary bodies for their enterprise and perseverance', he also had the conviction that this training contaminated the soul and essence of African art. Editress, 'Primitive African Art', 11.
39 Anitra Nettleton, 'Realism, Rurality and Modernity: Samuel Makoanyane, Julius Mfete, Zolani Mapente', *African Arts* 53, no. 2 (2020): 66–79.
40 Ntongela Masilela, *An Outline of the New African Movement in South Africa* (Trenton, NJ: Africa World Press, 2013), xvii.
41 Poncho, 'Successful Show of Bantu Arts and Craft Held at Pokwani', *The Bantu World*, 1 September 1934, 7.
42 Poncho, 'Successful Show', 11.
43 'African Sculptor Given a Chance', *The Bantu World*, 18 April 1936, 12.

REFERENCES

'African Sculptor Given a Chance'. *The Bantu World*, 18 April 1936.
'Bantu Crafts Attract Notice'. *The Bantu World*, 27 August 1932.
'Bantu Dramatic Society Stages Its First Show'. *The Bantu World*, 15 April 1933.
'Bantu Dramatic Society Surprises Its Audience'. *The Bantu World*, 6 May 1933.
'Bantu Jazz Band'. *The Bantu Wold*, 30 April 1932.
Berman, Esmé. *Art and Artists of South Africa: An Illustrated Biographical Dictionary and Historical Survey of Painters and Graphic Artists since 1875*. Cape Town: A.A. Balkema, 1970.
Biko, Steve. *I Write What I Like: A Selection of His Writings*. Edited by Aelred Stubbs. London: Heinemann, 1987.
Cobley, Alan. 'Introduction'. In *From Cattle Herding to Editor's Chair: A Forgotten Founder of the ANC*, by Richard V. Selope Thema, 9–41. Cape Town: Kwela Books, 2018.
Coka, Jameson G. 'The Bantu Would Soon Advance if All Minded Their Own Business'. *The Bantu World*, 6 August 1932.
Couzens, Tim. 'History of the Black Press in South Africa 1836–1960'. Paper presented at the University of Witwatersrand Institute for Advanced Social Research, Johannesburg, 1984.
Couzens, Tim. *The New African: A Study of the Life and Work of H.I.E. Dhlomo*. Johannesburg: Ravan Press, 1985.
Couzens, Tim. 'Pseudonyms in Black South African Writing, 1920–1950'. *Research in African Literatures* 6, no. 2 (1975): 226–231.
Editress [R.R.R. Dhlomo]. 'Primitive African Art'. *The Bantu World*, 2 June 1934.
Hobbs, Philippa and Elizabeth Rankin. *Printmaking in a Transforming South Africa*. Cape Town: David Philip, 1997.
Koloane, David N. 'Art Criticism for Whom?' In *Art Criticism and Africa*, edited by Katy Deepwell, 69–72. London: Saffron Books, 1998.
'League for Bantu Crafts'. *The Bantu World*, 5 October 1935.
Masilela, Ntongela. *An Outline of the New African Movement in South Africa*. Trenton, NJ: Africa World Press, 2013.
Nettleton, Anitra. 'Realism, Rurality and Modernity: Samuel Makoanyane, Julius Mfete, Zolani Mapente'. *African Arts* 53, no. 2 (2020): 66–79.
Nicodemus, Everlyn and Kristian Romare. 'Africa, Art Criticism and the Big Commentary'. *Third Text* 11, no. 41 (1997): 53–65.
Peterson, Bhekizizwe. '*The Bantu World* and the World of the Book: Reading, Writing, and "Enlightenment"'. In *Africa's Hidden Histories: Everyday Literacy and Making the Self*, edited by Karin Barker, 236–257. Bloomington: Indiana University Press, 2006.
Plomin, Robert. *Blueprint: How DNA Makes Us Who We Are*. London: Allen Lane, 2018.
Poncho. 'Successful Show of Bantu Arts and Craft Held at Pokwani'. *The Bantu World*, 1 September 1934.
'Printers in Demand'. *The Bantu World*, 20 August 1932.
Rankin, Elizabeth. 'Black Artists, White Patrons: The Cross-Cultural Art Market in Urban South Africa'. *Africa Insight* 20, no. 1 (1990): 25–32.
Selope Thema, Richard V. 'Editorial'. *The Bantu World*, 9 April 1932.
Selope Thema, Richard V. *From Cattle Herding to Editor's Chair: A Forgotten Founder of the ANC*. Edited by Alan Cobley. Cape Town: Kwela Books, 2018.
'Study of European Music Helps Africans to Understand Their Own'. *The Bantu World*, 2 December 1934.

Sweet Pea. 'European Pictures in Bantu Homes'. *The Bantu World*, 26 October 1935.
Switzer, Les. '*Bantu World* and the Origins of a Captive African Commercial Press in South Africa'. *Journal of Southern African Studies* 14, no. 3 (1988): 351–370.
Switzer, Les and Donna Switzer. *The Black Press in South Africa and Lesotho: A Descriptive Bibliographic Guide to African, Coloured and Indian Newspapers, Newsletters and Magazines 1836–1976*. Boston: G.K. Hall & Co., 1979.
'The Bantu Carpenter'. *The Bantu World*, 6 August 1932.
Thomas, Lynn M. 'The Modern Girl and Racial Respectability in 1930s South Africa'. *Journal of African History* 47, no. 3 (2006): 461–490.
Van Robbroeck, Lize. 'Unsettling the Canon: Some Thoughts on the Design of *Visual Century: South African Art in Context*'. *Third Text Africa* 3, no. 1 (2013): 27–29.

CHAPTER

4

In Conversation with the Nation: *Sowetan*'s Maverick Editor Aggrey Klaaste

Lesley Cowling

In the late 1980s the editor of *Sowetan*, Aggrey Klaaste, began a project to intervene in the fraught political situation in South Africa. Protest against the apartheid state in townships across the country was ongoing, two states of emergency had been declared and competing political groups warred with one another in deadly clashes. Klaaste's project sought to rebuild structures in black communities and to inspire local community projects. Klaaste called his idea 'nation-building' and promoted it through columns and articles, as well as events and community projects spearheaded by the newspaper.

Nation-building represented a significant shift from the radical activism of *Sowetan*'s newsroom, inherited from its predecessor paper, *The World*, which had aligned itself with the Black Consciousness struggles of the 1970s. Nation-building was strenuously opposed by militant journalists at the newspaper, as well as by many political activists, who argued that apartheid needed to be torn down before any 'building' could happen. As Phakama Mbonambi writes: 'In an atmosphere where the young lions exerted power through a box of matches, Klaaste's thinking was totally unconventional – perhaps even dangerous, given that it deviated from [the] received wisdom of waging the struggle right down to the last man standing.'[1]

However, by the 1990s, nation-building was integral to the ethos of the newspaper. *Sowetan*, successor to a long line of black-readership newspapers, increased in influence as circulation soared in the early 1990s.[2] It became the largest readership daily in the country, overtaking the white-readership *The Star*, and was widely distributed among black urban readers.[3] *Sowetan* journalists were closely connected to its township public, sharing in their lives through living and working in Soweto. But the newspaper's influence extended beyond the geographical borders of Soweto as it expanded into a national paper and was circulated in black residential areas across the country.[4]

Sowetan's nation-building project was thus a significant moment in South African public life. As I have argued elsewhere, nation-building allowed a collective re-imagining of black citizenship and positioned black South Africans as the leading public for an inclusive citizenry, which could unite competing political ideologies, religions and cultural loyalties, and also include white South Africans.[5] The newspaper thus convened 'a black public positioned as *the* public, and imagined as the nation'.[6] Klaaste's vision expressed more than the aspirations of his own 'African' majority,[7] denied citizenship in the South African state; it also imagined a future for all South Africans, fulfilling what Edward Said has argued is a key moral value for public intellectuals: to speak truth to power in service of a greater good, not simply for a special interest.[8]

This chapter is not concerned with the content of nation-building and where Klaaste can be positioned as part of the political landscape, but looks at how the media can shape public intellectual discussion. It hones in specifically on the ways in which Klaaste constructed and negotiated the idea of nation-building in his weekly column 'On the Line'.[9] In discussing nation-building, Klaaste moved away from conventional column styles, which tend to use reasoned argument, logic and evidence to make a case. Instead, he mixed a personal style with storytelling, scene-setting, characterisation and conversation to promote nation-building in its early days. The column modelled the ways different political players could be in dialogue and attempted to persuade readers to consider an inclusive politics. Klaaste played a role as a public interlocutor through presenting himself as uncertain, open to ideas, 'inside' the problem and looking for the best way forward. He did not operate from an 'all-knowing' elite position, despite the fact that he was an educated man and editor of a newspaper.

The case of Klaaste demonstrates the powers of media commentators and their role in intellectual discussion within mainstream media. The media provide a powerful platform, underwriting the 'public' in public intellectual, but they also circumscribe the influence of commentators. In South Africa, for example, the black press, once a collection of independent small publications, was largely bought up by white capital in the 1930s and became politically restricted, under-resourced and commercially oriented – a 'captive press'.[10] However, ownership by white conglomerates and the implementation of corporate approaches 'transformed the black press into a mass medium of communication', expanding readership significantly.[11] *Sowetan*, as a commercial tabloid, circulated the discussions in Klaaste's columns widely, across many black geographic communities and class, status and language identities. Following Michael Warner's contention that publics are created in relation to texts and their circulation, it could be argued that the distribution of *Sowetan* created nation-building publics across South Africa.[12]

However, the discussions in *Sowetan* did not circulate much beyond its 'African' readership to the readers of other newspapers. As Keyan Tomaselli notes: 'Apartheid prevented the development of an even minimally homogenous public sphere or "national culture" ... in terms of media consumption'.[13] Even when nation-building was reported on in other newspapers, it was often framed as a project by a black editor for black South Africans.

Klaaste's influence was also circumscribed in time: it appears that his conception of nation-building has not persisted in the public imagination. Although highly influential in the transition to democracy – some calling him visionary and far-sighted – Klaaste is not memorialised as a 'public intellectual' or influential public figure in the current moment.[14] It may be that the ephemeral nature of newspapers, which are concerned with current events, means that the ideas of media commentators do not persist much past the sell-by dates of their publications. Their columns go into the archives and are forgotten. Furthermore, as Richard Keeble notes, journalism 'retains a precarious position within literary culture and academe', which means that journalists' words are not given the same status as literary or academic works.[15]

The purpose of this chapter is not to memorialise Klaaste, but rather to revisit his role as a facilitator of public debate, examining how he made use of the media forms available to him in order to promote discussion of his ideas. In doing this, Klaaste continued a long tradition of African commentators, who explored ideas of identity and the role of indigenous people in southern African colonial territories through the pages of black-readership newspapers, from early black-owned and -managed presses to later commercial, white-owned newspapers. Klaaste was not an anomaly, then, in the history of African intellectualism through the press, but another chapter in that legacy.

INTELLECTUALS AND THE MEDIA

Normative ideas of democracies propose that they solve challenges best by involving the populace in reasoned discussion on important issues. Charles Taylor has argued that the public sphere – conceived of as a space between the people and the state in which reasoned public discussion can take place – is a key social imaginary that constitutes modernity.[16] In other words, the idea of the public sphere causes people to act collectively in relation to its precepts and drives certain operations and institutions in society. In this vision of societies debating the way forward, some individuals will emerge as critical to the discussions – experts who can provide knowledge on complex topics, proponents of various issues who set out a particular position and analysts who can explain context. Among the figures of the public sphere, the public intellectual is the most idealised and the most difficult to define. Said, in his Reith Lectures for BBC4, produced a picture of a highly moral individual, who speaks truth to power and sets aside sectional interests for the common good.[17]

In Africa, the role of intellectuals has been complicated by the colonial inheritances of the continent, in which Western approaches are seen to overdetermine local forms of knowledge and practice. Frantz Fanon argued in 1959 that the African intellectual 'should build up his nation'; in other words, African intellectuals in the pre-independence era needed to speak for their own societies, not for the world.[18] In the post-colonial era, intellectuals who once resisted colonial governments have often been called on to direct their efforts to building the new society, rather than keeping a critical eye on the state.

African intellectuals have also been expected to take the lead in 'decolonising the mind'.[19] Nicholas Creary argues that the juxtaposition of European modernity as humanist per se, against 'traditional' and 'cultural' Africa, created a binary in which Africa is 'a foil to Western humanity'.[20] Thus, even in the twenty-first century, Africans continue to struggle, in the words of Ngũgĩ wa Thiong'o, 'to seize back their creative initiative in history through a real control of all the means of communal self-definition in time and space'.[21] For African intellectuals, charting an authentic position in relation to systems of knowledge imposed by violent colonial dispossession is a challenging proposition.

In South Africa, African intellectuals began discussing issues that concerned them through the pages of newspapers in the nineteenth century. Hlonipha Mokoena argues that writing in the isiZulu-English newspaper *Ilanga lase Natal* in the 1900s created 'an assembly of readers', drawn from mission-educated literate *amakholwa* (believers).[22] They debated their identity and position in the British Empire, as subjects and citizens. In the Eastern Cape, 'the School People', as mission-educated people were called, 'initiated a significant change in black response to white power', moving from the battlefield to the political arena, from the spear to the pen.[23] The editors of black newspapers, such as the founder of *Imvo Zabantsundu*, John Tengo Jabavu, became powerful figures, able to intervene in political events.[24]

Black newspapers were instrumental in creating reading publics. Scholarship on South African media after the Second World War has shown that black-readership publications negotiated a range of factors to construct 'new possibilities for black self-representation' and 'alternative versions of black modernity' and to allow readers to imaginatively connect to black communities across the world, from elsewhere in Africa to the United States of America.[25]

During the apartheid era, certain publications positioned themselves as defiantly anti-apartheid and allied with political movements, such as *The World* (Black Consciousness) and *New Nation* (broadly aligned to the African National Congress, or ANC).[26] These forums made it possible for commentators to 'speak truth to power', attacking the system and its political and intellectual bases. Some activists were embedded in liberation, worker and anti-apartheid movements, others in universities or non-governmental organisations. Many espoused ideological positions, such as Marxist, workerist or liberal approaches, in the discussion of an imagined post-apartheid society.

As Said has noted, it is not easy for intellectuals to step into the public domain.[27] Access to the news media, in particular, is controlled and constrained by the processes of the production of debate and opinion.[28] Individuals who enter these arenas may not necessarily have control over their part in the debate or over the ways in which it unfolds. Commentators are selected according to a range of criteria that may not necessarily include intellectual prowess, but may relate to their ability to meet the demands of media forms, such as accessibility, reader interest and controversy.

There is one relatively independent form for commentators: the regular column, which appears on a daily or weekly basis. As Dan Nimmo and James Combs have noted: 'One of the oldest and most cherished public forums for punditry in the history of print journalism is the column.'[29] The 'pundit', according to Nimmo and Combs, is 'one who [commands] deference because of learned authority' and 'gives opinions in an authoritative manner'.[30] Such commentators rely on the media to provide a public forum. They are connected to the interpretive function of the media and empowered by their operation as figures in an imagined public sphere.[31]

On the other hand, newspapers rely on columnists to fulfil societal expectations that the media produce opinion and analysis.[32] Columnists 'constitute a source of opinion-formation and opinion-articulation, agenda-setting and agenda-evaluation' and contribute to a newspaper's personality.[33] Many writers argue that columnists become voices in society and that the best columns articulate a view of the world and contribute to national debate.[34]

However, Alistair Duff questions how much power and influence columnists actually have in a democracy. In his study of political commentators in Britain, he notes that the power of columnists depends very much on the power of the newspaper they write for.[35] He argues: 'The effectiveness of a so-called pundit is a function of his or her willingness to remain focused upon a theme; ... a columnist is most powerful when complying with a broader newspaper campaign.'[36]

Mastery of the skills of writing is also vital. Some have argued that a columnist's style should be individual and distinctive, while Nimmo and Combs note that the typical column has a common rhetorical style and an expected structure: 'statement of the problem, discussion of legitimate alternatives, argumentative defense of one choice and attack of others, conclusion and recommendation.'[37] They assert: 'Whether one is persuaded by a columnist's point of view may well depend not on what was written, but how.'[38]

FROM BLACK CONSCIOUSNESS TO NATION-BUILDING

Sowetan, as the name implies, was started as a community newspaper in Soweto in 1980 and distributed free. Its owners, white-owned media conglomerate the Argus Printing and Publishing Company, conceived of it as a project to grow black-readership publications in its stable and to attract advertisers. At the time, there were four major newspaper companies that dominated the market: Nasionale Pers and Perskor served mostly an Afrikaans-speaking, white readership, while the Argus Company and South African Associated Newspapers produced English-language newspapers for a mostly white market. Black-readership newspapers were largely owned by white capital and black journalists had to negotiate their professional role in relation to their politically marginalised readership, their subaltern position in white-owned media organisations and their outsider status in society.[39] Adrian Hadland suggests that this dominance by the big four white-owned companies prevented black-owned newspapers from entering the market and becoming a vibrant media sector.[40]

The new community paper was not produced at the Argus Company mothership in Johannesburg's city centre, but out of shabby, rundown offices in an industrial area of Soweto.[41] It was born at a time when the Black Consciousness movement of the 1970s, which had mobilised a generation of activists, had been quashed by the state, its organisations destroyed, its leaders detained, killed or exiled. The journalists at *The World*, a predecessor to *Sowetan*, had been at the coalface of that insurrection. As Craig Charney has argued, many *World* journalists embraced an activist role in response to the question: 'Are you a journalist first or black first', moving from a 'professional' journalistic ethos that drew on objectivity, accuracy and impartiality.[42] They also established an exclusively black journalists' organisation, the Union of Black Journalists (UBJ), in line with the Black Consciousness philosophy of self-reliance.[43]

Black journalists witnessed first-hand the protests of schoolchildren against the state in Soweto in 1976, the police action that killed and injured a number of children and the uprising that followed. Mbonambi makes this point with regard to Klaaste: 'Soweto 1976 was a watershed in Klaaste's life, an event he constantly revisited in his writing, using it as a potent lesson for what needs to be avoided if South Africa were to have a bright future. He particularly lamented the loss of innocence among youngsters, and viewed the uprising as a start of the inculcation of a culture of burning and destroying to achieve political ends.'[44]

The *World* was banned by the state in 1977, along with the UBJ and 19 Black Consciousness organisations. Many of its journalists were arrested, including its editor Percy Qoboza. Klaaste was imprisoned without trial for six months. Mbonambi writes that the detention frightened Klaaste, marking him for life. It gave him 'a taste of what the minority regime in Pretoria was capable of'.[45]

After the banning of the *World*, the Argus Company resuscitated the *Post*, another of its titles, and continued production using the same offices and staff. The journalists established another union in 1980, the Media Workers Association of South Africa (Mwasa), and opened its membership to all black workers at newspapers (including printers, drivers and messengers).[46] The staff of the *Post* joined a nationwide Mwasa strike for better working conditions and pay.[47] The strike shut down the *Post* in October 1980 and the authorities took the opportunity to remove it from circulation.[48]

The Argus Company then marshalled *Sowetan* into the *Post*'s position and staffed it with 18 *Post* journalists.[49] *Sowetan* thus became the carrier of the culture of the *World* and its Black Consciousness legacy. Qoboza's deputy, Joe Latakgomo, was made editor. A front page editorial and an article inside outlined a normative journalistic role for the newspaper and highlighted the contradictions of being a black journalist in apartheid South Africa.[50] The journalists and staff, however, mostly retained their adherence to the Black Consciousness movement and their membership of Mwasa. The journalists' espousal of Mwasa as their union was characterised in white-readership newspapers as evidence that the newspaper had been captured by Black Consciousness activists and thus did not produce objective journalism.[51]

The 1980s saw increased unionisation and worker strikes and the launch by civil society of the United Democratic Front (UDF) in 1983, which embarked on civil disobedience.[52] In 1984, violent insurrection burst out in many townships across the country, part of an effort to 'make the country ungovernable'.[53] Journalists found themselves in a tricky position, expected to report on developments while steering clear of a raft of press regulations.[54] For black editors, the difficulty was particularly acute. As the *Financial Mail* noted, black editors 'confronted great expectations and even greater pressures from rival social and political groups striving to claim their allegiance'.[55]

In May 1988, Aggrey Klaaste became editor of *Sowetan*. Unlike many of his colleagues, Klaaste was considered an educated man. He was the son of mission-educated teachers – 'tea drinkers', as educated, 'African', upper-class people were called. It was part of the family life to gather around the piano for a singalong.[56] He had a degree from the University of the Witwatersrand (Wits) and had spent a year at Harvard in the United States as a Nieman Fellow. He had also fought a battle against alcoholism and won.

Klaaste had written a column for the *Post*, titled 'Just for Today', before leaving for Harvard.[57] In 1981, he began writing a column about life under apartheid, 'On the Line', for *Sowetan*.[58] At the time of his promotion to editor, he was a senior member of staff, who had paid his dues at the paper. However, not everyone thought he was a good choice. The *Financial Mail* noted that Klaaste was thought of as highly educated, but weak on 'political commitment and leadership' and so 'might be swayed by forceful personalities on the newspaper who ardently espouse black consciousness (BC)'.[59]

This did not prove to be the case. Directly on taking up the mantle of editor, Klaaste began outlining his vision for nation-building, an idea he had been working on with a *Sowetan* colleague, Sam Mabe, for some time. He intended the newspaper to be a key driver of the project. In August 1988, Klaaste publicly introduced nation-building at a ceremony to honour him for excellence. *The Star* hailed the development, reporting: 'I have a dream, says top editor' (the headline echoing Martin Luther King).[60] The dream was 'to save this country', with black South Africans taking the lead in moving the country out of its 'political morass'.

There was a flurry of interest in other media and not only in the local press, but also in some international titles. Inside the newsroom of *Sowetan*, the response was very different: 'We actually confronted and fought Klaaste … saying, you know, "liberation now" and good stuff later. But he said, "No, no, no – it's got to go in parallel".'[61]

Journalist Len Maseko recalls: 'We were liberation fighters using a pen. We just saw ourselves as political soldiers and we were going out there to expose the brutalities of the system.'[62] Klaaste's friend and respected colleague Joe Thloloe, a former Pan Africanist Congress member and founder member of the UBJ, asked him how he could even think about nation-building in the middle of a revolution.[63]

However, Klaaste persisted in promoting the idea in discussions with his staff and in his columns. Mike Tissong, at the time a member of the Azanian People's Organisation, says that Klaaste had an open-door policy and any staff member could discuss things with him. The columns formed an important part of the debate in the newsroom. Tissong recalls: 'Aggrey developed the idea of nation-building through the columns, and they were passed to *Sowetan* journalists and editors for discussion and critique ... because he didn't come with a complete idea of nation building. It's something which evolved as he was editor of *Sowetan* so he would discuss it with everybody; you know "this is my idea what do you think of it?"'[64]

Klaaste won his staff over, as well as gaining the support of the executives of the Argus Company and the buy-in of white and black business to support the project. A year after Klaaste first launched nation-building, *Sowetan* published a 'Nation Building manifesto', committing the newspaper to community projects under its banner.[65] In October 1989, a 'Nation Building Week' followed, which consisted of a series of cultural and social events for black communities in Johannesburg and the Transvaal Province.[66] The 'highlights' included a non-denominational 'Prayers for the Nation' service at Regina Mundi Catholic Church in Soweto, a job market at Vista University in Soweto, a *Sowetan* Woman of the Year luncheon, a commemoration of the banning of the *World* newspaper and an advertising indaba.

According to Tissong, in those years, *Sowetan* was 'not just reporting on things but engaging and building'.[67] A journalist was assigned full-time to write about community projects and key figures who were making a difference. *Sowetan* linked up with township organisations, churches, community leaders and business people. One such initiative was to upgrade township areas, to make them 'as attractive and livable as we can'.[68]

By 1989, *Sowetan* averaged almost 175 000 in circulation and about two-thirds of this circulation was outside the greater Johannesburg area.[69] In 1990, the ANC was unbanned and its leaders were released from prison, inaugurating negotiations between the organisation and the apartheid government for a new democratic dispensation. By this stage, *Sowetan* had the biggest circulation of any daily newspaper, a position it held for the rest of the decade.

Nation-building continued to be a cornerstone of *Sowetan* after the democratic elections of 1994 and Klaaste moved from the day-to-day running of the newspaper to focusing on the nation-building projects themselves. He continued to write his column. In 2001, research showed that *Sowetan* was still the most-read daily in the country, with the All Media and Product Survey confirming that it had two million readers a day.[70] However, after two ownership changes, the migration of black readers to formerly white-readership newspapers and the rise of the tabloid newspaper, *The Sun*, it lost its prime position. Klaaste and his nation-building campaign were sidelined and he died in 2004. *Sowetan* continues to serve a mostly black readership, with a circulation of around 70 000.

THE COLUMNS

Klaaste was an experienced columnist by the time he became editor of *Sowetan*. He had shared personal stories, produced polemical attacks on the National Party state and discussed issues for the black community for a decade. His style in those years was in many respects typical of the conventional column; he would argue a position, backing up his points with evidence and reason, and unfold his argument over the space provided. Sometimes he made use of erudite ideas; sometimes he drew on other thinkers and he was able to marshal a range of materials from his large knowledge of scholars and writers, of history and of various philosophies, particularly related to African themes. Although not afraid to pose a question he had no answer to, he often occupied the space of learned authority. In those days, it was possibly easier to take strong positions, such as the oppressive nature of apartheid and its negative effects on the day-to-day lives of black South Africans, because they were generally agreed on by his peers and his readers.

Typical of his writing was an ability to share personal stories, make humorous self-deprecating remarks and to address the reader in a conversational way, creating intimacy between writer and reader. He was not afraid to detail feelings that were sad or difficult, which made him appear vulnerable, or to note the reactions of ordinary working people he encountered in his day-to-day life. 'My personal problem is that I cannot sleep because of Maritzburg,' he wrote in a column in early 1988, referring to political killings in that area.[71] In an article for the *Sunday Star* some weeks later, he wrote of his own life experience under apartheid: 'I have squirmed, protested, pleaded, sometimes fought, got arrested, got drunk as an excuse for my oppressed state and done all number of things to get the pressure off my neck.'[72]

Nation-building, which he referred to in the beginning stages as 'the big idea' (or, alternatively, 'the great idea'), was a greater challenge for him as a columnist. Not only did it fly in the face of the principle that the apartheid state should be pulled down before rebuilding happened, but it was initially a vague idea that needed to be defined and fleshed out. He introduced the 'big idea' as follows: 'I am preparing the ground, laying the bed so to speak for the seed of an idea I hope to be planting in the not too long future. Frankly, the idea excites and exhilarates me as it appears to have breathtaking possibilities.'[73]

The column went on to say that he was tempted to lay 'the total strategy behind the plan bare right now', but added that he was being cautious, going slowly. He then went on to argue that black South Africans were in a weak position, despite being in the majority, and that the weakness stemmed from a lack of unity, the lack of a 'central idea' to motivate all the various movements. He used the example of the Afrikaners, who, in 1948, were a divided people, poor, with no centre to unite them, but who became strong through building their nation. (This would not be the first time that Klaaste would draw on this historical example.) At this stage, he did not set out his plans. He took his readers into his confidence, though, about how he was choosing to approach the subject and what his concerns were, in a sense showing them the workings of his strategy for discussion.

This column inaugurated a long conversation with his readers about nation-building, discussion that took place on a weekly basis through his column over the space of about a year. By the next week (and the next column), Klaaste was officially editor of *Sowetan* and immediately announced that the newspaper would commit to nation-building.[74] His column was not the only space given to the idea: guest columnists were also invited to contribute and senior colleague Sam Mabe became a regular commentator. As discussed above, the campaign and its projects were also being built through collaborations with donors and community organisations, and reported on by the newspaper. However, Klaaste's column was the philosophical heart of the campaign, the space where the idea was offered, debated and fleshed out.

In the intense focus of 1988 and 1989, three phases can be discerned. In the first six months, from May to September 1988, nation-building was floated in a general way and Klaaste reported on reactions from the broader community on his plans, thus keeping the idea open for discussion. There was a lot of repetition of his concerns and hopes for the project, but he moved from a more argumentative approach to a questioning, uncertain position. In the second phase, from October 1988 to February 1989, there was an intensification of discussion, as nation-building received a lot more criticism and outright opposition, as well as being taken up with enthusiasm by certain sectors of society. At this stage, Klaaste (and also Mabe) engaged vigorously with a much greater set of counter-arguments and began to outline the concept in relation to other philosophical and political positions, such as ubuntu, Black Consciousness, African independence and so on. Alongside the debates, the discussion of projects such as support for failing schools and the upgrading of township areas also gave shape to nation-building as an approach.

By the final phase of the writing, nation-building was established in the newspaper and the columns record the successes and landmarks of the campaign, before moving on to other topics. In 1989, too, the apartheid government began talks with the ANC and released many political prisoners and detainees, which made nation-building highly relevant to the new era of creating inclusive citizenship for all South Africans. There was less need to constantly promote the idea.

Klaaste argued that people with differing political positions should talk to each other; however, he also modelled such bridge-building through the use of certain tactics in his writing. This was not so much a rational-critical debating position as an ongoing process of dialogue, in which everyone's point of view could be heard. In the first phase, when he is still floating nation-building as an idea, but without much detail, he tells his readers the various responses he has received – a tactic that could be called the 'report back'. For example, in the second column to discuss nation-building, in which he also announces his editorship of *Sowetan*, he notes: 'I might just mention that while the reaction to the first piece was not overwhelming, I have had some interesting responses. Some people have said I should come to the point and one white chap thought the idea had merit.'[75]

In another column, he writes: 'Like many good ideas, mine about rebuilding structures has raised expectations and a certain amount of scorn.'[76] He goes on to explain, again, that as the majority, black South Africans have a responsibility to save the country from ruin and to strengthen their own power structures in order to work with whites for 'our mutual survival'. At this stage, he tends to answer criticism with a reiteration of the necessity to rebuild structures in black communities, to work for a future. Gradually, however, he moves to a more substantive response to these questions, taking the critique of nation-building seriously and drawing on various philosophies in an attempt to answer concerns and shape the concept. He explicitly states that this is what he is doing, keeping readers informed of his thinking and experimenting.

This can be seen early on with the introduction of ubuntu as a foundational concept. This column fleshes out a theme Klaaste develops in his discussion of nation-building – the moral leadership of black South Africans in creating a future for the country, based on the practice of ubuntu. In a column titled '"Ubuntu" Will Rule', he writes: 'I am in a way forced by circumstances and other imperatives to reveal the awesome truth behind nation building. I have dropped hints here and there about where nation building will eventually, must eventually, lead to. I will go the whole hog today and put it on these lines.'[77]

Klaaste argued that nation-building would be driven by the 'wonderful characteristic', 'that undefinable attribute', the ethos of ubuntu, which was an essential value of black culture:

> It was our undoing in the beginning when our kings, our princes in black kingdoms that were thriving on the continent, allowed strangers from across the seas to break bread with them. They also allowed these strangers to build homes and own property. Because these strangers did not have *ubuntu*, they betrayed this hospitality ...
>
> Up to this very day we have this companionship with other people, this compassion for the total stranger or even the enemy.[78]

Klaaste went on to argue that, for black people to run the world, societal structures had to be underpinned by ubuntu. He connected the spirit of ubuntu to a range of black political leaders: 'The crazy thing about this is that it is not even unique. I think Robert Sobukwe's policy of Africanism spoke of Africa for humanity. I think Mr Mandela and the chaps in the ANC camp talk about a non-racial democracy ... The black Americans had a fleeting grasp of this when they said black is beautiful.'[79]

Although Klaaste's approach here could be read as promoting a romantic idea of ubuntu and referring to respected movements and members of the black community as a form of persuasion, his style of address creates the sense of a conversation. He also invited others to write about ubuntu to continue the dialogue. For example, a guest column in December 1988 offered a scholarly discussion of ubuntu as an African form of humanism. Lebamang Sebidi argued that Western humanism puts humans at the centre of things, but is 'bedevilled by two intractable elements: *individualism* and *atheism*'. He adds: 'Ubuntu – African humanism – is stubbornly and inherently anti-individualism while at the same time it is incurably religious.' Ubuntuism, as he called it, was inclusive, humane and concerned with the community: 'I am because they are and they are because I am.'[80]

Klaaste addressed a variety of hostile responses.

> I have said Nation Building is so many things. So that I should not be surprised by some of the interpretations people give it. There is an allegation that it has something to do with Pan Africanism, which is a bit of a risky thing to say about me seeing as I tend to get close attention from some quarters.
>
> There is a feeling that it is allied to Black Consciousness, which is in its way – and I stress – in its way – a reasonable interpretation. There is a view that it has something to do with Inkatha.[81]

He responded by positioning nation-building as not nailed to any political or ideological flag, but as 'the nation's forum to sort out divisiveness'. Then he uses the example of his extended family, in which each member had different political affiliations: 'I belong to an extended family, like most blacks ... we have leanings towards a whole range of diverse and ideological planks. We never fight over this ... On a more banal note, we also love sports in my family ... We hardly ever come to blows about the soccer teams we "favour" ... Nation Building is about the formation of such filial links.'[82]

As discussions over nation-building intensified, Klaaste used his column to explicitly model the 'for and against' of his idea. In early 1989, he puts his nation-building approach side-by-side with its main opposition, the 'liberation first' position, writing the column as a discussion between two friends who respect each other. His interlocuter, who remains unnamed, but could have been any one of a number of *Sowetan* senior colleagues or anti-apartheid activists, is described by Klaaste as 'a dear friend of mine', 'who has in various courageous, responsible ways, showed me what it means to be committed to the struggle'.[83] Klaaste 'hears' the friend's argument in the column by describing it in a respectful way, honouring both the speaker and his position: 'He has convinced me in his quite persuasive way that if the decision for the total revolution is taken in his unselfish totally responsible way, you must be a fool not to agree with him ... He has taught me that perhaps we are almost fated to pay the heaviest of prices for our mistakes. He believes we must go through the blood bath, almost as a cathartic exercise.'[84]

Klaaste then describes the attitude of his protagonist, which is respectful, listening and engaging with Klaaste's points: 'I have discussed Nation Building with this chap. In his usual courteous, attentive manner, he has listened. He has questioned and although I have the feeling he simply pities me for my idealism and naivety, he has said I should take a shot at it.'[85]

Throughout the column, Klaaste refers to his 'friend', his 'buddy', enumerates his good qualities and continues to set out a discussion that is in every way respectful:

> I have said to this buddy of mine that even if I accept his argument about the wastelands, that we have to smash everything and start from scratch I have a few problems and some suggestions ... I say to my friend, is it not better for us to build the hands, to develop the minds and skills that will rebuild this country if we go the whole hog to damnation?[86]

In his conclusion Klaaste writes that the friend 'smiles ruefully and says: "Give it a shot".' This implies that Klaaste has been given permission by a representative of the struggle and also that it is an open-ended project with no guarantee of success.

As well as the unnamed characters Klaaste was in conversation with in his columns, he also referred to an eclectic group of black thinkers in his writing. The individuals he mentioned, generally, were South African and African – Nigerian historian Chinweizu Ibekwe, Ghanaian independence leader Kwame Nkrumah and imprisoned Pan Africanist Congress leader Robert Sobukwe. He also wrote articles on the *Drum* writers of the 1950s and exiled artists. He seemed to reference their excellence, rather than interrogating their ideas – in effect, demonstrating African achievements.

Nation-building, as discussed in the second phase of Klaaste's columns, thus encompassed a range of different political positions, including Charterist, Africanist and Black Consciousness intellectual legacies. It provided a broad church for the variety of politics in black communities, as well as grounding nation-building in spiritual values, referencing eminent black figures and drawing on African traditions (such as ubuntu). The campaign also explicitly drew on one aspect of Black Consciousness, active self-reliance, to argue that black communities must take charge of their own empowerment.

After the first quarter of 1989, nation-building dropped off as a topic for the column, even as it gathered momentum as a set of projects and events in the community. In August of that year, *Sowetan* ran a 'Nation Building manifesto', which committed to 'picking up the pieces and rebuilding all the structures that have collapsed in our communities', 'creating an efficient leadership' and acquiring control of 'structures of power required for the survival' of the people.[87] The manifesto distilled the vision for a future society that Klaaste had been arguing for into a set of principles.

In October 1989 Klaaste wrote about the highlight, for him, of nation-building week – a prayer service at Regina Mundi Catholic Church in Soweto. In a column titled 'We've Got Inborn Dignity to Act Like Leaders', he observes: 'This meeting captured exactly the spirit, the resonance of Nation Building – a serious, thoughtful, painful, slightly old-fashioned set-piece of items; good but serious music, good speakers and the theme underlined that blacks have the innate dignity to act like leaders.'[88]

In this column, Klaaste did not argue for nation-building or debate its merits, but described his enjoyment and sense of satisfaction: 'And when Dr Stanley Mogoba spoke of ubuntu/botho he captured exactly the mood that pervaded this, our first Nation Building event. It did me a power of good; good about being black; good about being part of this movement.'[89]

Klaaste invoked memories of eminent African and African-American leaders from previous times:

> I was reminded strangely of people like Professor D.D.T. Jabavu and his ilk, who in days of yore displayed the type of dignity that a black man, given the right time and place, is able to exude.
>
> ... there was a feeling about this special event that reminded you of Martin Luther King, of Booker T. Washington, of Dr A.B. Xuma, men of a particular substance whose footprints will be implanted in our history books.[90]

In this phase of writing nation-building, Klaaste moves from the earlier style of debating and dialogue, storytelling and the position of questioning and reflective searcher, to a more exalted style. With nation-building established, he was able to enjoy the success of his project and to begin to place it, for his readers, in a historical context, as well as locating it in legacies of black leadership.

His final words in the column position nation-building more firmly as an alternative to what he sees as the populist/popular options offered to black South Africans:

> The problem these days is that the most events of significance are launched on twin poles of the extreme – they are either emotionally charged with a populist political anger, or they are flippant but extremely popular like a soccer game or a pop festival.
>
> There seems to be a paucity of the type of dignified affair, not actively religious nor purposively funereal, but laid on with the gravity that takes our lives, our sorrows and joys seriously.[91]

Klaaste fought for that dignity, for black South Africans to be taken seriously as potential leaders of the country, for black communities to create a future, not only for themselves as the majority, but for all South Africans. Part of the success of nation-building may have been the result of the changing times, so that the ideas met with a receptiveness that may not have been there in previous eras. The influence of nation-building also came, I would argue, from Klaaste's ability to wield words in his column to engage, to persuade and to offer constructive and ongoing dialogue, drawing his readers into the discussion of their collective future.

Klaaste's status as a public figure was driven not just by his vision for South Africa, but by the place he occupied in the media. As both editor of *Sowetan* and long-time columnist, he was able to draw *Sowetan* readers into considering nation-building as a possibility, to circulate his ideas widely and to gain the support of business and political interests of the day. Like the editors of black-owned publications of a previous era – John Tengo Jabavu, John Dube and Sol Plaatje – he used the press to promote the political aspirations of African communities and to discuss their role in South Africa. But by writing in the highest circulating daily of the 1990s, Klaaste enabled a process of ongoing discussion far beyond the educated and urban black middle class. His role as 'public intellectual' was thus amplified by his location in the popular space of a tabloid newspaper and his ideas and vision reached a range of communities across the country.

NOTES

[1] Phakama Mbonambi, 'Aggrey Klaaste: The Relentless Community-Builder' (Master's thesis, Rhodes University, 2014), 1.
[2] Lesley Cowling, 'Building a Nation: The *Sowetan* and the Creation of a Black Public', *Journal of Southern African Studies* 40, no. 2 (2014): 339.
[3] Cowling, 'Building a Nation', 339.
[4] Lesley Cowling, 'Saving the *Sowetan*: The Public Interest and Commercial Imperatives in Journalism Practice' (PhD diss., Rhodes University, 2015), 214.
[5] See Cowling, 'Building a Nation'.
[6] Cowling, 'Building a Nation', 326.
[7] The apartheid state categorised the indigenous black majority as 'African', denied them political rights and made them citizens of territories within South Africa called homelands. The term 'African', used here in quotation marks, signifies that political category in the apartheid state. In other parts of the chapter, the term African signifies inhabitants of Africa. This awkward difference in usage should be clear by the context.
[8] Edward Said, *Representations of the Intellectual* (London: Vintage, 1994), 63.
[9] A full set of Aggrey Klaaste's columns and other writings were provided to me by Jerome Klaaste and the Aggrey Klaaste Trust.
[10] On the commercial black press after the Second World War, see Tim Couzens, 'A Short History of "The World" (and Other Black South African Newspapers)' (paper presented at the African Studies Seminar, University of the Witwatersrand, Johannesburg, 1976); Cowling, 'Saving the *Sowetan*', 101–126; Shaun Johnson, 'An Historical Overview of the Black Press', in *The Alternative Press in South Africa*, ed. Keyan Tomaselli and P.E. Louw (Johannesburg: Anthropos, 1991), 15–32; Irwin Manoim, 'The Black Press 1945–1963: The Growth of the Black Mass Media and Their Role as Ideological Disseminators' (Master's thesis, University of the Witwatersrand, 1983); Les Switzer and Donna Switzer, *The Black Press in South Africa and Lesotho* (Boston: Hall, 1979).
[11] Switzer and Switzer, *The Black Press*, 8.
[12] Michael Warner, 'Publics and Counterpublics', *Public Culture* 14, no. 1 (2002): 62.

13 Keyan Tomaselli, 'Ownership and Control in the South African Print Media: Black Empowerment after Apartheid, 1990–1997', *Ecquid Novi* 18, no. 1 (1997): 67.
14 Cowling, 'Building a Nation', 340.
15 Richard Keeble, 'On Journalism, Creativity and the Imagination', in *The Journalistic Imagination: Literary Journalists from Defoe to Capote and Carter*, ed. Richard Keeble and Sharon Wheeler (New York: Routledge, 2007), 2.
16 Charles Taylor, 'Modern Social Imaginaries', *Public Culture* 14, no. 1 (2002): 91–124.
17 Said, *Representations of the Intellectual*, 63.
18 Frantz Fanon, 'On National Culture', in *Colonial Discourse and Post-Colonial Theory*, ed. Patrick Williams and Laura Chrisman (New York: Routledge, 2013), 51.
19 Ngũgĩ wa Thiong'o, *Decolonizing the Mind: The Politics of Language in African Literature* (Nairobi: East African Educational Publishers, 1986), 4.
20 Nicholas M. Creary, 'Introduction', in *African Intellectuals and Decolonization*, ed. Nicholas M. Creary (Athens: Ohio University Press, 2012), 1–11.
21 Ngũgĩ, *Decolonizing the Mind*, 4.
22 Hlonipha Mokoena, 'An Assembly of Readers: Magema Fuze and His *Ilanga lase Natal* Readers', *Journal of Southern African Studies* 35, no. 3 (2009): 595.
23 Couzens, 'A Short History', 3.
24 Couzens, 'A Short History', 4.
25 Michael Titlestad, 'Jazz Discourse and Black South African Modernity, with Special Reference to "Matshikese"', *American Ethnologist* 32, no. 2 (2005): 211; Tom Odhiambo, 'Inventing Africa in the Twentieth Century: Cultural Imagination, Politics and Transnationalism in *Drum* Magazine', *African Studies* 65, no. 2 (2006): 160; Shane Graham and John Walters, eds, *Langston Hughes and the South African Drum Generation* (New York: Palgrave, 2010).
26 Guy Berger, 'Publishing for the People: The Alternative Press 1980–1999', in *The Politics of Publishing in South Africa*, ed. Nicholas Evans and Monica Seeber (Pietermaritzburg: University of Natal Press, 2000), 73–103.
27 Said, *Representations of the Intellectual*, 63.
28 See, for example, Kenichi Serino, 'The Origin of Ideas in "the Paper for the People": Research into How the *Sunday Times* Chooses Topics and Commentators for Its Opinion Pages' (Master's thesis, University of the Witwatersrand, 2009); Lesley Cowling and Carolyn Hamilton, 'Thinking Aloud/Allowed: Pursuing the Public Interest in Radio Debate', *Social Dynamics* 36, no. 1 (2010): 85–98.
29 Dan D. Nimmo and James E. Combs, *The Political Pundits* (New York: Praeger, 1992), 12.
30 Nimmo and Combs, *The Political Pundits*, 6.
31 Nimmo and Combs, *The Political Pundits*, 11.
32 Cowling and Hamilton, 'Thinking Aloud/Allowed', 88.
33 Nimmo and Combs, *The Political Pundits*, 7; Alistair Duff, 'Powers in the Land? British Political Columnists in the Information Era', *Journalism Practice* 2, no. 2 (2008): 233.
34 Duff, 'Powers in the Land', 233.
35 Duff, 'Powers in the Land', 238.
36 Duff, 'Powers in the Land', 230.
37 Duff, 'Powers in the Land', 233.
38 Nimmo and Combs, *The Political Pundits*, 13.
39 See Manoim, 'The Black Press 1945–1963'.
40 Adrian Hadland, 'State-Media Relations in Post-Apartheid South Africa: An Application of Comparative Media Systems Theory', *Communicare* 26, no. 2 (2007): 1–17.

41. Lesley Cowling, 'Understanding the "Sowetans": Journalism as a Product of Organisational Culture', *African Journalism Studies* 38, no. 1 (2017): 9.
42. Craig Charney, 'Black Power, White Press: Literacy, Newspapers, and the Transformation of Township Political Culture' (paper presented at the African Studies Seminar, University of the Witwatersrand, Johannesburg, 10 May 1993), accessed 10 August 2012, http://wiredspace.wits.ac.za/handle/10539/8510, 11.
43. Cowling, 'Building a Nation', 328.
44. Mbonambi, 'Aggrey Klaaste', 55.
45. Mbonambi, 'Aggrey Klaaste', 1.
46. 'New Name for Black Writers Association', *The Argus*, 19 October 1980, 2.
47. Jon Qwelane, 'For Many It Was a Year of Surprises', *The Star*, 8 January 1981, 16.
48. 'The Post Is Silenced', *The Star*, 20 January 1981, 1.
49. 'The Sowetan Nou Dagblad', *Beeld*, 27 January 1981, 14.
50. Joe Latakgomo, 'Onslaught on the Press', *Sowetan*, 2 February 1981, 8.
51. 'The Future of the Black Press', *The Star*, 23 January 1981, 4.
52. Eric P. Louw, 'Rethinking the Leftist Struggle in South Africa', *Critical Arts* 6, no. 1 (1992): 5.
53. J.A. Marais, 'Politieke Forum', *Tempo*, 23 August 1985, 4.
54. Les Switzer, 'Introduction: South Africa's Resistance Press in Perspective', in *South Africa's Resistance Press: Alternative Voices in the Last Generation under Apartheid*, ed. Les Switzer and Mohamed Adhikari (Athens: Ohio University Press, 2000), 50.
55. 'Aggrey Klaaste and Joe Latakgomo: Putting on Heirs', *Financial Mail*, 11 March 1988, 69.
56. Mbonambi, 'Aggrey Klaaste', 5.
57. See, for example, Aggrey Klaaste, 'Just for Today: Who Are Our Leaders?' *Post*, 30 April 1979, 4; Aggrey Klaaste, 'Just for Today: When Dr Koornhof Becomes Mr Hyde', *Post*, 11 June 1979, 4.
58. See, for example, Aggrey Klaaste, 'On the Line: Astronomical Price of Progress', *Sowetan*, 9 February 1981, 6; Aggrey Klaaste, 'On the Line: Telling the Truth about the Ghettos', *Sowetan*, 23 February 1981, 4.
59. 'Aggrey Klaaste and Joe Latakgomo', 70.
60. Kaizer Nyatsumba, 'I Have a Dream, Says Top Editor', *The Star*, 12 August 1988, 13.
61. Quoted from my interview with Mike Tissong, former publisher of *Sowetan*, in Johannesburg, 2009.
62. From my interview with Len Maseko, long-time journalist at *Sowetan*, in Johannesburg, 2010.
63. Joe Thloloe, 'The Aggrey I Knew', *Sowetan*, 21 June 2004, 15.
64. Tissong, interview.
65. 'Nation Building Manifesto', *Sowetan*, 31 August 1989, 5.
66. Kaizer Nyatsumba, 'The Sowetan Launches Nation-Building Week', *The Star*, 1 September 1989, 7.
67. Tissong, interview.
68. 'Comment', *Sowetan*, 23 November 1988, 8.
69. 'A Changing Scene for Newspapers', *The Star*, 5 September 1989, 17.
70. 'Sowetan Remains SA's Best-Read Daily', *Sowetan*, 20 August 2001, 2.
71. Aggrey Klaaste, 'On the Line: Mirror Image of the Tragedy of SA', *Sowetan*, 1 February 1988, 5.
72. Aggrey Klaaste, 'A Nightmare Life of Fear, Suspicion and Degradation', *Sunday Star*, 22 May 1988, 11.

73   Aggrey Klaaste, 'On the Line: Looking into the Future', *Sowetan*, 25 April 1988, 9.
74   Aggrey Klaaste, 'On the Line: We Must Build a Stronger SA', *Sowetan*, 2 May 1988, 9.
75   Klaaste, 'We Must Build a Stronger SA', 9.
76   Aggrey Klaaste, 'On the Line: Something within Us Not Easily Definable', *Sowetan*, 20 June 1988, 7.
77   Aggrey Klaaste, 'On the Line: Ubuntu Will Rule', *Sowetan*, 12 October 1988, 7.
78   Klaaste, 'Ubuntu Will Rule'.
79   Klaaste, 'Ubuntu Will Rule'.
80   Lebamang Sebidi, 'Ubuntu Is African Humanism', *Sowetan*, 2 December 1988, 9–10.
81   Aggrey Klaaste, 'On the Line: Expounding on the Great Idea', *Sowetan*, 11 November 1988, 5.
82   Klaaste, 'Expounding on the Great Idea', 5.
83   Aggrey Klaaste, 'On the Line: Let's Give It a Shot', *Sowetan*, 23 January 1989, 5.
84   Klaaste, 'Let's Give It a Shot', 5.
85   Klaaste, 'Let's Give It a Shot', 6.
86   Klaaste, 'Let's Give It a Shot', 6.
87   'Nation Building Manifesto', 5.
88   Aggrey Klaaste, 'On the Line: We've Got Inborn Dignity to Act Like Leaders', *Sowetan*, 16 October 1989, 4.
89   Klaaste, 'We've Got Inborn Dignity', 4.
90   Klaaste, 'We've Got Inborn Dignity', 4.
91   Klaaste, 'We've Got Inborn Dignity', 4.

REFERENCES

'A Changing Scene for Newspapers'. *The Star*, 5 September 1989.
'Aggrey Klaaste and Joe Latakgomo: Putting on Heirs'. *Financial Mail*, 11 March 1988.
Berger, Guy. 'Publishing for the People: The Alternative Press 1980–1999'. In *The Politics of Publishing in South Africa*, edited by Nicholas Evans and Monica Seeber, 73–103. Pietermaritzburg: University of Natal Press, 2000.
Charney, Craig. 'Black Power, White Press: Literacy, Newspapers, and the Transformation of Township Political Culture'. Paper presented at the African Studies Seminar, University of the Witwatersrand, Johannesburg, 10 May 1993. Accessed 10 August 2012. http://wiredspace.wits.ac.za/handle/10539/8510
'Comment'. *Sowetan*, 23 November 1988.
Couzens, Tim. 'A Short History of "The World" (and Other Black South African Newspapers)'. Paper presented at the African Studies Seminar, University of the Witwatersrand, Johannesburg, 1976.
Cowling, Lesley. 'Building a Nation: The *Sowetan* and the Creation of a Black Public'. *Journal of Southern African Studies* 40, no. 2 (2014): 325–341.
Cowling, Lesley. 'Saving the *Sowetan*: The Public Interest and Commercial Imperatives in Journalism Practice'. PhD diss., Rhodes University, 2015.
Cowling, Lesley. 'Understanding the "Sowetans": Journalism as a Product of Organisational Culture'. *African Journalism Studies* 38, no. 1 (2017): 1–18.
Cowling, Lesley and Carolyn Hamilton. 'Thinking Aloud/Allowed: Pursuing the Public Interest in Radio Debate'. *Social Dynamics* 36, no. 1 (2010): 85–98.

Creary, Nicholas M. 'Introduction'. In *African Intellectuals and Decolonization*, edited by Nicholas M. Creary, 1–11. Athens: Ohio University Press, 2012.
Duff, Alistair. 'Powers in the Land? British Political Columnists in the Information Era'. *Journalism Practice* 2, no. 2 (2008): 231–244.
Fanon, Frantz. 'On National Culture'. In *Colonial Discourse and Post-Colonial Theory*, edited by Patrick Williams and Laura Chrisman, 36–52. New York: Routledge, 2013.
Graham, Shane and John Walters, eds. *Langston Hughes and the South African Drum Generation*. New York: Palgrave, 2010.
Hadland, Adrian. 'State-Media Relations in Post-Apartheid South Africa: An Application of Comparative Media Systems Theory'. *Communicare* 26, no. 2 (2007): 1–17.
Johnson, Shaun. 'An Historical Overview of the Black Press'. In *The Alternative Press in South Africa*, edited by Keyan Tomaselli and P. Eric Louw, 15–32. Johannesburg: Anthropos, 1991.
Keeble, Richard. 'On Journalism, Creativity and the Imagination'. In *The Journalistic Imagination: Literary Journalists from Defoe to Capote and Carter*, edited by Richard Keeble and Sharon Wheeler, 1–14. New York: Routledge, 2007.
Klaaste, Aggrey. 'Just for Today: When Dr Koornhof Becomes Mr Hyde'. *Post*, 11 June 1979.
Klaaste, Aggrey. 'Just for Today: Who Are Our Leaders?' *Post*, 30 April 1979.
Klaaste, Aggrey. 'A Nightmare Life of Fear, Suspicion and Degradation'. *Sunday Star*, 22 May 1988.
Klaaste, Aggrey. 'On the Line: Astronomical Price of Progress', *Sowetan*, 9 February 1981.
Klaaste, Aggrey. 'On the Line: Expounding on the Great Idea'. *Sowetan*, 11 November 1988.
Klaaste, Aggrey. 'On the Line: Let's Give It a Shot'. *Sowetan*, 23 January 1989.
Klaaste, Aggrey. 'On the Line: Looking into the Future'. *Sowetan*, 25 April 1988.
Klaaste, Aggrey. 'On the Line: Mirror Image of the Tragedy of SA'. *Sowetan*, 1 February 1988.
Klaaste, Aggrey. 'On the Line: Something within Us Not Easily Definable'. *Sowetan*, 20 June 1988.
Klaaste, Aggrey. 'On the Line: Telling the Truth about the Ghettos'. *Sowetan*, 23 February 1981.
Klaaste, Aggrey. 'On the Line: Ubuntu Will Rule', *Sowetan*, 12 October 1988, 7.
Klaaste, Aggrey. 'On the Line: We Must Build a Stronger SA'. *Sowetan*, 2 May 1988.
Klaaste, Aggrey. 'On the Line: We've Got Inborn Dignity to Act Like Leaders'. *Sowetan*, 16 October 1989.
Latakgomo, Joe. 'Onslaught on the Press'. *Sowetan*, 2 February 1981.
Louw, Eric P. 'Rethinking the Leftist Struggle in South Africa'. *Critical Arts* 6, no. 1 (1992): 1–25.
Manoim, Irwin. 'The Black Press 1945–1963: The Growth of the Black Mass Media and Their Role as Ideological Disseminators'. Master's thesis, University of the Witwatersrand, 1983.
Marais, J.A. 'Politieke Forum'. *Tempo*, 23 August 1985.
Mbonambi, Phakama. 'Aggrey Klaaste: The Relentless Community-Builder'. Master's thesis, Rhodes University, 2014.
Mokoena, Hlonipha. 'An Assembly of Readers: Magema Fuze and His *Ilanga lase Natal* Readers'. *Journal of Southern African Studies* 35, no. 3 (2009): 595–607.
'Nation Building Manifesto'. *Sowetan*, 31 August 1989.
'New Name for Black Writers Association'. *The Argus*, 19 October 1980.
Ngũgĩ wa Thiong'o, *Decolonizing the Mind: The Politics of Language in African Literature*. Nairobi: East African Educational Publishers, 1986.

Nimmo, Dan D. and James E. Combs. *The Political Pundits*. New York: Praeger, 1992.
Nyatsumba, Kaizer. 'I Have a Dream, Says Top Editor'. *The Star*, 12 August 1988.
Nyatsumba, Kaizer. 'The Sowetan Launches Nation-Building Week'. *The Star*, 1 September 1989.
Odhiambo, Tom. 'Inventing Africa in the Twentieth Century: Cultural Imagination, Politics and Transnationalism in *Drum* Magazine'. *African Studies* 65, no. 2 (2006): 157–174.
Qwelane, Jon. 'For Many It Was a Year of Surprises'. *The Star*, 8 January 1981.
Said, Edward. *Representations of the Intellectual*. London: Vintage, 1994.
Sebidi, Lebamang. 'Ubuntu Is African Humanism'. *Sowetan*, 2 December 1988.
Serino, T. Kenichi. 'The Origin of Ideas in "the Paper for the People": Research into How the *Sunday Times* Chooses Topics and Commentators for Its Opinion Pages'. Master's thesis, University of the Witwatersrand, 2009.
'Sowetan Remains SA's Best-Read Daily'. *Sowetan*, 20 August 2001.
Switzer, Les. 'Introduction: South Africa's Resistance Press in Perspective'. In *South Africa's Resistance Press: Alternative Voices in the Last Generation under Apartheid*, edited by Les Switzer and Mohamed Adhikari, 1–75. Athens: Ohio University Press, 2000.
Switzer, Les and Donna Switzer. *The Black Press in South Africa and Lesotho*. Boston: Hall, 1979.
Taylor, Charles. 'Modern Social Imaginaries'. *Public Culture* 14, no. 1 (2002): 91–124.
'The Future of the Black Press'. *The Star*, 23 January 1981.
'The Post Is Silenced'. *The Star*, 20 January 1981.
'The Sowetan Nou Dagblad'. *Beeld*, 27 January 1981.
Thloloe, Joe. 'The Aggrey I Knew'. *Sowetan*, 21 July 2004.
Titlestad, Michael. 'Jazz Discourse and Black South African Modernity, with Special Reference to "Matshikese"'. *American Ethnologist* 32, no. 2 (2005): 210–221.
Tomaselli, Keyan. 'Ownership and Control in the South African Print Media: Black Empowerment after Apartheid, 1990–1997'. *Ecquid Novi* 18, no. 1 (1997): 21–68.
Warner, Michael. 'Publics and Counterpublics'. *Public Culture* 14, no. 1 (2002): 49–90.

CHAPTER

5

William Pretorius and the Public Intellectualism of the Film Critic

Chris Broodryk

Working in a Pretoria video store as an Afrikaans-speaking teenager in the 1990s, I was drawn to movie reviews as a way to access film content. Age restrictions and distribution issues meant that I was at least temporarily prohibited from seeing many films and reviews provided valuable knowledge about these unseen films. I read movie reviews in two Afrikaans newspapers, the *Rapport* on Sundays and the *Beeld* on Fridays. On occasion, my father would treat me to the *Sunday Times*. My exposure to mostly Afrikaans publications in a pre-internet era meant that I was familiar with the film criticism of Leon van Nierop and Barrie Hough, as well as Barry Ronge's writing in English for the *Sunday Times* (he would eventually publish pieces of non-fiction in a column, later collected in a book titled *Spit 'n Polish*).[1] Van Nierop and Hough were both also novelists; film criticism was a part of what they did for a living, not their solitary endeavour. Hough gained fame for his sensitive Afrikaans novels for young adults, while Van Nierop wrote popular thrillers and radio dramas, as well as appearing regularly on television and radio to speak about new film releases.

As generally informative as these reviews were, the Afrikaans film critic who most informed my own thinking about film, and specifically film and politics, was William Pretorius. While I initially read Pretorius's writing in Afrikaans in the *Beeld*, I later discovered exactly how prolific he had been, as he had published regularly in the English print (and later online) media and occasionally in academic contexts. Pretorius occupied a dual position: he was academically active and involved in teaching film, but also aired his views on film for non-academic film-going readers in popular print and online publications. His movie reviews demonstrated his propensities and concerns, which were communicated to a readership who sought out his voice among other critics for a politically committed, cine-literate film criticism.

As this chapter shows, Pretorius's political commitment is demonstrated in how he consistently foregrounded a film's sociopolitical contextual concerns; he was cinematically informed because he watched and referred to films outside of the Hollywood classical narrative and promoted these films in his criticism. In positioning Pretorius as a public intellectual, I argue that his film criticism throughout his career remained dedicated to a call for a politically committed South African cinema, a cinema (an art form and a film industry) that is sociopolitically responsive.

In this chapter, I focus on selected writings from the 1980s and early 1990s that explicate Pretorius's challenges to Afrikaans cinema and also on his more popular writing that appeared online in the *Mail & Guardian* and online in *Artslink*. Taken together, these selections crystallise the image of Pretorius the film critic as a public intellectual whose primary directive was to emphasise the sociopolitical contextual significance of film, especially South African and Afrikaans films, to a readership familiar with more commercial and politically inert forms of entertainment.

THE PUBLIC INTELLECTUALISM OF FILM CRITICISM

The argument that film criticism should be sociopolitically responsive and politically committed has been put forward from several critical positions. For instance, reflecting on criticism in England in the early 1980s, Terry Eagleton comments that the criticism of that time lacks 'all substantive social function'.[2] Issuing a dire warning against critics being 'incapable of unlocking the most lethal power-struggles now confronting us', Eagleton argues that the future of sustained and acute criticism should be 'defined as a struggle against the bourgeois state'.[3] In this struggle, the critic is a nomad; put differently, 'the critic is a *flaneur* or *bricoleur*, rambling and idling among diverse social landscapes where he is everywhere at home'.[4] These social landscapes point to the sociopolitical contexts that film critics such as William Pretorius emphasised in the 1980s and beyond, ensuring that the potential moviegoer was made aware of the dominant affirmations or contradictions that a film may or may not deliberately point out. Importantly, criticism 'can be the engine not only of aesthetic reassessment, but also *of social change*'.[5]

As Herman Wasserman notes, arts journalists in their arts criticism perform an evaluative function that foregrounds how these journalists disseminate their views on art.[6] In addition, this evaluative function casts light on how the individual arts journalist conceives of the relationship between art, the media and society. In writing film reviews, for instance, critics evaluate a work of art such as film in a particular sociopolitical context and the critic should be cognisant of this context and its nuances.[7] In the post-apartheid South African context arts journalists have a responsibility to critically reflect on 'cultural and aesthetic value production' in a highly diverse and unequal society and to tease out the ways in which the work of art is part of and responds to what Wasserman refers to as contextual imperatives.[8] These 'obligations' already existed in Pretorius's criticism before the official end of apartheid in 1994. In addition, arts journalism is vulnerable to the mandate of profit or 'commercial pressures' in contemporary journalism.[9] Or, as A.O. Scott puts it: 'Every critic has to contend with the forces of publicity and hype, with a cultural apparatus that exists for the purpose of blunting and marginalizing critical voices.'[10] As I discuss later in this chapter, Pretorius's own criticism demonstrates the responsibility of the individual critic to promote the presence and voice of the marginalised. Pretorius would, for instance, champion queer causes such as the 13th Gay and Lesbian Film Festival in 2007.[11]

This emphasis on the sociopolitical context of a work of art's production and reception is, of course, not unique to South African or Afrikaans film criticism. In the United States, public intellectuals such as James Baldwin engaged with the politics of art and film in a manner that was deeply personal, as well as committed to a collective political reality. In his lyrical and socially acute *The Devil Finds Work*, Baldwin weaves his film criticism into his autobiography and uses his autobiography as a lens through which to explore the political ambivalences of a number of high-profile American films.[12] Baldwin understands how film cannot but respond to social change and to processes that impede creativity, such as censorship: 'In 1952, I was in America, just in time for the McCarthy era. I had never seen anything like it.' Later, Baldwin adds that the political realities of the United States meant that 'I loved my country, but I could not respect it.'[13]

It is on the silver screen that Baldwin sees the invalidation of his father's views: film star Bette Davis, whom Baldwin thought had similar 'pop-eyes' to his own, was white and rich even though she was 'ugly' by his father's disparaging standards.[14] Moving from such personal reflections to lucid and acute political commentary, Baldwin's criticism is appropriately cut-throat where it needs to be: D.W. Griffith's racist epic *The Birth of a Nation*, for instance, is essentially 'an elaborate justification of mass murder'.[15] Baldwin amplifies the way certain images play into the film's racist narrative: 'The plot is entirely controlled by the image of the mulatto', an image that would not have been so evident to the moviegoer.[16] Baldwin writes about critically acclaimed films such as *The Defiant Ones* and *Lawrence of Arabia*, challenging the racial dynamics of cross-racial partnerships in the former and the idea of the blue-eyed British saviour in the latter.[17] Turning his inspection away from these explicitly political films to the horror genre, Baldwin interrogates the vapid supernaturalism of the acclaimed popular horror film *The Exorcist* by once again challenging the film's politics and locating the devil not in hell, or in a young girl's demonically possessed body, but in humanity: the moment of the encounter with the devil is in the eyes of others and in the mirror, 'that moment when no other human being is real for you, nor are you real for yourself'.[18] For Baldwin, the horror of *The Exorcist* is not the horror of demonic possession, but an embodied inhumanity.

Outside of the film dominance of the United States, one of the instances in which film criticism had the most tangible effects on film as an art that was politically aware was in France in the 1950s and 1960s. In this period, French film criticism gave birth to the French New Wave. Several politically left-leaning film-makers, such as Jean-Luc Godard, not only wrote film criticism but also practised film-making as a demonstration of their criticism. 'Like the best critics,' writes James Naremore, 'the young Godard was not only what Wilde would call an artist but also what Walter Benjamin would call a producer. He appropriated a film to his own ends, showing how it could be used in defense of an attitude.'[19]

Both Godard and Baldwin's practice of film criticism correlates with Scott's explanation that the critic embodies an internal antagonism – 'scapegoat and paragon, scold and saint, id and superego'.[20] This paradox makes the critic 'at once superfluous and ubiquitous, indispensable and useless, to be trusted and reviled'. In his book *Better Living through Criticism*, Scott describes criticism as 'an art of the voice', of personality; this voice is characterised by its honesty and it is a voice that can be trusted.[21]

As Wasserman points out, arts criticism involves evaluation.[22] For the renowned film scholar V.F. Perkins, evaluation is 'the articulation of value, the grateful effort to spell out the nature of a significant achievement'.[23] Evaluation is not judicial judgement but 'a contribution to a discussion which positions the critic performing the evaluation as one of a collective, or community of critics' whose voices are multiple and whose evaluations may or may not be aligned.[24] Here, Perkins presses the point that evaluation is about understanding, but it also involves exchanging and sharing the understanding of the film. 'Good criticism,' Perkins maintains, 'is motivated by gratitude for the achievement of the filmmakers.'[25] Criticism 'is an effort that we join together to explain why films matter to us' – again one notices the emphasis on criticism as a collaborative, collective activity – in which the critic rewards 'the artists' attention to detail with an equal attentiveness in the viewing'. The ideas that stand out in Perkins's discussion of criticism and evaluation concern understanding, collectivity and attentiveness. Even when watching and evaluating what he calls a 'bad film', understanding and attentiveness remain in play.

In his discussion of badness in cinema, Perkins criticises the 'bad film' *Dead Poets Society* for using 'crude but effective devices of emotional manipulation that may disguise contradictions between its declared projects (anti-authoritarian) and its dramatic structure (which validates the authority of the hero)'.[26] One of this film's most important transgressions is 'offering a dishonestly simplified viewpoint on conflict', but then Perkins points out that it is only in a single scene that this happens: 'Whether we agree to take it as an instance of highly effective but corrupt filmmaking must depend on whether we think the scene accurately represents the film as a whole.'[27] Importantly, Perkins' criticism here is not rooted in a technicist account of the film, that is, an evaluation founded on primarily technical matters such as continuity errors, a choice of camera filter or lens selection. Instead, he focuses on the film's internal contradictions that the film itself cannot resolve, which become the responsibility of the film critic (and the viewer) to evaluate and respond to.

The South Africa in which Pretorius practised film criticism for nearly 20 years was itself a space of sociopolitical contradiction even when apartheid was explicitly oppressive and regressive. Afrikaans film, in particular, had a clear political position in the South African cultural landscape, where the salience of whiteness was continuously affirmed. Consider this quote from Afrikaans film director Rudi Meyer: 'Blacks don't understand film language. This means that if you show a guy going into a house, you have to show him coming out as well. If you cut from the house to a car on the highway, your audience won't know what the hell's going on.'[28] This inequitable view of black film audiences as somehow incapable of understanding how a film works in creating time and space speaks to historical visibility and power in the South African and Afrikaans film industry. As Jeremy Nathan says: 'Since the first moving images were ever seen [in South Africa], they have been largely American, or British, controlled by and from either America or Britain', which contributed to masking the sociopolitical realities of South African society.[29] The cultural boycott of 1987 isolated South African audiences from American and international cinema, but in reality very few American film-makers – such as Woody Allen and Spike Lee – were able to withhold their films from

South African release.[30] In 1988, then president P.W. Botha pronounced the film industry a strategic player towards government ends and against those who resist the hegemony.[31]

It is against this cultural and political backdrop that Pretorius demonstrated a political commitment – a political consciousness critical of South African and Hollywood-style commercial entertainment – which informed his writing on cinema across films of various quality (from 'good' to 'bad'). Pretorius challenged South African cinema, and Afrikaans cinema in particular, to be critical of power and to refuse to glance over or ignore the sociopolitical realities that many of these films masked.

WILLIAM PRETORIUS (9 JUNE 1941 TO 26 JUNE 2007)

Pretorius's challenge to South African films and their critics echoed Robert Greig's lamentation about what he saw as South African film critics making few demands on local cinema output.[32] Whereas Greig investigated myths and stereotypes in South African cinema, the popular print and television critic Barry Ronge practised auteur criticism.[33] For these and other critics, such as the politically oriented John van Zyl, film criticism 'was an *intellectual* activity not directly connected with the stimulation of alternative or oppositional filmmaking or popular movements'.[34] Pretorius's criticism embraced this intellectualism and encouraged both audiences and film-makers to seek out films from outside their demographics and geographies in order to enhance their understanding of the film art. Keyan Tomaselli and Martin Botha also discuss Pretorius's contribution to film criticism in South Africa.[35] For Botha, Pretorius's film criticism complemented the work of academic scholarship on South African cinema by Pieter J. Fourie, Harriet Gavshon and Tomaselli himself. This relationship is significant, as it positions film scholars as part of the film critic's public, with whom they are in sustained conversation about the politics of film.

Botha recounts that Pretorius wrote film criticism and other forms of critical writing in both English and Afrikaans for publications as diverse as the Afrikaans weekly newspaper *Rapport* and the liberal English weekly *Mail & Guardian* (previously the *Weekly Mail*). He occasionally published criticism under the pseudonym of Fabius Burger. Having studied Practical Criticism at the University of South Africa, Pretorius was also an accomplished script reader and an outspoken critic of censorship.[36]

In the 1980s Pretorius complained about how lenient English-language critics were towards the narrative inadequacies of many Afrikaans films.[37] For Pretorius,

Afrikaans films often provided a 'concise little formula', which celebrated the exclusivity of the Afrikaner as social group.[38] In what is arguably his most academically accomplished written work, published in *Movies, Moguls, Mavericks*, Pretorius critically discusses the Afrikaans cinema of the 1980s as a cinema of 'soothing images'.[39] These 'soothing images' masked the sociopolitical realities of South Africa and provided a comfortably escapist narrative and aesthetic to placate white Afrikaans-speaking audiences who did not want to think about their country's moral demise. In his chapter, Pretorius describes how often Afrikaans films centre on the 'soapie-style melodrama about mismatched couples overcoming obstacles on the path to true love'.[40] When watching such a film, it is the critic – or the reviewer – who has to bring politics to the film, 'to measure the gap between the lifestyles depicted on film and their own experience'. Later in the chapter, Pretorius comments that Afrikaans films have to acknowledge political change or risk becoming 'irrelevant when their themes are measured against the viewer's own experience'.[41] In this regard, it is as important to consider what is excluded from an Afrikaans film as it is to notice what is included; these creative decisions reflected 'the Afrikaner psyche'.[42] Cognisant of the linkages between culture, politics and economics, Pretorius is further critical of the financial motivation behind making *Circles in the Forest* in English rather than in Afrikaans.[43] In the early 1980s, Afrikaans films did not critically explore Afrikanerdom. In those Afrikaans films of the 1980s that offered more diverse casts, Pretorius finds an 'honest colonialism' in which black individuals are either servants of whiteness or threats to whiteness.[44] He further notes the role of comedy in 1980s Afrikaans cinema in 'suggesting that all is well amongst Afrikaners' and that political difference is addressed with humour.[45] Not only were many Afrikaans films during the time made for television, but the Afrikaans film industry of the 1980s became a television-based industry.[46] Pretorius found it concerning that the four Afrikaans films released between 1990 and 1991 were partly financed by the television company M-Net, an instance in which industry support shaped the films' aesthetics.[47] Here, Pretorius prefigured a similar concern that would materialise among certain critics about Afrikaans-language entertainment provider kykNET's financial and aesthetic input in Afrikaans films since it founded the annual Silwerskermfees (Silver Screen Festival).

In 1984, Pretorius notes a positive development in South African cinema with the emergence of a new type of Afrikaans film that 'shows a willingness to consider political issues as part of their theme'; at the time, such a consideration was not available for television, given South Africa's strict television censorship.[48] *Broer Matie* and *Die Groen Faktor* are often acclaimed as a politically progressive drama and a satire respectively.[49] In Pretorius's view, however, *Broer Matie* is a patronising melodrama with little meaningful political power because of how the film celebrates the good nature of white clergy. Pretorius finds that *Die Groen Faktor* is the more innovative, progressive and even radical film: the film suggests that Afrikaners have to experience rejection before they can be human.[50] An equally important film of the 1980s was *Mamza*, which breaks with the conventions of Afrikaans cinema by focusing on a clearly identified social group (coloured South Africans) instead of telling a story of individual triumph.[51]

Another dominant presence in 1980s Afrikaans cinema was war and Pretorius describes films such as *Grensbasis 13* as blatant 'war-time propaganda', in which the enemy is consistently abstract and faceless.[52] Pretorius notes that the 'new' Afrikaans comedy of the 1980s produced candid camera films and established the comedic supremacy (at least in box-office terms) of Leon Schuster, whose film *Oh Schucks ... Here Comes UNTAG* conveyed the idea that 'whites know best'.[53] In 2020, Schuster's films came under fire for their use of blackface and seven of his comedy films were summarily removed from the streaming platform Showmax for reasons of racial insensitivity.[54]

Towards the end of his chapter in *Movies, Moguls, Mavericks*, Pretorius alleges that Afrikaans cinema 'remains parochial and provincial' and is essentially a cinema of soothing escapism.[55] What interests me more, however, is what Pretorius says in the third-to-last paragraph of his chapter: 'Why bother, then, with Afrikaans films? Because there are stories to be told. Afrikaans is not the property of a white elite, but an Africa-language, part of the multicultural reality of South Africa, and has to be freed from its role as the language of the oppressor.' Here, Pretorius foregrounds the politics of the Afrikaans language and how it had been the language of the minority white power who also made films for, and about, minority white power. Afrikaans and Afrikaans-language cinema had to embrace the multiculturalism of South Africa and in so doing break from the elitism around the language and its cultural artefacts.

Pretorius's criticism of the Afrikaans film industry discussed above is mirrored in a piece he wrote for *The SAFTTA Journal* in December 1985, seven years before the publication of *Movies, Moguls, Mavericks*.[56] In his article, titled 'Afrikaans Cinema', Pretorius first confirms that Afrikaans cinema suffered aesthetically and stylistically from the introduction of television in South Africa in 1976.[57] (It was also in this article that Pretorius first used the idea of Afrikaans films representing its black characters by way of an 'honest colonialism'.[58]) He even refers to the Afrikaans feature film as 'a spin-off of television' aimed at the widest possible Afrikaans-speaking audience, which formed part of the South African moviegoing audiences of the 1980s.[59] These 'made-for-cinema TV movies' employed familiar formulas often in the comedy genre that presented homogeneous Afrikaans audiences with images of comfort and safety; that is, with soothing images.[60] Afrikaans comedies sacrificed the potential of satire for the sake of the illusion of political solidarity, suggesting that 'all is well amongst Afrikaners'.[61] Comedies would foreground characters' innocence by putting them in compromising situations and this plot dynamic would become a staple of Afrikaans comedy.

Pretorius provides a brief overview of his main critique against the border war films in evaluating *Boetie Gaan Border Toe!*, which was released to considerable box-office success.[62] The film oscillates between being a light satire of patriarchy and 'pure comic-book adventure'. 'Again,' Pretorius writes, 'the "enemy" remains an abstract, inhuman factor', which exists unembodied and mostly unrepresented outside of the film frame. Pretorius ends his contribution by underlining once again that the Afrikaans cinema of the late 1970s and early 1980s was essentially an escapist cinema for Afrikaans audiences.[63]

Comparing Pretorius's concerns about the failings of specifically the Afrikaans cinema of 1980s South Africa to his film criticism and culture writing of the 1990s and beyond, it is clear that some of his concerns had remained, reshaped or resurfaced. Writing about Pat Hopkins's book *Cringe, the Beloved Country*, Pretorius frames the book as a 'necessary corrective' to the exploits of local sports celebrities, former president Thabo Mbeki's stance on AIDS and the Boeremag's 'political pornography'.[64] From the book, Pretorius singles out the image of a lampshade with the head of so-called apartheid architect H.F. Verwoerd underneath the bulb: 'With hindsight, there's an ironic contrast between the light bulb above the head and the utterly stupid ideas he put into practice.'[65]

For his 'FreeWheeling' column writing for the online *Artslink*, Pretorius visited the set of Darrell James Roodt's adaption of *Cry, the Beloved Country*, 'South Africa's first major post-election film project'.[66] In conversation with Pretorius, director Roodt prematurely notes that 'confrontational protest films are over'. Nonetheless, Pretorius is positive: making this film, at this time, he says, the film-makers are 'thinking South Africa', which 'takes enormous courage and faith in film'.

In an impassioned article for *News24*, Pretorius once again reflects on his experiences of watching Afrikaans films during apartheid.[67] These movies were a 'safe, lowest common denominator product'. Then he turns his attention to South African movies he describes as 'unseen' and 'invisible', films that suffered from poor distribution. Pretorius champions the unseen films, films that may not have been 'great artworks' but signalled any kind of difference from mainstream South African products:

> Francois Coertse ... has two unreleased movies, the slapstick farce *Lyk Lollery* [Corpse Trouble] and the road movie *Desert Diners* ... Rotten movies.[68] Maybe they are. I've seen *Desert Diners*. It's by no mean a great film, but it is a genuine attempt to do something different, to localise an American genre. It fails. But it is still worth seeing – even bad movies ... are ... educational and also contribute towards an understanding of film in SA.[69]

Although Coertse's films are in content and form very different from the awards-bait of *Dead Poets Society*, Pretorius's approach to 'bad' films evokes Perkins's earlier discussion of so-called bad films. Like Perkins, Pretorius's approach is non-technicist because his attention, as much as the idea of the value of the films, is on the films' capacities to challenge industry norms and not on their technical polish.

On occasion, Pretorius titles an opinion piece with an acute sociopolitical comment: 'Needed: A Local Moviemaker to Do Our Own *Bowling for Columbine*'.[70] Pretorius contrasts the visceral violence of Michael Moore's documentary film about gun control in America with a series of photos on violence in an Italian magazine, *Colors*, valuing the film's critical stance on culture and violence more than the magazine's glossy pictures: violence should not be glorified, not on film and not in the pages of a magazine. However prestigious and necessary such politically acute films may be, they generally have a limited theatrical run and are perceived as financial risks. With these constraints in mind, Pretorius contends that the cinema of the early 2000s was subjected to a new, different kind of censorship from the political censorship South Africa was infamous for during apartheid. Later, Pretorius would write: 'I dislike censorship as it wants to be the final word ... Censorship, as we learnt in the old South Africa, preferred silence to debate, negotiation or understanding.'[71] This new censorship is 'a democratic censorship: *market values*. Give the mass market what it wants. The rest is unimportant.'[72] This new censorship limits success to predominantly financial terms, the kind of censorship that would make productive failures such as *Desert Diners* and *Lyk Lollery* difficult to finance. Pretorius continues: 'Market values have become the filter, not the cultural boycott.'[73] The cultural and political boycott of previous years had been supplanted by the rule of profit, of the artistically limiting logic of giving audiences (the market) what they want (a product tailored to the market). When Pretorius writes about popular culture, such as J.K. Rowling's bestselling Harry Potter books, his interest is not on the individual hero wizard's journey or the magic of Hogwarts, but on how expensive the books are to purchase in South Africa: 'Harry Potter's going to do zilch for literacy in this country ... Harry Potter was really only a marketing fest for rich kids or, at least, privileged kids.'[74]

In writing about popular culture, Pretorius wrote regularly about American film and its conservatisms and he evidently had fun writing about the pleasures and perils of sex in cinema.[75] Unlike other critics, Pretorius finds that in too many American films, sex and sexuality have become 'safe, self-reflexive romances'. The risk of sex, as well as its pleasures, have abated. Explicit sex means a higher age restriction, which means fewer individuals see a film in cinemas.

Writing about class in American comedy in his review of *Joe Dirt*,[76] Pretorius turns autobiographical and is worth quoting at length:

> I know a bit about the white SA working class, having started my career as a fitter and turner and worked with dinkum working class people. They were diverse. Sure, there were guys into motorbikes and you'd look at them and think 'thugs', but they were ordinary, sweet guys ... Their lifestyles didn't differ much their [sic] middleclass counterparts: there was the same conservatism in taste. How do you symbolise working class? I didn't come across ducks on the wall – my family, middle-class white [sic], favoured them.[77]

Pretorius adds that his family's favourite art was by Tretchikoff and returns to the issue of class and representation: 'I found that it's mostly among the rich that one starts getting a kind of consensus on style and symbols, mostly because the style's used to show money.'[78] In the absence of such conspicuous consumption, Pretorius recognises in his childhood home and family an approach to art that is risky, preference-based, not dictated by the safe mundanity of market value.

Pretorius's concern with social class (including his own) materialises again in his review of Leon Schuster's broad comedy of infrastructure, *Mr Bones*.[79] Reviewing *Mr Bones*, Pretorius cheerfully notes that classes are equal in their bathroom affairs, striking an almost Žižekian appreciation of scatology: 'Shit's the great leveller' in Schuster's film, which makes him, in the critic's view, the prankster to Jamie Uys's myth-maker with *The Gods Must Be Crazy*.[80] Pretorius is not condescending to Schuster or to his audiences: 'Every cinema needs a Schuster, even if it's just to remind us that moviemaking is mainly for viewers, although we [critics] also have fun moaning from the sidelines.'[81]

Pretorius's emphasis on a film's political context and meanings cannot be disassociated from a film's position in the entertainment industry, or from its style and form. Consider when he amplifies a shot from *Apocalypse Now Redux*: 'It's a shot from a helicopter. All you see is a soldier's knee framed in the square opening in which he is sitting, and way below a bit of beach and an azure sea.'[82] For Pretorius, this film is one the last real American epics: Francis Coppola's war film is far removed from the world of *Titanic*, which for all of its digital effects cannot convey the same kind of visual depth.[83] 'Spectacular excess,' writes Pretorius, 'is now a common, everyday medium.'[84] He understood that excess had its place in the entertainment industry, specifically in the new censorship of the market and its risk-averse approach to popular film. Years before *Avatar* and *Titanic*, Pretorius recounts the experience of watching the 1970s disaster movie *Earthquake* in the Cinerama in Johannesburg Sensurround: 'I had the queasy feeling the balcony was about to shake loose and tumble on the stalls.'[85] In general, he remained wary of Hollywood's influence on film, since Hollywood 'projects its obsessions and idealistic paradigms on history ... The global blockbuster, the mass art de luxe for the 21st century, has no other option or peer.'[86] Occasionally, a critically acclaimed film with considerable box-office appeal would demonstrate how in the eyes of the critic, even star-studded feature films can invite the viewer towards compassion and sensitivity. Reviewing the hypertext film *Babel*, Pretorius praises the film's use of silence.[87] In one scene, a wounded American tourist (played by Cate Blanchett) is watched by an older Moroccan woman, who simply sits in silence as she smokes her opium pipe. Pretorius's description again emphasises class: 'Two diametrically opposed worlds, rich and poor, connect. This is an E.M. Fosterian moment: only connect.'[88]

The humanity of this kind of connection is often absent from films that may claim historical veracity, religious insight and documentary truth. With the excesses of *Titanic* in mind and now writing about Mel Gibson's historical blockbusters *Apocalypto* and *The Passion of the Christ*, Pretorius observes that Gibson's two films' relentless linearity is reflective of his religious absolutism, as indicated in the Stations of the Cross section in the latter film and the chase sequence that makes up the middle part of the former.[89] Reviewing the documentary *Long Night's Journey into Day*, Pretorius notes that a 'documentary like this ... tends to date as soon as it's made. History goes on' and therefore a documentary film cannot claim any absolute truth.[90] Turning his attention to the ever-popular horror genre, Pretorius wonders if perhaps 'television, CNN, has killed off horror ... The horror genre's been outdone and killed off by actuality.'[91] With reference to both the documentary film and the horror genre, Pretorius is saying that film cannot afford to exclude itself from the sociopolitical and other realities in which films are produced. Spectacles, horrors and documentaries need to be responsive to these realities and meet them head on.

Since film critics read other critics who also partake in the collective activity of criticism, Pretorius reads 'people for who they are, not who they recycle. Among my favourite movie reviewers are 3 Black Chicks ... James Berardinelli, Armond White and Johnathan Rosenbaum. What if they started recycling each other and sacrifice diversity of opinion?'[92] It is evident that Pretorius pursued and valued distinctive voices in film criticism with whom he could engage intellectually and politically. Armond White, for instance, remains one of the most divisive voices in American film criticism.[93]

In a 'FreeWheeling' column for *Artslink* in 2003, Pretorius describes how he constructs the basis for a film review. Taking 'the Susan Sontag-stance of secular observer', he started reviewing films in 1976, from a background in journalism.[94] Comparing how his approach to film is both objective and subjective, Pretorius suggests that 'reading a film is trying to understand the selection out of the possibilities available to you.'[95] Returning to his training in Practical Criticism, Pretorius writes about how sense, intuition, feeling and imagery inform how he reads a film. To demonstrate his point, he recounts the contrasting use of tracking shots in the films *Thirteen Days* (Donaldson 2000), set against the Cuban Missile Crisis of 1962, and Paul Verhoeven's 1980 gay suspense drama *Cruising* (which Pretorius misremembers as being titled *Cruise*).[96] In the former, American officials are shown to walk towards the camera in tracking shots, while in the latter it is the tracking shot that guides the protagonist and the audience into an unfamiliar and strange place. 'Tracking shots aren't neutral,' comments Pretorius.[97]

Pretorius refers to examples from world cinema to demonstrate his understanding and practice of film criticism, including the poetic Iranian drama *Baran* and the Brazilian gang drama *City of God*.[98] Admittedly, both these films were at the very top of international film releases at the time and he refers to them specifically, I suspect, because of their familiarity to the Cinema Nouveau moviegoer. Pretorius also names *Understanding Movies* by Louis Giannetti and *How to Read a Film* by James Monaco as key texts that informed his approach to film criticism.[99] He later refers to Nicolas Tredell's edited volume *Cinemas of the Mind* in this regard.[100] Provocatively, Pretorius highlights the importance of revisiting and developing new film vocabularies to accommodate and help individuals to develop a diversified and diversifying film culture.[101]

Reviewing the stage musical *Hair*'s revival at Montecasino in 2007, Pretorius uses his review to once again address the politics of popular culture by bringing *Hair*'s resistance to the Vietnam War – which 'created a surge of creativity' – into parallel with cultural expressions of resistance to United States President George W. Bush's invasion of Iraq.[102] For Pretorius, *Hair* is the musical counterpoint to the safety and domesticity of *Mary Poppins*, which 'was allowed in South Africa under the apartheid regime' while *Hair*'s soundtrack was banned.[103] Two weeks after his death, the *Mail & Guardian* posthumously published Pretorius's opinion piece titled 'Painful Past, Present and Future?'.[104] He offered an overview of an unreleased edited volume on contemporary South African cinema by Martin Botha.[105] Once again, Pretorius used the opportunity to contrast the energetic dynamism of world cinema with its lack in much South African film and its adherence to the 'wisdom' of the market; South Africa overvalues 'commercial distribution patterns and [places] an overemphasis on Hollywood films'.[106] It was within this distribution pattern that South African distributors could not find their way towards releasing the South African-Canadian co-production *Proteus*.[107] Pretorius then contemplates the ways in which new social and digital media may impact on the production and reception of film, and finally remarks: 'There are now numerous film schools teaching people how to make films, but hardly any to *teach the public how to look at them*, also an important part of the growth of a film culture.'[108]

A POLITICALLY COMMITTED FILM CRITIC

In an imagined dialogue Scott has with himself in his book, he asks: can anything that exists be criticised? In response, he pins down one of the cornerstones of the relationship between the work of art and the critic who engages with it: 'The question is whether the thing in question can bear the scrutiny, which is really to say whether the act of scrutinizing it can be made interesting.'[109]

Pretorius was uninterested in convincing any reader to agree with him about a film's quality. Instead, his writing reveals a commitment to the productive conflict that the best film criticism can make possible by pointing out contradictions between a film and its context of production, and by challenging possible preconceptions about a film or about the role of art in society. Overall, his film writing was politically committed, as demonstrated by his staunch opposition to censorship; his suspicion of the market as an indicator of content value; his wariness of the dominance of American film; and his perpetual challenge to South African and Afrikaans films to be more politically invested and reflective. Insofar as Pretorius's criticism had an evaluative function, it was to locate and lay bare a film's political content and form, as if in a sustained response to Fredric Jameson's call to 'always historicise'.[110]

NOTES

1   Barry Ronge, *Spit 'n Polish* (Johannesburg: Penguin, 2006).
2   Terry Eagleton, *The Function of Criticism* (London: Verso, 2005), 7.
3   Eagleton, *The Function of Criticism*, 124.

4   Eagleton, *The Function of Criticism*, 20.
5   A.O. Scott, *Better Living through Criticism: How to Think about Art, Pleasure, Beauty, and Truth* (London: Penguin, 2017), 203; emphasis added.
6   Herman Wasserman, 'Revisiting Reviewing: The Need for a Debate on the Role of Arts Journalism in South Africa', *Literator* 25, no. 1 (2004): 143.
7   Wasserman, 'Revisiting Reviewing', 144.
8   Wasserman, 'Revisiting Reviewing', 150–151.
9   Wasserman, 'Revisiting Reviewing', 149.
10 Scott, *Better Living through Criticism*, 163.
11 William Pretorius, 'Wretched and Confused', *Artslink*, 3 February 2007, accessed 25 April 2019, https://www.artlink.co.za/news_article.htm?contentID=3095
12 James Baldwin, *The Devil Finds Work* (New York: Vintage Books, 2011).
13 Baldwin, *The Devil Finds Work*, 85, 95.
14 Baldwin, *The Devil Finds Work*, 7.
15 D.W. Griffith, dir., *The Birth of a Nation* (Los Angeles: David W. Griffith Corp., 1915); Baldwin, *The Devil Finds Work*, 47.
16 Baldwin, *The Devil Finds Work*, 49.
17 Stanley Kramer, dir., *The Defiant Ones* (New York: Curtleigh Productions, 1958); David Lean, dir., *Lawrence of Arabia* (London, Horizon Pictures, 1962).
18 William Friedkin, dir., *The Exorcist* (Burbank, CA: Warner Bros Pictures, 1973); Baldwin, *The Devil Finds Work*, 126.
19 James Naremore, 'Authorship and the Cultural Politics of Film Criticism', *Film Quarterly* 44, no. 1 (1990): 22.
20 Scott, *Better Living through Criticism*, 123.
21 Scott, *Better Living through Criticism*, 159, 165.
22 Wasserman, 'Revisiting Reviewing', 143.
23 V.F. Perkins, 'Badness: An Issue in the Aesthetics of Film', ed. Andrew Klevan, *Movie: A Journal of Film Criticism* 8, no. 1 (2019): 34.
24 Perkins, 'Badness', 36.
25 Perkins, 'Badness', 37.
26 Peter Weir, dir., *Dead Poets Society* (Burbank, CA: Touchstone Pictures, 1989); Perkins, 'Badness', 34.
27 Perkins, 'Badness', 36.
28 Cited in James Burns, 'Watching Africans Watch Films: Theories of Spectatorship in British Colonial Africa', *Historical Journal of Film, Radio & Television* 20, no. 2 (2000): 197.
29 Jeremy Nathan, 'Movies and Monopolies: The Distribution of Cinema in South Africa', *Staffrider* 9 no. 4 (1991): 61, 62.
30 Nathan, 'Movies and Monopolies', 69.
31 Nathan, 'Movies and Monopolies', 71.
32 Keyan Tomaselli, *The Cinema of Apartheid: Race and Class in South African Film* (London: Routledge, 1989), 116.
33 Tomaselli, *The Cinema of Apartheid*, 114, 123.
34 Tomaselli, *The Cinema of Apartheid*, 136.
35 Martin Botha, ed., *Marginal Lives & Painful Pasts: South African Cinema after Apartheid* (Cape Town: Genugtig!, 2007), 152.
36 Botha, *Marginal Lives*, 153.
37 Tomaselli, *The Cinema of Apartheid*, 102.

38 Tomaselli, *The Cinema of Apartheid*, 112.
39 William Pretorius, 'Afrikaans Cinema in the Eighties: Soothing Images', in *Movies, Moguls, Mavericks: South African Cinema 1979–1991*, ed. Johan Blignaut and Martin Botha (Cape Town: Showdata, 1992).
40 Pretorius, 'Afrikaans Cinema in the Eighties', 375.
41 Pretorius, 'Afrikaans Cinema in the Eighties', 393.
42 Pretorius, 'Afrikaans Cinema in the Eighties', 376.
43 Regardt van den Bergh, dir., *Circles in a Forest* (Johannesburg: Philo Pieterse Productions, 1988).
44 Pretorius, 'Afrikaans Cinema in the Eighties', 378.
45 Pretorius, 'Afrikaans Cinema in the Eighties', 380.
46 Pretorius, 'Afrikaans Cinema in the Eighties', 381.
47 Pretorius, 'Afrikaans Cinema in the Eighties', 382.
48 Pretorius, 'Afrikaans Cinema in the Eighties', 383.
49 Jans Rautenbach, dir., *Broer Matie* (My Brother, My Mate) (n.p.: Satbel Films, 1984); Koos Roets, dir., *Die Groen Faktor* (The Green Factor) (Johannesburg: Heyns Films, 1984).
50 Pretorius, 'Afrikaans Cinema in the Eighties', 385.
51 Johan Blignaut, dir., *Mamza* (n.p.: Everis Films, 1985); Pretorius, 'Afrikaans Cinema in the Eighties', 386.
52 Elmo de Witt, dir., *Grensbasis 13* (Johannesburg: Brigadiers Films, 1979); Pretorius, 'Afrikaans Cinema in the Eighties', 387, 388.
53 David Lister, dir., *Oh Schucks … Here Comes UNTAG* (Johannesburg: Koukus Films and Toron Screen Corporation, 1990); Pretorius, 'Afrikaans Cinema in the Eighties', 390.
54 H. Eloff, 'Showmax Removing 7 Titles from Its Platform after Concluding Review of Racially Insensitive Content', *News24*, 3 July 2020, accessed 12 August 2020, https://www.news24.com/channel/movies/news/showmax-removing-7-titles-from-its-platform-after-concluding-review-of-racially-insensitive-content-20200703
55 Pretorius, 'Afrikaans Cinema in the Eighties', 392.
56 William Pretorius, 'Afrikaans Cinema', *The SAFTTA Journal* 5, no. 1–2 (1985): 23–28; Johan Blignaut and Martin Botha, eds, *Movies, Moguls, Mavericks: South African Cinema 1979–1991* (Cape Town: Showdata, 1992).
57 Pretorius, 'Afrikaans Cinema in the Eighties'.
58 Pretorius, 'Afrikaans Cinema', 24.
59 Pretorius, 'Afrikaans Cinema', 27.
60 Pretorius, 'Afrikaans Cinema', 23.
61 Pretorius, 'Afrikaans Cinema', 24, 25.
62 Regardt van den Bergh, dir., *Boetie Gaan Border Toe!* (Johannesburg: Philo Pieterse Productions, 1984); Pretorius, 'Afrikaans Cinema', 27.
63 Pretorius, 'Afrikaans Cinema', 28.
64 Pat Hopkins, *Cringe, the Beloved Country* (Cape Town: Zebra Press, 2003); William Pretorius, 'Schlock Keeps Coming Back', *Artslink*, 14 November 2003, accessed 25 April 2019, https://www.artlink.co.za/news_article.htm?contentID=19778. The Boeremag was an Afrikaans nationalist separatist group that had plotted a number of terrorist attacks in 2002. See Kathryn Henne, 'Enemies and Citizens of the State: Die Boeremag as the Face of Postapartheid Otherness', *Critical Criminology* 19 (2011): 285–286.
65 Pretorius, 'Schlock Keeps Coming Back'.
66 *Artslink* can be found at https://www.newslink.co.za/. Darrell J. Roodt, dir., *Cry, the Beloved Country* (Los Angeles: Miramax Films, 1994); William Pretorius, 'New Life

67 for Old Classic', *Artslink*, 9 December 1994, accessed 25 April 2019, https://mg.co.za/article/1994-12-09-new-life-for-old-classic
68 William Pretorius, 'SA's Unseen Movies', *News24*, 14 February 2002, accessed 25 April 2019, https://www.news24.com/xArchive/Archive/Sas-unseen-movies-20020214
69 Francois Coertze, dir., *Lyk Lollery* (Johannesburg: Abyss Productions, 2001); Francois Coertze, dir., *Desert Diners* (Johannesburg: Abyss Productions, 2000).
70 Pretorius, 'SA's Unseen Movies'.
71 William Pretorius, 'Needed: A Local Moviemaker to Do Our Own *Bowling For Columbine*', *Artslink*, 14 June 2003, accessed 25 April 2019, https://www.artlink.co.za/news_article.htm?contentID=19090
72 William Pretorius, 'The Big Big B', *Artslink*, 13 April 2007, accessed 25 April 2019, https://www.artlink.co.za/news_article.htm?contentID=3366
73 William Pretorius, 'The Limits of Knowledge', *Artslink*, 15 September 2003, accessed 25 April 2019, https://www.artlink.co.za/news_article.htm?contentID=19495; emphasis added.
74 Pretorius, 'The Limits of Knowledge'.
75 William Pretorius, 'Last Saturday I Happened to Be in an Upmarket Shopping Mall', *Artslink*, 27 June 2003, accessed 25 April 2019, https://www.artlink.co.za/news_article.htm?contentID=19144
76 William Pretorius, 'No Snakes in Paradise', *Mail & Guardian*, 17 February 1995, accessed 2 April 2019, https://mg.co.za/article/1995-02-17-no-snakes-in-paradise
77 Dennie Gordon, dir., *Joe Dirt* (Culver City: Columbia Pictures, 2001).
78 William Pretorius, '*Joe Dirt*', *News24*, 17 August 2001, accessed 25 April 2019, https://www.news24.com/xArchive/Archive/Joe-Dirt-20010816
79 Pretorius, '*Joe Dirt*'.
80 Gray Hofmeyr, dir., *Mr Bones* (La Lucia: Videovision Entertainment, 2001).
81 Jamie Uys, dir., *The Gods Must Be Crazy* (Johannesburg: Mimosa Films, 1980); William Pretorius, '*Mr Bones*', *News24*, 30 November 2001, accessed 25 April 2019, https://www.news24.com/xArchive/Archive/Mr-Bones-20011129-2
82 Pretorius, '*Mr Bones*'.
83 William Pretorius, 'There's a Shot in *Apocalypse Now Redux*', *Artslink*, 11 April 2003, accessed 25 April 2019, https://www.artlink.co.za/news_article.htm?contentID=18775; Francis F. Coppola, dir., *Apocalypse Now Redux* (Los Angeles: Miramax Films, 1979).
84 James Cameron, dir., *Titanic* (Hollywood: Paramount Pictures, 1997).
85 Pretorius, 'There's a Shot'.
86 James Cameron, dir., *Avatar* (Los Angeles: 20th Century Fox, 2009); Cameron, *Titanic*; Mark Robson, dir., *Earthquake* (Universal City: Universal Pictures, 1974); William Pretorius, 'Watching *The Ring*', *Artslink*, 14 February 2003, accessed 25 April 2019, https://www.artlink.co.za/news_article.htm?contentID=18472
87 William Pretorius, 'What's It All About, Mel?' *Artslink*, 26 January 2007, accessed 25 April 2019, https://www.artlink.co.za/news_article.htm?contentID=2864
88 Alejandro G. Iñárritu, dir., *Babel* (Los Angeles: Anonymous Content, 2006); William Pretorius, 'The Way the World Is – in Movies', *Artslink*, 24 February 2007, accessed 25 April 2019, https://www.artlink.co.za/news_article.htm?contentID=3046
89 Pretorius, 'The Way the World Is'.
90 Mel Gibson, dir., *Apocalypto* (Burbank, CA: Touchstone Pictures, 2006); Mel Gibson, dir., *The Passion of the Christ* (Los Angeles: Newmarket Films, 2004); Pretorius, 'What's It All About, Mel?'.

90 William Pretorius, 'Long Night's Journey', *News24*, 25 May 2001, accessed 25 April 2019, https://www.news24.com/xArchive/Archive/Long-Nights-Journey-20010524; Frances Reid and Deborah Hoffmann, dir., *Long Night's Journey into Day* (n.p.: Reid-Hoffman Productions, 2000).
91 Pretorius, 'Watching *The Ring*'.
92 William Pretorius, 'Duplicitous Duplications', *Artslink*, 29 August 2003, accessed 25 April 2019, https://www.artlink.co.za/news_article.htm?contentID=19416
93 Walter Biggins, 'In Defense of Armond White', *RogerEbert.com*, 14 January 2014, accessed 13 August 2020, https://www.rogerebert.com/features/in-defense-of-armond-white
94 Pretorius, 'The Big Big B'.
95 William Pretorius, 'Open Cards', *Artslink*, 19 September 2003, accessed 25 April 2019, https://www.artlink.co.za/news_article.htm?contentID=19520
96 William Friedkin, dir., *Cruising* (Culver City: Lorimar Film Entertainment and CiP-Europaische Treuhand, 1980).
97 Pretorius, 'Open Cards'.
98 Majid Majidi, dir., *Baran* (Los Angeles: Miramax Films, 2002); Fernando Meirelles and Kátia Lund, dir., *City of God* (São Paulo: 02 Filmes, 2002); Pretorius, 'Open Cards'.
99 Louis Gianetti, *Understanding Movies*, 13th edition (Boston: Pearson, 2014); James Monaco, *How to Read a Film*, 3rd edition (New York: Oxford University Press, 2000); Pretorius, 'Open Cards'.
100 Nicolas Tredell, ed., *Cinemas of the Mind: A Critical History of Film Theory* (Cambridge: Icon, 2002); Pretorius, 'The Way the World Is'.
101 Pretorius, 'Open Cards'.
102 William Pretorius, 'Flowers and Hair', *Artslink*, 20 April 2007, accessed 25 April 2019, https://www.artlink.co.za/news_article.htm?contentID=3410
103 Pretorius, 'Flowers and Hair'.
104 William Pretorius, 'Painful Past, Present and Future?' *Mail & Guardian*, 11 July 2007, accessed 25 April 2019, https://mg.co.za/article/2007-07-11-painful-past-present-and-future
105 The book was published as *Marginal Lives & Painful Pasts*, edited by Martin Botha, who dedicated the book to his long-time friend Pretorius.
106 Pretorius, 'Painful Past'.
107 John Greyson and Jack Lewis, dir., *Proteus* (n.p.: Pluck Productions, 2003).
108 Pretorius, 'Painful Past'; emphasis added.
109 Scott, *Better Living through Criticism*, 255.
110 Fredric Jameson, *The Political Unconscious: Narrative as a Social Symbolic Act* (London: Methuen, 1981), 9.

REFERENCES

Baldwin, James. *The Devil Finds Work*. New York: Vintage Books, 2011.
Biggins, Walter. 'In Defense of Armond White'. *RogerEbert.com*, 14 January 2014. Accessed 13 August 2020. https://www.rogerebert.com/features/in-defense-of-armond-white
Blignaut, Johan, dir. *Mamza*. N.p.: Everis Films, 1985.
Blignaut, Johan and Martin Botha, eds. *Movies, Moguls, Mavericks: South African Cinema 1979–1991*. Cape Town: Showdata, 1992.

Botha, Martin, ed. *Marginal Lives & Painful Pasts: South African Cinema after Apartheid.* Cape Town: Genugtig!, 2007.
Burns, James. 'Watching Africans Watch Films: Theories of Spectatorship in British Colonial Africa'. *Historical Journal of Film, Radio & Television* 20, no. 2 (2000): 197–211.
Cameron, James, dir. *Avatar.* Los Angeles: 20th Century Fox, 2009.
Cameron, James, dir. *Titanic.* Hollywood: Paramount Pictures, 1997.
Coertze, Francois, dir. *Desert Diners.* Johannesburg: Abyss Productions, 2000.
Coertze, Francois, dir. *Lyk Lollery.* Johannesburg: Abyss Productions, 2001.
Coppola, Francis F., dir. *Apocalypse Now Redux.* Los Angeles: Miramax Films, 1979.
De Witt, Elmo, dir. *Grensbasis 13.* Johannesburg: Brigadiers Films, 1979.
Donaldson, Roger, dir. *Thirteen Days.* New York: New Line Cinema, 2000.
Eagleton, Terry. *The Function of Criticism.* London: Verso, 2005.
Eloff, H. 'Showmax Removing 7 Titles from Its Platform after Concluding Review of Racially Insensitive Content'. *News24*, 3 July 2020. Accessed 12 August 2020. https://www.news24.com/channel/movies/news/showmax-removing-7-titles-from-its-platform-after-concluding-review-of-racially-insensitive-content-20200703
Friedkin, William, dir. *Cruising.* Culver City: Lorimar Film Entertainment and CiP-Europaische Treuhand, 1980.
Friedkin, William, dir. *The Exorcist.* Burbank, CA: Warner Bros Pictures, 1973.
Gianetti, Louis. *Understanding Movies*, 13th edition. Boston: Pearson, 2014.
Gibson, Mel, dir. *Apocalypto.* Burbank, CA: Touchstone Pictures, 2006.
Gibson, Mel, dir. *The Passion of the Christ.* Los Angeles: Newmarket Films, 2004.
Gordon, Dennie, dir. *Joe Dirt.* Culver City: Columbia Pictures, 2001.
Greyson, John and Jack Lewis, dir. *Proteus.* N.p.: Pluck Productions, 2003.
Griffith, D.W., dir. *The Birth of a Nation.* Los Angeles: David W. Griffith Corp., 1915.
Henne, Kathryn. 'Enemies and Citizens of the State: Die Boeremag as the Face of Postapartheid Otherness'. *Critical Criminology* 19 (2011): 285–299.
Hofmeyr, Gray, dir. *Mr Bones.* La Lucia: Videovision Entertainment, 2001.
Hopkins, Pat. *Cringe, the Beloved Country.* Cape Town: Zebra Press, 2003.
Iñárritu, Alejandro G., dir. *Babel.* Los Angeles: Anonymous Content, 2006.
Jameson, Fredric. *The Political Unconscious: Narrative as a Social Symbolic Act.* London: Methuen, 1981.
Kramer, Stanley, dir. *The Defiant Ones.* New York: Curtleigh Productions, 1958.
Lean, David, dir. *Lawrence of Arabia.* London: Horizon Pictures, 1962.
Lister, David, dir. *Oh Schucks ... Here Comes UNTAG.* Johannesburg: Koukus Films and Toron Screen Corporation, 1990.
Majidi, Majid, dir. *Baran.* Los Angeles: Miramax Films, 2002.
Meirelles, Fernando and Kátia Lund, dir. *City of God.* São Paulo: 02 Filmes, 2002.
Monaco, James. *How to Read a Film*, 3rd edition. New York: Oxford University Press, 2000.
Naremore, James. 'Authorship and the Cultural Politics of Film Criticism'. *Film Quarterly* 44, no. 1 (1990): 14–23.
Nathan, Jeremy. 'Movies and Monopolies: The Distribution of Cinema in South Africa'. *Staffrider* 9 no. 4 (1991): 61–75.
Perkins, V.F. 'Badness: An Issue in the Aesthetics of Film'. Edited by Andrew Klevan. *Movie: A Journal of Film Criticism* 8, no. 1 (2019): 34–37.
Pretorius, William. 'Afrikaans Cinema'. *The SAFTTA Journal* 5, no. 1–2 (1985): 23–28.

Pretorius, William. 'Afrikaans Cinema in the Eighties: Soothing Images'. In *Movies, Moguls, Mavericks: South African Cinema 1979–1991*, edited by Johan Blignaut and Martin Botha, 375–394. Cape Town: Showdata, 1992.

Pretorius, William. 'Duplicitous Duplications'. *Artslink*, 29 August 2003. Accessed 25 April 2019. https://www.artlink.co.za/news_article.htm?contentID=19416

Pretorius, William. 'Flowers and Hair'. *Artslink*, 20 April 2007. Accessed 25 April 2019. https://www.artlink.co.za/news_article.htm?contentID=3410

Pretorius, William. '*Joe Dirt*'. *News24*, 17 August 2001. Accessed 25 April 2019. https://www.news24.com/xArchive/Archive/Joe-Dirt-20010816

Pretorius, William. 'Last Saturday I Happened to Be in an Upmarket Shopping Mall'. *Artslink*, 27 June 2003. Accessed 25 April 2019. https://www.artlink.co.za/news_article.htm?contentID=19144

Pretorius, William. '*Long Night's Journey*'. *News24*, 25 May 2001. Accessed 25 April 2019. https://www.news24.com/xArchive/Archive/Long-Nights-Journey-20010524

Pretorius, William. '*Mr Bones*'. *News24*, 30 November 2001. Accessed 25 April 2019. https://www.news24.com/xArchive/Archive/Mr-Bones-20011129-2

Pretorius, William. 'Needed: A Local Moviemaker to Do Our Own *Bowling For Columbine*'. *Artslink*, 14 June 2003. Accessed 25 April 2019. https://www.artlink.co.za/news_article.htm?contentID=19090

Pretorius, William. 'New Life for Old Classic'. *Artslink*, 9 December 1994. Accessed 25 April 2019. https://mg.co.za/article/1994-12-09-new-life-for-old-classic

Pretorius, William. 'No Snakes in Paradise'. *Mail & Guardian*, 17 February 1995. Accessed 2 April 2019. https://mg.co.za/article/1995-02-17-no-snakes-in-paradise

Pretorius, William. 'Open Cards'. *Artslink*, 19 September 2003. Accessed 25 April 2019. https://www.artlink.co.za/news_article.htm?contentID=19520

Pretorius, William. 'Painful Past, Present and Future?' *Mail & Guardian*, 11 July 2007. Accessed 25 April 2019. https://mg.co.za/article/2007-07-11-painful-past-present-and-future

Pretorius, William. 'SA's Unseen Movies'. *News24*, 14 February 2002. Accessed 25 April 2019. https://www.news24.com/xArchive/Archive/Sas-unseen-movies-20020214

Pretorius, William. 'Schlock Keeps Coming Back'. *Artslink*, 14 November 2003. Accessed 25 April 2019. https://www.artlink.co.za/news_article.htm?contentID=19778

Pretorius, William. 'The Big Big B'. *Artslink*, 13 April 2007. Accessed 25 April 2019. https://www.artlink.co.za/news_article.htm?contentID=3366

Pretorius, William. 'The Limits of Knowledge'. *Artslink*, 15 September 2003. Accessed 25 April 2019. https://www.artlink.co.za/news_article.htm?contentID=19495

Pretorius, William. 'The Way the World Is – in Movies'. *Artslink*, 24 February 2007. Accessed 25 April 2019. https://www.artlink.co.za/news_article.htm?contentID=3046

Pretorius, William. 'There's a Shot in *Apocalypse Now Redux*'. *Artslink*, 11 April 2003. Accessed 25 April 2019. https://www.artlink.co.za/news_article.htm?contentID=18775

Pretorius, William. 'Watching *The Ring*'. *Artslink*, 14 February 2003. Accessed 25 April 2019. https://www.artlink.co.za/news_article.htm?contentID=18472

Pretorius, William. 'What's It All About, Mel?' *Artslink*, 26 January 2007. Accessed 25 April 2019. https://www.artlink.co.za/news_article.htm?contentID=2864

Pretorius, William. 'Wretched and Confused'. *Artslink*, 3 February 2007. Accessed 25 April 2019. https://www.artlink.co.za/news_article.htm?contentID=3095

Rautenbach, Jans, dir. *Broer Matie*. N.p.: Satbel Films, 1984.

Reid, Frances and Deborah Hoffmann, dir. *Long Night's Journey into Day*. N.p.: Reid-Hoffman Productions, 2000.
Robson, Mark, dir. *Earthquake*. Universal City: Universal Pictures, 1974.
Roets, Koos, dir. *Die Groen Faktor*. Johannesburg: Heyns Films, 1984.
Ronge, Barry. *Spit 'n Polish*. Johannesburg: Penguin, 2006.
Roodt, Darrell J., dir. *Cry, the Beloved Country*. Los Angeles: Miramax Films, 1994.
Scott, A.O. *Better Living through Criticism: How to Think about Art, Pleasure, Beauty, and Truth*. London: Penguin, 2017.
Tomaselli, Keyan. *The Cinema of Apartheid: Race and Class in South African Film*. London: Routledge, 1989.
Tredell, Nicolas, ed. *Cinemas of the Mind: A Critical History of Film Theory*. Cambridge: Icon, 2002.
Uys, Jamie, dir. *The Gods Must Be Crazy*. Johannesburg: Mimosa Films, 1980.
Van den Bergh, Regardt, dir. *Boetie Gaan Border Toe!* Johannesburg: Philo Pieterse Productions, 1984.
Van den Bergh, Regardt, dir. *Circles in a Forest*. Johannesburg: Philo Pieterse Productions, 1988.
Wasserman, Herman. 'Revisiting Reviewing: The Need for a Debate on the Role of Arts Journalism in South Africa'. *Literator* 25, no. 1 (2004): 139–157.
Weir, Peter, dir. *Dead Poets Society*. Burbank, CA: Touchstone Pictures, 1989.

CHAPTER

6

Cultural Policy and the Arts: Mewa Ramgobin and Public Dialogue

Keyan G. Tomaselli

The inclusive post-apartheid cultural policy that emerged from the political transition of the 1990s is in clear contrast with the Rhodes Must Fall movement of the mid-2000s. Initially focused on a statue at the University of Cape Town (UCT) that commemorated arch-imperialist Cecil Rhodes, one of UCT's early benefactors, the campaign for the statue's removal generated a global movement to 'decolonise' education.

The two contrasting 'transformation' discourses of cultural policy and Fallism can be compared to the reassuring branding campaign of deterritorialised and evanescent ethnic harmony propagated by the Spur steakhouse chain from the late apartheid era to the present day. In contrast to Spur's depiction of pre-lapsarian innocence was the scathing Nando's fast-food chicken political satire during the same period. A third example is Castle Lager, which pioneered multiracial advertising from the late 1970s. These examples illustrate Mewa Ramgobin's positive, inclusive, dialectical and historically informed view of cultural policy in the redefinition of post-apartheid identities. Monological, ahistorical and path-dependent solutions perpetuate social conflict, he argues. A cultural activist in Gandhian vein, Ramgobin (1932–2016) was a public figure who helped to revitalise the Natal Indian Congress.[1] He was a founding member of the United Democratic Front (UDF), active in the Congress of South African Writers (Cosaw) and he served as an African National Congress (ANC) Member of Parliament. Though not an academic, Ramgobin's independently constructed theory of cultural policy bore similarities to Foucauldian derivations of Australian cultural policy studies.

This chapter examines Ramgobin's cultural philosophy with regard to ethnic representational inclusivity in his attempt to reorientate discussion from the narrow structuralist pessimistic Marxism of the 1970s and 1980s towards a fluid post-Marxism. Post-Marxism recognises that individuals embody contradictory consciousnesses and multiple subject positions, and that they play multiple roles in cosmopolitan societies.

A BRIEF HISTORY

In contrast to conservative cultural theory (CCT), which developed coherent principles of cultural mobilisation during the first half of the twentieth century, 'culture' and 'media' studies as potential sites of anti-apartheid struggle were largely ignored by liberal and radical scholars from the 1960s until the mid-1970s.[2] The mechanistic left-wing assumption was that that since the apartheid state owned the means of production, distribution and regulation in broadcasting, performing arts councils and some print media, it therefore also de facto controlled interpretation, effects, uses and responses. In this view, the arts also lacked hard social theory. This reductive view feared that cultural struggle would result in the co-optation of activists into the 'ruling ideas' – dangerous, since Karl Marx and Friedrich Engels equated a direct and determining structural relationship between material and mental production.[3] In other words, receivers of messages were seen as lacking the means to engage with them critically.

A theory of affirmation with an identifiable anti-apartheid constituency was, until the mid-1980s, largely lacking. Some literary scholars even rejected the application of political economy to the study of the arts and film.[4] Not surprisingly, therefore, CCT theorists understood Marxist pessimism as the failure of historical materialism. This was because it had, until the mid-1970s, surrendered possibilities of counter-mobilisation. Similarly, in the absence of an affirming cultural programme – such as had eventually emerged from the 1982 culture and resistance meeting in Botswana – Afrikaner conservatives would have understood anti-apartheid cultural activists as proposing an abstract optimism without vision, content or strategy.

EVADING VICTIMHOOD

Cultural activists of the 1980s, however, were not axiomatically interpellated into 'apartheid ideology' or the 'ruling ideas'. Rather, they invented a new culture, new kinds of lived experience – new practices, new discourses and new ways of being in the world. The resultant cultural energy that they unleashed in the early 1980s had, by the end of the decade, become highly visible.[5]

The arts, drama and related activities took academics and practitioners into the communities, to the streets and to 'the people'. Indeed, academics often lagged behind those organising in the townships, the unions and in formal cultural sectors. Challenging magazines that appeared in the 1970s and 1980s such as *Staffrider* (edited by Mike Kirkwood), *S'ketch* (edited by Robert Kavanagh), *Speak* (Eve Bertelsen) and *Die Suid-Afrikaan* (Hermann Giliomee), which even interviewed banned ANC members, populated the 1980s. *Critical Arts*, *Pretexts* and the *South African Theatre Journal* interrogated the nature of meaning-making in the context of Arnoldian-derived assumptions about the civilising role of high art in contrast to popular culture.[6] Such publications opened spaces for critical analysis within and beyond the academy, challenging not only the way that universities were interpreting Western thought, but also, along with other journals like *Perspectives in Education*, they were contesting the academy itself.

Germinal intermediations penned by Njabulo Ndebele, for example, queried a proclivity for narratives of repression and victimhood.[7] Yet, an abiding victimology chained to a fixation with 'the past' underpinned thematic path dependencies where traditional practices continued in the face of better alternatives. This occurred to such an extent that returning ANC activist Albie Sachs questioned this imagined recurrent rhetorical recovery,[8] a turning point in the fracturing of internal debates.[9]

The following sections sketch some anti-apartheid arts initiatives of the 1980s in relation to CCT, which was in the early twentieth century mobilising against industrialisation and British imperialist hegemony.

PARADIGM CLASH

The early 1980s witnessed organisational developments that coalesced into the Mass Democratic Movement (MDM). The MDM incorporated anti-apartheid universities,[10] academics, artists and over 1 000 civic organisations that had earlier made up the UDF.[11]

Many of the personalities located on the anti-apartheid English-language campuses were teaching (more or less) in a Marxist structuralist vein the ineffectiveness of struggle, even as revolution was dramatically unfolding in the streets of 1976 Soweto and beyond. Louis Althusser's functionalism had appealed to sections of the left during the late 1970s and early 1980s as it very effectively explained how ideology is materialised within social practices and how it shapes class behaviour accordingly.[12]

Only later was this affirmative street/place/space movement explained by application of Antonio Gramsci's earlier studies, which offered a strategy of resistance.[13] Labour sociology, for example, was a motor of the Federation of South African Trade Unions (Fosatu) resistance, creating worker theatre.[14] Notwithstanding this single-site understanding of resistance, the UDF had made alternative media central to its strategy, while Black Consciousness theatre drove explicit dramaturgical considerations that enabled a shift from a rigid structuralist Marxism to a more nuanced position (à la Chantal Mouffe, via Gramsci and Michel Foucault).[15] Mouffe counters essentialism, decentres the economy as foundational of politics and addresses the proliferation of 'new subject positions'.[16] Ian Steadman writes of his shift from Marxism to post-Marxism:

> I prefer to view the creative practitioners of South African theatre as being inscribed in a multiplicity of social relations ranging from relations of production to relations of race, sex, vicinity, language and religion ... The playwrights I study might well be inscribed in relations of production as workers or petit-bourgeois intellectuals, but they are also either male or female, white or black, Zulu or English.[17]

Classical Marxism's class reductionism is questioned by Mouffe. She affirms instead multiple subject positions corresponding both to the different social relations in which the individual is inserted and to the discourses that constitute these relations.[18] Thus, the subjectivity of a given social agent is always precariously and provisionally fixed or, to use the Lacanian term, sutured at the intersection of various discourses. There is no reason to privilege, a priori, a class position as the articulation of subjectivity, as was the case with some sections of the left's analysis of apartheid.[19]

Another dramatist who shifted similarly from Marxism to post-Marxism is Robert Kavanagh, as evidenced in the 30 years between the first and second editions of *Theatre as Cultural Struggle*.[20] The second edition examines the conflicting interplay between class, nation and race and evaluates the merits and limitations of multiracial theatre projects created by white liberals, the popular commercial musicals staged for black audiences by emergent black impresarios, and the efforts of the Black Consciousness movement to forge a distinctly African form of revolutionary theatre during the 1970s.[21]

CONSERVATIVE CULTURAL THEORY

While anti-imperialist Afrikaners of the 1930s and 1940s had developed an affirmative CCT to mobilise their own early struggle against English-dominated capital, the anti-apartheid resistance initially tried to generate a cultural moment via the campus-based National Union of South African Students (Nusas), which was formed in 1924 and disbanded in 1991.[22] The cultural wing of Nusas, Aquarius, was active at the four liberal English-language universities from 1970.[23] Nusas is now, however, cast as a small, whites-only grouping that had failed to understand the 'struggle story'.[24] Ramgobin, in an interview with Iain Edwards, explains:

> In the days when NUSAS was established there was no doubt of the fact that at the time it had an impact on student affairs, had an impact on race relations – as did the South African Institute of Race Relations – and they were respected for this. But the ethos that they were confronted with was in many ways different from the ethos that we were confronted with ... What were the founders of NUSAS seeing? Was it the mobilization of English-speaking white students? I'd say yes. That was a motivation. Was it a question of liberalism with a capital L? I'd say yes, there is no doubt of the fact. Was it a challenge to the social system? I'd say no. Was it a challenge to Afrikaner nationalism as manifested in a political organization called the Nationalist Party and the student bond and the Afrikaner Broederbond? I'd say yes. Was there a desire to resolve the intricate problems of race? Yes. Was there a resolution on the part of NUSAS to alter the social contradictions and the political manifestations in our country? I would say no.[25]

Nevertheless, as Glenn Moss reminds us, Nusas was directly involved on many fronts and had in 1968 adopted a policy decision to continue mobilisation on white English-language campuses, while the breakaway South African Student Organisation (SASO) mobilised on black campuses.[26] Given the racial and ethnic spatial structuring of apartheid, this tactic of working in one's 'own' community was later successfully propagated by the UDF.

Arts activities during the 1970s, but less so in the 1980s, were uncoordinated, un-theorised and anarchic. Much of the discussion, debate and contestation related to how this broad terrain of cultural activity could be integrated and developed more coherently with a political and oppositional commitment. Apart from Aquarius's activities were efforts to theorise the place of 'culture' in society, its relationship to other structures (such as politics, ideology and the economy) and the place of the committed artist. This Nusas moment coincides with Steve Biko's Black Consciousness intervention, a Gramsci-type affirmative strategy.[27] There were always fissures through which questioning and outright resistance could occur.

CCT was articulated in the 1930s and 1940s by Afrikaner intellectuals wanting a recovery of pastoralism, re-imagining a psycho-spiritual connection to 'the farm' before the successive British genocidal invasions that occurred between 1886 and 1903. Though marginalised from the urbanising and industrialising Afrikaner mainstream, CCT offered, firstly, a critical dimension consistently defining itself against liberal humanism and English culture. In contrast, during the 1980s racial capitalism was identified by the UDF as the adversary, though the liberation government after 2000 reconfigured racial capitalism as black economic empowerment (BEE).[28] This is a racially selective allocative mechanism aimed at the redistribution of ownership, procurement and job eligibility that largely excludes white people in an effort to rebalance economic opportunities.

Second, CCT's affirmative utopian dimension strove for a positive set of moral values to enable collective action. Rituals, cultural festivals and a preoccupation with the 'past' soon anchored a tactical ideological stasis. Conversely, idealist, utopian and policy thinking was pilloried by sections of the left during the 1980s. Among early twentieth-century Afrikaners the pastoral/ist-based CCT lost favour as the Broederbond de-emphasised pastoralism – a back-to-the-land migration – and took the Afrikaner struggle to the cities, where it confronted English-dominated capital on its own ground.[29] CCT failed because, unlike the Broederbond, it squandered the support of pragmatic Afrikaners who chose to adapt to the cities, while yearning for pastoral life characterised by 'the farm'. Founded on the nostalgia of the pre-Anglo-Boer War period, at its height, CCT evaded the onset of modernity and industrialisation, as urbanisation was equated with depravity and cultural impotence.

Third, clear constituencies were addressed by both the MDM and the CCT. The MDM, which had absorbed the UDF and Fosatu's successor, the Congress of South African Trade Unions (Cosatu), together with civic associations, provided the necessary consolidated left-wing constituency, while CCT had worked primarily through cultural, language and religious organisations. For CCT activists this involved awareness of the relationship between culture and power; they had placed film at the centre of their popular cultural and religious programmes.[30] The key CCT text for film was Hans Rompel's two-part *Die Bioskoop in Diens van die Volk* (The Bioscope in Service of the *Volk*). Rompel also published in *Huisgenoot* and *Brandwag*. This Reddingsdaadbond (Salvation Deed) series included 'Die Afrikaanse Universiteit en Sy Taak in Ons Volkslewe' (The Afrikaans University and Its Task in Our Nation's Life).[31] Rompel did not emphasise the terms 'White' or 'Nationalist'. He rather used '*volk*' (nation), '*publiek*' (public) and '*volkskuns*' (folk art), assuming a white, rural, Afrikaner nation state. In contrast, until the Culture and Resistance Conference (1982), this culture-power relationship was minimally appreciated by anti-apartheid activists, though academics were addressing this lacuna, if against the ideological tide.

Philosophical popular dimensions, a fourth component, were intrinsic to CCT programme implementation. CCT film directors appropriated aspects of Soviet film theory and mixed it with radical Griersonian documentary practices that had characterised the socially conscious British Documentary Film Movement of the 1930s.[32] In contrast, the anti-apartheid left in the 1980s had generated *in situ* aesthetics drawn from a much wider, though less coherent or theorised, overtly struggle repertoire. CCT's idealised rural and well-theorised film aesthetic was a driving theoretical force, while for the MDM, a less well-theorised, agitprop, anti-apartheid aesthetic largely sufficed.

Flexibility for both local and national mobilisation was a fifth element. This occurred during the early twentieth century via the Dutch Reformed Church. The *dominee* (pastor) was the literary, film and television character through which social flexibility was navigated, in alerting the rank and file to affirmative alternatives and the necessary urbanisation and associated cultural change in confronting liberalism and capitalism in the cities, and later even criticising aspects of apartheid.[33] In contrast, MDM-linked organisations were primarily labour oriented.

Finally, an empowering discourse was organisationally manifested in cultural festivals linked to historical events and the parallel establishment of Afrikaner-owned financial institutions such as Sanlam, financed from the rural Afrikaner population and designed to compete with, and then appropriate, English-dominated, urban-based capital.[34] Apart from black union pension funds that were mobilised to purchase some media companies in the 1990s, the MDM had no accumulation strategy other than the ANC's BEE redistributive requirement. BEE resulted in the creation of a few mega-rich oligarchs, on the one hand, and the financial catastrophe of state-owned enterprises, on the other.[35]

In commenting on the place of structuralism, Moss observes that some academics had applied Althusserian thought to loosening mechanistic determinism and structuralism, developing a nuanced notion of causality in opposition to the ahistorical Marxism of Soviet theorists. Artists' undermining of 'structuralist pessimism' meshed well with political scientist Rick Turner's insistence that imagination of an alternative – the necessity of utopian thinking – was integral to any oppositional and transformative project.[36] The operating principles underlying CCT are evident here.

CULTURE AND RESISTANCE CONFERENCE, BOTSWANA

Symbolic energy emerged from often-fragmented sites across all forms of expression, within and beyond the labour movement, coalescing in the 1982 Culture and Resistance Conference, hosted in Gaborone, Botswana. Here, 900 exiles and internal artists negotiated something of a testy, if unifying and transformative cultural front.

The single critique of the conference identified undialectical arguments over race and class and their interrelation.[37] Exiles justifiably personalised repression through the primary prism of race, while white delegates from within South Africa spoke abstractly, each group of exiles and internals respectively reproducing their different lived class relations. Traditional and rural/Bantustan artists were excluded, indicating the othering of cultural workers whose location in terms of apartheid geography was predetermined to disqualify them.

Theories of representation and reception were largely absent; that is, there was limited critical engagement with the determining reception theory of 'ruling ideas'. Populist resentment arose when academics raised such epistemological issues, thus impeding discussion of affirmative cultural theory. Such definitional inconsistency reappeared in the 1995 *ACTAG* (Arts and Culture Task Group) *Report*, leading to a static fixing of 'culture' in terms of past practices, manifested in assumptions of culture as instrumentalist, measured primarily in terms of its use and value in the 'struggle'.[38]

Relative autonomy from the state as a necessary condition of artistic practice was rejected by delegates supporting the Soviet option while mechanistic agitprop metaphors, such as 'the typewriter is a machine gun', assumed the discredited stimulus-response 'ruling ideas' definition of communication, or what Nadine Gordimer dismissed as 'phony sub-art'.[39] In addressing such myopia a decade later, Sachs proposed a five-year moratorium on clichéd phrases.[40] He appealed for 'real criticism', which rigorously debates contradictions, to replace 'solidarity criticism'. The desire to defeat and exclude the enemy, rather than in Gramscian strategy to win him over, observes Graham Hayman, impeded possibilities of restructuring state, racial and class systems.[41]

Organisations were formed to represent each art discipline, where not already in place, such as Cosaw and the Film and Allied Workers Organisation. From the organising Medu Art Ensemble's perspective, the Culture and Resistance Conference offered a cornerstone for the Towards a People's Culture Arts Festival (Cape Town, 1986) and the Culture in Another South Africa (CASA) Conference, held in Amsterdam in 1987, and others that followed.[42] Resolutions stemming from the 1987 conference included flexibility and the cultural boycott now focused on isolating the apartheid regime while simultaneously empowering internal democratic culture.

By the mid-1980s CCT theorists had become concerned with the organisational coherence that was emerging from these cultural jamborees. Coming as they did from a once identifiable constituency and utopian vision, the CCT theorists apprehensively understood that the Marxist (structuralist) pessimism that had previously surrendered the possibility of mobilisation was being now replaced with an affirmative discourse.[43] Theoretical abstraction was not considered a threat, but implementation in practice as a critical mass began to develop, led by the alternative press, video-makers, artists, writers and dramatists.

The chapter now turns to the post-apartheid era in identifying continuities and discursive substitutions through the prism of cultural policy developments.

CULTURAL POLICY

During 1995 the Centre for Communication, Media and Society at the University of KwaZulu-Natal was employed by the Convention for a Democratic South Africa (Codesa), via the Human Sciences Research Council (HSRC), to propose post-apartheid cultural policy.[44] The government-aligned HSRC had previously led a national research programme in the early 1980s that concluded that apartheid was the prime cause of failing intergroup relations.[45] As with the second example discussed below relating to a change of thinking in other sectors of the state on monuments, the HSRC had facilitated a radical reorientation. One researcher working on the project observed that a 'window of opportunity' was opened up: 'The transition period (1990–1994) and the tenure of the Government of National Unity (1994–1999) opened up all kinds of opportunities for the type of academic-state relationships which will not exist after 1999, the year when the "winner takes all" kind of politics returns to South Africa.'[46]

Policy work was informed by international best practice, as well as positions that were being articulated within the MDM prior to 1990 and, thereafter, the ANC. Ramgobin, despite being the target of endless state machinations against him, promoted reconciliation and subsequently issued the ANC Southern Natal Region statement on cultural policy, which derived from his lectures on the Freedom Charter at the University of KwaZulu-Natal. Ramgobin's stated twin reference points were, on the one hand, Mikhail Gorbachev's attempts at addressing Soviet economic stagnation by creating an interrelationship between policymaking – *glasnost* (openness) and *perestroika* (structural reform) – in relation to Gandhian passive resistance strategies.[47] *Perestroika* implied the retention of the command economy to effect a more efficient socialism that would enhance delivery to Soviet citizens.[48]

Ramgobin's hybrid approach was, however, akin to Australian cultural studies that pioneered the 'cultural policy moment' from the late 1980s, promoting co-operative relationships between the academy and government, redefining relations between policy workers and various arms and levels of the state in jointly enhancing the public sphere: 'This sphere of democratic political discourse and participation is supposedly capable of achieving the dialectical reconciliation of the technical and the substantive, administration and "culture", the state and "civil society" and, of course, political expertise and democratic decision. It is thus envisaged as being able to provide bureaucratic government with a normative orientation to the public good.'[49]

For Ian Hunter, critical debate in Australia stemmed from an assured ethical position of critical practice, enshrined in the university and completing a sociopolitical triad of citizen, critic and bureaucrat, in which the state was understood to be morally and ethically neutral. Australian researchers had applied Foucault's writings on governmentality that were helpful in displacing oppositions that locate the academy and the state as different realms. The academy operates as a branch of government for the purposes of cultural policy debates.[50]

Until 1990 in South Africa, however, criticism of the apartheid state was discouraged, often violently. The state changed in 1994, but civil society generally retained the culture of distrust. Post-apartheid policy research, however, could proceed from a clear vision of what *not to do*. Government functionaries are supposed to implement policies that emerge from legitimate consultative processes entrenched in civil, intellectual and political society, a process that underpinned Ramgobin's implicit Weberian practice that involves non-elected government officials.

Early cultural studies as an *oppositional* strategy was thus re-articulated into a discourse of policymaking and co-operation between state and civil agencies. The intention was to concretise democratic structures, which themselves facilitate access to resources and expertise, and give voice to popular concerns. This shift emerged in the late 1980s in some Australian states that had elected progressive governments espousing policies enabling democratic cultural practices and access to media, the arts and other forms of popular expression. In contrast, anyone on the South African left proposing policy studies was marked as 'counter-revolutionary' and despite Turner's affirmative position, as 'utopian' and thereby discursively marginalised. Thus, both prior to and immediately after the liberation movements were unbanned in 1990, South Africans were still learning how to engage in constructive critical policy work and to negotiate post-Marxist formulations of class, ethnicity and new subject positions.[51]

A critical rhetoric of affirmation was needed. The Australian cultural theory that underpinned Codesa was in fact to become the basis of Nelson Mandela's government's cultural policy under the direction of the Department of Arts, Culture, Science and Technology. The South African proposals: (a) recognised the symbolic value of colonial and post-colonial (the period of the Union/Republic) monuments; (b) advocated for a discursive re-articulation of these inherited statues and icons; and (c) sought to enable inclusion rather than exclusion.[52] The next section explains how these goals could be achived.

Conservation of Culture Conference

When Ramgobin and I were jointly invited to the Conservation of Culture Conference in Cape Town in 1988, we quickly realised that this site was a contestation of left-wing, liberal and right-wing factions.[53] The organising committee was surprisingly amenable to our request that the Freedom Charter be circulated on the first day of the five-day event. At the conference, many anti-apartheid activists were arguing the merits of affirmative cultural theory, social critique and democracy with their conservative colleagues, some of whom vacated the conference in dismay. Ramgobin, however, took the wind out of the sails of the inheritors of CCT. When asked, 'What will *you* [the ANC] do with "our" monuments when *you* take over?', Ramgobin would flip the question: 'It's not what will the ANC do with your monuments, but what will *you* do with them? Will they be used to continue to signify oppression and dispossession or will you re-articulate them into multicultural symbols of reconciliation?'[54] As Edwards observed of Ramgobin's life-long corpus and ability to strategically manoeuvre between subjectivities and interpretive communities:

> Ramgobin's core mental worlds seek spiritual and political richness in cultures and societies emergent from centuries of oppression and exploitation. His views are longitudinal, not of latitudes. And looking into South Africa he recognises these very same dynamics, but now through centuries of migration, existing within one country. In landmark speeches to the National Assembly Ramgobin showed how all South Africa's languages have words for the same vital set of human emotions: of humanity and compassion.[55]

The response from the Afrikaner conservatives was utter astonishment at how their question/accusation was re-articulated by Ramgobin into an opportunity for reconciliation, one that they themselves could express by taking a different subject position. The *verligte* (enlightened) liberals and left wing won the day and, extraordinarily, the conference issued a consensus statement based on the Freedom Charter.[56] Nicolaas Vergunst, an artist covering the event, observed: 'A declaration on the fifth day accepted that cultural preservation is not possible in an apartheid state, and also not under the tri-cameral system or where communities and organisations are destroyed in the name of the Group Areas Act and other legislation. The conference unambiguously rejected apartheid. In the light of the many delegates from the public service this was a notable change to the status quo.'[57]

Even Nusas had been reluctant to accept the Charter. Not Marxist, as Ramgobin observed, 'it was a non-racial document and NUSAS as a student body could not be allowed to take that kind of a position'. Much earlier, practising what he had laid out at the Conservation of Culture Conference, Ramgobin had debated with the Afrikaans Studentebond (students' organisation) on how destiny is linked to non-racialism. While he was Nusas's Director of Studies, he argued: 'We had to reach out to NUSAS leadership and NUSAS rank and file to persuade them to say this is a course for us.' It was also necessary 'to reach out to the instrument of our own oppression': the Studentebond was a wing of the Broederbond. 'So in taking on the Broederbond, we were literally taking on the system.'[58]

The conference's constituencies that saw out the five days accepted that historical imaginaries were to be re-articulated into the present for a post-apartheid future that was, to everyone's surprise, just 19 months away. One such attempt in 1995 was made by the Pretoria City Council. The objective of the television advertisement that animated monuments in Church Square was to 'reposition the image of the city from one of grey bureaucrats, red tape, and staidness associated with typical Afrikanerdom, to one of interracial and intercultural tolerance, unity and reconciliation – not acceptance of, but embracing change and cooperation in the New South Africa'.[59]

Offered thus as a form of cultural negotiation on the part of the outgoing Afrikaner city fathers, they were attempting to symbolically disarticulate Pretoria's historically conservative image and repressive mission, by re-articulating it as the locus of non-racial democracy and national unity, multiculturalism and economic growth. Successive shots of colonial-era statues of Queen Victoria, Jan van Riebeeck, King Shaka, Paul Kruger and Mohandas K. Gandhi are revealed in the visuals of the advertisement. The image of Kruger coincides with a midnight chime of the Pretoria City Hall clock, whereupon the grey 'statues' successively come to life to house music and climb off their pedestals. Next, the queen and Kruger are foregrounded in conversation at the base of Kruger's plinth. The dialogue occurs in Afrikaans, with English subtitles. The action is frozen and the logo for Pretoria's bid for commercial viability is superimposed on the scene. As this sequence comes to an end, the ringing sound of a cell phone is heard. The Kruger 'statue' pulls a phone from his jacket:

> KRUGER: Ja? (Looks knowingly at Queen Victoria) Madiba! [Mandela's clan name.] (Queen Victoria gives a knowing smile in return.) So tell me, Nelson, when are all these foreigners supposed to be coming to town?

By re-presenting Kruger as asking eagerly of President Mandela when all these foreigners, against which CCT was previously mobilised, are coming to Pretoria, the advertisement signals that Pretoria's once racial, political and cultural exclusivity was being discarded following the April 1994 elections.[60] Notwithstanding this momentary mid-1990s symbolic reconciliation, these statues were defaced in 2014 as a result of the Rhodes Must Fall campaign, which claimed that such monuments are signifiers of 'black pain', despite a notice issued by the minister of Arts and Culture that explicitly recalled the inclusive cultural policy that inaugurated the post-apartheid era.[61]

Among other responses to the new inclusive era of re-articulation and conciliation were the Castrol Motor Oil and Nando's advertisements that superseded the pioneering Castle Lager series on the mythical Charles Glass's increasingly multiracial beer-drinking community. South African Breweries advertising had portended an earlier shift from race-based to multiracial, class-based market profiles as reconstructed by its agency, J. Walter Thompson. P.W. Botha, during the 1980s, had planned to implement a Constitution based on a consociational democracy within a confederation of states. Some critics prematurely judged the advertising industry to be involved with what was seen as a neo-apartheid concept of power sharing. Alex Holt argues that the Castle commercials, broadcast from the mid-1980s onwards, signified the historical turning point from where the leading sector of South African capitalism distanced itself from the government and began a realignment with a future government under the ANC, then still banned.[62]

These commercialised aesthetic changes anticipated ANC cultural policy, as issued by Ramgobin on behalf of the Department of Arts and Culture, Southern Natal region. They mirrored Mouffeian analysis that was open to inscriptions of a multiplicity of social relations, incorporating multiple subjectivities with regard to race, sex, ethnicity, gender, language and religion. Ramgobin expressed these relations thus:

> The idea of a Bill of Rights admits that the ANC does not claim a monopoly on truth ...
>
> > In our own experience only the perverse will disregard:
> > the inter-facing of the Bible, the Koran and the Gita;
> > the inter-facing of the African drum and the rhythm of Spain;
> > the admission of the Roman script into our indigenous oral language.
>
> Whilst we <u>are</u> these and an array of more, there also are differences. While our cultural workers can harmonise or synthesise these differences, these differences must be allowed to coexist.
>
> > Coexistence of differences can only enrich our society. Cultural workers must constantly guard society against those practices that can suck us into the quagmire of intolerance, bigotry and cultural arrogance.[63]

The Cultural Reconstruction and Development initiative's post-Marxist framing paper adopted the Latin idea of culture: to nurture, tend, look after and live in a place.[64] Crucially, Ramgobin's nurturing approach insisted, in opposition to UDF cultural desk instrumentalist edicts mobilising culture as a weapon, that 'cultural workers must also demand the right from politicians to decide not only on *their* rights, but the rights of those who preceded us.'[65] The challenge, he said, was for 'us to enter the future without the fears and the hatred of the past'. Reconstruction, concluded Ramgobin, does not mean destruction or to build from scratch: 'The Voortrekker Monument, for example, is the symbol of the white Afrikaner's socio-political culture. Equally, the 1820 Settlers Monument is the symbol of the English-speaking white's socio-political culture ... In the interest of culture per se, and reconciliation in general, cultural workers need to burden themselves with the conservation of such works, spaces and symbols'.[66]

Drawing correspondences, Ramgobin observed that the destruction of political cultural symbols of the Soviet Union, or burning the works of Marx and Lenin, was immature, just as it was wrong for Stalin and others to destroy the symbols, artefacts, works and writings of those who opposed them. The plea of the ANC statement was for cultural workers to rather constitute themselves into an influential interest group to keep government in check and to respect cultural expressions. Cultural workers, argued Ramgobin, must vigilantly demonstrate their tolerance and the rejection of dogma: 'We now have to bring together different custodians of the diverse cultural experiences in our country.'[67]

The following section briefly discusses two further manifestations of the contradictory cultural discourses that characterised the year 2015: Rhodes Must Fall and the marketing iconography of Spur. My aim is to draw out the iconographic contradictions relating to representations of imagined pasts and the branded present.

What to do with monuments?

The fruitful policy dialogue of the 1990s was disrupted with a populism inaugurated at UCT, where students demanded the removal of the Rhodes statue in early 2015.[68] Few institutions were prepared for the new ahistorical monologue as they had failed to re-articulate the monuments located on their campuses, as Ramgobin had suggested at the Conservation and Culture Conference. The incident that sparked the national campaign of defacement occurred when students, themselves beneficiaries of Rhodes's largesse, smeared faeces over the statue and successfully forced its removal.

In contrast, the principal of the University of the Free State (UFS) had re-articulated the Boer President Steyn statue located next to the administration building as a site of reconciliation and compassion, leveraging it as a means of intercultural communication.[69] The Steyn monument alone stood tall and largely unmolested, if on occasion guarded because at this university they had engaged in dialogue about the future. As Andrew Nash might have concluded, UFS had met the conditions as outlined by Ramgobin, where a dialogue occurs in which one view is not seen as a threat to another, but as 'meaningful co-existence'. This is where 'dialogue meets other people as autonomous beings, who have their own roles to play, which do not fit into the monological system. The dialogical form requires the other because of the importance of contact with other people, and especially with different-minded people, in order to be part of that meaning and learning for yourself.'[70]

The UFS feat is on a par with the Conservation of Culture charter, given the appalling racism that had previously characterised UFS's white student residences.[71] As Ramgobin wrote in the late 1980s: 'It will be to the credit of the current generation of South Africans a source of pride for the generations that will follow, if, for instance, the statues of General Louis Botha and Jan Smuts, though symbolising a particular kind of cultural ethic, can soon be interfaced with the statues of Nelson Mandela, Albert Luthuli and Mahatma Ghandi.'[72]

The UCT students and the faeces-led moral panic they engendered across the nation dis-articulated the dialectical potential of monuments as sites for reconciliation, re-articulating them into now-recovered, path-dependent indicators of continued oppression (rather than defeat), emphasising victimology, rather than the robust emancipatory dialogue intended by Ramgobin and early ANC cultural policy. The strategy of the new, self-styled class-empowered is to repudiate previous dominant imagined pasts, monologues and oppressions, to suppress the social dialectic that could have been engendered by these monuments and to impose a new single ahistorical interpretation. This requires a strategy of 'doing something *to*' (defacement, damage, removal, relocation) an ideologically offending monument ('removal' *of*, was the UCT institutional response), rather than working *with* such statues (and those constituencies that valorise them) in pursuing a re-articulated inclusive democratic vision in which we all move on together.[73]

Today's positive stereotypes and icons become tomorrow's villains and the sacrificial lambs of monologically driven detractors. King Shaka was disappeared from the new Durban airport well before the Rhodes Must Fall incident – the militaristic Zulu nationalist Inkatha decriers opposed the allegedly 'soft' appearance of Andries Botha's re-articulated (reconciliatory) sculpture. Botha's Durban city elephants fell into disrepair because the ANC's one-dimensional vision objected to what they saw as an Inkatha symbol. The University of KwaZulu-Natal's King George V statue remained in place, still coated after many years with multicoloured paint. In the Soviet Union it was Lenin; in Iraq, Saddam Hussein, while the Taliban and Isis have destroyed millennia-old religious icons.

The previous tyrants, colonialists and benefactors – if removed – no longer caution and watch over us; neither do they remind us of what not to become. History is not about the past, but as Ramgobin argued, it should be about the future and what we do with it. The Rhodes Trust led the way in re-articulating itself into the future by linking with the Mandela Foundation. Students who have benefited from this relationship wanted to drag it back into the past. Without the social dialectic, debate and democracy cease, a new, destructive, one-dimensional analysis emerges and the ability of individuals, communities and social movements to practise empathy is gone, as Ramgobin suggests, with the dire consequences that have faced the world for millennia.

Depending on one's subject position, sometimes re-articulation goes off the ideological rails. One example is the Spur branding campaign.

Spur people: Native American tribal myth

While hosting American students, one of the stops is always a Spur restaurant. They do not relate to the brand or Spur marketing iconography. Their (literal) response is that the use of infantilised 'Indian' (Native American) representational icons (drawings) is politically incorrect.

However, in South Africa, Spur's sanitised iconography of the pre-settler American West integrates into historical Afrikaner idyllic myths about 'the farm'. The Spur myths of Native Americans is peacefully merged with the impression of the quintessential South African. Spur's partnership with the Springbok rugby team ceded the restaurant chain the rights for the flag-bearer activations at all inbound rugby test matches. Where some early Spur television advertisements involved a heart-warming and embracing deep male Afrikaner voice-over accent, later the chain became associated with the multilingual national anthem. Through this symbolic multilayering, Spur creates a sense of the 'good' old days of the romanticised old West (or *platteland*, countryside) before the *uitlanders* (foreigners, settlers) intruded, on the one hand, and of 'the (tranquil) farm' before the fall in the South African *bundu* (bushveld) occurred, on the other, when all was well, before ethnic and racial conflicts occurred over land and other scarce resources.

Spur created a new hybrid, a non-racial, internationalist, unthreatening, fun-loving, mythical, all-inclusive naturalised indigene. Nothing needs to fall in this scenario. While the Spur image calls on Native Americans, rather than 'Bushmen' for its indigenous iconography, this is merely a symbolic transposition for branding purposes. Race, colour, national origin, ethnicity and language are all erased in this internationalised imaginary that like the now-discontinued Kalahari-imaged Castrol Oil advertisements only works in South Africa. Consumer subjectivities, sutured at the intersection of various contradictory discourses, mask the discontinuities that shape individual consciousness.

The imaginary of 'Spur people' creates a new kind of consumer citizen who relates to a wonderfully convivial, cohesive and family-oriented community. This neverland is starkly contrasted to the highly satirical, cutting-edge Nando's chicken brand that engaged in critical social commentary, drawing on a different overtly politicised populist recent history of South Africa. Neither Spur nor Nando's has to fall in such discursive environments, unlike monuments that cannot be easily re-articulated in sections of the public mind.

Both the Spur and the Nando's campaigns respond to historical context, but construct the consumer-as-citizen very differently. Nando's' satire pilloried politicians and confronted social taboos, articulating what ordinary people were thinking and saying. Most South Africans are able, via a contradictory consciousness and by taking multiple subject positions, to identify with both brands and both identities. Both restaurant chains, despite their starkly different racial iconography, secured the highest multiracial customer bases of any restaurant groups. Something is working well in their strategic positioning within the new multiracial South African middle class that is able to manage its different subject positions.

Where the Nando's campaign admitted that historical conflict as driven by stereotypes (both positive and negative, depending on which ideological side consumers locate themselves), Spur naturalises innocence and ethnic harmony – the rainbow nation idea. Histories are forgotten, timeless pasts are remade and become something else – postmodernist experiences to be consumed. Reality is a social construction, which is why individuals differ in their responses to lived conditions, media and to Spur and Rhodes and other statues. Ordinary South Africans are far removed from American discourses and debates about ethnic representation. They do not easily recognise connotations in the Spur branding that would be questionable in a different context.

Spur is advertised as recalling the days before endemic crime isolated middle- and upper-class families who lock themselves within gated communities. The Spur experience is located in a contrived but welcome and safe fantasy land where the children can play happily in the activity room. In contrast, Nando's fractured this nirvana in its advertisements, recognising divisions and dystopia, and acting as trickster.

Whereas reference to the Native American past has been found to work negatively in marketing in the United States, the use of such iconography and myth is popular with some customers for products or services in other environments.[74] A possible explanation for this contradiction might lie in the fact that advertising is a distorted mirror of society by virtue of its tendency to conceal the ugliness of social reality by depicting people who are free, contented and find meaning through consumption. In this respect, associating products or services with the Native American historical and cultural past can elicit negative connotations in the United

States because of close proximity to conquered peoples who have been subjected to 'Anglo' genocide, similar to that systematically dished out to Boers in South Africa by the British coloniser between 1899 and 1902.

In the same way, one would have to think twice before using 'Voortrekker' as a brand name for denim jeans in South Africa, even though it might signify connotations of toughness, hardy people and heavy-duty cloth, whereas it might well work as a niche brand in the United States. And, in a South African context, the Native American myth, safely divorced from the grounds of death and destruction of its people, achieves only the positive aspects of its potential connotations. It is therefore a suitable marketing tool to a cross-section of the social formation, inclusive of all the various local victims of cultural wounds, to which it provides happy escapism.[75]

POST-COLONIALITY

While cultural theory has significantly matured since the 1982 Culture and Resistance Conference and now embraces the idea of post-coloniality, the intellectual crisis remains familiar. The difference is that a new generation of scholars is examining memories of the period and their relevance for current analysis from the perspective of the affirmative, the self-reflexive and the future.[76] For the most part, however, we remain fixed in apartheid-derived racial classifications, in which individuals are legislatively consigned to officially imposed subject positions. These have been reconfigured to administer micro-ethnic BEE imperatives and we have yet to rethink our globalising subjectivities, positions and associated practices. Where do we really stand culturally, inter-culturally or within broader hybridities?[77]

The analyses offered by John Williams and Graham Hayman have yet to be systematically addressed in developing an affirmative and democratised critical cultural theory.[78] The Rhodes Must Fall incidents are graphic reminders of this path dependency and how it has entrapped us in a reassuring victimology provided by history in contrast to a Ramgobian affirmation for the future.

Michael Chapman's notion of value is linked to critical self-reflection on our creative practices.[79] Valorisation of these in the post-colonial era requires that we re-interrogate, re-articulate and move beyond the agitprop slogans of old and 'de-colonise the mind' of the entropy that many new state regulators and their adherents have taken on.[80] As Sachs and Ramgobin pleaded, we need to escape temporal limiting conscriptions and the rhetorical phrases that are misappropriated from the preferred gurus, into which politically correct nonsense is shoehorned. Critique of inherited aesthetics also needs to be re-articulated in terms of ensuring a role for the arts that remains a key contributor to a dialectical public sphere. The interaction of two kinds of implementation (creation, vandalism) did, however, generate public debate, though the defacers themselves hardly engaged in a policy dialectic of the kind envisaged by Ramgobin. The post-apartheid debate thus remains incomplete:

> Things are left buried under the surface in the name of *'wat verby is, is verby'* [what's past is passed], without cathartic verbal discussion, critical reflection and co-enquiring, analysis and the catharsis of verbalization and analysis – delving inside matters, deconstructing, reconstructing, understanding and articulating the meanings and history of things and conveying of ontological verbal enquiries and analysis of feelings and experiences of historical phenomena, present events and living lives at the present and going towards the future.[81]

However, among the frameworks for reconciliation that did occur in the mid-1990s, were Codesa, the Truth and Reconciliation Commission, university restructuring and all the charters, missions and visions in many state and private sectors – squandered under Jacob Zuma's reign of rapacious looting. It is the reminders of these that have fallen from public sight. What the above examples indicate is an ahistorical new class response, one that educators failed to shape adequately, in terms of the complexities and contradictions of history. Different classes respond differently: where frustrated workers burn their civic infrastructure, the middle class largely protect their infrastructure and rather target iconic representations like paintings and statues, while they readily accept the consumerist brandings of Spur and Nando's and the contradictions that accompany them.

Government exists precisely to prevent affairs from getting out of hand: the bureaucrat, for example, is in principle professionally excluded from conducting any kind of business beyond that prescribed by the rules of the agreed-upon process. As Ramgobin pleads, we need to start re-imagining ourselves, self-reflexively rethinking our practices and repositioning our identities as inclusive, rather than as exclusive. The destructive incidents, though rooted in class-bound imagined pasts, linked to a victimology of the present, could have, in Chapman's terms, released a fissure of art and heritage talk about the future. But the future is what we make of it. This was the strategy used by media and cultural workers during apartheid – whether for or against. Cultural policy best practice must engage in a public critical dialogue on names, naming, monuments, artefacts and statues. These should be considered symbolic and material resources open to dis-articulation from crude meanings and re-articulated via creative dialectical engagement into new reconciliatory images and social practices. Transformation cannot be undialectical or monological; it must also be historical and dialogical. This was Ramgobin's contribution, regrettably under-acknowledged, which joined a dialectical activism that leveraged previous path dependencies into a dialogical future, one that Rhodes Must Fall tactically squandered.

NOTES

1. For a brief biography, see 'Mewa Ramgobin', *KZN Literary Tourism*, accessed 2 December 2020, http://www.literarytourism.co.za/index.php?option=com_content&view=article&id=387:mewa-ramgobin&catid=13:authors&Itemid=28
2. A detailed history is elaborated in Keyan G. Tomaselli, 'Arts, Apartheid Struggles, and Cultural Movements', *Safundi* 20, no. 3 (2019): 338–358.
3. Karl Marx and Frederich Engels, *The German Ideology* (London: Lawrence & Wishart, 1970).
4. Guy Willoughby, 'Keyan Tomaselli and the Task of Cultural Criticism', *Journal of Literary Studies* 7, no. 1 (1991): 64–75.
5. See, for example, Poster Book Collective, *Images of Defiance: South African Resistance Posters of the 1990s* (Johannesburg: Ravan Press, 1991).
6. Mathew Arnold, *Culture and Anarchy: An Essay in Political and Social Criticism* (London: Smith, Elder and Co., 1869). Arnold's thesis was predominant in literary and drama programmes during the 1970s: see Lynn Dalrymple, 'Some Thoughts on Identity, Culture and the Curriculum; and the Future of South African Theatre', *South African Theatre Journal* 1, no. 2 (1987): 20–51.
7. Njabulo Ndebele, 'Turkish Tales and Some Thoughts on South African Fiction', *Staffrider* 6, no. 1 (1984): 42–48.
8. Albie Sachs, 'Preparing Ourselves for Freedom: Culture and the ANC Guidelines', *The Drama Review*, 35, no. 1 (1991): 187–193.
9. Eve Bertelsen, 'Phasing the Spring: An Open Letter to Albie Sachs', *Pretexts* 2, no. 2 (1990): 129–136; Geoffrey V. Davis, *Voices of Justice and Reason: Apartheid and Beyond in South African Literature* (Amsterdam: Rodopi, 2003); Pitika Ntuli, 'Fragments under a Telescope: A Response to Albie Sachs', *Third Text* 7, no. 23 (1993): 69–78.
10. Glenn Moss, *The New Radicals and Anti-Apartheid Politics at Wits in the 1970s* (Johannesburg: Jacana Media, 2014). See also Rachel Matteau Matsha, *Real and Imagined Readers: Censorship, Publishing and Reading under Apartheid* (Pietermaritzburg: University of KwaZulu-Natal Press, 2018).
11. Ineke van Kessel, *Beyond Our Wildest Dreams* (Charlottesville: University Press of Virginia, 2000).
12. Louis Althusser, *Lenin and Philosophy and Other Essays* (London: New Left Books, 1971).
13. Antonio Gramsci, *Prison Notebooks* (London: Lawrence & Wishart, 1971). For when, how and in what order Marxist theories travelled to South Africa, see Keyan G. Tomaselli, 'Reading Stuart Hall in Southern Africa', in *Without Guarantees: In Honour of Stuart Hall*, ed. Paul Gilroy, Larry Grossberg and Angela McRobbie (London: Verso, 2000), 375–387.

14 Astrid von Kotze, *Organise & Act: The Natal Workers Theatre Movement 1983–1987* (Durban: Culture and Working Life Publications, 1988).
15 Ian Steadman, 'Towards Popular Theatre in South Africa', in *Politics and Performance: Theatre, Poetry and Song in South Africa*, ed. Liz Gunner (Johannesburg: Wits University Press, 1994); Chantal Mouffe, 'Hegemony and New Political Subjects: Toward a New Concept of Democracy', trans. S. Gray, in *Marxism and the Interpretation of Culture*, ed. Cary Nelson and Larry Grossberg (London: MacMillan Education, 1988).
16 Chantal Mouffe and Ernesto Laclau, *Hegemony and Socialist Strategy* (London: Verso, 1985); Iain McLean and Alistair McMillan, *The Concise Oxford Dictionary of Politics* (Oxford: Oxford University Press, 2003).
17 Ian Steadman, e-mail to author, 25 July 2019.
18 Mouffe, 'Hegemony and New Political Subjects', 89–90.
19 Steadman, 'Towards Popular Theatre'.
20 Robert Mshengu Kavanagh, *Theatre as Cultural Struggle* (London: Zed Books, 2017).
21 See Steadman, 'Towards Popular Theatre'; Kavanagh, *Theatre as Cultural Struggle*.
22 The CCT framework is drawn from Johan Muller and Keyan G. Tomaselli, 'Becoming Appropriately Modern: Towards a Genealogy of Cultural Studies in South Africa', in *Knowledge and Method in the Human Sciences*, ed. Johann Mouton and Dian Joubert (Pretoria: Human Sciences Research Council, 1990).
23 See National Union of South African Students, 'Fifty-Seven Years of NUSAS: Have We Learned Our Lessons?', accessed 2 December 2020, http://psimg.jstor.org/fsi/img/pdf/t0/10.5555/al.sff.document.cnf19811100.026.022.000_final.pdf; Arlene Faranof, 'Nusas 1966–1986: An Introduction', accessed 2 December 2020, http://disa.ukzn.ac.za/sites/default/files/pdf_files/ess20060915.000.026.pdf. Andy Durbach, ed., *Dead in One's Own Lifetime* (Cape Town: Nusas, 1979) was the first publication to emerge from Aquarius.
24 Peter Vale, 'NUSAS, Justice and Rock 'n Roll', *Mail & Guardian*, 8 September 2014, accessed 2 December 2020, https://mg.co.za/article/2014-09-08-nusas-justice-and-rock-n-roll/
25 'Mewa Ramgobin Interviewed by Iain Edwards, Ramgobin's Parliamentary Office, Old Assembly Building, South African Parliament, Cape Town, 3 February 2003', accessed 2 December 2020, https://www.researchgate.net/profile/Iain_Edwards/publication/317106271_Ramgobin_Edwards_Edited_Interview_Transcript_0083203022003/data/5926c16faca27295a8fb9404/008-RAMGOBIN-EDWARDS-EDITED-INTERVIEW-TRANCRIPT.pdf
26 SASO was formed after some members of the University of Natal's black campus's student representative council broke with Nusas. See South African Democracy Education Trust, *The Road to Democracy in South Africa, Volume 2 (1970–1980)* (Pretoria: Unisa Press, 2006), 858–859.
27 Steve Biko, *I Write What I Like: A Selection of His Writings*, ed. Aelred Stubbs (London: Bowerdean Press, 1978).
28 John Saul and Stephen Gelb, *The Crisis in South Africa: Class Defence, Class Revolution* (New York: Monthly Review Press, 1980).
29 Dan O'Meara, *Volkskapitalisme: Class, Capital and Ideology in the Development of Afrikaner Nationalism* (Johannesburg: Ravan Press, 1983). The Broederbond (Brotherhood) was a secret, policy-influential, Calvinist, male organisation in South Africa, dedicated to the advancement of Afrikaner interests.
30 Hans Rompel, *Die Bioskoop in Diens van die Volk* (*Deel I* and *Deel II*) (Bloemfontein: Nasionale Pers, 1942).

31 Rompel, *Die Bioskoop*.
32 Keyan G. Tomaselli and Michael Eckardt, 'Brown-Red Shadows: The Influence of the Third Reich and Soviet Cinema on Afrikaans film', in *Cinema and the Swastika: German Influence over National Film Industries 1933–1945*, ed. Roel Vandewinkel and David Welch (Basingstoke: Palgrave Macmillan, 2007), 231–242.
33 Keyan G. Tomaselli and Mikki van Zyl, 'Themes, Myths and Cultural Indicators: The Structuring of Popular Memories', in *Movies, Moguls, Mavericks: South African Cinema 1979–1991*, ed. Johan Blignaut and Martin Botha (Cape Town: Showdata, 1992), 427–430.
34 O'Meara, *Volkskapitalisme*.
35 Moletsi Mbeki, *Architects of Poverty: Why African Capitalism Needs Changing* (Johannesburg: Picador Africa, 2009); Mark Swilling et al., *Betrayal of the Promise: How South Africa Is Being Stolen*, 2017, accessed 2 December 2020, http://pari.org.za/wp-content/uploads/2017/05/Betrayal-of-the-Promise-25052017.pdf
36 Rick Turner, *The Eye of the Needle* (originally published in 1978), accessed 2 December 2020, https://www.sahistory.org.za/archive/eye-needle-rick-turner. This paragraph is thanks to Glenn Moss, written communication, 22 June 2015.
37 Graham Hayman, 'Class, Race or Culture: Who Is the Enemy? The Botswana Culture and Resistance Conference', *Critical Arts* 2, no. 3 (1983): 33–48.
38 Arts and Culture Task Group, 'Report for the Ministry of Arts, Culture, Science and Technology', 1995. The White Paper deriving from this group was published in 1996, accessed 2 December 2020, http://www.dac.gov.za/content/white-paper-arts-culture-and-heritage; John J. Williams, 'Report of the Arts and Culture Task Group presented to the Minister of Arts, Culture, Science and Technology, June 1995', *Critical Arts* 10, no. 2 (1996): 107–112.
39 Nadine Gordimer, 'Relevance and Commitment: Apprentices of Freedom' (paper delivered at Culture and Resistance Conference, Gaborone, 1982).
40 Sachs, 'Preparing Ourselves for Freedom', 187–188.
41 Hayman, 'Class, Race'.
42 David Bunn and Jane Taylor, eds, *From South Africa: New Writing, Photographs & Art*, special issue of *Triquarterly* 69, 1987. See also William Campschreur and Joost Divendal, eds, *Culture in Another South Africa* (New York: Olive Branch Press, 1987).
43 Republic of South Africa, *Report of the Commission of Inquiry into the Mass Media*, 1981. For a critique of the Commission's use of Gramsci to explain how the black press had become the vanguard of the revolution, see Ruth E. Tomaselli and Keyan G. Tomaselli, '"How to Set Your House in Order": Read All about It in Steyn Commission II', *Critical Arts* 2, no. 3 (1982): 1–22. The Medu Art Ensemble, established in 1977, was composed of exiles living in Gaborone, Botswana. Its sub-groups specialised in music, theatre, graphics and visual arts, photography and research.
44 Donald Guambe and Arnold Shepperson, 'Developing Development Policy Research Programmes: A Focus on the Material Communities of Cultural Practice' (Pretoria: Human Sciences Research Council, 1995). Advising CURED was Australian academic Tom O'Regan – see his article in a special issue he edited, 'Thinking about Policy Utility: Some Aspects of Australian Cultural Policy Development in a South African Context', *Critical Arts* 12, no. 1–2 (1998): 1–23. See also Keyan G. Tomaselli, Arnold Shepperson and Alum Mpofu, 'National Symbols: Cultural Negotiation and Policy beyond Apartheid', *Communicatio* 22, no. 1 (1996): 50–54.
45 Main Committee: HSRC Investigation into Intergroup Relations, *The South African Society: Realities and Future Prospects*. Pretoria: HSRC, 1985.

46 Arnold Shepperson, 'Cultural Studies and Policy Initiatives in South Africa after 1990' (unpublished paper).
47 Mewa Ramgobin, *An Overview of the Freedom Charter: The People Shall Govern* (Durban: Centre for Communication, Media and Society, University of Natal, n.d.). Ramgobin headed the non-European section of the Students' Representative Council at the University Natal. He was the facilitator of Gandhi's passive resistance philosophy in the late 1980s and was banned for 17 years. He recounts his experiences in *Prisms of Light* (East London: iQula Publishing, 2009). See Iain Edwards, ed., *Faith & Courage: The Political Papers of Mewa Ramgobin: Anti-Apartheid and Democracy Struggles South Africa, 1960s to 1994* (Kindle edition, 2016).
48 Mikhail Gorbachev, *Perestroika* (New York: Harper Collins, 1987). Quoted in Mark Kishlansky, ed., *Sources of the West: Readings in Western Civilization*, vol. 2, 4th ed. (New York: Longman 1995), 200.
49 Ian Hunter, 'Bureaucrat, Critic, Citizen: On Some Styles of Ethical Life', *Arena* 2, no. 4 (1993): 80.
50 Tony Bennett, personal communication with author, 23 September 1996. Bennett pioneered cultural policy studies.
51 Charles Malan, 'The Politics of Self and Other in Literary and Cultural Studies: The South African Dilemma', *Journal of Literary Studies* 11, no. 2 (1995): 16–28.
52 Jonathan Sterne, 'Cultural Policy Studies and the Problem of Political Representation', *The Communication Review* 5, no. 1 (2002): 59–89.
53 Ingrid Coetzee and Gerhard-Mark van der Waal, eds, *Conservation of Culture: Changing Context and Challenges: Proceedings of the South African Conference on the Conservation of Culture, Cape Town, 6–10 June 1988*. Pretoria: South African Conference on the Conservation of Culture. The conference was organised by the HSRC, the Department of Environmental Affairs, the National Monuments Council and the South African Society for Cultural History. The irony was that this event opened on the same day as the third renewal of the state of emergency ('Kultuurpolitiek en die Noodtoestand' (Cultural Politics and the State of Emergency), editorial, *Die Suid-Afrikaan*, 16 August 1988: 2). I had been invited, but I made it a condition of my acceptance that Ramgobin be included as my co-presenter.
54 Nicolaas Vergunst, 'Staatsamptenare, Kultuur en die Freedom Charter' (State Officials, Culture and the Freedom Charter), *Die Suid-Afrikaan*, 16 August 1988: 37.
55 Cited in Edwards, *Faith & Courage*.
56 Coetzee and Van der Waal, *Conservation of Culture*, 491–501.
57 Vergunst, 'Staatsamptenare', 37; translated from Afrikaans.
58 'Mewa Ramgobin Interviewed by Iain Edwards'.
59 D.B.J. van Rensburg, 'Pretoria Television Commercial: Post Testing', mimeo (Sandton: The Agency, 1995).
60 For an analysis of this advertisement, see Keyan G. Tomaselli and Arnold Shepperson, '"Pretoria, Here We Come": Re-historicising the Post-Apartheid Future', *Communicatio* 23, no. 2 (1997): 24–33.
61 Genevieve Quintal, 'Mantashe, You Can't Take a Hammer to History', *News24*, 13 April 2015, accessed 2 December 2020, http://www.news24.com/SouthAfrica/News/You-cannot-take-a-hammer-to-history-Mantashe-20150413
62 Alex Holt, 'Political Economy of Racial Stereotyping in Advertising of Reform as an Influence on Advertising', in *Political Economy of Media Transformation in South Africa*, ed. Anthony A. Olorunnisola and Keyan G. Tomaselli (New Jersey: Hampton Press,

63   2011), 45–80. See also Nyasha Mboti, 'Who Is (South) African? A Re-reading of Thabo Mbeki's "I Am an African" Speech in the Context of the Banned (Later Unbanned) Nando's "Diversity" Television Commercial', *Communicatio* 39, no. 4 (2013): 449–465.
64   Mewa Ramgobin, one-page mimeo in possession of the author, untitled, undated.
65   Arnold Shepperson, 'Can SA Culture be Cured?' *Subtext* 5 (1996): 1–4, accessed 28 May 2020, http://ccms.ukzn.ac.za/files/articles/Publications/sub%20text%20no.%205,%201996.pdf
66   Mewa Ramgobin, one-page mimeo in possession of the author, untitled, undated.
67   ANC cultural policy, as issued by Ramgobin on behalf of the Department of Arts and Culture, Southern Natal region.
68   ANC cultural policy, as issued by Ramgobin on behalf of the Department of Arts and Culture, Southern Natal region.
69   Rhodes Must Fall Movement, *Rhodes Must Fall: The Struggle to Decolonise the Racist Heart of Empire* (London: Zed Books, 2018).
70   Jonathan Jansen, *Leading for Change: Race, Intimacy and Leadership in Divided University Campuses* (London: Routledge, 2016). See also Jonathan Jansen, 'There Is a Terrifying Silence in the Storm over Statues', *Rand Daily Mail*, 8 April 2015.
71   Andrew Nash, *The Dialectical Tradition in South Africa* (London: Routledge, 2009).
72   Willemien Marais and Johann de Wet, 'The Reitz Video: Inviting Outrage and/or Pity?' *Communitas* 14 (2009): 27–42.
73   ANC cultural policy, as issued by Ramgobin on behalf of the Department of Arts and Culture, Southern Natal region.
74   Pitika Ntuli noted: 'When I see a statue fall, I see someone destroying a precious work. These statues that we do not want in public, let us have a sculpture garden where people can go to learn about history.' Pitika Ntuli, 'The Bone Connector', *Sunday Times*, 21 June 2020, 19.
75   G.L. Abrams, *The Art of Advertising* (New York: Harry N. Abrams, 1977).
76   My thanks to Alex Holt for these observations.
77   Natasha N. Distiller, *Shakespeare and the Coconuts: On Post-Apartheid South African Culture* (Johannesburg: Wits University Press, 2012); Farieda Nazier, 'Beyond the "After Math": Exploring Psychological Decolonisation in a Post-Apartheid Context of Artistic Praxis', *Critical Arts* 28, no. 2 (2014): 199–215. See also Michael Chapman, 'To Be a Coconut? Thoughts Provoked by Natasha Distiller's *Shakespeare and the Coconuts: On Post-Apartheid South African Culture*', *Critical Arts* 28, no. 2 (2014): 165–177; Derek Hooks, *(Post) Apartheid Conditions* (London: Palgrave, 2013).
78   Zimitri Erasmus, *Race Otherwise: Forging a New Humanism for South Africa* (Johannesburg: Wits University Press, 2017).
79   Williams, 'Report of the Arts and Culture Task Group', 107–112.
80   Michael Chapman, *Art Talk, Politics Talk* (Pietermaritzburg: University of KwaZulu-Natal Press, 2006).
81   Ngũgĩ wa Thiong'o, *Decolonising the Mind* (London: James Currey, 1986).
   Nash, *The Dialectical Tradition*, 185.

REFERENCES

Abrams, G.L. *The Art of Advertising*. New York: Harry N. Abrams, 1977.
Althusser, Louis. *Lenin and Philosophy and Other Essays*. London: New Left Books, 1971.
Arnold, Matthew. *Culture and Anarchy: An Essay in Political and Social Criticism*. London: Smith, Elder and Co., 1869.

Arts and Culture Task Group. 'Report for the Ministry of Arts, Culture, Science and Technology'. 1995.
Bertelsen, Eve. 'Phasing the Spring: An Open Letter to Albie Sachs'. *Pretexts* 2, no. 2 (1990): 129–136.
Biko, Steve. *I Write What I Like: A Selection of His Writings.* Edited by Aelred Stubbs. London: Bowerdean Press, 1978.
Bunn, David and Jane Taylor, eds. *From South Africa: New Writing, Photographs & Art.* Special issue of *Triquarterly* 69 (1987).
Campschreur, William and Joost Divendal, eds. *Culture in Another South Africa.* New York: Olive Branch Press, 1987.
Chapman, Michael. *Art Talk, Politics Talk.* Pietermaritzburg: University of KwaZulu-Natal Press, 2006.
Chapman, Michael. 'To Be a Coconut? Thoughts Provoked by Natasha Distiller's *Shakespeare and the Coconuts: On Post-Apartheid South African Culture*'. *Critical Arts* 28, no. 2 (2014): 165–177.
Coetzee, Ingrid and Gerhard-Mark van der Waal, eds. *Conservation of Culture: Changing Context and Challenges: Proceedings of the South African Conference on the Conservation of Culture, Cape Town, 6–10 June 1988.* Pretoria: South African Conference on the Conservation of Culture.
Dalrymple, Lynn. 'Some Thoughts on Identity, Culture and the Curriculum; and the Future of South African Theatre'. *South African Theatre Journal* 1, no. 2 (1987): 20–51.
Davis, Geoffrey V. *Voices of Justice and Reason: Apartheid and Beyond in South African Literature.* Amsterdam: Rodopi, 2003.
Distiller, Natasha N. *Shakespeare and the Coconuts: On Post-Apartheid South African Culture.* Johannesburg: Wits University Press, 2012.
Durbach, Andy, ed. *Dead in One's Own Lifetime.* Cape Town: Nusas, 1979.
Edwards, Iain, ed. *Faith & Courage: The Political Papers of Mewa Ramgobin: Anti-Apartheid and Democracy Struggles South Africa, 1960s to 1994.* Kindle edition, 2016.
Erasmus, Zimitri. *Race Otherwise: Forging a New Humanism for South Africa.* Johannesburg: Wits University Press, 2017.
Faranof, Arlene. 'Nusas 1966–1986: An Introduction'. Accessed 2 December 2020. http://disa.ukzn.ac.za/sites/default/files/pdf_files/ess20060915.000.026.pdf
Gorbachev, Mikhail. *Perestroika.* New York: Harper Collins, 1987.
Gordimer, Nadine. 'Relevance and Commitment: Apprentices of Freedom'. Paper delivered at Culture and Resistance Conference, Gaborone, 1982.
Gramsci, Antonio. *Prison Notebooks.* London: Lawrence & Wishart, 1971.
Guambe, Donald and Arnold Shepperson. 'Developing Development Policy Research Programmes: A Focus on the Material Communities of Cultural Practice'. Pretoria: Human Sciences Research Council, 1995.
Hayman, Graham. 'Class, Race or Culture: Who is the Enemy? The Botswana Culture and Resistance Conference'. *Critical Arts* 2, no. 3 (1983): 33–48.
Holt, Alex. 'Political Economy of Racial Stereotyping in Advertising of Reform as an Influence on Advertising'. In *Political Economy of Media Transformation in South Africa*, edited by Anthony A. Olorunnisola and Keyan G. Tomaselli, 45–80. New Jersey: Hampton Press, 2011.
Hooks, Derek. *(Post) apartheid Conditions.* London: Palgrave, 2013.
Hunter, Ian. 'Bureaucrat, Critic, Citizen: On Some Styles of Ethical Life'. *Arena* 2, no. 4 (1993): 77–102.

Jansen, Jonathan. *Leading for Change: Race, Intimacy and Leadership in Divided University Campuses*. London: Routledge, 2016.
Jansen, Jonathan. 'There Is a Terrifying Silence in the Storm over Statues'. *Rand Daily Mail*, 8 April 2015.
Kavanagh, Robert M. *Theatre as Cultural Struggle*. London: Zed Books, 2017.
Kishlansky, Mark, ed. *Sources of the West: Readings in Western Civilization*. Volume 2, 4th edition. New York: Longman, 1995.
'Kultuurpolitiek en die Noodtoestand' (Cultural Politics and the State of Emergency). Editorial. *Die Suid-Afrikaan*, 16 August 1988.
Main Committee, HSRC Investigation into Intergroup Relations. *The South African Society: Realities and Future Prospects*. Pretoria: HSRC, 1985.
Malan, Charles. 'The Politics of Self and Other in Literary and Cultural Studies: The South African Dilemma'. *Journal of Literary Studies* 11, no. 2 (1995): 16–28.
Marais, Willemien and Johann de Wet. 'The Reitz Video: Inviting Outrage and/or Pity?' *Communitas* 14 (2009): 27–42.
Marx, Karl and Frederick Engels. *The German Ideology*. London: Lawrence & Wishart, 1970.
Matsha, Rachel Matteau. *Real and Imagined Readers: Censorship, Publishing and Reading under Apartheid*. Pietermaritzburg: University of KwaZulu-Natal Press, 2018.
Mbeki, Moletsi. *Architects of Poverty: Why African Capitalism Needs Changing*. Johannesburg: Picador Africa, 2009.
Mboti, Nyasha. 'Who Is (South) African? A Re-reading of Thabo Mbeki's "I Am an African" Speech in the Context of the Banned (Later Unbanned) Nandos "Diversity" Television Commercial'. *Communicatio* 39, no. 4 (2013): 449–465.
McLean, Iain and Alistair McMillan. *The Concise Oxford Dictionary of Politics*. Oxford: Oxford University Press, 2003.
'Mewa Ramgobin'. *KZN Literary Tourism*. Accessed 2 December 2020. http://www.literary-tourism.co.za/index.php?option=com_content&view=article&id=387:mewa-ramgobin&catid=13:authors&Itemid=28
'Mewa Ramgobin Interviewed by Iain Edwards, Ramgobin's Parliamentary Office, Old Assembly Building, South African Parliament, Cape Town, 3 February 2003'. Accessed 2 December 2020. https://www.researchgate.net/profile/Iain_Edwards/publication/317106271_Ramgobin_Edwards_Edited_Interview_Transcript_0083203022003/data/5926c16faca27295a8fb9404/008-RAMGOBIN-EDWARDS-EDITED-INTERVIEW-TRANCRIPT.pdf
Moss, Glenn. *The New Radicals and Anti-Apartheid Politics at Wits in the 1970s*. Johannesburg: Jacana Media, 2014.
Mouffe, Chantal. 'Hegemony and New Political Subjects: Toward a New Concept of Democracy'. Translated by S. Gray. In *Marxism and the Interpretation of Culture*, edited by Cary Nelson and Larry Grossberg. London: MacMillan Education, 1988.
Mouffe, Chantal and Ernesto Laclau. *Hegemony and Socialist Strategy*. London: Verso, 1985.
Muller, Johan and Keyan G. Tomaselli. 'Becoming Appropriately Modern: Towards a Genealogy of Cultural Studies in South Africa'. In *Knowledge and Method in the Human Sciences*, edited by Johann Mouton and Dian Joubert. Pretoria: Human Sciences Research Council, 1990.
Nash, Andrew. *The Dialectical Tradition in South Africa*. London: Routledge, 2009.
National Union of South African Students. 'Fifty-Seven Years of NUSAS: Have We Learned Our Lessons?' Accessed 2 December 2020. http://psimg.jstor.org/fsi/img/pdf/t0/10.5555/al.sff.document.cnf19811100.026.022.000_final.pdf

Nazier, Farieda. 'Beyond the "After Math": Exploring Psychological Decolonisation in a Post-Apartheid Context of Artistic Praxis'. *Critical Arts* 28, no. 2 (2014): 199–215.

Ndebele, Njabulo. 'Turkish Tales and Some Thoughts on South African Fiction'. *Staffrider* 6, no. 1 (1984): 42–48.

Ngũgĩ wa Thiong'o. *Decolonising the Mind*. London: James Currey, 1986.

Ntuli, Pitika. 'The Bone Connector'. *Sunday Times*, 21 June 2020, 19.

Ntuli, Pitika. 'Fragments under a Telescope: A Response to Albie Sachs'. *Third Text* 7, no. 23 (1993): 69–78.

O'Meara, Dan. *Volkskapitalisme: Class, Capital and Ideology in the Development of Afrikaner Nationalism*. Johannesburg: Ravan Press, 1983.

O'Regan, Tom. 'Thinking about Policy Utility: Some Aspects of Australian Cultural Policy Development in a South African Context'. *Critical Arts* 12, no. 1–2 (1998): 1–23. Special issue, edited by Tom O'Regan.

Poster Book Collective. *Images of Defiance: South African Resistance Posters of the 1990s*. Johannesburg: Ravan Press, 1991.

Quintal, Genevieve. 'Mantashe, You Can't Take a Hammer to History'. *News24*, 13 April 2015. Accessed 2 December 2020. http://www.news24.com/SouthAfrica/News/You-cannot-take-a-hammer-to-history-Mantashe-20150413

Ramgobin, Mewa. *An Overview of the Freedom Charter: The People Shall Govern*. Durban: Centre for Communication, Media and Society, University of Natal, n.d.

Ramgobin, Mewa. *Prisms of Light*. East London: iQula Publishing, 2009.

Republic of South Africa. *Report the Commission of Inquiry into the Mass Media*. 1981.

Rhodes Must Fall Movement. *Rhodes Must Fall: The Struggle to Decolonise the Racist Heart of Empire*. London: Zed Books, 2018.

Rompel, Hans. *Die Bioskoop in Diens van die Volk. Deel I* and *Deel II*. Bloemfontein: Nasionale Pers, 1942.

Sachs, Albie. 'Preparing Ourselves for Freedom: Culture and the ANC Guidelines'. *The Drama Review* 35, no. 1 (1991): 187–193.

Saul, John and Stephen Gelb. *The Crisis in South Africa: Class Defence, Class Revolution*. New York: Monthly Review Press, 1980.

Shepperson, Arnold. 'Can SA Culture be Cured?' *Subtext* 5 (1996): 1–4. Accessed 28 May 2020. http://ccms.ukzn.ac.za/files/articles/Publications/sub%20text%20no.%205,%20 1996.pdf.

Shepperson, Arnold. 'Cultural Studies and Policy Initiatives in South Africa after 1990'. Unpublished paper.

South African Democracy Education Trust. *The Road to Democracy in South Africa, Volume 2 (1970–1980)*. Pretoria: Unisa Press, 2006.

Steadman, Ian. 'Towards Popular Theatre in South Africa'. In *Politics and Performance: Theatre, Poetry and Song in South Africa*, edited by Liz Gunner, 11–34. Johannesburg: Wits University Press, 1994.

Sterne, Jonathan. 'Cultural Policy Studies and the Problem of Political Representation'. *The Communication Review* 5, no. 1 (2002): 59–89.

Swilling, Mark, Bhorat Haroon, Mbongiseni Buthelezi, Ivor Chipkin, Sikhulekile Duma, Lumkile Mondi, Camaren Peter, Mzukisi Qobo and Hannah Friedenstein. *Betrayal of the Promise: How South Africa Is Being Stolen*. 2017. Accessed 2 December 2020. http://pari.org.za/wp-content/uploads/2017/05/Betrayal-of-the-Promise-25052017.pdf

Tomaselli, Keyan G. 'Arts, Apartheid Struggles, and Cultural Movements'. *Safundi* 20, no. 3 (2019): 338–358.

Tomaselli, Keyan G. 'Reading Stuart Hall in Southern Africa'. In *Without Guarantees: in Honour of Stuart Hall*, edited by Paul Gilroy, Larry Grossberg and Angela McRobbie, 375–387. London: Verso, 2000.

Tomaselli, Keyan G. and Michael Eckardt. 'Brown-Red Shadows: The Influence of the Third Reich and Soviet Cinema on Afrikaans Film'. In *Cinema and the Swastika: German Influence over National Film Industries 1933–1945*, edited by Roel Vandewinkel and David Welch, 231–242. Basingstoke: Palgrave Macmillan, 2007.

Tomaselli, Keyan G. and Arnold Shepperson. '"Pretoria, Here We Come": Re-historicising the Post-Apartheid Future'. *Communicatio* 23, no. 2 (1997): 24–33.

Tomaselli, Keyan G., Arnold Shepperson and Alum Mpofu. 'National Symbols: Cultural Negotiation and Policy beyond Apartheid'. *Communicatio* 22, no. 1 (1996): 50–54.

Tomaselli, Keyan G. and Mikki van Zyl. 'Themes, Myths and Cultural Indicators: The Structuring of Popular Memories'. In *Movies, Moguls, Mavericks: South African Cinema 1979–1991*, edited by Johan Blignaut and Martin Botha, 427–430. Cape Town: Showdata, 1992.

Tomaselli, Ruth E. and Keyan G. Tomaselli. '"How to Set Your House in Order": Read All about it in Steyn Commission II'. *Critical Arts* 2, no. 3 (1982): 1–22.

Turner, Rick. *The Eye of the Needle*. Originally published in 1978. Accessed 2 December 2020. https://www.sahistory.org.za/archive/eye-needle-rick-turner

Vale, Peter. 'NUSAS, Justice and Rock 'n Roll'. *Mail & Guardian*, 8 September 2014. Accessed 2 December 2020. https://mg.co.za/article/2014-09-08-nusas-justice-and-rock-n-roll/

Van Kessel, Ineke. *Beyond Our Wildest Dreams*. Charlottesville: University Press of Virginia, 2000.

Van Rensburg, D.B.J. 'Pretoria Television Commercial: Post Testing'. Mimeo. Sandton: The Agency, 1995.

Vergunst, Nicolaas. 'Staatsamptenare, Kultuur en die Freedom Charter' (State Officials, Culture and the Freedom Charter). *Die Suid-Afrikaan*, 16 August 1988.

Von Kotze, Astrid. *Organise & Act: The Natal Workers Theatre Movement 1983–1987*. Durban: Culture and Working Life Publications, 1988.

Williams, John J. 'Report of the Arts and Culture Task Group presented to the Minister of Arts, Culture, Science and Technology, June 1995'. *Critical Arts* 10, no. 2 (1996): 107–112.

Willoughby, Guy. 'Keyan Tomaselli and the Task of Cultural Criticism'. *Journal of Literary Studies* 7, no. 1 (1991): 64–75.

CHAPTER

7

'*Kaalgat* Critique': The Public Intellectualism of Koos Roets as Afrikaans Satirist

Anna-Marié Jansen van Vuuren

[An] uncomfortable presence ... who brings disruption and conflict ... that is what intellectuals are for.

— Tony Judt (cited in Posner 2003)

Public intellectuals have long used and engaged with the arts to communicate ideas about power, identity and society. John Issit and Duncan Jackson discuss the difficulty of trying to determine the role of a public intellectual: 'I am looking for what the public intellectual might be, what it might become, its tensions, its changes, its history, its roles and its ideological condition.'[1] They are quite clear that confining the term 'public intellectual' to its Oxford Dictionary description of 'an intellectual who expresses views intended to a general audience' is a narrow definition, 'which lacks explanatory precision on the one hand' and is 'excessively restrictive in scope on the other.'[2] In propagating a less restrictive use of the term 'public intellectual', I argue that two films directed by Koos Roets can be considered a form of 'symbolic goods' that disrupted the status quo within the Afrikaner community.[3]

Roets is not known as a critically engaging media presence, or for writing thought-provoking criticism in newspaper columns (like many of the other public intellectuals discussed in this book). However, as a cinematographer he made immense contributions to films by dissident film-makers Jans Rautenbach and

Emil Nofal that would change the course of the South African film industry. The films he collaborated on as a writer, cinematographer and director received attention from scholars, critics and general film audiences. In considering these films, I posit with other scholars that the term 'public intellectual' could be broadened to include verbal or published goods that make a contribution to other individuals' thinking.[4] Therefore, I propose it is not Roets's public persona that deserves to be credited with being a public intellectual; rather, it is that his films are symbolic goods that have contributed to the public sphere, as well as the history of South African film.

To construct this argument, I refer to two feature films Roets directed: *Die Groen Faktor* (The Green Factor, 1984) and *Kaalgat tussen die Daisies* (Naked among the daisies, 1997).[5] These films were created and released 13 years apart and I read them as demonstrating Roets's approach within two different socio-historical contexts. The films selected for analysis in this chapter constitute a mere sample of Roets's *oeuvre* that uses satire to prick people's consciences and challenge the powerful notions within so-called Afrikaner society. I would argue that he is like a poker player: with a poker face he never openly speaks against the grain of Afrikaner society, but rather uses his cards to speak for him.

ROETS'S SYMBOLIC CAPITAL AND SUCCESSFUL ENTRY INTO THE INDUSTRY

Matthys Jacobus (Koos) Roets left his education studies midway for a low-ranking assistant position at Jamie Uys Films in 1962, where he was trained in the camera department by cinematographer Judex Viljoen and technician David Mashilo. After assisting on a variety of documentaries and feature films, he graduated as a camera operator working on international features at SA Film Studios in Lonehill, Johannesburg.

Roets gives credit to film-makers Jans Rautenbach and Emil Nofal as great mentors and collaborators who would have a lasting influence on his film career. Nofal was of Lebanese origin and often at the receiving end of apartheid laws, since Lebanese people were classified as 'non-white' for a certain time during this era.[6] In the late 1960s Nofal first got backlash with his bilingual film *Wild Season*, which featured black actors prominently in leading roles.[7] At around the same time, Rautenbach drew contempt from the Publications Control Board for his film *Katrina*.[8] Based on the stage play *Try for White* by Basil Warner, it tells the story of a 'coloured' woman who pretends to be white in segregated South Africa. Then came the groundbreaking *Jannie Totsiens* (Jannie Goodbye), a psychological thriller that allegorises Afrikaners as being trapped in a psychiatric institution because of their ideological beliefs.[9] Because of these films Rautenbach has been described as the only film-maker of the so-called Sestigers ('Sixty-ers') who, in a similar way as his literary counterparts, challenged apartheid policy and contributed to the intellectual struggle of the Afrikaner.[10]

Rautenbach credits Roets's cinematography as one of the distinguishing factors making *Jannie Totsiens* an avant-garde art film.[11] Rautenbach and Roets's experiment garnered attention from intellectuals and has been described as comparable to its international counterparts of the time.[12] After *Jannie Totsiens*, Roets did the cinematography for director Manie van Rensburg's first feature film, *Freddie's in Love* (1971).[13] Although Roets would continue to collaborate with Rautenbach and other notable directors throughout the 1970s, he also began directing his own feature films in the same period, beginning with *Die Erfgenaam* (The Heir Apparent) in 1971.[14]

Moving with ease from behind the camera to the director's chair, Roets is one of the most diverse film-makers in the South African film and television industry, with skills ranging from lighting to editing. Though Roets observed many directors closely while serving as their cinematographers, in a personal interview he emphasised that with the exception of his mentor, Rautenbach, he learnt more from these directors in terms of how *not* to direct a good film.[15]

According to Ken Dancyger: 'Each director has a distinct personality that makes the work of that director different from the work of others, depending on the character, beliefs, and interests of that specific filmmaker.'[16] Actors working with Roets as a director, from Cobus Rossouw to Sandra Prinsloo, describe him as a quiet and contemplative director, driven by a desire to use engaging images to tell stories. This skill has led to his direction of television series and films that still stand out in the Afrikaans entertainment *oeuvre*, such as *Koöperasiestories, Die Mannheim-Sage, Die Mannakwalanners, Kootjie Emmer* and *Faan se Trein*.[17]

In most of these productions Roets collaborated with talented authors such as P.G. du Plessis, Pieter Fourie and Jeanne Goosen. But in many cases he adapted and reworked their stories into suitable screenplays. Thereafter he had to elicit strong performances from actors, co-ordinate the *mise en scène*, choreograph character blocking and navigate between the commercial expectations often created by both producers and audiences. Roets uses all of these to create the wonder of the moving picture, the same wonder he experienced many decades ago when he used cardboard and a candle to project moving images on the wall of his school hostel.

DIE GROEN FAKTOR (THE GREEN FACTOR)

Die Groen Faktor was made in the politically tumultuous context of 1980s' South Africa. Released one year prior to the state of emergency declared in 1985, the film uses fantasy and satire to parody the apartheid state. The film's narrative premise is centred on a white Afrikaans politician in the National Party who has aspirations to become a Cabinet minister. However, when Koos Visagie's skin literally begins to turn green after an accident with a bowl of green punch, it creates a political dilemma: in a segregated South Africa (where race and white supremacy are dominant features of society) a 'green' person could never be elected as a parliamentarian.[18] In his widely acclaimed publication *The Cinema of Apartheid* (1989), Keyan G. Tomaselli (himself a public intellectual in his own right) wrote about this film: '*Die Groen Faktor* is a hardhitting satire ... in which the "greens" are ostracized by white Afrikaners who classify them [as] "non-white". The malady is contagious and eventually even the prime minister turns green. His solution: "The question is, what are we going to do with the whites?"'[19]

The story idea behind the *Die Groen Faktor* originally came from Roets's longtime collaborator Emil Nofal.[20] He had previously written successful comedies such as *Rip van Wyk*, *Lord Oom Piet* and *Kimberley Jim*.[21] Nofal found the English-Afrikaans rivalry between white South Africans a successful filmic trope and wanted to continue along that vein. According to Roets, Nofal initially wanted to make the film with either Jamie Uys or his then partner Jans Rautenbach; however, after a fallout with the latter, the film never came to fruition. When the producer Paul Raleigh (then affiliated to the company Heyns Films) asked Roets to direct a film for them, he immediately recalled Nofal's story.[22]

Although Nofal and Marie du Toit were immediately contracted to write a screenplay, because of timelines they did not have a completed script when they went into production. According to Roets, this was the norm, rather than an exception, in the film industry of those days. In an interview, the lead actor of the film, Cobus Rossouw, complained to me that it was precisely this lack of completed and polished screenplays that plagued the industry at that point: 'Production companies were in too much of a hurry to release a film and claim the subsidy. Thus, they often neglected the most important part: the script.'[23] According to Rossouw, an unfinished script also plagued him with director Manie van Rensburg's film *Die Square*, in which he portrayed a staunch nationalist (similar to Roets's character of Koos Visagie).[24] As Roets only received the pages of dialogue the evening before the next day's shoot, he would then have to decide within limited time what would work and whether any of the scenes needed additional writing. If he thought a scene needed a rewrite, he would brainstorm it with Nofal again, especially in terms of its significance and contribution to the overall narrative.

Despite its edgy theme that criticised apartheid, *Die Groen Faktor* fared much better than Rautenbach's *Broer Matie*, which was released in the same year and likewise exposed Afrikaner hypocrisy, albeit in the church. Knowing what Nofal achieved with *Die Kandidaat*, where he is credited as screenwriter alongside Rautenbach, one might not be surprised by his deliberate political approach in *Die Groen Faktor*.[25] Still, in the 1980s, when censorship was rife and many anti-apartheid films were made underground, there is something to be said for the tenacity of the daring white male team behind the production.[26] In a time where deplorable Afrikaans films were being made because of the state subsidy, *Die Groen Faktor* is one that producer Paul Raleigh fondly remembers as an exception.[27]

The film opens with unnerving music over a static visual of a mountain. It is overlaid by the names of the lead cast centred in the middle of the screen. The opening sequence is reminiscent of Stanley Kubric's thriller *The Shining* and smoothly transitions from a panning shot of the mountain, accompanied by eerie music to an upbeat musical track, as a green Lotus motorcar drives down the mountainous road into the fictitious town Meyersburg.[28] The vehicle's green colour semiotically foreshadows and gives a comic wink to the colour that would become the nightmare of many of the film's characters. Thus Roets uses colour as a semiotic sign in his *mise en scène* and the colour of the car is 'not at all arbitrary or anarchic'.[29]

Meyersburg is having a traditional *plattelandse kermis* or *kerkbasaar* (rural church fair), aesthetically reminiscent of the glory days of farms and small towns in South Africa. Most notable in this scene is how Roets references the political tension experienced by South Africans in the 1980s by visually illustrating the divide among the townsfolk: on the one side are the followers of the National Party (NP) and on the other side the more liberal supporters of the Progressive Federal Party (PFP).

Inside the church hall, at the time socially considered to be the 'castle' equivalent of small-town society, the NP caucus is having a heated debate about selecting their candidate for the next by-election. After some swindling on the part of the main character, Koos Visagie (portrayed by Cobus Rossouw), and his close ally Hannes Jooste (George Ballot), Visagie gets elected as the NP candidate. Their challenge at this point is to create a sense of belonging and solidarity among the rest of the town – and, of course, to get Koos Visagie elected.

The members of the caucus come out of the building and prepare to announce their new candidate to the people at the fair – notably against the blue and orange backdrop of the NP's colours. Visagie decides to steal the thunder of the other party's candidate, William Honniball (Graham Armitage), who is at the time busy making his own speech to his constituency.[30] One of Visagie's henchmen cuts off the sound system, thereby interrupting Honniball's speech. Honniball is quick to counter-attack and Visagie finds that after the first few opening lines of his own speech (in which he notably wants to present his five-point plan for South Africa's race policy), his speech is drowned out by music on the PFP's public address system.

After an altercation between the two opposing candidates, Honniball climbs into his car and (accidentally) drives over Koos's foot. While Koos is jumping up and down from the pain, a bowl of green punch is spilled over the same foot. This serves as the inciting incident of the narrative and sets in motion the series of events that ultimately change the fictitious South African society setting of the film. At home that evening, Koos puts his foot up on the coffee table and inspects his injury. His big toe appears to be turning green. Following doctor's orders, he goes to bed and as an audience member one can but guess that he is hoping that the toe will be less green in the morning. However, the next day Koos witnesses how the greenness has spread from his toe to the rest of the foot. The discolouration of his skin from white to green will continue throughout the rest of the narrative until Koos's skin colour (as with many of the other characters) is entirely green at the end of the film.[31] Colour thus serves a mode of communication and postmodern device within the film.[32]

When analysing *Die Groen Faktor*, one needs to consider the context within which this film was made, notably at a time when Afrikaans films 'unabashedly and predominantly served Afrikaner nationalism'.[33] Martin Botha argues that in most cases these film-makers merely appropriated the themes and motifs of the Afrikaner nationalistic narrative, instead of 'interrogating the philosophical assumptions on which the order was based'.[34] However, when considering David Rodowick's statement that 'all films are ideological', Chris Broodryk affirms the potential power of Afrikaans cinema: '[It] has the capacity to shape and inform cultural memory of both past and present, acknowledging how social and cultural processes interact with memory and perception.'[35] I regard the following scene from *Die Groen Faktor* as a case in point.

The morning after Koos is nominated as NP candidate, the country's prime minister phones him. Apart from congratulating him, the prime minister also emphasises that 'the party' must remain in control of the constituency. Thereafter Koos's friend Hannes arrives to advise him on his political strategy. Hannes explains to Koos that the word 'apartheid' has fallen out of favour and that the emphasis is now on 'collaboration' between the different races. The dialogue in this scene serves to illustrate the political discourse taking place in South African society at the time.[36] Instead of paying attention to what Hannes is saying, Koos is worrying about his toe and comments on a case of wine he acquired at an auction. When Hannes berates him for this, the stubborn Koos argues that there is nothing that he can be taught about the new dispensation: 'I know my sales pitch. After all, I'm a car salesman – acquiring votes should be child's play.'[37] This scene reveals how ignorant NP politicians believed their voters to be. Satirical humour is used to subvert the country's dominant centre of authority – the government.

Released at a time in South Africa when censors cut up films and banned music, literature and almost any form of popular culture that criticised the ruling NP, one might have expected the film to be banned.[38] Nonetheless, Roets's use of comedic punchlines and sharp wit left audiences smiling while planting a seed of unease about the absurdities of the apartheid regime.[39] The film's narrative functioned in a way 'to short-circuit the dominant culture's repressive impulses' and I therefore argue that Roets created an intellectual product that drew attention to issues within society, exposed the errors and absurdity of the government's racial policy and ignited public debate.[40]

For many a South African child watching the film, it was their first awakening to the 'ideology of race', as Sallas de Jager, writer and producer behind thought-provoking feature films such as *Roepman*, *Verraaiers* and *Free State*, explains: 'I watched *Die Groen Faktor* as a small boy on the platteland. It literally changed my life. It portrays the political questions of the time realistically and with humour, without taking away of the seriousness of the issue.'[41] The film has been revisited by journalists and political commentators, including John Scott, who wrote in an opinion column titled 'We'll All Be Green in the End, if Life Imitates Art': 'Helen Zille's announcement in Kroonstad that the DA is a party for "blue people" reminds me of a time when many South Africans turned green. It happened in a movie, one of the funniest I've seen, poking fun at racism at a time when you did so at your own peril.'[42]

Die Groen Faktor is not flawless and has been criticised for its ending, in which 'the ethnic solution prevails'.[43] Accenting the oddities of the characters and film's narrative, the film-makers employed magical realism as a plot device.[44] Initially the 'green epidemic' is blamed on Honniball's punch. The drink's key ingredient is a green potion that had been passed on from generation to generation in Honniball's family. However, most of the characters who turned green did not come into contact with the punch. Whether through osmosis or any other magical trope, at the end of the story there are so many green citizens that they form a different population group and Koos establishes his own political party, the Green Party.[45] He is joined by the prime minister, who has also changed skin colour. During a fiery political meeting, the prime minister announces: 'The green people are ... we know, are here to stay. The question is now: what to do with the white people?'[46] Scott argues that this foreshadows the complexity of race issues that the government still grapples with more than 20 years after the end of apartheid: 'Sometimes I think the ANC hierarchy asks the same question: What to do with us whiteys?'[47]

Roets not only poked fun at the NP's emphasis on racial purity, but also at the so-called race question. When Koos's black employee Lukas (portrayed by Timmy Kwebulana) turns green as well, Koos refuses to accept that they are now on an equal footing. He explains to Lukas, 'Hell, no, you're dark green, I'm light green. There's a helluva difference.'[48] This references the 'colour question' that was first touched on by Nofal and Rautenbach in *Die Kandidaat* and *Katrina*, which Rautenbach revisited in *Broer Matie*.

While *Broer Matie* was criticised by audiences for being 'too heavy-handed' in terms of its complex theme, *Die Groen Faktor* was 'financially successful because [it] appealed to the traditional Afrikaner cinema audience in terms of narrative, aesthetic and quality of production'.[49] The film might be traditional in these ways, but it questioned the ideology of race and apartheid in a way that was easier for audiences to understand than Rautenbach's *Jannie Totsiens* – an avant-garde film that followed an unconventional storytelling and aesthetic approach.[50] In *Die Groen Faktor*, Roets's Koos Visagie supposedly 'ticks all the boxes': he is an NP candidate, identifies with Afrikaner culture and espouses the 'values' of the Afrikaner while believing in the ideology of Afrikanerdom. But, because his skin colour becomes green, he is reclassified as 'non-white' and cannot serve in the NP government.

Though he is assured by his friend Hannes that *'een keer 'n Afrikaner, altyd 'n Afrikaner'* (once an Afrikaner, always an Afrikaner), Koos is ostracised by the same community that previously had supported him as their mayoral candidate. He is forcefully removed from his house and required to become a gardener in order to stay in the servant's quarters. Still, Koos stubbornly defends the apartheid policy to the PFP leader, Honniball. Koos only comes to the realisation of the detrimental aspects of the policy when he is forced to acquire a pass in order to move around in the white neighbourhood. Thus, fantastical elements (such as the character literally turning green) are used to present to the audience the absurdity and chaos resulting from their commonly held beliefs.[51]

Because of Roets's probing use of satire in criticising the apartheid system, *Die Groen Faktor* fits Richard Posner's description of public intellectual goods as entertainment goods – as Posner says: 'I am not such a killjoy as to disparage intellectuals for entertaining an audience.'[52] Because of the criticism of the film's open ending, one could consider Lance Olsen's distinction between traditional and postmodern satire and classify the film as the latter.[53] Astrid Klocke says: 'Whereas traditional satire relies on clear and unmistakable references to the reader's world to make the correction effective, postmodern humour leaves these references open to interpretation.'[54] Furthermore, as Tomaselli argues, *Die Groen Faktor* falls into the category of the more commercially orientated films made in the period: 'These more commercially orientated films constitute the majority of films made and are therefore seen to reflect more accurately the mass psychology and social orientations of a society than the less popular serious or art movie.'[55]

While the 'mind circus' of apartheid's racial ideology was explored in this first film under discussion, the second deals with fluid sexuality and the church.

KAALGAT TUSSEN DIE DAISIES (NAKED AMONG THE DAISIES)

Set in post-apartheid South Africa, *Kaalgat tussen die Daisies* explores a Dutch Reformed minister's fall from grace. When he is thrown out of his church, he is coerced into a job as the manager of a 'gentleman's club' (actually a strip club). What follows is a humorous account of his encounters with the 'unsavoury' elements of society that many a *volksmoeder* (mother of the nation) would have warned against. These include gangsters, strippers, cross-dressers and, of course, the upstanding Afrikaans men who frequent venues of ill repute.

In his book about the history of Afrikaans film, critic Leon van Nierop describes *Kaalgat tussen die Daisies* as the low point for Afrikaans cinema for its forced performances, insulting language and unnecessary sexual innuendos.[56] Similarly, Broodryk argues that the comedy 'mocks religious hypocrisy, but the form of its mockery lacks political purpose and permanence'.[57] Still, the film won both the critics' and audience choice awards at an Australian film festival. This has led to Roets describing the film as an enigma, or perhaps a 'sure indicator of how tastes differ'.[58]

In *Kaalgat tussen die Daisies* the protagonist is a Dutch Reformed Church minister in a small West Coast town. It is poignant that Roets chose this background for his lead character because of the 'centrality of the Afrikaans church in cultural activity'.[59] As Shaun Joynt and Chris Broodryk argue: 'South African cinema has a long film history in which religion and the image serve narratives of spiritual salvation as well as nationalism.'[60] Considering the decades of censorship that South Africans had to endure, it seems a bold choice for Roets to make fun of Afrikaans clergy. Given that the film was made in 1997, one must admit that film-makers such as Willie Esterhuizen had already shocked audiences in 1994 with *Lipstiek Dipstiek*'s 'scatological excesses'.[61] Roets wanted to differentiate himself by telling stories that Nofal would have appreciated: jolly and humorous, but without the banality that would make audiences cringe in their seats.[62]

Roets developed the idea for *Kaalgat* while serving as the cinematographer and co-producer of the series *'n Rand 'n Droom* (A Rand a Dream) in Philadelphia on the West Coast.[63] At the local hotel one of the townsfolk told him the story of the real life *kaalgat dominee* (a stark naked preacher) – a story he swore was true. Later on, Roets retold it to Nofal, who thought it the ideal storyline for a film. However, by the time Nofal passed away ten years later, he had still not made the film.

In the early 1990s Afrikaans producers faced harsh economic conditions. After the end of apartheid, the state broadcaster was rebranded as the public broadcaster and the once generous budgets for Afrikaans productions were cut to the bone.[64] The film industry was in dire straits as well and, according to Roets, many production companies had to close down. Veteran producer Dirk de Villiers made one last desperate attempt in a waning industry by investing his last capital in a feature film.[65] He decided upon *Kaalgat*'s story and chose Roets to write and direct the film, based on the fact that *Kootjie Emmer* and *Koöperasiestories* had proven Roets's track record with character-driven stories.[66] Both the producer and director understood the risk they took in challenging the perception of an esteemed Dutch Reformed minister. Still, the distributor Ster Kinekor trusted them and gave them free rein to pursue their vision.[67]

The film opens with the narrator Kareltjie (Soli Philander) getting dressed for a performance as a drag queen. Breaking the fourth wall, he explains to the audience that it is actually someone else's fault that he now performs this role. He then invites us to listen to the larger-than-life tale of the culprit, Dominee (Reverend) Isak Meiring (played by Frank Opperman). Roets uses Kareltjie's character to bring sarcasm, irony and dark humour to the story, all distinctive elements of satire in film.[68] The opening scene establishes him as a drag queen, nonchalantly taking off his socks and using them to serve as make-believe breasts, and sets the film's tone.

Kareltjie serves as a stark contrast to the protagonist, the uptight and naive Dominee Isak, whom the audience meets in the next scene. Isak, preparing to officiate at a wedding, is lecturing the groom, Gert (Willie Esterhuizen), on his '*katoolsgeit*' (ruttish nature). Gert is hesitant to proceed with the shotgun wedding, but since the bride is the daughter of the local mafioso, Petrus (Zack du Plessis), he does not really have a choice. While they are waiting for the bride to arrive, Isak suffers from severe toothache. Since the groom is looking for any excuse to delay (or avoid) the wedding, he suggests the clergyman should go to the dentist to repair his tooth before they conduct the ceremony.

When they arrive at the dentist, Frik (Tolla van der Merwe) is on his way to go fishing. He reluctantly agrees to pull Dominee Isak's tooth, but informs them that he has already had a couple of drinks and is therefore not in the best condition to perform the procedure. Because of his drunken state, he drops the syringe with local anaesthetic on the floor. Looking at the shattered glass, he informs them that he does not have any other anaesthetic in stock. Isak offers to go ahead without anaesthetic. However, his loud screams soon convince the other two that this is not going to work. Frik gives the clergyman a good dose of witblits and pulls the tooth.[69] Isak, not used to drinking such strong alcohol, passes out, along with the groom who has also had his fair share to drink. The dentist (who finds the situation quite humorous) loads the two men on his trailer and takes them along on his 'fishing trip'. However, on the road Frik stops to meet up with a couple of lobster smugglers. He discovers that Isak and the groom have finished the entire five litres of box wine he had loaded into the back of his trailer. It is in this scandalous drunken state that an officer of the law, Sergeant Bokkie Bredell (Gys de Villiers), also an elder of the church, finds them when he pulls Frik over in a roadblock.

In this film Roets plays with social taboos that still existed in conservative Afrikaans culture, a conservatism that remained after the fall of apartheid. With his use of satirical humour, he subtly plays the role of critical commentator, 'addressing a nonspecialist audience on matters of broad public concern'.[70] As Roets mostly employs dark humour, I argue that the film contains aspects of grotesque comedy, which contains 'the incongruous presence of some laughable and disgusting things' and is 'at least as strongly emotional as it is intellectual'.[71]

In *Humour and Irony in Dutch Post-War Fiction Film* Peter Verstraten discusses various Dutch films that use the paradoxical effect of the grotesque to satirise religion.[72] Two of his case studies, namely *De Mantel der Liefde* and *De Vierde Man*, ridicule Christianity and the hypocrisy of the (Catholic) church. *De Mantel der Liefde* mocks the rules set out by the Ten Commandments and employs blasphemy through its representation of Moses and Jesus Christ with 'a definite purpose to ridicule and discourage'.[73]

If Roets had attempted these techniques, he would have undoubtedly been ostracised by the Afrikaans-speaking community, which is a deeply religious cultural grouping. The film would definitely have flopped at the box office, as even the Dutch films mentioned above had proved to be too much for their mostly secular audience to swallow. Verstraten aptly describes his case studies as 'box office poison'.[74] However, it was not Roets's intent to ridicule religion per se, but rather the way clergy, church councils and pious parishioners often set higher standards for their reverends than for themselves.[75] This theme is clearly addressed in the film, when the same members of the church council who fired Isak for his debauchery visit a strip club and and gamble. Roets uses satire as a form of critique and protest against the misplaced standards and values of society.

Unable to find work and deeply in debt, Isak is hired by his cousin Petrus to manage a gentleman's club in Saldanha. Although he initially refuses, his friend and 'mentor' Kareltjie convinces him to accept the job, as he is now an unemployed white Afrikaans male he cannot be picky in the new dispensation. In this scene, as the archetypal trickster, Kareltjie reveals the deep-rooted fear and plight of many Afrikaans men in the 1990s whose job security was threatened by affirmative action. Much more persuasion was needed, but in the end Isak decides to make the best of the situation. After all – as Kareltjie assures him – where else would he be able to minister to so many of his 'lost sheep'? Isak dons an Egyptian costume, calls himself Potifar and performs traditional Afrikaans folk songs (with a twist) to his makeshift congregation – those who frequent the strip club. The formerly holier-than-thou Isak must swallow his pride and work alongside those whom he had previously disdained, notably the entertainers, strippers and (as we would later discover) cross-dressers. Consequently, through its use of satire, the film 'derides aberrations from the norm, ridicules faulty character, censures "uncivilized" behaviour and denigrates ineffective social institutions'.[76] In an interview Roets expressed the opinion that the film might still be too risqué for the Afrikaans public.[77]

Many critics reviewing *Kaalgat* commented on the exaggerated acting (especially Dominee Isak), the in-your-face art design, including portraits of women with naked breasts in the club and the use of dark humour in the last part of the film when one of the senior citizens who visits the club dies of a heart attack while watching a striptease, leaving Isak and Kareltjie to dispose of the body. Yet already in the opening scene, and through all the elements described, the film is clearly a farce that uses hyperbole (in its acting and otherwise) to poke fun at the limits of what was then allowed in the entertainment made for South African society.[78] 'Yes, I could have made a film that portrayed society's rejection of gay cross-dressers,' Roets told me in a personal interview. 'But audiences would have stayed away or even boycotted it on television. I chose to showcase the taboos of society in a jolly way. We all knew that many of those men who spoke out against pornography hid a *Scope* or a *Loslyf* underneath their pillow, but it was not allowed to talk about it in society back then.'[79] Thus, the film could also be regarded as an oral historical record of chauvinistic nationalism's hypocrisy.

Although Broodryk considers *Kaalgat* one of the Afrikaans films made in the period between 1994 and 2014 that displayed 'political impotence', this statement is refuted by those who worked alongside Roets on the film, such as actor Soli Philander and composer Charl-Johan Lingenfelder (who also appears in multiple scenes of the film dressed as a woman playing the piano in the club).[80] When Philander read Roets's screenplay for the first time, he felt that it conformed to the conventions of satire and that it would shift boundaries for Afrikaans film, especially in terms of depicting those who had thus far been under-represented – cross-dressers and gay men.[81] 'These were big and important questions to ask the (mostly) conservative nation at that point in time. And Roets could get away with it because he used satire. He would never have gotten away with it otherwise,' Philander told me in a personal interview.[82]

Philander disputes some critics' viewpoint that Roets casts experienced actors and then allows them to tailor their performances according to their own free will: 'He respects your craft as an actor, and he does not prescribe how the actor must perform. But he has a clear vision for a character in terms of the structure and motifs of the story. It is your job as an actor to fulfil that vision.'[83]

At the end of the narrative Petrus is exposed for being the crook he actually is and is arrested for his corrupt business dealings, as well as for attempted murder. The club's lead singer, Charmaine, is revealed to be an undercover policeman, Brand Boshoff (Charl Engelbrecht). The latter device of using a male character in drag for the duration of most of the film is one of the elements that Lingenfelder describes as being especially 'fresh' and 'edgy'.[84] In fact, throughout the entire film Kareltjie pokes fun at gayness and the Afrikaners' denial of its existence in their community. Kareltjie as the narrative's trickster therefore fulfils the role of 'grotesque artist' who 'plays half laughingly, half horrified, with the deep absurdities of existence'.[85]

In hindsight, Lingenfelder feels the film should have crossed more boundaries. He describes collaborating with Roets as pleasurable in terms of subverting and undermining traditional Afrikaans value systems, but he was consciously aware of the pressure exerted by financiers, distributors and a deeply conservative audience: 'This film is a good example of where the Afrikaner found himself in the mid-nineties: in search of a new identity but still trapped after decades of apartheid that had a strong ideological hold on them.'[86] With this statement, he reasserts Broodryk's argument that 'given the censorious apartheid regime's hold on cinematic outputs and the ease with which any work of art could be banned, Afrikaans filmmakers had to produce films that would be financially profitable while not opposing dominant white Afrikaans ideologies of exclusion'.[87] Given that it would take 20 years for Lingenfelder himself to produce a commercially successful Afrikaans film where audiences accepted the sympathetic portrayal of gay characters (*Kanarie*, released in 2018), he credits *Kaalgat* with playing an important entertainment and educative role in South Africa's years of transition.

Since its release in cinemas, the film has gathered a cult following. It frequently appears on YouTube, gets taken down by the administrators because of copyright issues, to be uploaded again a couple of months later by a fan.[88] In YouTube's public comments section one can witness the fierce debate among users about the film's representation of a Dutch Reformed minister, small town communities and the prudishness that still exists in South Africa, even at the time of writing. Therefore, it serves as a point of departure for viewers to discuss aspects of their society. In these comments the film is also commended by its staunch supporters for its well-plotted narrative structure and adult humour. Therefore I maintain that the film can be considered a 'public intellectual good' as defined by Posner.

In the end, the tragedy of *Kaalgat*'s reception was that it was lambasted by some critics as not being political enough, disdained for its use of sexual innuendo to portray gay characters and rejected by some members of the Afrikaans community for depicting their culture as one that frequents strip clubs and appreciates drag queens. In the same manner that Dominee Isak, himself dressed in drag, shouts '*Ek glo dit nie! Ek glo dit nie!*' (I don't believe it! I don't believe it!), they refused to believe in the diverse and complex nature of Afrikaners and their sexuality – a theme that Philander believes the film portrayed very well. This brings to mind Verstraten's words when he implies that the reception of most satirical films could be regarded as tragic: 'For the one the work of art will be nauseating, for another funny, and a third will consider it both horrifying and comic.' As he points out: 'Life is alternately comic and tragic. The world is now a vale of tears, now a circus.'[89]

'N PAWPAW VIR MY DARLING (A PAWPAW FOR MY DARLING)

More recently, in *'n Pawpaw vir My Darling*, the dog Tjaka narrates the story about a group of Afrikaners living in the suburb of Damnville (referencing the poor suburb of Danville in Pretoria).[90] Based on Jeanne Goosen's novel, Roets wrote the screenplay, served as director and edited the film as well. A combination of good scripting, directing, pacing and editing (especially the cross-cutting between the scenes of the dogs and the humans) leads to a strong viewing experience.[91] In an interview Roets commented that before even going on set he had already seen all the images (and how they should be edited together) in his mind's eye.[92] Roets directed the film in a manner that he felt would have the most visual impact.

What resonates most is the empathy with which Roets sketches the lives of the 'poor white' Afrikaners who are frowned upon or more often than not neglected by their highbrow counterparts. During the apartheid years films such as *Siener in die Suburbs* and *'n Seder Val in Waterkloof* addressed this issue, but it also needed representation in the new dispensation. One such attempt was made with Michael

Raeburn's *Triomf*, which won best South African film at the Durban International Film Festival in 2008, but was a dismal box office failure. Using comedy in *h Pawpaw vir My Darling*, Roets underscores the theme of class while attracting audiences to the theatres and selling large quantities of DVDs. Audiences watching films containing social commentary often complain that the film-maker tried too hard to teach them a moral lesson.[93] I propose that it is precisely because of his use of wit and humour and carefully crafted characters that Roets could communicate provocative ideas about gender and conservatism while avoiding this trap.

* * *

Roets has never really been fully appreciated by South African film scholars, except as background to the better-known directors (such as Rautenbach and Van Rensburg). Yet, in his collaborations, with Nofal and Rautenbach, in particular, you had the doyens of critical Afrikaans cinema (dubbed the 'triumvirate' by Tomaselli) who created alternative Afrikaans cinema that defied the censors, challenged Afrikanerdom and took their films directly to white Afrikaans audiences.[94] These audiences not only included ordinary people, but also high-ranking politicians, Cabinet ministers and members of the intelligentsia, such as the South African Academy of Arts and Sciences.[95] In the context of the late 1960s and early 1970s, there was an excitement among Afrikaner intellectuals (such as the academy) about the potential of these type of films to uplift the rest of the industry.[96] Even among NP members 'there was an excitement in the air about the quality of these productions, even if they had to navigate the contradistinctions of the PCB's [Publications Control Board's] notorious moralistic minefields'.[97]

This chapter demonstrates that Roets has made a valuable contribution to Afrikaans cultural discourse over the last four decades. He could be considered 'public' because his cultural work is screened for large audiences in the public sphere. Roets might be better known as a cinematographer, but I argue that he deserves to be recognised as a notable director in his own right. Through his use of grotesque comedy in the films discussed in this chapter, he created watershed narratives that could ignite significant debate among viewers and cultural institutions alike, without alienating his audience (which is often the case with serious art films). Roets demonstrates a knowledge of his target audience through creating films that would appeal to their sensibilities and standards, while touching on relevant political and societal themes.[98]

One may look at a work of art to carry a public intellectual's message and Roets has decided to let his films speak for him, while he stands quietly behind the camera.

NOTES

In writing this chapter, I owe a great deal to the assistance of Koos Roets and his partner Eunice Visser. They patiently answered all my questions and were generous with their input, but also encouraged me to critically reflect and interpret Roets's work from my own perspective. I would like to acknowledge the generous support of my mentor, Keyan Tomaselli, and Chris Broodryk, who acted as readers for this text, improving it immeasurably. Lastly, I need to thank Anna-Mart Bonthuys and Peter Goldsmid who initially proofread this chapter.

1. John Issit and Duncan Jackson, 'What does It Mean to Be a Public Intellectual?', 2013, accessed 15 November 2018, https://www.heacademy.ac.uk/system/files/resources/12_march_presentation.pdf
2. Issit and Jackson, 'Public Intellectual', 2.
3. Goods with the function to express or inform.
4. Helen Small, 'Introduction', in *The Public Intellectual*, ed. Helen Small (Oxford: Blackwell Publishing, 2002), 2.
5. Koos Roets, dir., *Die Groen Faktor* (The Green Factor) (Johannesburg: Heyns Films, 1984); Koos Roets, dir., *Kaalgat tussen die Daisies* (Naked among the Daisies) (Cape Town: C-Films, 1997).
6. Koos Roets, 'Reminiscing about Koos Roets's Old Films' (unpublished interview with Anna-Marié Jansen van Vuuren, Klaarstroom, 3 April 2018).
7. Emile Nofal, dir., *Wild Season* (Johannesburg: Emil Nofal Films, 1967).
8. Jans Rautenbach, dir., *Katrina* (Johannesburg: Emil Nofal Films, 1969).
9. Jans Rautenbach, dir., *Jannie Totsiens*. Johannesburg: Sewentig Films, 1970.
10. Franklin Sonn, 'Preface', in *Jans Rautenbach: Dromer, Baanbreker en Auteur*, by Martin Botha (Parklands: Genugtig Uitgewers, 2006), ii. See also Keyan Tomaselli, *The South African Film Industry* (Johannesburg: African Studies Institute, 1979), 48. The Sestigers, or Sixties Generation, included writers such as André Brink, Breyten Breytenbach and Chris Barnard, who contested the dominant system through formal experimentation and the provocative nature of their subject matter.
11. Anna-Marié Jansen van Vuuren, 'Waar Is die "Magic" Heen?' *Litnet*, 11 January 2018, accessed 7 December 2020, https://www.litnet.co.za/waar-die-magic-heen/
12. Martin Botha, *South African Cinema 1896–2010* (Bristol: Intellect, 2012), 66.
13. Manie van Rensburg, dir., *Freddie's in Love* (Johannesburg: Visio Films, 1971).
14. Koos Roets, dir., *Die Erfgenaam* (The Heir Apparent) (Johannesburg: Quadro Films, 1971).
15. Koos Roets, unpublished interview with Anna-Marié Jansen van Vuuren, Klaarstroom, 17 October 2017.
16. Ken Dancyger, *The Director's Idea: The Path to Great Directing* (Burlington, MA: Focal Press, 2006).
17. Koos Roets, dir., *Koöperasiestories* (Johannesburg: Pendulum, 1983); *Die Mannheim Sage* (Johannesburg: Satbel, 1986); *Die Manakwalanners* (Johannesburg: Quantum Produksies, 1993); *Kootjie Emmer* (Johannesburg: Brigadier Films, 1977); *Faan se Trein* (Faan's Train) (Johannesburg: Helena Spring/Faan Films, 2014).
18. Roets, *Die Groen Faktor*.
19. Keyan G. Tomaselli, *The Cinema of Apartheid: Race and Class in South African Film* (London: Routledge, 1989), 219.
20. Roets, 'Reminiscing'.

21. Jamie Uys, dir., *Rip van Wyk* (Johannesburg: Mimosa Films, 1960); *Lord Oom Piet* (Johannesburg: Mimosa Films, 1962); Emil Nofal, dir., *Kimberley Jim* (Johannesburg: Mimosa Films, 1963).
22. Roets, 'Reminiscing'. Roets credits Nofal's sharp storytelling skills as a major contributing factor to the film's success.
23. Cobus Rossouw, 'Cobus Rossouw on Some of his Historical Roles and Experiences within the Film Industry' (unpublished interview with Anna-Marié Jansen van Vuuren, Cape Town, 26 August 2018).
24. *Die Square* is also considered to be a satire on so-called Afrikaner hegemony within the South African context of that period. See Botha, *South African Cinema*.
25. Jans Rautenbach, dir., *Die Kandidaat* (Johannesburg: Emil Nofal Films, 1968).
26. The team included Heyns Films' executive producers, Thys Heyns and Johan Heyns and producer Paul Raleigh. Their production company was relatively successful in the 1980s.
27. Paul Raleigh, email correspondence with the author, 1 March 2019.
28. Roets's actual location was the town of Tulbagh in the Western Cape.
29. Gunther Kress and Theo van Leeuwen, 'Colour as a Semiotic Mode: Notes for a Grammar of Colour', *Visual Communication* 1, no. 3 (2002): 345.
30. Graham Armitage was a British actor. Between 1979 and 1985 he portrayed the role of Sherlock Holmes for a Springbok Radio drama serial.
31. There is a myth that many white South Africans referred to black people during apartheid as '*groenes*' or 'greenies' because the municipal buses reserved for black people were green, while those reserved for whites were red. I could not find evidence to corroborate that this was the reason the film-makers chose to use the colour green as an aesthetic driving force for their story.
32. Kress and Van Leeuwen, 'Colour as a Semiotic Mode': 345.
33. Botha, *South African Cinema*, 51.
34. Botha, *South African Cinema*, 57; see also Bill Ashcroft, Gareth Griffiths and Helen Tiffin, *The Empire Writes Back* (London: Routledge, 1989), 33.
35. Chris W. Broodryk, 'Absences, Exclusivities and Utopias: Afrikaans Film as a Cinema of Political Impotence, 1994–2014' (PhD diss., University of Cape Town, 2015), 1.
36. See Hermann Giliomee, *The Afrikaners: Biography of a People* (London: Hurst & Company, 2003), 623.
37. My translation from Afrikaans.
38. Tomaselli, *The Cinema of Apartheid*, 221.
39. J. Scott, 'We'll All Be Green, if Life Imitates Art', *Pretoria News*, 24 April 2014, 14.
40. My translation from Afrikaans; M. Fockema, 'Dié Rolprente Bly Hulle by: Grotes in Bedryf se Gunstelinge', *Volksblad*, 13 October 2014, 9; see also Astrid Klocke, 'Subverting Satire: Edgar Hilsenrath's Novel *Der Nazi und der Friseur* and Charlie Chaplin's Film *The Great Dictator*', *Holocaust and Genocide Studies* 22, no. 3 (2008): 499.
41. Fockema, 'Dié Rolprente Bly Hulle by', 9.
42. Scott, 'We'll All Be Green', 14. The column subsequently appeared in many other regional newspapers, such as the *Cape Times*.
43. Tomaselli, *The Cinema of Apartheid*, 219.
44. Peter Verstraten, *Humour and Irony in Dutch Post-War Fiction Film* (Amsterdam: Amsterdam University Press, 2016), 299.
45. No connection or relevance to the environmentally conscious Green Parties that one finds in many countries.
46. My translation from Afrikaans; Roets, *Die Groen Faktor*.
47. Scott, 'We'll All Be Green', 14.

48 Roets, 'Reminiscing', as translated and quoted by Scott, 'We'll All Be Green'.
49 Keyan G. Tomaselli, *Encountering Modernity: Twentieth-Century South African Cinemas* (Pretoria: Unisa, 2006), 40.
50 Roets was the cinematographer of *Jannie Totsiens* and was credited by Rautenbach for having realised the 'madhouse' effect that he wanted to create in the film; see Jans Rautenbach, personal interview with Anna-Marié Jansen van Vuuren, De Rust, 30 June 2016. *Jannie Totsiens* was one of 'the occasional breakaway film[s] that question the status quo [but] has little chance of success fighting against the preferences of a preconditioned audience, an industry unable to cope with genre innovation and a theoretical and critical heritage rooted somewhere else' (Tomaselli, *The South African Film Industry*, 3).
51 Klocke, 'Subverting Satire', 499.
52 Richard A. Posner, *Public Intellectuals: A Study of Decline* (Cambridge: Harvard University Press, 2003), 3.
53 Lance Olsen, *Circus of the Mind in Motion: Postmodernism and the Comic Vision* (Detroit: Wayne State University Press, 1990), 18.
54 Klocke, 'Subverting Satire', 499.
55 Tomaselli, *The South African Film Industry*, 4.
56 Leon van Nierop, *Daar Doer in die Fliek: 'n Persoonlike Blik op die Geskiedenis van die Afrikaanse Rolprent* (Pretoria: Protea Boekhuis, 2016), 242.
57 Broodryk, 'Absences, Exclusivities and Utopias', 3.
58 Roets, 'Reminiscing'.
59 Shaun Joynt and Chris Broodryk, 'Screening the Church: A Study of Clergy Representation in Contemporary Afrikaans Cinema', *HTS Teologiese Studies/Theological Studies* 74, no. 2 (2018): 1.
60 Joynt and Broodryk, 'Screening the Church': 1.
61 Broodryk, 'Absences, Exclusivities and Utopias', 6. Translated into English *Lipstiek Dipstiek* means 'Lipstick Dipstick'.
62 Despite differing viewpoints from the above-mentioned critics, Roets maintains that his characters walk the fine line between '*stoutigheid*' (naughtiness) and banality in this film, whereas many other film-makers do not hesitate to show sexual acts in their films.
63 Written by P.G. du Plessis and directed by Katinka Heyns, it won the South African Broadcast Corporation's best single television drama prize in 1978.
64 Tomaselli, *Encountering Modernity*.
65 Dirk de Villiers made 25 feature films and is probably most well known for the award-winning series *Arende* (1989). His series *Jantjie Kom Huis Toe* is regarded as the first Afrikaans television production consisting of an entirely coloured cast.
66 Roets suspects that Nofal told the 'Kaalgat' story to Rautenbach while they produced the film *King Hendrik* and that he later retold it to the producer Dirk de Villiers, as they were drinking buddies.
67 Roets, 'Reminiscing'.
68 Klocke, 'Subverting Satire', 499.
69 Witblits is a traditional South African homemade grape brandy.
70 Posner, *Public Intellectuals*.
71 Verstraten, *Humour and Irony*.
72 Verstraten, *Humour and Irony*, 295.
73 Verstraten, *Humour and Irony*, 311.
74 Verstraten, *Humour and Irony*, 313.
75 This theme is again investigated in Sallas de Jager's film *Dominee Tienie* (Johannesburg: Bosbok Ses Films, 2019).

76 Klocke, 'Subverting Satire', 499.
77 Roets, 'Reminiscing'.
78 Broodryk, 'Absences, Exclusivities and Utopias', 144.
79 Roets, 'Reminiscing'. *Loslyf* is an Afrikaans pornographic magazine that was founded in 1995, a year after the harsh apartheid censorship laws were lifted. Annie Coombes, *History after Apartheid: Visual Culture and Public Memory in a Democratic South Africa* (Durham: Duke University Press, 2003), 40.
80 Broodryk, 'Absences, Exclusivities and Utopias', 204.
81 Soli Philander, 'Working with Koos Roets on *Kaalgat tussen die Daisies*' (unpublished interview with Anna-Marié Jansen van Vuuren, Cape Town, 30 August 2019).
82 Philander, 'Working with Koos Roets'.
83 Philander, 'Working with Koos Roets'.
84 Lingenfelder, C-J. '*Grense, Drag* en *Kaalgat tussen die Daisies*' (unpublished interview with Anna-Marié Jansen van Vuuren, Cape Town, 25 March 2019).
85 Verstraten, *Humour and Irony*, 295.
86 Lingenfelder, '*Grense*'.
87 Broodryk, 'Absences, Exclusivities and Utopias', 144.
88 YouTube and its online discussion of the film were monitored between November 2018 and September 2019.
89 Verstraten, *Humour and Irony*, 296.
90 Koos Roets, dir., *'n Pawpaw vir My Darling* (Johannesburg: Krisan Productions, 2015).
91 Van Nierop, *Daar Doer in die Fliek*.
92 Roets, 'Reminiscing'.
93 Carole Cox, 'Film as Documentation, Social Comment, Satire, and Spoof', *The English Journal* 76, no. 4 (1987): 85.
94 Keyan Tomaselli, email communication with the author, 3 August 2020.
95 Martin Botha, *Jans Rautenbach: Dromer, Baanbreker en Auteur* (Parklands: Genugtig Uitgewers, 2006), 46.
96 Botha, *Jans Rautenbach*, 46.
97 Tomaselli, email, 3 August 2020.
98 John S. Nelson, *Popular Cinema as Political Theory: Idealism and Realism in Epics, Noirs, and Satires* (New York: Springer, 2013), 53.

REFERENCES

Ashcroft, Bill, Gareth Griffiths and Helen Tiffin. *The Empire Writes Back*. London: Routledge, 1989.

Botha, Martin. *Jans Rautenbach: Dromer, Baanbreker en Auteur*. Parklands: Genugtig Uitgewers, 2006.

Botha, Martin. *South African Cinema 1896–2010*. Bristol: Intellect, 2012.

Broodryk, Chris W. 'Absences, Exclusivities and Utopias: Afrikaans Film as a Cinema of Political Impotence, 1994–2014'. PhD diss., University of Cape Town, 2015.

Coombes, Annie. *History after Apartheid: Visual Culture and Public Memory in a Democratic South Africa*. Durham: Duke University Press, 2003.

Cox, Carole. 'Film as Documentation, Social Comment, Satire, and Spoof'. *The English Journal* 76, no. 4 (1987): 85–87.

Dancyger, Ken. *The Director's Idea: The Path to Great Directing*. Burlington, MA: Focal Press, 2006.
De Jager, Sallas, dir., *Dominee Tienie*. Johannesburg: Bosbok Ses Films, 2019.
Fockema, M. 2014. 'Dié Rolprente Bly Hulle by: Grotes in Bedryf se Gunstelinge'. *Volksblad*, 13 October 2014, 9.
Giliomee, Hermann. *The Afrikaners: Biography of a People*. London: Hurst & Company, 2003.
Issit, John and Duncan Jackson. 'What Does It Mean to Be a Public Intellectual?' 2013. Accessed 15 November 2018. https://www.heacademy.ac.uk/system/files/resources/12_march_presentation.pdf
Jansen van Vuuren, Anna-Marié. 'Waar Is die "Magic" Heen?' *Litnet*, 11 January 2018. Accessed 7 December 2020. https://www.litnet.co.za/waar-die-magic-heen/
Joynt, Shaun and Chris Broodryk. 'Screening the Church: A Study of Clergy Representation in Contemporary Afrikaans Cinema'. *HTS Teologiese Studies/Theological Studies* 74, no. 2 (2018): 1–8.
Klocke, Astrid. 'Subverting Satire: Edgar Hilsenrath's Novel *Der Nazi und der Friseur* and Charlie Chaplin's Film *The Great Dictator*'. *Holocaust and Genocide Studies* 22, no. 3 (2008): 497–513.
Kress, Gunther and Theo van Leeuwen. 'Colour as a Semiotic Mode: Notes for a Grammar of Colour'. *Visual Communication* 1, no. 3 (2002): 343–368.
Lingenfelder, C-J. '*Grense, Drag* en *Kaalgat tussen die Daisies*'. Unpublished interview with Anna-Marié Jansen van Vuuren, Cape Town, 25 March 2019.
Nelson, John S. *Popular Cinema as Political Theory: Idealism and Realism in Epics, Noirs, and Satires*. New York: Springer, 2013.
Nofal, Emil, dir. *Kimberley Jim*. Johannesburg: Mimosa Films, 1963.
Nofal, Emil, dir. *Wild Season*. Johannesburg: Emil Nofal Films, 1967.
Olsen, Lance. *Circus of the Mind in Motion: Postmodernism and the Comic Vision*. Detroit: Wayne State University Press, 1990.
Philander, Soli. 'Working with Koos Roets on *Kaalgat tussen die Daisies*'. Unpublished interview with Anna-Marié Jansen van Vuuren. Cape Town, 30 August 2019.
Posner, Richard A. *Public Intellectuals: A Study of Decline*. Cambridge: Harvard University Press, 2003.
Rautenbach, Jans, dir. *Jannie Totsiens*. Johannesburg: Sewentig Films, 1970.
Rautenbach, Jans, dir. *Die Kandidaat*. Johannesburg: Emil Nofal Films, 1968.
Rautenbach, Jans, dir. *Katrina*. Johannesburg: Emil Nofal Films, 1969.
Rautenbach, Jans. Personal interview with Anna-Marié Jansen van Vuuren, De Rust, 30 June 2016.
Roets, Koos, dir. *Die Erfgenaam* (The Heir Apparent). Johannesburg: Quadro Films, 1971.
Roets, Koos, dir. *Faan se Trein* (Faan's Train). Johannesburg: Helena Spring/Faan Films, 2014.
Roets, Koos, dir. *Die Groen Faktor* (The Green Factor). Johannesburg: Heyns Films, 1984.
Roets, Koos, dir. *Die Manakwalanners*. Johannesburg: Quantum Produksies, 1993.
Roets, Koos, dir. *Die Mannheim Sage*. Johannesburg: Satbel, 1986.
Roets, Koos, dir. *Kaalgat tussen die Daisies* (Naked among the Daisies). Cape Town: C-Films, 1997.
Roets, Koos, dir. *Kootjie Emmer*. Johannesburg: Brigadier Films, 1977.
Roets, Koos, dir. *Koöperasiestories*. Johannesburg: Pendulum, 1983.
Roets, Koos, dir. *'n Pawpaw vir My Darling*. Johannesburg: Krisan Productions, 2015.
Roets, Koos. 'Reminiscing about Koos Roets's Old Films'. Unpublished interview with Anna-Marié Jansen van Vuuren. Klaarstroom, 3 April 2018.

Roets, Koos. Unpublished interview Anna-Marié Jansen van Vuuren. Klaarstroom, 17 October 2017.
Rossouw, Cobus. 'Cobus Rossouw on Some of his Historical Roles and Experiences within the Film Industry'. Unpublished interview with Anna-Marié Jansen van Vuuren. Cape Town, 26 August 2018.
Scott, J. 'We'll All Be Green, if Life Imitates Art'. *Pretoria News*, 24 April 2014, 14.
Small, Helen. 'Introduction'. In *The Public Intellectual*, edited by Helen Small, 1–18. Oxford: Blackwell Publishing, 2002.
Sonn, Franklin. 'Preface'. In *Jans Rautenbach: Dromer, Baanbreker en Auteur*, by Martin Botha, i. Parklands: Genugtig Uitgewers, 2006.
Tomaselli, Keyan G. *The Cinema of Apartheid: Race and Class in South African Film*. London: Routledge, 1989.
Tomaselli, Keyan G. *Encountering Modernity: Twentieth-Century South African Cinemas*. Pretoria: Unisa, 2006.
Tomaselli, Keyan. *The South African Film Industry*. Johannesburg: African Studies Institute, 1979.
Uys, Jamie, dir. *Lord Oom Piet*. Johannesburg: Mimosa Films, 1962.
Uys, Jamie, dir. *Rip van Wyk*. Johannesburg: Mimosa Films, 1960.
Van Nierop, Leon. *Daar Doer in die Fliek: 'n Persoonlike Blik op die Geskiedenis van die Afrikaanse Rolprent*. Pretoria: Protea Boekhuis, 2016.
Van Rensburg, Manie, dir. *Freddie's in Love*. Johannesburg: Visio Films, 1971.
Verstraten, Peter. *Humour and Irony in Dutch Post-War Fiction Film*. Amsterdam: Amsterdam University Press, 2016.

CHAPTER

8

The Public Intellectualism of Artivist Mandisi Sindo

Katlego Chale

This chapter focuses on the artistic and activist practice of Cape Town-based theatre maker Mandisi Sindo, in order to gain an understanding of artivism and locating this praxis as an alternative form of public intellectualism. According to José María Mesías-Lema, 'artivism is a neologism derived from "art" and "activism", where the order of words has its rationale; the term describes artists who are committed to creative processes of an activist nature but not activists who resort to art as a form of vindication'.[1]

Mandisi Sindo is a South African theatre maker, social entrepreneur and artivist based in Cape Town. Writing for *Lead SA*, Lilford Lesabe describes Sindo as 'the founder, artistic director, and CEO of Makukhanye Art Room'.[2] The Makukhanye Art Room is Khayelitsha's 'first ever shack theatre' and was run by Sindo alongside 'technical director Bamanye Yeko, Siphosethu Runqu and Sivuwe Sigudu (maintenance) and Siphosethu Dyonase and Lwazi Thezaphi (operations and co-ordination)'.[3] The space first came into use in 2007, when, as a shack, it 'served mainly as a rehearsal space for the Makukhanye Entertainment Act Group run by Thando Mpengezi and Siphosethu Runqu'. The shack was also used as a shared public space for members of the community of Khayelitsha, the second largest township in South Africa, to share knowledge and ideas on how to make life better for themselves.[4] Following his graduation from the University of Cape Town with a Drama degree, Sindo became more actively involved with the space, leading to his becoming artistic director and producer in 2015.[5] Since he took over, the shack has come to be known as the Makukhanye Art Room, South Africa's first recognised shack theatre.

Sindo has since left Makukhanye Art Room to start another shack theatre with a wider scope of interest. Founded in 2017, Khayelitsha Art School & Rehabilitation Centre (KASI RC), writes Shifaan Ryklief, 'is a shack theatre based in the heart of Khayelitsha where locals and visitors can enjoy the performing arts and partake in educational workshops'.[6]

Sindo's contribution to the arts sector within his community provides a basis for engaging with the ways he uses artistic devices to frame his activism, thus becoming an artivist. Artivism gives artists who would be social actors alternative modes of practising intellectualism, which for the most part has been and is expressed through the act of writing. Beyond penning responses to complex phenomena, which enables ordinary citizens to understand and respond to the multiplicity of happenings around them, this chapter considers other ways of practising public intellectualism.

ARTIVISM

Artists, through their talents and creative approaches to problem solving and awareness creation, occupy a vital role in generating moments of public conversation about issues pertinent to the collective consciousness of a particular place at a particular time. Speaking about the origins of the term 'artivism', Nina Felshin locates its roots in the cultural, political and artistic revolution that manifested in the United States during the 1960s and 1970s.[7] The atmosphere of rebellion and the social and cultural movements championing the efforts to expose the systematic oppression of racism, sexism and gender discrimination were the impetus for artists to grapple with and speak back to social ills. Gabriella Leon suggests a different origin, positing that artivism is a 'term coined by critic and contemporary art theorist Rosalind Krauss in relation to sculpture, and is a concept widely explored in contemporary art'.[8] Leon argues that artivism 'operates from the intersection of the "expanded fields" ... of art and activism to create scenarios that advance social criticism'. Both definitions signal a merging of art and activism initiated by artists with the intention of producing social comment. These artists, according to Lucy Lippard, practise their artivism 'through alternative images, metaphors and information made with humour, irony, indignation and compassion, with the aim of making those previously invisible and powerless voices and faces heard and seen'.[9]

There is a link here to the intentions of the Subaltern Studies Collective, a group of intellectuals coming together to speak for those on the lowest rungs of society, which is discussed later in this chapter when considering the post-colonial and its intersections with Sindo's artivism.

When the first artivists set out to create work, according to José María Mesías-Lema, the environment upheld by human rights movements offered them a space to effectively reach the audience/s for which a work was intended.[10] Mesías-Lema alludes to 'the success of performance, feminism and queer theory which demanded more efficient communication strategies ... capable of demanding and institutionalising the non-existent rights of those groups in a situation of risk and social exclusion'. Artivism became a means to sensitise a society to the issues its people collectively faced, with the intention of making space for the marginalised to speak from a place of understanding their rights and responsibilities.[11] Leon offers an expanded view of the rising popularity of recorded public interventions by artivists, suggesting that artivism 'began to be popular in the late 90s'. At the same time, she acknowledges its development 'throughout the history of social and artistic movements, including the situationism interwoven with the revolutionary movements of May 1968, "zapatismo" in Mexico, the uprising of 2006 in Oaxaca, and the Occupy movements in Madrid and Wall Street in 2011'.[12] At the core of the various theories of origin and definition of the term 'artivism' is an agreement that 'artivism harnesses the critical imagination to design events and strategies that provoke new questions and new meaning in pursuit of more respectful ways of being'.[13] Ramsden goes a step further, arguing that 'artivism is not simply a communication device or a campaign tool, but a way of understanding where we are located in the world and expressing the depth of our feeling about it'.[14]

Examples of artivism

Artivist interventions have occurred in many ways around the world and only a few examples are mentioned here. Ché Ramsden, commenting on the 13th Association for Women's Rights in Development International Forum, notes: 'Murals and graffiti are some of the most commonly used forms of artivism – activism through art – around the world.'[15] At this forum, multidisciplinary approaches to artivism were brought to life through a series of interventions, including the *Equal Airtime* project, which was put together by the Sisonke Sex Worker Movement and the African Centre for Migration and Society (University of the Witwatersrand), with the aim of exploring 'the lived experiences of migrant sex workers in the Limpopo province of South Africa', through a collaborative workshop, employing 'visual, narrative and theatrical exercises'.[16] In these works, artivism became a catalyst 'to centre people who are marginalised, ignored or erased by society', giving voice to otherwise silenced struggles.

One of the most famous graffiti artists in the world, whose work continues to stir social and political debate, is a stencil artist known by the pseudonym Banksy. According to Eva Aladro-Vico, Olga Bailey and Dimitrina Jivkova-Semova, Banksy is a 'graffiti artist, political activist and unidentified film director, who carries out his work from Bristol in the United Kingdom anonymously'.[17] The artworks of Banksy have gained worldwide recognition because of the artist's unique ability to allow 'an individual to wrestle power, territory, and glory, in front of a larger and better-equipped enemy'. Banksy's street art, which has gained traction through social media, addresses 'various political and social issues, including anti-war, anticonsumerism, and anti-fascism'. As an artivist, Banksy is not only preoccupied with the aesthetic quality of the work, but also the message and the meanings emanating from the work. This is an important element in the work of artivism, as Simon Sheikh points out: 'Activist art subverts the very notion of the aesthetic object, entering into a process of involvement more important than the creative process itself.'[18] The idea of meaning construction supersedes artistic intentions, as 'artivism changes materials and media, practices and styles, roles and rituals, and ceases to be idiomatic in the art world, to become pragmatic in social life'.

Banksy's work, by making the controversial statements it does, forces large entities to reflect on their impact in society. One of Banksy's more recent artivist works, according to Aladro-Vico, Bailey and Jivkova-Semova, 'draws attention to realities and situations … in the border territories dividing Israel and Palestine'.[19] Banksy's artivism is about finding ways of converting public spaces into murals with the single intention of speaking truth to power.

Another recent artivist intervention can be seen in France after the terrorist attacks that turned Paris upside down on 13 November 2015, leaving 130 people dead and another 368 wounded.[20] In response to the mass shooting, President Francois Holland 'closed France's borders and declared a state of national emergency', which only really came to an end, according to Yannicke Goris and Saskia Hollander, in July 2017. The impact of these security measures was carried by French citizens who were at the mercy of a government, which had given itself the immense power 'to set curfews, limit the movement of people and prohibit mass gatherings'. These measures, in effect, made it impossible for any form of organised collective action or protest to take place in Paris, effectively taking away the public's ability to speak out.

With the Climate Conference to be held in Paris only two weeks away, where 'for the first time in over 20 years of UN negotiations, world leaders aimed to achieve a universal, legally-binding climate agreement', environmental groups that had mass actions planned needed to find alternative strategies of activism without breaking the law.[21] For Parisians, in the environment of terrorist attacks, followed by extreme government interventions limiting social freedoms and modes of expressing not just the anguish of the moment, but the overarching ills of society, there was a need to generate interventions in unprecedented ways:

> 29 November 2015, at the start of COP21, people passing by the Assemblée Nationale building in the heart of Paris were stunned. Staring back at them were the faces of over 500 people from all over the world, projected on the building's massive façade. The video projection – titled 'The Standing March' – was created by renowned French artist JR and Brooklyn-based film director Darren Aronofsky. These 'Artivists' used their skill and creativity to protest when protesting in traditional ways was forbidden.[22]

By transforming a recognised public space into an artwork, the Standing March became an act of artivism, 'by addressing an issue on the minds of a broad audience (the COP21) and depicting a big crowd of people in a place where mass protests are not allowed'.[23] This act of peaceful artistic resistance gained even wider recognition when it was mounted at several public points in Paris during the conference, such as 'the Louvre, the Pantheon, the Musée Picasso, and the Bibliotheque Sainte Genevieve'. This intervention speaks to the fact that artivism is an unconventional form of peaceful resistance that manages to find expression in spite of measures taken to stifle conventional forms of resistance.

In South Africa, a collaboration between Nondumiso Msimanga and Jenny Nijenhuis on the issue of rape culminated in an artivism campaign titled *SA's Dirty Laundry*: 'A 10-day creative project which ... aimed to provoke a public and open dialogue about rape in our country, by radically creating the space for a difficult-to-ignore conversation ... through artistic intervention.'[24] The collaborators chose the recently gentrified Maboneng precinct in Johannesburg as the site for an installation piece, which saw '3600 pairs of used underwear hanging on a 1.2 km washing line between Fox, Albrecht and Kruger Streets'.[25] The artivism thus became a sociopolitical metaphor that gave a new meaning to the phrase 'airing your dirty laundry' – in this case, the 'dirty laundry' consisted of the undergarments of many of South Africa's rape survivors. Msimanga and Nijenhaus took the personal experience of rape and created art with the aim of disrupting our societal sensibilities.

They state the project's purpose: 'We wanted to reveal what the socio-political system covers up by shunning rape survivors. Rape survivors are abandoned, alone, with very little support or justice from our social, policing or legal systems ... Police officers are incentivised to reduce violent crime (performance is measured in this way), which does not motivate police officers to record violent crimes.'

The artists managed to take their private struggle – shared by many womxn – into a public space. This not only demonstrates that activism is useful for 'creating a space for the renewed agency of those who encounter oppression', but also shows that participation in the public discourse can be an effective tool for meaningful change.[26] With regard to the 'new genre' of artivism:

> Artistic productions within this new genre appear as formulas for public or contextualized art, in that they interpellate the spaces they interact with – the street, the plaza, semi-public areas – in order to address the inherent qualities that demonstrate their willingness to cover up all types of ruptures and cracks, signs of vulnerability in a socio-political system that these artistic productions reject and discard.[27]

For Msimanga and Nijenhaus, South Africa's extremely high incidence of rape cannot remain swept under the carpet if the question of transformative social change is to be truly addressed.

ARTIVISM AND PUBLIC INTELLECTUALISM

Edward Said provides multiple conceptions of what an intellectual is, relying on the arguments of seminal theorists to develop his own conception of the intellectual.[28] In thinking about the role of the intellectual in society, Said frequently draws on the work of Antonio Gramsci, an important figure in public intellectual discourse as a political thinker, activist, journalist and Marxist. Gramsci sets out a primary differentiating factor: 'All men are intellectuals, one could therefore say: but not all men have in society the function of intellectuals.'[29] Said informs us of Gramsci's two types of intellectuals: traditional intellectuals and organic intellectuals.[30] The traditional intellectuals include 'teachers, priests, and administrators, who continue to do the same thing from generation to generation', whereas the organic intellectuals are those professionals used by different entities 'to organize interests, gain more power, get more control'. The core difference between Gramsci's two categories of intellectuals is that the traditional intellectuals tend to regurgitate the same knowledge over and over again, whereas organic intellectuals constantly seek out different ways to influence decisions and continuously aim to grow their reach.

Of interest in the South African context is whether there is scope for the two types to interact in the practice of an intellectual, particularly considering the post-colonial drive towards decolonisation. The movement towards uncovering erased or suppressed knowledge requires those whose intellectual practice has been traditional – at least as Gramsci puts it – to become, if at least for the decolonising moment, organic.

An alternative view is offered by Julien Benda, who considers 'intellectuals as a tiny band of super-gifted and morally endowed philosopher-kings who constitute the conscience of mankind'.[31] Benda's examples of this type of intellectual include Jesus, Socrates, Spinoza and Voltaire. Said suggests that for Benda, the true intellectuals are 'very rare creatures indeed, since what they uphold are eternal standards of truth and justice that are precisely not of this world'.[32] Benda's conception of the intellectual, like Gramsci's, emanates from a patriarchal frame and suggests that ordinary individuals must first ascend to certain levels of enlightenment to be considered intellectuals. To an extent one could suggest that objectivity or immunity from the human condition is an essential trait of Benda's intellectual, as we can see in his continued definition of true intellectuals: 'Those whose activity is essentially not the pursuit of practical aims, all those who seek their joy in the practice of an art or science or metaphysical speculation, in short in the possession of non-material advantages, and hence in a certain manner say: "My kingdom is not of this world."'[33]

One may get a sense of Benda proposing a sort of ivory tower theory of the intellectual. However, Said explains that Benda goes on to clarify 'that he does not endorse the notion of totally disengaged, other worldly, ivory-towered thinkers'.[34] Benda criticises the modern intellectuals of his era for laying down their 'moral authority' to the interests of a commissioning entity, thus becoming a mouthpiece for governments and companies to justify predetermined positions, 'which could disguise the truth of what was occurring in the name of institutional "expediency" or "national honour"'.[35] Perhaps the clearest marker of Benda's conception being divorced from the ivory tower is the element of true risk associated with being an intellectual. Benda encourages intellectuals to carry out their work whilst confronting the risk of 'being burned at the stake, ostracized or crucified'.[36] The idea of being a non-conformist in order to be an intellectual resonates in Benda's theory and while Said appreciates the drive towards truth in this conception, it is Gramsci whom he thinks offers a realistic view of the intellectual. Quoting the surge of new vocations emerging in the twentieth century, Said mentions that 'broadcasters, academic professionals, computer analysts ... government advisors ... and indeed the whole field of modern mass journalism' can be seen as modern-day vindications of Gramsci's intellectual.[37] Said ends this comparison between Benda and Gramsci with the suggestion of his preferred conception, stating that 'everyone who works in any field connected with the production or distribution of knowledge is an intellectual in Gramsci's sense', clearly advocating for this more accommodating definition.[38] He goes on to look at how intellectuals carry out their practice and noteworthy for this chapter is the idea of specialised language: 'Each intellectual, the book editor and the author, the military strategist and the international lawyer, speaks and deals in a language that has become specialized and usable by other members of the same field, specialized experts addressing other specialized experts in a lingua franca unintelligible to unspecialized people.'

Here, the public role of the intellectual comes into focus. When an intellectual engages with knowledge, the idea of doing intellectual work for a greater purpose than one's own enlightenment should guide the inquiry. It is clear from both Benda's and Gramsci's visions that intellectuals are not self-serving creatures in that the work they undertake often has greater objectives than appeasing the intellectual's fancy. The idea of accountability to society permeates both conceptions to suggest that as much as intellectuals work for themselves, they also conduct their intellectual work in service to a public. The notion of an intellectual echo chamber becomes a real danger when the knowledge under exploration becomes exclusive to only those who have dedicated themselves to that intellectual vocation. This is particularly problematic when it comes to the use of intellectuals by governments to consolidate policy positions that may be to the detriment of ordinary people. Here we can see how intellectuals can become weapons that ensure that elite, powerful minority forces controlling global happenings continue to subjugate and oppress the disenfranchised majorities they so often refer to as 'the people', 'the poorest of the poor' or 'the masses'.

Said offers a compelling argument for the public role of the intellectual:

> The intellectual is an individual with a specific public role in society that cannot be reduced simply to being a faceless, professional, a competent member of a class just going about his or her business. The central fact, for me is, I think, that the intellectual is an individual endowed with a faculty for representing, embodying, articulating, a message, a view, an attitude, philosophy, or opinion to, as well as for, a public.[39]

Despite the fact that different publics are able to access, intellectually, different types of knowledge, the factor of representation must never be forgotten by intellectuals, whether they use specialised language or not. Said continues:

> And this role has an edge to it, and cannot be played without a sense of being someone whose place it is publicly to raise embarrassing questions, to confront orthodoxy and dogma (rather than produce them), to be someone who cannot easily be co-opted by governments or corporations, and whose *raison d'être* is to represent all those people and issues that are routinely forgotten or swept under the rug.[40]

Here we start to see a common thread linking the work of an artivist with the work of an intellectual. Both these designations require individuals practising as artivists or intellectuals to place at the core of their actions the representation of marginalised or suppressed voices. The link is further grounded in Said's argument: 'The intellectual does so on the basis of universal principles: that all human beings are entitled to expect decent standards of behavior concerning freedom and justice from worldly powers or nations, and that deliberate or inadvertent violations of these standards need to be testified and fought against courageously.'[41]

Writing in 1944, Charles Wright Mills suggested that intellectuals were faced with two choices in terms of the manner of their practice: the first, the struggle of a 'despondent sense of powerlessness' at being relegated to the margins of society and the second, 'joining the ranks of institutions, corporations or governments', as unaccountable members of self-regulating, decision-making elite groups.[42] The two choices, obscurity or assimilation, determined, in Mills's opinion, to a great extent the trajectory of the intellectual's career. The danger of institutional affiliation is that the intellectual may surrender the sound of their own voice to echo the institutional imperative, whereas non-affiliation could mean that the intellectual's practice is so obscure or minuscule in the face of a knowledge economy dominated by tertiary institutions that it never reaches the public/s for which it is intended. Mills, who seems to support the cause of the independent intellectual, suggests that for this intellectual there is a singular primary objective: 'The independent artist and intellectual are among the few remaining personalities equipped to resist and to fight stereotyping and consequent death of genuinely living things. Fresh perception now involves the capacity to continually unmask and to smash the stereotypes of vision and intellect with which modern communications [i.e. modern systems of representation] swamp us. These worlds of mass-art and mass-thought are increasingly geared to the demand of politics.'[43]

The beauty of this statement is the inclusion of the artist in this objective. We come to see how both the praxes of intellectuals and artists can become pacifying agents, advancing the unscrupulous interests of governments and corporations. Mills argues: 'That is why it is in politics that intellectual solidarity and effort must be centered. If the thinker does not relate himself to the value of truth in political struggle, he cannot responsibly cope with the whole of live experience.'[44]

The responsibility of artivists echoes in Mills's sentiment in that artivist action is about direct action that seeks to disrupt the order of the day by finding creative strategies to the limitations provided by conditions born out of repressive political situations. Said suggests that Mills argued that the public role of the intellectual is to stand up against the immense power of governments and large organisations in defence of 'the relative weakness not just of individuals but of human beings considered to have subaltern status, minorities, small peoples and states, inferior or lesser cultures and races'.[45] Said clarifies that for him, 'the intellectual belongs on the same side with the weak or unrepresented', suggesting that intellectuals must, in their practice, champion the causes of the subalterns of the society. I return to this point later in this chapter.

MANDISI SINDO: THE PUBLIC INTELLECTUAL AS ARTIVIST

South African theatre director Greg Karvellas offers a glimpse into Sindo's character: 'Mandisi Sindo is an incredible driving force in the South African Theatre landscape ... He works tirelessly to create opportunities for young artists. He works day and night in pursuit of bridging the divide in the arts sector in South Africa and I feel he needs to be recognised. Without him, many young artists would not have a platform to express themselves.'[46]

As Karvellas points out, there is generally a lack of support and tolerance for the type of activism undertaken by Sindo. His drive towards activism emanates from multiple realisations that led him to go beyond the call of being only an artist. The first of these realisations was that black theatre makers were excluded from major mainstream theatre events in the city of Cape Town. He also gradually discovered that the city was not interested in building cultural and recreational facilities in the townships. As a skilled theatre maker with local and international credits as an actor and director, Sindo could have opted to survive on the work his agency found for him and focused on developing his own career by doing what many township-born youths do when they get a break: leave the township. Sindo, however, chose to stay and put his hard-earned degree, his passion for human development and a raging fire to battle the injustices faced by black people in marginalised communities to good use. Referring to what is now the award-winning shack theatre, Makukhanye Art Room, Sindo says: 'The venue is an increasingly important gathering space for dramatic productions, dance recitals, educational workshops, mentorship programs and community meetings. It provides for an ever-growing audience and network of actors, musicians, dancers, writers, directors, and artists based in Khayelitsha, who find it difficult to access the cultural infrastructure that otherwise exists in Cape Town's city centre.'[47]

The well-worn trope about the small audiences in theatres nowadays, usually coupled with 'we need to take theatre to the people', is not just a buzz phrase for Sindo, but a daily lived experience. Rather than shying away from the poverty that is often glamourised by the middle-class and upper circles of society, Sindo is adamant on the need for revitalisation of township spaces as opposed to migration to the suburbs when considering the prospects of youth currently living in these spaces. 'We proudly call this space a shack theatre, because it is a huge shack surrounded by hundreds of shacks,' posits Sindo, boldly affirming the intentional positioning of Makukhanye Art Room.[48] Faye Kabali-Kagwa illustrates the surroundings of Makukhanye: 'It sits next to the market stalls in Site B ... The Makukhanye Art Room logo takes up an entire wall, painted proudly against a black backdrop. Another wall is painted red with the words "Kasi-2-Kasi" ... other walls are decorated with colourful murals, and the rest are covered with the names of productions that have graced its stage. It is a history made alive and visible.'[49]

Makukhanye's growth has had a definite impact on the community of Khayelitsha through productions by theatre makers who would have otherwise never performed in the township. Sindo is affecting his immediate environment through Makukhanye by bringing illustrious productions to what he often refers to as 'the forgotten township'. These have included two productions that both claimed top honours at the Zabalaza Theatre Festival hosted by the Baxter Theatre, including *Fruit* by Paul Noko and *Worst of Both Worlds* by Bulelani Mabutyana.[50] Though both works were staged in Cape Town, there was very little chance for the audiences of Khayelitsha to watch these shows because the costs associated with going to theatres in town make the trip too expensive. This fact moved Sindo to start looking further than just sharpening the tools of his own craft and in an effort to make quality work and opportunities more accessible to his people, he set out to become an artivist.

Unlike the artivist interventions in the examples above, Sindo's conception of artivism is not only tangible and event-based, but is also a philosophy for his praxis as an artist. Once an artist has decided to become a voice for their people, they set aside personal ambition in service to the needs of the community they represent. Artivism goes from becoming an interventionist strategy for responding to particular events or crises that affect groups of the society and evolves into an ideology that governs their approach to the practice of their art. In accordance with the standing tradition of artivist intervention, Sindo staged the work *Mari and Kana* as a response to the Marikana tragedy at Lonmin mine in 2012 when 34 miners were shot dead by the police.[51] The piece was staged in a public space as part of the Infecting the City Festival in Cape Town in 2015 and was mounted as a performance art installation accompanied by physical theatre and live vocals. Crosses representing the graves of the fallen miners were strewn around the space, encouraging members of the public to actively engage with and move through the artwork.

Sindo's decision to set his base of operations in Khayelitsha serves to concretise his practice of artivism beyond reactionary interventions. Kabali-Kagwa muses on the mystification associated with African storytelling: 'We are told that we conjure stories out of thin air and tell them with flair. Advertising campaigns constantly remind us that we sing well and have innate rhythm – bursting into song at the slightest provocation.'[52] She affirms that the honing of these abilities, which are perceived to be innate, is essential, but cautions that 'schools and arts programmes are located in the suburbs and city centres', excluding those who cannot access these spaces, mainly because of financial constraints. The problem is further exacerbated when township community festivals are used as spaces 'for mining talent' that is 'then validated elsewhere'.

Makukhanye Art Room has been breaking this narrative to widen the scope of the arts in Cape Town and to promote inclusivity in township spaces 'by being an independent, multifaceted, high-quality performance and rehearsal space for artists and audiences who want to make and access work in Khayelitsha'.[53] Beyond merely providing a space for the philosophy and practice of artivism to thrive, Sindo has also used Makukhanye Art Room and now KASI RC as spaces for art education, performance, public dialogue and debate for issues at the heart of the black artist's experience in Cape Town's entertainment industry. On 16 June 2017, a four-part conversation series, titled *Black Art & Communities at Heart*, was launched at Makukhanye. Kabali-Kagwa explains that 'Sindo conceptualised the series of "decolonial conversations in a space where it matters". All four conversations were hosted at Makukhanye and dealt with various topics affecting black art, artists and communities such as "State of the townships", "Homophobia, Queerness and Patriarchy in the township", "Defining Community Theatre" and "Liberating Black Artists".'[54]

Further considering the public value of Makukhanye, Kabali-Kagwa refers to 'an industry meeting held at the theatre', where 'artists and stakeholders met in reaction to violent attacks that had left a number of artists injured or dead', leading the theatre to call for all sectors of the entertainment industry 'to respond to the violence as one voice'.[55] Sindo does not consider himself some sort of messiah, but functions and encourages others to function as beacons of truth and justice in their environments. Unlike most public intellectuals, Sindo's intellectualism emanates outside of the traditional written word. Keeping in mind the public he serves, perhaps Sindo has come to realise that writing for academic journals or advancing the mandate of tertiary institutions as a scholar may serve to disconnect him from the people he feels a need to represent.

THE SUBALTERN AND POST-COLONIALITY

The Subaltern Studies Collective is a group of Indian historians whose major focus is colonialism and post-colonialism with an emphasis on historiography.[56] According to Jane Hiddlestone: 'Founded by [the influential historian Ranajit] Guha in 1982, *Subaltern Studies* was an annual publication of historiographical essays ... whose objective ... was to rewrite the political history of colonial India from the point of view of the people.'[57] The collective borrowed the term 'subaltern' from Gramsci, who coined it in reference to those inhabitants belonging to the lowest class status in society. The collective characterised their use of the term in the following manner: 'The disenfranchised peasantry exploited by the colonists and deprived at the same time of a voice with which to express their response to their condition.' The aim of the journal was to illustrate how historical accounts of India in relation to colonialism and post-colonialism were written from one of two perspectives; the first being that of the colonising nation and the second, 'a native bourgeois elite'.[58]

Part of the scope of the journal's publications included writings by Guha, Partha Chatterjee and Dipesh Chakrabarty, with an emphasis on and critique of Marxist principles and Michel Foucault's positions on the complicity of power and knowledge.[59] These views were complemented by revelations on 'how economic oppression is directly mirrored by the suppression of the voice'. Guha sketches the problematic situation that brought about the journal's existence, through an interrogation of historical texts on colonial and post-colonial India: 'The colonial elitist form of history presents Indian nationalism as the sum of activities and ideas by which the Indian hegemonic class responded to the colonial establishment.

The bourgeois elitist version defines Indian nationalism as an idealist venture in which the indigenous elite led the people from subjugation to freedom.'[60]

The exclusion of an account that represents the agency of the subaltern class in liberating themselves from the clutches of colonialism provided a gap, which Guha and the collective sought to explore. A noteworthy voice from the collective is post-colonial intellectual Gayatri Spivak, who, while she associates with the group, criticises it for the danger of doing the same thing done by colonial texts written from the perspectives of the two groups mentioned above.[61] One of her most famous essays, 'Can the Subaltern Speak?', shows clearly that any person claiming to speak for the subaltern also suppresses the subaltern voice.[62] The risks faced by the collective led to a lack of 'self-conscious reflection on its own ethics', due in part to the fact that sources for their inquiries were limited, forcing them to rely to an extent on texts written by the two groups they aimed to counter. As Hiddlestone points out: 'If they set out to rewrite Indian history from the point of view of the masses, it was ultimately difficult for them to know the complex facets of that occluded and subjugated perspective. In asserting a new form of historiography ... the movement did not fully take on board the ethical difficulties of its own project.'[63]

The composition of the Subaltern Studies Collective was representative not of the subaltern, but of those claiming to speak for them, thereby posing the same threat that colonial and native bourgeois accounts of colonialism and post-colonialism did. To return to the point made above about the role of artivism in giving a voice to the voiceless, Spivak concludes her essay with two revelations: first that the term 'subaltern', in her context referred to Indian women of the lower class and, second, in relation to the question posed by the essay's title, she argues that the subaltern cannot, in fact, speak.[64]

However, when one considers the interventions presented as examples of artivism earlier in this chapter, it becomes clear how artivism can make space for the subaltern to find a voice, to speak and to be heard. The intellectual role of the collective is expressed by means of the journal – a text-based medium for knowledge production and engagement – whereas artivism offers multidisciplinary platforms for providing a space for those affected by injustices (such as colonialism) to respond to and fight back against their oppressors, much like the journal aimed to do. Artivists do not claim to speak for, but rather attempt to speak with and collaborate with the subaltern, not for the subaltern. In this way, artivism offers intellectuals such as Mandisi Sindo the opportunity to find alternative forms of engaging with various publics and exploring their public role.

SINDO AND THE SUBALTERN

Spivak's criticism of the Subaltern Studies Collective is countered by Sindo's active, non-text-based engagements with the societal ills plaguing the public to which he feels obligated.

The conversation series *Black Art & Communities at Heart*, which was held in partnership with the Institute for the Creative Arts at the University of Cape Town, according to Kate-Lyn Moore, 'prompted healing', but was 'also disturbing and provoking for many in attendance' – an allusion to Sindo's unapologetic stance on the positions he assumes.[65] As Kabali-Kagwa suggests, 'Makukhanye simultaneously highlights structural oppression and subverts the expectations caused by racism and classism.'[66] Sindo often speaks publicly about the divides that rule the theatre sector in Cape Town and his rhetoric frequently centres on the segregation and marginalisation that still exists today in one of South Africa's most divided cities.

Deemed notorious by some for asking 'difficult' questions, Sindo unashamedly asks: 'Why is there no art centre or a theatre in the townships in Cape Town?' In doing so, he pinpoints immediately the core of the problem, arguing : 'It is a problem that mainstream or white practiced work is still seen as superior', in opposition to community-based theatre made by black theatre practitioners.[67] Perhaps Sindo's most formidable public address came at a conference at Ghent University in Belgium titled 'Removing Apartheid'. He argued: 'The trauma of the collective black past keeps us looking back on where we come from as black people and our creativity, just like our identity, is based on those traumatic moments. Apartheid, racism, discrimination is something psychological, something that one is taught while growing up. It will never be easy to remove these issues from our society.'[68]

He followed up his opening remarks with an allusion to the student protests that came to be known as #FeesMustFall and #RhodesMustFall, which brought attention to the plight experienced by tertiary-level students from the marginalised communities of which Sindo himself is a product. 'These movements are initiated and fuelled by young people fighting for their educational rights. This is a fight against their own government … It's a sign of the ages', a reminiscing Sindo elaborated, as he was reminded of the Soweto Uprising of 1976.[69] He continued: 'It takes us back to the olden days when young people of 1976 fought the National Party and Afrikaner rule – now they want free education and the land to be returned to its rightful owners.' Critical in his rhetoric not only of governance in his city, but also of coverage and reportage of events at the time, Sindo lambasted the media for 'steering information regarding Fees/Rhodes Must Fall along very windy roads', arguing that 'the comradeship and intellectual qualities of a strike aimed at the future of the country is swept under the carpet'. When he eventually arrives at the theme of the conference, 'Removing Apartheid', Sindo's position is clear and unequivocal:

> The removal of statues and renaming of streets will never remove the apartheid. Apartheid cannot be removed ... Apartheid needs to be demolished ... We do not need to remove apartheid; we must destroy it. Segregation is a predominant social issue in Cape Town. There exists very little integration between black, white and coloured communities in and around the city. Forced removals during Apartheid and Industrialisation led to this artificial geographic. This ever-present system continues to place white people in a more superior and socio-economically affluent space than the black and coloured population. By pushing us to the outskirts of society we are also facing impossible challenges to be and make the change we desire to see in our country ... The problematic cycle continues.[70]

The artificial geographic to which Sindo refers can be seen in all the major cities in South Africa: Pretoria – the proximity of Mamelodi, Soshanguve and Atteridgeville to the city centre; Johannesburg – Alexandra, Soweto, Diepsloot and Tembisa; Durban, Cape Town and many other places across the vast expanse of this land. In each of these cities, townships designed during apartheid prevail on the outskirts of the major cities and yet the divide between the two can be whittled down to a single road, bridge, rivulet or structure that symbolises the end of the township and the beginning of the town. The even greater tragedy is the commute taken by workers who live in townships, but work in town – people who can literally see the built environment improve as they get closer to work, mirrored by the deterioration suffered on the commute back home. Sindo illustrates his argument with an example: 'Think about it this way: if you REMOVE that chair you are planning to put it down somewhere else, but if you DESTROY that chair you will throw it in the dust bin and move on. That is what needs to be done with apartheid. It needs to be destroyed ... not just removed.'[71]

Sindo ended his speech with the tragic story of his mother getting run over by a car – effectively crippling her – while she was on her way to work, as a domestic worker. The dehumanisation suffered by many domestic workers in South Africa, like his mother, led to a generation of children who were adamant that their exhausted parents were entitled to some rest while they enjoy the fruits of the labour of their children, and Sindo was no different. He concluded his speech stating that for him, it is most depressing that the apartheid system 'suppressed black women into the position of being domestic workers', leading him to the conclusion: 'The trauma of the black people of South Africa is too complex for a speech. It is an experience. It is embedded in our genetic identity.'[72]

Perhaps more work is required to strengthen the links between artivism and intellectualism and the different streams of each as practised by different artists. Today, Sindo is engaged with two new ventures, namely Mandimila Casting Agency, Khayelitsha's first casting agency, and KASI RC, where youths in the communities surrounding Khayelitsha can have a space that provides alternatives to the dangers lurking in every township, responsible for taking many young lives.

***

Future studies may pull at threads found in this chapter, towards further considering how different vocations can practise alternative forms of public intellectualism. Artivism provides a dual approach: firstly, through events-based interventions, such as that staged at at the Climate Conference in Paris, or Banksy's graffiti art, and second, through embodying the philosophy of artivism and allowing it to become the modus operandi of one's practice as an artist, as we see Mandisi Sindo do.

Sindo's wide-ranging contributions to the arts as a theatre and film practitioner, coupled with his community activism, centred on providing truthful knowledge and opportunities to people living in disadvantaged communities not only resonates with Said's conception of what an 'intellectual' should be, but also provides an alternative mode for considering how public intellectualism can be practised through artivism. The possibilities provided by the arts have proved effective in advancing many a mass struggle and there is still much more work to be done to probe and concretise the concept of artivism. However, in its current state, one can draw the conclusion that in the South African arts, at least, artivism – and thus alternative public intellectualism – has a future.

NOTES

[1] José María Mesías-Lema, 'Artivism and Social Conscience: Transforming Teacher Training from a Sensibility Standpoint', *Communicar: Media Education Research Journal* 26, no. 57 (October 2018): 20.

[2] Lilford Lesabe, 'Makukhanye Art Room: The First Shack Theatre in Khayelitsha', *Lead SA*, 13 June 2018, accessed 2 February 2019, http://capetalk.co.za/articles/306989/makukhanye-art-room-the-first-shack-theatre-in-khayelitsha

3   Lesabe, 'Makukhanye Art Room'; Faye Kabali-Kagwa, 'Where Theatre Dreams Are Made Real', *Mail & Guardian*, 24 November 2017, accessed 2 February 2019, https://mg.co.za/article/2017-11-24-00-where-theatre-dreams-are-made-real
4   Kabali-Kagwa, 'Theatre Dreams'.
5   Kabali-Kagwa, 'Theatre Dreams'.
6   Shifaan, Ryklief, 'Khayelitsha Art School Turns Shack Theatre into Soup Kitchen', *Coronavirus Monitor*, 1 May 2020, accessed 30 July 2020, https://www.coronavirusmonitor.co.za/people/khayelitsha-artschool-turns-the-shack-theatre-into-soup-kitchen/
7   Nina Felshin, '¿Pero esto es arte? El espiritu del arte como activismo', in *Modos de hacer: Arte crítico esfera pública y acción directa*, ed. Paloma Blanco, Jesús Carrillo, Jordi Claramonte and Marcelo Expósito (Salamanca: Unversidad de Salamanca, 2001), 73–94.
8   Gabriella Leon, 'Artivism', *Beautiful Rising*, 2019, accessed 2 February 2019, https://beautifulrising.org/tool/artivism
9   Lucy Lippard, 'Mirando alrededor: Donde estamos y donde podriamos estar', in *Modos de hacer: Arte crítico esfera pública y acción directa*, ed. Paloma Blanco, Jesús Carrillo, Jordi Claramonte and Marcelo Expósito (Salamanca: Unversidad de Salamanca, 2001), 57.
10 Mesías-Lema, 'Artivism and Social Conscience', 21.
11 Mesías-Lema, 'Artivism and Social Conscience', 22.
12 Leon, 'Artivism'.
13 Leon, 'Artivism'.
14 Che Ramsden, 'Artivism: Art as Activism, Activism as Art', *Open Democracy*, 10 September 2016, accessed 2 February 2019, https://www.opendemocracy.net/ch-ramsden/artivism-art-as-activism-activism-as-art
15 Ramsden, 'Artivism'.
16 Ramsden, 'Artivism'.
17 Eva Aladro-Vico, Olga Bailey and Dimitrina Jivkova-Semova, 'Artivism: A New Educative Language for Transformative Social Action', *Communicar: Media Education Research Journal* 57, no. 4 (July 2018): 13.
18 Simon Sheikh, 'Positively Trojan Horses Revisited', *e-flux*, October 2009, accessed 15 February 2019, https://www.e-flux.com/journal/09/61372/positively-trojan-horses-revisited/
19 Aladro-Vico, Bailey and Jivkova-Semova, 'Artvisim', 13.
20 Yannicke Goris and Saskia Hollander, *Activism, Artivism and Beyond: Inspiring Initiatives of Civic Power* (Amsterdam: Partos, 2017), 8.
21 Goris and Hollander, *Activism*, 8–9.
22 Goris and Hollander, *Activism*, 9.
23 Goris and Hollander, *Activism*, 9.
24 Nondumiso Msimanga and Jenny Nijenhuis, 'SA's Dirty Laundry and the Things We Do for Love: Love and Artivism as Process-Protest', *Agenda* 31, no. 3–4 (2017): 52.
25 Msimanga and Nijenhaus, 'SA's Dirty Laundry', 54.
26 Msimanga and Nijenhaus, 'SA's Dirty Laundry', 55.
27 Manuel Delgado, 'Artivism and Post-Politics: On the Aestheticization of Social Struggles in Urban Contexts', 2013, accessed 21 December 2020, https://www.researchgate.net/publication/293141699_Artivism_and_post-politics_On_the_aestheticization_of_social_struggles_in_urban_contexts
28 Edward Said, *Representations of the Intellectual* (New York: Vintage Books, 1996).

29 Antonio Gramsci, *Selections from Prison Notebooks*, trans. Quintin Hoare and Geoffrey N. Smith (London: Lawrence & Wishart, 1971), quoted in Said, *Representations of the Intellectual*, 3.
30 Said, *Representations of the Intellectual*, 4.
31 Julien Benda, *The Treason of Intellectuals*, trans. Richard Aldington (New York: Norton, 1969); Said, *Representations of the Intellectual*, 4–5.
32 Said, *Representations of the Intellectual*, 5.
33 Benda, *The Treason of Intellectuals*, 43.
34 Said, *Representations of the Intellectual*, 5–6.
35 Said, *Representations of the Intellectual*, 6.
36 Said, *Representations of the Intellectual*, 7.
37 Said, *Representations of the Intellectual*, 8–9.
38 Said, *Representations of the Intellectual*, 9.
39 Said, *Representations of the Intellectual*, 11.
40 Said, *Representations of the Intellectual*, 11.
41 Said, *Representations of the Intellectual*, 11–12.
42 Said, *Representations of the Intellectual*, 20. Charles Wright Mills, *Power, Politics and People: The Collected Essays of C. Wright Mills*, ed. Irving L. Horowitz (New York: Ballantine, 1963).
43 Mills, *Power, Politics and People*, 299.
44 Mills, *Power, Politics and People*, 299.
45 Said, *Representations of the Intellectual*, 22.
46 In Lesabe, 'Makukhanye Art Room'.
47 In Lesabe, 'Makukhanye Art Room'.
48 In Kabali-Kagwa, 'Theatre Dreams'.
49 Kabali-Kagwa, 'Theatre Dreams'.
50 Kabali-Kagwa, 'Theatre Dreams'.
51 Mandisi Sindo, dir., *Mari and Kana*, Infecting the City Festival, Cape Town, 2015, accessed 2 February 2019, http://infectingthecity.com/2015/artist/mandisi-sindo/?p=1
52 Kabali-Kagwa, 'Theatre Dreams'.
53 Kabali-Kagwa, 'Theatre Dreams'.
54 Kabali-Kagwa, 'Theatre Dreams'.
55 Kabali-Kagwa, 'Theatre Dreams'.
56 Jane Hiddlestone, *Understanding Postcolonialism* (London: Routledge, 2014), 68.
57 Hiddlestone, *Understanding Postcolonialism*, 68.
58 Hiddlestone, *Understanding Postcolonialism*, 68–69.
59 Hiddlestone, *Understanding Postcolonialism*, 69.
60 Ranajit Guha, 'On Some Aspects of the Historiography of Colonial India', in *Subaltern Studies I: Writings on South Asian History and Society*, ed. Ranajit Guha (Delhi: Oxford University Press, 1982), 2.
61 Gayatri C. Spivak, 'Subaltern Studies: Deconstructing Historiography', in *The Spivak Reader*, ed. Donna Landry and Gerald MacLean (London: Routledge, 1996), 203-235.
62 Gayatri C. Spivak, 'Can the Subaltern Speak?' in *Marxism and the Interpretation of Culture*, ed. Cary Nelsen and Lawrence Grossberg (Urbana: University of Illinois Press, 1988), 271–313.
63 Hiddlestone, *Understanding Postcolonialism*, 74.
64 Spivak, 'Can the Subaltern Speak?'

65 Kate-Lyn Moore, 'Art and the Township', *UCT News*, 20 June 2017, accessed 2 February 2019, https://www.news.uct.ac.za/article/-2017-06-20-art-and-the-township
66 Kabali-Kagwa, 'Theatre Dreams'.
67 Moore, 'Art and the Township'.
68 Mandisi Sindo, 'Let's Destroy Apartheid' (paper presented at On: Removing Apartheid Conference, Ghent University, Belgium, 30 September, 2016).
69 Sindo, 'Let's Destroy Apartheid'.
70 Sindo, 'Let's Destroy Apartheid'.
71 Sindo, 'Let's Destroy Apartheid'.
72 Sindo, 'Let's Destroy Apartheid'.

REFERENCES

Aladro-Vico, Eva, Olga Bailey and Dimitrina Jivkova-Semova. 'Artivism: A New Educative Language for Transformative Social Action'. *Communicar: Media Education Research Journal* 57, no. 4 (July 2018): 9–18.

Benda, Julien. *The Treason of Intellectuals*. Translated by Richard Aldington. New York: Norton, 1969. Originally published in 1928.

Delgado, Manuel. 'Artivism and Post-Politics: On the Aestheticization of Social Struggles in Urban Contexts'. 2013. Accessed 21 December 2020. https://www.researchgate.net/publication/293141699_Artivism_and_post-politics_On_the_aestheticization_of_social_struggles_in_urban_contexts

Felshin, Nina. '¿Pero esto es arte? El espiritu del arte como activismo'. In *Modos de hacer: Arte crítico esfera pública y acción directa*, edited by Paloma Blanco, Jesús Carrillo, Jordi Claramonte and Marcelo Expósito, 73–94. Salamanca: Unversidad de Salamanca, 2001.

Goris, Yannicke and Saskia Hollander. *Activism, Artivism and Beyond: Inspiring Initiatives of Civic Power*. Amsterdam: Partos, 2017.

Gramsci, Antonio. *Selections from Prison Notebooks*. Translated by Quintin Hoare and Geoffrey N. Smith. London: Lawrence and Wishart, 1971.

Guha, Ranajit. 'On Some Aspects of the Historiography of Colonial India'. In *Subaltern Studies I: Writings on South Asian History and Society*, edited by Ranajit Guha, 1–8. Delhi: Oxford University Press, 1982.

Hiddlestone, Jane. *Understanding Postcolonialism*. London: Routledge, 2014.

Kabali-Kagwa, Faye. 'Where Theatre Dreams Are Made Real'. *Mail & Guardian*, 24 November 2017. Accessed 2 February 2019. https://mg.co.za/article/2017-11-24-00-where-theatre-dreams-are-made-real

Leon, Gabriella. 'Artivism'. *Beautiful Rising*, 2019. Accessed 2 February 2019. https://beautifulrising.org/tool/artivism

Lesabe, Lilford. 'Makukhanye Art Room: The First Shack Theatre in Khayelitsha'. *Lead SA*, 13 June 2018. Accessed 2 February 2019. http://capetalk.co.za/articles/306989/makukhanye-art-room-the-first-shack-theatre-in-khayelitsha

Lippard, Lucy R. 'Mirando alrededor: Donde estamos y donde podriamos estar'. In *Modos de hacer: Arte crítico esfera pública y acción directa*, edited by Paloma Blanco, Jesús Carrillo, Jordi Claramonte and Marcelo Expósito, 51–71. Salamanca: Unversidad de Salamanca, 2001.

Mesías-Lema, José María. 'Artivism and Social Conscience: Transforming Teacher Training from a Sensibility Standpoint'. *Communicar: Media Education Research Journal* 26, no. 57 (October 2018): 19–28.

Mills, Charles Wright. *Power, Politics and People: The Collected Essays of C. Wright Mills*. Edited by Irving L. Horowitz. New York: Ballantine, 1963.

Moore, Kate-Lyn. 'Art and the Township'. *UCT News*, 20 June 2017. Accessed 2 February 2019. https://www.news.uct.ac.za/article/-2017-06-20-art-and-the-township

Msimanga, Nondumiso and Jenny Nijenhuis. 'SA's Dirty Laundry and the Things We Do for Love: Love and Artivism as Process-Protest'. *Agenda* 31, no. 3–4 (2017): 50–59.

Ramsden, Che. 'Artivism: Art as Activism, Activism as Art'. *Open Democracy*, 10 September 2016. Accessed 2 February 2019. https://www.opendemocracy.net/ch-ramsden/artivism-art-as-activism-activism-as-art

Ryklief, Shifaan. 'Khayelitsha Art School Turns Shack Theatre into Soup Kitchen'. *Coronavirus Monitor*, 1 May 2020. Accessed 30 July 2020. https://www.coronavirusmonitor.co.za/people/khayelitsha-artschool-turns-the-shack-theatre-into-soup-kitchen/

Said, Edward. *Representations of the Intellectual*. New York: Vintage Books, 1996.

Sheikh, Simon. 'Positively Trojan Horses Revisited'. *e-flux*, October 2009. Accessed 15 February 2019. https://www.e-flux.com/journal/09/61372/positively-trojan-horses-revisited/

Sindo, Mandisi. 'Let's Destroy Apartheid'. Paper presented at the On: Removing Apartheid Conference, Ghent University, Belgium, 30 September 2016.

Sindo, Mandisi, dir. *Mari and Kana*. Infecting the City Festival, Cape Town, 2015. Accessed 2 February 2019. http://infectingthecity.com/2015/artist/mandisi-sindo/?p=1

Spivak, Gayatri C. 'Can the Subaltern Speak?' In *Marxism and the Interpretation of Culture*, edited by Cary Nelsen and Lawrence Grossberg, 271–313. Urbana: University of Illinois Press, 1988.

Spivak, Gayatri C. 'Subaltern Studies: Deconstructing Historiography'. In *The Spivak Reader*, edited by Donna Landry and Gerald MacLean, 203–235. London: Routledge, 1996.

CHAPTER

9

The Janus-Faced Public Intellectual: Dr Thomas Duncan Greenlees at the Institute for Imbecile Children, 1895–1907

Rory du Plessis

In June 1907, Dr Thomas Duncan Greenlees informed the Colonial Office of the Cape of his intention to retire. He testified that since 1890, 'I have worked strenuously for the good of the institutions I have had charge of.'[1] The institutions were situated in Makhanda, formerly known as Grahamstown, and included the Grahamstown Lunatic Asylum (hereafter 'the asylum'), where he was the medical superintendent from 1890 to 1907; the Chronic Sick Hospital, where he was the surgeon-superintendent from 1890 to 1903; and the Institute for Imbecile Children, which he founded in 1895 and was its visiting medical officer until 1907.[2] During his tenure at these institutions, Greenlees was prolific in his public and professional engagements. He gave numerous public lectures, hosted public activities at the asylum, as well as founding and editing an asylum magazine titled the *Fort England Mirror*. Greenlees achieved prominence in the Cape medical fraternity as a member of the Eastern Province branch of the British Medical Association and he served as its president in 1897 and again in 1903. He was also a member of the Eastern Province Literary and Scientific Society, the South African Medical Association and the South African Association for the Advancement of Science.[3] He was a prolific author of psychiatric studies, some of which were published in journals of critical acclaim, including the *South African Medical Journal*, the *British Journal of Psychiatry* and the *American Journal of Psychiatry*.

In his public engagements, two of Greenlees's priorities were addressing the stigma of the asylum and mental illness and encouraging the public to provide charitable aid to the institutionalised patients under his care. Greenlees was a laudable public campaigner for destigmatising the asylum and mental illness, and magnanimous in fostering public charity for the institutionalised patients. This is in stark contrast to his professional engagements, where he denounced children with intellectual disabilities as 'helpless waifs' and declared them 'monstrosities' that should be condemned by the government to 'destruction'.[4] Greenlees was thus Janus-faced: in his public intellectualism, he successfully produced and promoted a positive image of the asylum, but in his professional tenure, he denied children with intellectual disabilities their personhood and their humanness and advocated for their extermination.

This chapter seeks to investigate the Janus-faced nature of Greenlees, by adopting John Law's pinboard approach.[5] A pinboard account can be 'understood as the inverse of narrative. If narrative is about tying things together, then a pinboard works to keep things apart and separate. If narrative is about erasing non-coherence, then a pinboard is instead about exploring and articulating these differences and non-coherencies.'[6]

Law points out that a 'common predicament of the storyteller' is identification of the 'rough edges', the non-coherence, contradictions and inconsistencies of reality.[7] The storyteller seeks to erase the '"messiness" of reality', by adopting a singular narrative, where differences are explained away as instances of 'faulty vision, biased perspective, inadequate information, local interests, whatever else'.[8] The pinboard approach seeks to 'juxtapose' the conflicting and diverging elements, to raise the 'prospect that there are different and valid knowledges that can be neither entirely reconciled nor dismissed, and suggests that knowing is or might properly be, a process that is also decentered, distributed, but also partially connected. The logic of juxtaposition renders it inappropriate, even impossible, to draw things together into singularity.'[9]

By identifying the unviability of offering a singular narrative account – through foregrounding juxtaposition and the diverging fractures contained in a story – the pinboard approach resists and refuses the possibility of redemptive narratives.[10] The main motivation for adopting a pinboard approach in this chapter is the refusal to construct a redemptive narrative for the Janus-faced Greenlees. To this end, I seek to juxtapose Greenlees's public intellectualism with the stance that he projected in his professional tenure. By highlighting the contrasts between Greenlees's public face and his professional face, in 'such a way that it does not attempt to render any of those points of interest more important, true, real or general than the others', any attempt at redemption is rendered a fallacy.[11] In this way, Greenlees's derogatory and dehumanising stance towards children with intellectual disabilities can on no account be redeemed by his successful philanthropic campaign or by his creation of a positive public image of the asylum. One outcome of refusing redemptive narratives is that it opens up the possibility to explore areas of knowledge that have previously been neglected.[12] Accordingly, I explore the Institute for Imbecile Children's casebook as an untapped resource, in order to recover the personhood and humanness of the children.

THE FACE OF THE PUBLIC INTELLECTUAL

Over several days in May 1892, a lecture in the town's assembly rooms was advertised on the front page of the local newspaper, *The Grahamstown Journal*. The presenter of the lecture was Greenlees and the lecture was titled 'The Brain: Its Development, Architecture, Functions, and Education'. The proceeds from the ticket sales were in aid of the Chronic Sick Hospital's entertainment fund. The day after the lecture, the newspaper reported that a large audience was enthralled by the lecture.[13] Shortly thereafter, Greenlees's lecture was published in the newspaper.

Greenlees opened his lecture by outlining the objectives of the evening, which were twofold. One of the objectives was to boost the entertainment fund of the Chronic Sick Hospital: 'By coming here to-night you are aiding ... in cheering the lives of many who are rapidly descending into the valley of shadows, and for this little deed done in kindness, you may rest assured you will not be forgotten by those who appreciate your liberty.'[14] The other objective entailed correcting the audience's understanding of mental illness: 'You are accustomed to look upon madness as something beyond the common. Some of you think the insane must be possessed of the evil one; this is all a delusion on your part; there is nothing more wonderful in a madman than there is in a man with a broken leg.'[15]

These two aims – to enlist the public's 'active philanthropy' to support the care of the institutionalised patients and to destigmatise the asylum and mental illness – are recurrent themes in Greenlees's engagements with the public.[16] In these engagements, Greenlees sought to cultivate a positive public image of the asylum as 'a Hospital for the treatment of acute and recoverable cases of insanity' that is ideally suited to the care of white, middle-class, paying patients.[17] The public image of the asylum was carefully crafted in multiple platforms and events, each of which publicised the achievements and the advantages of the establishment. These included acts of 'institutional display', in which the asylum was opened to the public for entertainments and activities, and the publication of the *Fort England Mirror*, which functioned as a brochure designed to present the asylum's ethos to the broader community and to attract custom from paying patients.[18]

OPENING THE ASYLUM TO VISITS FROM THE PUBLIC

During Greenlees's tenure, he sought to address and correct the public's misperceptions of asylums.[19] In general, the public were still frightened of asylums and they believed them to be closely allied with jails.[20] To remedy the public's misperceptions of the asylum, Greenlees aimed to open the asylum to visits from the public. He boldly posited that such events helped to mitigate the stigma regarding asylums: 'The more the public know of the internal working of an asylum the sooner will their prejudice against such institutions disappear.'[21] While the asylum afforded unlimited access to visits by government officials and appointed inspectors, it did not afford the same access to the public. Instead, public access was, for the most part, limited to attendance of the annual ball, cricket matches and the opening of new wards, facilities or buildings at the asylum. Thus, it becomes evident that Greenlees's aim for public visiting was less concerned with providing knowledge of the asylum's 'internal workings' – its therapeutic and disciplinary regimen – and more concerned with exhibiting to the public a curated view of the asylum and thereby its suitability for inclusion in the sociocultural landscape of the community.

Significantly, Greenlees extolled the asylum's annual ball as 'one of the excellent methods I occasionally adopt here of giving the public an opportunity of seeing for themselves the working of this establishment, on every occasion in which a Ball has been held, several members of Parliament receiving invitations, and availing themselves of this opportunity of inspecting the asylum'.[22] The asylum's annual ball included performances by the town's local band, the guests engaged in dancing and the 'supper was a work of art'.[23] Curiously, there is no mention of the public visiting the institution's wards or witnessing the care and treatment of the patients. In this sense, the asylum ball did not afford an inclusive view of the institution, but a 'dressed-up view', in which an immaculately neat and extravagantly decorated hall served as the backdrop to fine dining and dancing, and these were possibly interspersed with speeches about the asylum's ethos, goals and future direction.[24] Asylum balls, in the history of psychiatry, were never geared to afford an unmediated view of the establishment, but provided the medical superintendent with a 'highly controlled public relations opportunity between the asylum and the broader community, official visitors and invited guests'.[25] Thus, the ball gave Greenlees a means to present a carefully orchestrated positive image of the asylum, to counter sullied perceptions of the establishment held by the public.

Hosting asylum balls, along with inviting members of the public and the press to the ceremonial openings of new buildings and wards at the asylum, were important avenues through which Greenlees established links between the community and the asylum.[26] The activities offered at the asylum were important events for the citizens of the town and were regularly featured in *The Grahamstown Journal*. For example, the newspaper reported on the entertainment events hosted by the staff of the asylum, as well as the additions and alterations to the buildings of the asylum.[27] The press's reporting on the asylum established it as a community institution that offered events and festivities of local importance.

By inviting the press to the asylum's events, Greenlees caused the asylum to become a prominent establishment in the community. Rather than a stigmatised conception of the asylum as a stain on the community, the asylum under Greenlees's custodianship became rooted in the community's 'social and cultural landscape'.[28] It is imperative to foreground that the asylum's integration into the community landscape was largely directed at the population who were white and middle class: gala events, balls, ceremonial openings and inaugurations were public events that were part of the social circle of citizens who were white and who had leisure time and disposable income. Greenlees thus sought to secure positive integration of the asylum into the white and middle class community, rather than embracing all the communities that constituted the town. This is manifestly apparent in the importance that Greenlees attached to cricket matches for public engagements with the asylum.

Cricket matches were played with outside teams from as far afield as Port Elizabeth and when the matches were played at the asylum, Greenlees noted that they were very popular events with the local community and resulted in the asylum's grounds looking 'bright and cheerful with visitors, patients and cricketers'.[29] As cricket encouraged self-respect, self-control and appreciation for orderly behaviour, patients who participated in the sport were seen as respectable and self-disciplined and closely modelling the gentlemanly behaviour of the middle class.[30] Accordingly, visitors to the match were witness to the patients' behaviour, which countered stereotypes of the insane as wild, dishevelled and bestial. This point is evocatively expressed by Dr Dodds, the Cape Colony's Inspector of Asylums, who stated that cricket matches 'tend to correct the extravagant ideas that many even educated people still have in relation to asylums and the insane, and to enlist their sympathy on behalf of the sufferers who need all that enlightened medical science can do for them'.[31]

In Dodds's discussion, of interest is how an asylum's events can also be used to enlist the support of the public. We should not lose sight of how the aim of destigmatising the asylum, by forging connections with the community, consequently gave rise to some members of the public engaging in acts of charity.[32] Members of the community were able to contribute to the well-being, comfort and happiness of patients by offering entertainment and a range of recreational activities. Examples recorded in the asylum's annual reports were concerts, dramatic performances and magic lantern shows.

THE *FORT ENGLAND MIRROR*

Greenlees launched the publication of an asylum magazine called the *Fort England Mirror*.[33] The intention of the magazine was to provide a source of amusement and instruction to the asylum patients and the outside world at large.[34] Greenlees edited the magazine, with literary contributions obtained from the public, as well as reprints by established authors. Every issue contained a number of articles on the asylum. The authors of these articles were anonymous, but in the body of the text, it was indicated that they were patients. On reviewing the content of the articles, however, it is patently clear that Greenlees wrote them, as they explicitly reflect his image-making of the asylum. For example, in an article titled 'Ins and Outs of Asylum Life', an 'observer' declares: 'I am aware and rejoice in the fact, that in this institution there are billiards, weekly concerts and dancing, cricket, swimming bath, cards ... May I just add, Sir, that it would be better for all concerned if Christians and others, who are enjoying freedom and liberty, would in some practical way show more sympathy with their afflicted brethren.'[35]

The article is a brazen mouthpiece of Greenlees's interest in destigmatising the asylum and enlisting the public to support the care of the mentally ill. This is the basis of every issue of the magazine, where numerous articles depict the asylum as a hive of activity, in which amusements and entertainments take centre stage: the results of cricket and billiards tournaments held at the asylum were regularly reported, as well as accounts of the annual ball, visits to the seaside and evening entertainments. These events do not reflect the daily routine of the asylum, but rather the highlights of the asylum's entertainment calendar, which were far outweighed by periods of inertia, boredom and mundane routines, as well as sporadic outbreaks of contagious diseases, such as dysentery. Moreover, it was mainly the paying patients who had access to the seaside and to the whole gamut of the asylum's entertainment offerings. It is precisely the articles' shared focus on the amenities and activities for paying patients that link them explicitly to the content of asylum brochures. A number of studies explicate that asylum brochures relied on providing an account of activities and marketing the amenities and recreational facilities to gain custom.[36]

Typical of a brochure's content, the magazine showcases the ethos of the asylum and its curative aims, through 'testimonies' presented by ex-patients. For example, the article 'Asylums' is purportedly written from the perspective of a patient who had spent two years at the asylum:

> Within the walls of Fort England, the Master of Assemblies has taken note, that many of 'his little ones' have been lovingly nursed and cared for, not 'grudgingly or of necessity,' but with a glad heart and free. The staff have vied with each other who should show the greatest kindness ... Apparently hopeless cases that have been carried in, in a few months' time have recovered, and been sent home in excellent health.[37]

Instead of providing statistics of the asylum's cure rate, or discussions of the treatment regimen of the asylum, or even an examination of its disciplinary regimen to manage suicidal, dangerous and disruptive patients in ferocious fits of rage, the magazine published 'testimonies' that served to endorse the asylum's ethos, which may have served to advertise the curative potential of the asylum.[38] The magazine may have declared that its intention was to entertain and educate the public and patients, but it most certainly was part of a larger 'public relations exercise' to disseminate and endorse Greenlees's image-making of the asylum.[39]

Overall, the public engagements that Greenlees offered – hosting public events at the asylum and producing the asylum magazine – were acts of presenting and disseminating a positive public image of the asylum as a curative institution suitable for paying patients. Although Greenlees's public engagements have been shown to be exceedingly mediated and overwhelmingly stage-managed executions,[40] they did result in his attaining some measure of success in destigmatising the asylum and mental illness, as well as fostering public support and charity for the patients.[41]

Greenlees's efforts at destigmatising the asylum played a decisive role in contributing to 'the increased confidence' that the public had in the institution.[42] On one level, this is manifested in the town cementing its close connections with the asylum, by including it in the *Album of Grahamstown*, published to coincide with the Industrial and Arts Exhibition hosted in the town from 1898 to 1899.[43] On another level, this is evident in the *South African Medical Journal*, which reported in 1897 that 'people do not hesitate now as they formerly did to send a friend for treatment to the Asylum'.[44] The asylum enjoyed not only an increase in the number of paying patients – which Greenlees triumphantly proclaimed 'provided continued proof that we retain the confidence of the public of a better class' – but also increased interest from non-paying patients.[45]

THE FACE OF THE PROFESSIONAL

Although Greenlees successfully established a public image of the asylum as curative and suitable for the care of paying patients, the patient population remained a heterogeneous mix of individuals from various walks of life, suffering from acute and chronic states of insanity.[46] Worryingly, the asylum had a relatively low recovery rate, coupled with a high death rate. Greenlees attributed the unfavourable statistics to the 'large number of incurable cases admitted', in particular, 'the chronic residuum of dements and imbeciles'.[47] As these patients held no prospect of cure, Greenlees, like his international contemporaries, endorsed eugenic practices aimed at putting an end to chronic and hereditary forms of illness.[48] To this end, he called on general practitioners to condemn marriage between people who were suffering from hereditary physical and/or mental illness:

> We are certainly all agreed that 'Love is blind;' only it is sad to think how much suffering might be avoided if the bandages were removed from Cupid's eyes, and men were to exercise the same care in the selection of their mate as they do when breeding their cattle. If such a plan were carried out although there might be fewer ... idiots, the race would certainly be healthier and happier.[49]

In this quote, and in several other scientific texts, Greenlees isolates 'idiots' as an ignominious omen of the 'degeneracy of the Anglo-Saxon race'.[50] Put differently, the cornerstone of Greenlees's eugenic discourse is a conception of the 'idiot' as the depraved progeny of parents who failed to uphold the health of the Anglo-Saxon race and the imperial rule of the Colony.[51] Greenlees's propaganda of eugenics was not only an act of pathologising those with intellectual disabilities as an offence to imperial constructions of whiteness and a menace to white control of the Colony, but also an ungodly exercise in dehumanisation. People with intellectual disabilities were described by Greenlees as 'monstrosities' and an 'awful curse', who are 'handicapped in every sphere of life'.[52] By divesting these people of humanness, Greenlees sets the stage for motioning the government to sanction 'the destruction of infants known to be hereditarily tainted with disease'.[53]

Although Greenlees advocated 'sterilisation of degenerates, and even the lethal chamber', he also acknowledged that 'society is not yet ripe for such drastic measures'.[54] While these two 'treatment' options remained off the table, Greenlees established the Institute for Imbecile Children in April 1895, to offer the children 'the best known methods of educating and training'.[55] It is important to note here that the Institute was reserved for white children. Black children with intellectual disabilities were admitted to the Chronic Sick Hospital and the Colony's network of asylums. The Institute aimed for the children to become 'useful units in the world's hive of industry', so that they would no longer be economic burdens on their families or the state by joining the 'increasing crowds within the walls of our asylums'.[56] The Institute never achieved this objective and by 1905 Greenlees conceded that the Institute had abandoned its aim and was operating as a 'home where mental waifs are cared for, nursed, and their simplest wants attended to'.[57] Although the Institute deserves praise for providing a home and care for the children, this does not redeem Greenlees of the dehumanised account of the children that he promoted to medical fraternities and government officials. In this regard, over more than a decade of the Institute's annual reports submitted to the government, Greenlees constructed the children as the 'most hopeless and helpless of stray waifs of humanity'.[58] Thus, he dehumanised the children by consigning them to a collective subjectivity that is fixed to a negative portrait of ignominy.

RECOVERING THE HUMANITY OF THE CHILDREN

One means to counter Greenlees's dehumanised account of the children is to explore the Institute's casebook. Interspersed among the clinical and medical reports in the casebook are important biographical and personal narratives, which present a portrait of the children's humanity.[59] Despite the predominance of a clinical gaze deployed by the doctors when completing the casebook, there are slivers of information that describe a patient's personality, their engagements at an institution and their interpersonal relations. Although these statements authored by the doctors do not capture the patient's own voice and views, they afford 'unparalleled insight into the lives' of the patients.[60] Casebooks also offer a glimpse of the patients' lives before they were institutionalised.[61] The casebooks contain a section titled 'History of the Case', which records the life experiences of the patient prior to being committed, as well as the family's relationship with the patient. Thus, by examining such material, 'historians may be able to "walk out the gates" of the asylum and discover the lives intellectually disabled individuals led before they were institutionalized'.[62]

The framework for maintaining perspective of an individual's humanness, established by Robert Bogdan and Steven J. Taylor, guides the investigation of the Institute's casebook.[63] Bogdan and Taylor identify several dimensions that sustain a view of persons with disabilities as 'valued and loved human beings'.[64] For the purposes of this chapter, I explore three of the dimensions as an aid to recover an understanding of the children's humanness and personhood: (i) defining social place for the Other, (ii) viewing the Other as reciprocating, and (iii) seeing individuality in the Other.

DEFINING SOCIAL PLACE FOR THE OTHER

The emphasis in this dimension of humanness is how the children performed specific roles and participated in certain activities, to become part of the human relations and community that constituted the Institute.[65] In the casebook, for example, it is noted that Andrea delighted in attending the weekly dances and her brother, Gysbert, shared in the pleasure derived from participating in the event. Willie was portrayed as relishing the amusements offered at the Institute.[66] These entries identify the children as engaging with the opportunities for 'meaningful activities' presented by the Institute, but, more importantly, they identify them as being capable of cherishing life and savouring its pleasures.[67] For example, Gysbert's participation in the dances suggested to the authors of the casebook that he was 'quite capable of enjoying life'.[68]

Taking on general household work within the wards of the Institute and assisting the staff with the care of frail patients was a means by which the children established their role and their sense of belonging in the human community of the Institute. By way of example, Myrtle was described as working well at 'housework and the care of the more helpless of the children'.[69] The use of patient labour was a common occurrence in institutions for the care of disabled children and it was encouraged as a means of reducing costs.[70] The work performed by the children also demonstrates their personal character traits. Myrtle was depicted as being diligent in her work commitments and Andrea was praised for being 'very willing and anxious to help with the housework'.[71] What becomes evident is that the children did not approach their work duties as automatons, but as individuals with unique temperaments and dispositions.

For some children, work duties indicate the occurrence of interactions with staff and the other patients. For instance, Gideon would alternate his time between 'working with the asylum staff' and 'assisting the other children'.[72] In this way, work afforded Gideon an opportunity to establish relationships with both the staff and the patients. Although the quality of these relationships is not outlined in the casebook, it can be suggested that his having these relationships had a beneficial influence on how the staff and fellow patients viewed Gideon. The casebook describes Gideon as a 'good little fellow', whom the staff may have regarded as an honorary assistant and this may have resulted in preferential treatment and even friendships developing.[73] In his interactions with his fellow patients, bonds of solidarity, companionship and camaraderie may have developed between the children.[74] What is certain is that Gideon's work duties firmly cemented his inclusion in the human community and relationships of the Institute.

VIEWING THE OTHER AS RECIPROCATING

To be a participant in a relationship, for Bogdan and Taylor, an individual has to be 'contributing something to the partnership'.[75] Put differently, a relationship is about reciprocation, where both parties 'receiv[e] as much as they give'. For the children at the Institute, the casebook offers a potential means to consider them as reciprocating contributors in a relationship. After the Institute abandoned 'systematic education' for the children, the teaching duties were taken over by several female patients from the asylum.[76] For the brother and sister, Andrea and Gysbert, the casebook indicates that their education improved under the care and tuition of a female patient. For example, Andrea, after being 'taken in hand' by a female patient, made 'wonderful progress' and she was able for the first time to spell simple words.[77] Although the casebook indicates that the children benefited from their relationship with the female patients, it is silent on the benefits that the children offered to the women. Yet it is possible to conclude that one of the potential benefits that the relationship provided to the women was that the children gave the women companionship and maybe even love.[78] In other words, the children may have reciprocated in the 'coin and currency [of] love'.[79] Indeed, the casebook occasionally draws attention to the love and affection that the children showed. For example, Andrea was fondly described by the staff as being 'affectionate' in her relationships with them.[80]

SEEING INDIVIDUALITY IN THE OTHER

To counter Greenlees's view of the children as a homogeneous body of helpless and hopeless waifs, we need to identify and describe the children as 'distinct, unique individuals with particular and specific characteristics that set them apart from others'.[81] One dimension involves describing the children as having individual tastes and preferences. Johan had an 'excellent ear for music' and despite having underdeveloped speech function, was described as always singing and as a 'happy little fellow'.[82] Henry liked to hear the piano, while John was very fond of his toys and would often be found trying to cram into his pockets the ones he cherished the most.[83]

The casebook reveals that each of the children had a distinct personality. A case in point is Maria, who is portrayed as being a 'little mischief, bold and fearless'.[84] And for the children who stayed a considerable time at the Institute, it becomes evident that their personalities had multiple facets. Maggie was at first described as being 'very shy', but in later years she became more confident and was even 'liable to fits of temper'.[85] George is depicted in the first few years of his institutionalisation as being 'full of mischief but [a] happy laughing little fellow', who would sometimes have uncontrollable fits of temper.[86] For several years later, his playful and mischievous nature gave way to bad behaviour, where he would urinate on the other children and knock them about. Such recalcitrant behaviour was resented by the staff and resulted in George's mischievousness being described in the casebook as 'his only sign of intelligence'. However, soon thereafter, his behaviour and personality changed for the better. He became helpful with ward duties, assisted with the care of the younger children and was praised for being able to appreciate kindness.[87]

A further way to foreground the humanness of the children is to explore their relationships with their families.[88] The casebook abounds in evidence of families loving, caring for and supporting their children.[89] This is evident, for instance, in the family maintaining their relationship with the child during the period of institutional care and offering the child a return to the family fold following their discharge. For example, Maggie was visited regularly at the Institute by her family and was later discharged into their care.[90] For several years after that, the family continued to provide the Institute with feedback on her progress. In other cases, a family might seek a range of methods and treatments for the care and improvement of their child, both before and after institutionalisation.[91] The parents of Henry were citizens of the Zuid-Afrikaansche Republiek and resided in Pietersburg (now known as Polokwane) and they sought to bathe Henry in the hot springs of the area as a means of improving his condition.[92] The bathing resulted in some improvement, after which they sought further progress by sending him to the Institute. After several years of limited progress at the Institute, the family removed Henry and returned to the hot springs in their search for long-term healing and improvement for their son.

* * *

As should be clear from the material presented in this chapter, during his tenure at the asylum and the Institute, Greenlees was Janus-faced: in his public engagements, he advanced a positive public image of the asylum, but in his professional engagements he presented a dehumanised account of children with intellectual disabilities and, horrifyingly, he advocated their extermination. In adopting Law's pinboard method, this chapter refuses to redeem Greenlees's dehumanised view of the children, either by accounting the good that came out of his public engagements or by justifying his assertions as being the product of the beliefs of the time. The chapter made use a previously neglected resource – the Institute's casebook, which reflected that the children were individuals, each with their unique preferences and personalities. It shows that they were capable of enjoying life and, above all, they were loved human beings, who were able to reciprocate with love and affection. By affirming the humanness of the children, this chapter hopes to bring into the spotlight the value of their lives, their rights to care and dignity and the 'deep sense of the irreplaceable and distinctive worth of each human being'.[93]

In the nineteenth century, at institutions for people with intellectual disabilities, the medical superintendents 'were experts on the conditions and individuals housed within the institution's walls, and they represented the public and political face of intellectual disability'.[94] The indictment of Greenlees is that in his political and professional face he propagated a discourse of the children as deficient. In this discourse, the focus was exclusively on the children's impairments. In propagating this discourse, he contributed to the devaluation of the lives of people with intellectual disability. For Wolf Wolfensberger, the devaluation of people with disabilities is a menacing trope throughout the twentieth century and he cautioned, already in 1974, against the beginnings of a 'systematic and large-scale "death-making" of afflicted people'.[95] Death-making encompasses the 'erosion of the sense of sanctity of the lives' of disabled people and is evidenced in them being 'dumped into the community without support systems' where they become victimised, assaulted, suffer from gross neglect and consequently succumb to an untimely death.[96] It is distressing to witness how current events around the globe can be considered to be expressions of death-making.[97]

A contemporary example of death-making in South Africa is the Gauteng Mental Marathon Project, where, beginning in October 2015, over 1 700 mental health care users were transferred from a long-term care facility, Life Esidimeni, to facilities provided mainly by non-governmental organisations (NGOs). Unlike the 'structured and non-stop caring environment' that the mental health care users received at Life Esidimeni, the NGOs were likened to 'concentration camps'.[98] Ultimately, 140 mental health care users – people with intellectual disabilities and individuals suffering from chronic mental illnesses – lost their lives. Many of the mental health care users died from exposure to the cold, starvation, dehydration, neglect, abuse and infection.[99] The cost of care at the NGOs was estimated at R112 per day, compared to R320 at Life Esidimeni. The Health Ombud, Malegapuru Makgoba, had this to say: 'One has to ask what quality health care service can be delivered anywhere for an estimated cost of R112 per day. This surely must represent a serious form of neglect and denial of quality health care to one of the most vulnerable populations of our society.'

To avoid further manifestations of death-making, an extensive set of social injustices must be addressed.[100] Intellectuals in their public and political faces are called on to 'draw the attention of people to the tendency among the majority of our citizens to devalue a significant proportion of fellow citizens'.[101]

NOTES

1. CO 7950, 22 June 1907, Colonial Office correspondence, Western Cape Archives and Records Service.
2. The institution still operates today as the Fort England Hospital. The Chronic Sick Hospital functioned to care for the 'chronic sick of the colony' and thus the majority of the admitted patients were 'infirm from old age or physical disease'. The hospital also admitted poor pensioners, as well as individuals who were 'utterly destitute and starving'. Reports on the Government and Public Hospitals and Asylums; Report on the Inspector of Asylums, Cape of Good Hope Official Publications, G24-1894, 67; G37-1891, 44; G24-1893, 11, Western Cape Archives and Records Service.
3. C. Plug, 'Greenlees, Dr Thomas Duncan (Psychiatry)', *S2A3 Biographical Database of Southern African Science*, 18 May 2020, accessed 12 January 2017, http://www.s2a3.org.za/bio/print_action.php?sernum=1137&q_name=./includes/biofinal_query.inc&pf_name=./content/biofinal/biofinal_display.inc
4. Reports on the Government and Public Hospitals and Asylums; Report on the Inspector of Asylums, Cape of Good Hope Official Publications, G27-1896, Western Cape Archives and Records Service; Thomas D. Greenlees, 'The Etiology, Symptoms and Treatment of Idiocy and Imbecility', *South African Medical Record* 5, no. 2 (1907): 21;

Thomas D. Greenlees, *Insanity: Past, Present, and Future* (Grahamstown: Grahamstown Asylum Press, 1903), 19. Where possible, this chapter uses the current terminology of 'intellectual disability', instead of the nineteenth-century terms 'imbecile' and 'idiot'.
5   For a critical evaluation and application of the pinboard method, see William A. Craige, 'The Pinboard in Practice: A Study of Method through the Case of US Telemedicine, 1945–1980' (PhD diss., Durham University, 2015) and Alex Crawley, 'Method in His Madness: Enacting Male Normativity in Holloway Sanatorium for the Insane, 1880–1910' (PhD diss., University of Illinois at Chicago, 2018).
6   Craige, 'The Pinboard in Practice'.
7   John Law, *Aircraft Stories: Decentering the Object in Technoscience* (Durham: Duke University Press, 2002), 195.
8   Craige, 'The Pinboard in Practice', 2; Law, *Aircraft Stories*, 195; John Law, 'Pinboards and Books: Juxtaposing, Learning and Materiality', 28 April 2006, accessed 12 January 2017, http://www.heterogeneities.net/publications/Law2006PinboardsAndBooks.pdf
9   Law, *Aircraft Stories*, 197.
10 Law, *Aircraft Stories*, 195.
11 Craige, 'The Pinboard in Practice', 217.
12 Law, *Aircraft Stories*, 191.
13 'Lecture on the Brain', *The Grahamstown Journal*, 19 May 1892, 2.
14 Thomas D. Greenlees, *The Brain: Its Development, Architecture, Functions, and Education* (Grahamstown: J. Slater Printers, 1892), 3–4.
15 Greenlees, *The Brain*, 25.
16 Thomas D. Greenlees, 'Remarks on Lunacy Legislation in the Cape Colony', *The Cape Law Journal* 14 (1897): 23.
17 Reports on the Government and Public Hospitals and Asylums; Report on the Inspector of Asylums, Cape of Good Hope Official Publications, G37-1891, 42, Western Cape Archives and Records Service. For recent scholarship that pertains to image-making at asylums, see Dolly MacKinnon, '"The Trustworthy Agency of the Eyes": Reading Images of Music and Madness in Historical Context', *Health and History* 5, no. 2 (2003): 123–149; Leslie Topp, 'The Modern Mental Hospital in the Late Nineteenth-Century Germany and Austria: Psychiatric Space and Images of Freedom and Control', in *Madness, Architecture and the Built Environment: Psychiatric Spaces in Historical Context*, ed. Leslie Topp, James E. Moran and Jonathan Andrews (London: Routledge, 2007), 241–262.
18 Erving Goffman, *Asylums: Essays on the Social Situation of Mental Patients and Other Inmates* (Harmondsworth: Penguin, 1968).
19 Thomas D. Greenlees, 'An Address on the Ethics of Insanity: An Address before the Norwood Division of the British Medical Association', *British Medical Journal* 2, no. 2588 (1910): 301.
20 Thomas D. Greenlees, 'Medical, Social, and Legal Aspects of Insanity', *South African Medical Record* 1, no. 8 (1903): 122.
21 Reports on the Government and Public Hospitals and Asylums; Report on the Inspector of Asylums, Cape of Good Hope Official Publications, G20-1897, Western Cape Archives and Records Service.
22 CO 7166, 17 July 1896, Colonial Office correspondence, Western Cape Archives and Records Service.
23 'Our Annual Ball', *The Fort England Mirror* 6 no. 3 (1897): 50.
24 Goffman, *Asylums*, 95.

25   Dolly MacKinnon, '"Amusements Are Provided": Asylum Entertainment and Recreation in Australia and New Zealand c.1860–c.1945', in *Permeable Walls: Historical Perspectives on Hospital and Asylum Visiting*, ed. Graham Mooney and Jonathan Reinarz (Amsterdam: Rodopi, 2009), 270.
26   See MacKinnon, 'Amusements Are Provided', 272; Janet Miron, '"In View of the Knowledge to Be Acquired": Public Visits to New York's Aylums in the Nineteenth A. Century', in *Permeable Walls: Historical Perspectives on Hospital and Asylum Visiting*, ed. Graham Mooney and Jonathan Reinarz (Amsterdam: Rodopi, 2009), 249; Graham Mooney and Jonathan Reinarz, 'Hospital and Asylum Visiting in Historical Perspective: Themes and Issues', in *Permeable Walls: Historical Perspectives on Hospital and Asylum Visiting*, ed. Graham Mooney and Jonathan Reinarz (Amsterdam: Rodopi, 2009), 14.
27   'Entertainment at the Asylum', *The Grahamstown Journal*, 12 July 1892; 'Fort England Asylum', *The Grahamstown Journal*, 13 December 1894; 'Red-Letter Day', *The Grahamstown Journal*, 20 November 1894.
28   Miron, 'Knowledge to Be Acquired', 250.
29   Reports on the Government and Public Hospitals and Asylums; Report on the Inspector of Asylums, Cape of Good Hope Official Publications, G17-1893; G37-1891, Western Cape Archives and Records Service.
30   Dolly MacKinnon, 'Divine Service, Music, Sport, and Recreation as Medicinal in Australian Asylums 1860s–1945', *Health and History* 11, no. 1 (2009): 145.
31   Reports on the Government and Public Hospitals and Asylums; Report on the Inspector of Asylums, Cape of Good Hope Official Publications, G36-1892, Western Cape Archives and Records Service.
32   Miron, 'Knowledge to Be Acquired', 248.
33   For studies of asylum magazines published internationally, see M. Eannace, 'Lunatic Literature: New York State's *The Opal* 1850–1860' (PhD diss., State University of New York, 2001); Miron, 'Knowledge to Be Acquired'; Benjamin Reiss, 'Letters from Asylumia: *The Opal* and the Cultural Work of the Lunatic Asylum, 1851–1860', *American Literary History* 16, no. 1 (2004): 1–28.
34   Reports on the Government and Public Hospitals and Asylums; Report on the Inspector of Asylums, Cape of Good Hope Official Publications, G36-1892, Western Cape Archives and Records Service.
35   'Ins and Outs of Asylum Life', *The Fort England Mirror* 7, no. 3 (1898): 34.
36   William L.I. Parry-Jones, *The Trade in Lunacy: A Study of Private Madhouses in England in the Eighteenth and Nineteenth Centuries* (London: Routledge, 1972), 105; Rebecca I. Wynter, '"Diseased Vessels and Punished Bodies": A Study of Material Culture and Control in Staffordshire County Gaol and Lunatic Asylum, c.1793–1866' (PhD diss., University of Birmingham, 2007), 211.
37   'Asylums', *The Fort England Mirror* 5, no. 2 (1896): 8–11.
38   See also Reiss, 'Letters from Asylumia': 4.
39   Pauline Prior and Gillian McClelland, 'Through the Lens of the Hospital Magazine: Downshire and Holywell Psychiatric Hospitals in the 1960s and 1970s', *History of Psychiatry* 24, no. 4 (2013): 401.
40   See also Mooney and Reinarz, 'Hospital and Asylum Visiting', 15.
41   See also Rory du Plessis, 'Promoting and Popularising the Asylum: Photography and Asylum Image-Making at the Grahamstown Lunatic Asylum, 1890–1907', *Image & Text* 22, no. 1 (2013): 99–132; Rory du Plessis, 'The Principles and Priorities of Dr T.D.

Greenlees, Medical Superintendent of the Grahamstown Lunatic Asylum, 1890–1907', *Historia* 60, no. 1 (2015): 22–46.

42 Reports on the Government and Public Hospitals and Asylums; Report on the Inspector of Asylums, Cape of Good Hope Official Publications, G55-1904, Western Cape Archives and Records Service.

43 *Grocott and Sherry's Album of Grahamstown* (Grahamstown: Grocott and Sherry, 1898).

44 Cited in Felicity Swanson, 'Colonial Madness: The Construction of Gender in the Grahamstown Lunatic Asylum, 1875–1905' (Honours thesis, University of Cape Town, 1994), 38–39.

45 Reports on the Government and Public Hospitals and Asylums; Report on the Inspector of Asylums, Cape of Good Hope Official Publications, G60-1903; G55-1904, Western Cape Archives and Records Service.

46 Rory du Plessis, *Pathways of Patients at the Grahamstown Lunatic Asylum, 1890 to 1907* (Pretoria: Pretoria University Law Press, 2020).

47 Thomas D. Greenlees, 'Statistics of Insanity in Grahamstown Asylum', *South African Medical Record* 3, no. 11 (1905): 222.

48 Theodore M. Porter, *Genetics in the Madhouse: The Unknown History of Human Heredity* (Princeton: Princeton University Press, 2018), 6.

49 Greenlees, 'Medical, Social, and Legal Aspects', 123. See also Greenlees, 'The Etiology, Symptoms and Treatment', 17; Greenlees, *Insanity*, 18.

50 Greenlees, 'The Etiology, Symptoms and Treatment', 20. See also Greenlees, 'Statistics of Insanity'; Thomas D. Greenlees, 'A Contribution to the Statistics of Insanity in Cape Colony', *The American Journal of Psychiatry* 50, no. 4 (1894): 519–529.

51 Greenlees, 'The Etiology, Symptoms and Treatment', 21. For a discussion of the eugenic discourses in the *South African Medical Journal* during this period, see Rebecca Hodes, 'Kink and the Colony: Sexual Deviance in the Medical History of South Africa, c.1893–1939', *Journal of Southern African Studies* 41, no. 4 (2015): 715–733 and Susanne Klausen, '"For the Sake of the Race": Eugenic Discourses of Feeblemindedness and Motherhood in the South African Medical Record, 1903–1926', *Journal of Southern African Studies* 23, no. 1 (1997): 27–50.

52 Thomas D. Greenlees, *On the Threshold: Studies in Psychology* (lecture delivered to the Eastern Province Literary and Scientific Society, Grahamstown) (Grahamstown: Asylum Press, 1899), 36.

53 Greenlees, *Insanity*, 19.

54 Greenlees, 'Etiology, Symptoms and Treatment', 21. See also Greenlees, 'Statistics of Insanity', 222.

55 Greenlees, 'Remarks on Lunacy Legislation', 36.

56 Reports on the Government and Public Hospitals and Asylums; Report on the Inspector of Asylums, Cape of Good Hope Official Publications, G27-1896, Western Cape Archives and Records Service; Greenlees, *On the Threshold*, 36.

57 Reports on the Government and Public Hospitals and Asylums; Report on the Inspector of Asylums, Cape of Good Hope Official Publications, G57-1905, Western Cape Archives and Records Service.

58 Reports on the Government and Public Hospitals and Asylums; Report on the Inspector of Asylums, Cape of Good Hope Official Publications, G21-1899, Western Cape Archives and Records Service.

59 Rory du Plessis, 'The Life Stories and Experiences of the Children Admitted to the Institute for Imbecile Children from 1895 to 1913', *African Journal of Disability* 9 (2020): 1–10.

60   See Nic Clarke, 'Opening Closed Doors and Breaching High Walls: Some Approaches for Studying Intellectual Disability in Canadian History', *Histoire Sociale/Social History* 39, no. 78 (2006): 479; Jean D. Hoole, 'Idiots, Imbeciles, and the Asylum in the Early Twentieth Century: Bevan Lewis and the Boys of Stanley Hall' (PhD diss., University of Aberdeen, 2012), 179, 211.
61   Hoole, 'Idiots, Imbeciles, and the Asylum'.
62   Clarke, 'Opening Closed Doors': 481.
63   Robert Bogdan and Steven J. Taylor, 'Relationships with Severely Disabled People: The Social Construction of Humanness', *Social Problems* 36, no. 2 (1989): 135-148.
64   Bogdan and Taylor, 'Relationships with Severely Disabled People', 135.
65   Bogdan and Taylor, 'Relationships with Severely Disabled People', 145.
66   HGM 24, Grahamstown Lunatic Asylum Casebooks, Western Cape Archives and Record Service, 45, 46, 52.
67   Stef Eastoe, 'Playing Cards, Cricket and Carpentry: Amusement, Recreation and Occupation in Caterham Imbecile Asylum', *Journal of Victorian Culture* 24, no. 1 (2019): 72.
68   HGM 24, Grahamstown Lunatic Asylum Casebooks, 46.
69   HGM 24, Grahamstown Lunatic Asylum Casebooks, 17.
70   Eastoe, 'Playing Cards', 76-77; Lee-Ann Monk, 'Exploiting Patient Labour at Kew Cottages, Australia, 1887-1950', *British Journal of Learning Disabilities* 38, no. 2 (2010): 86-94; Stephen J. Taylor, *Child Insanity in England, 1845-1907* (London: Palgrave Macmillan, 2017), 93; David Wright, *Mental Disability in Victorian England: The Earlswood Asylum, 1847-1901* (Oxford: Clarendon Press, 2001), 143.
71   HGM 24, Grahamstown Lunatic Asylum Casebooks, 17, 45.
72   HGM 24, Grahamstown Lunatic Asylum Casebooks, 60.
73   HGM 24, Grahamstown Lunatic Asylum Casebooks, 60. See also Hoole, 'Idiots, Imbeciles, and the Asylum', 237; Monk, 'Exploiting Patient Labour', 91.
74   Goffman, *Asylums*, 244; Geoffrey Reaume, *Remembrance of Patients Past: Patient Life at the Toronto Hospital for the Insane, 1870-1940* (Toronto: Oxford University Press, 2000), 64.
75   Bogdan and Taylor, 'Relationships with Severely Disabled People', 143.
76   Reports on the Government and Public Hospitals and Asylums; Report on the Inspector of Asylums, Cape of Good Hope Official Publications, G57-1905; G32-1906, Western Cape Archives and Records Service.
77   HGM 24, Grahamstown Lunatic Asylum Casebooks, 45.
78   Bogdan and Taylor, 'Relationships with Severely Disabled People', 144; Eva F. Kittay, *Love's Labor: Essays on Women, Equality, and Dependency* (New York: Routledge, 1999), 152.
79   Kittay, *Love's Labor*, 152.
80   HGM 24, Grahamstown Lunatic Asylum Casebooks, 45.
81   Bogdan and Taylor, 'Relationships with Severely Disabled People', 141.
82   HGM 24, Grahamstown Lunatic Asylum Casebooks, 7.
83   HGM 24, Grahamstown Lunatic Asylum Casebooks, 26, 38.
84   HGM 24, Grahamstown Lunatic Asylum Casebooks, 22.
85   HGM 24, Grahamstown Lunatic Asylum Casebooks, 20.
86   HGM 24, Grahamstown Lunatic Asylum Casebooks, 48.
87   HGM 24, Grahamstown Lunatic Asylum Casebooks, 48.
88   Bogdan and Taylor, 'Relationships with Severely Disabled People', 142-143; Maureen Gillman, John Swain and Bob Heyman, 'Life History or "Case" History: The Objectification of People with Learning Difficulties through the Tyranny of Professional Discourses', *Disability & Society* 12, no. 5 (1997): 687; Hoole, 'Idiots, Imbeciles, and the Asylum', 209.

[89] Jessa Chupik and David Wright, 'Treating the "Idiot" Child in Early 20th-Century Ontario', *Disability & Society* 21, no. 1 (2006): 77–90; Nic Clarke, 'Sacred Daemons: Exploring British Columbian Society's Perceptions of "Mentally Deficient" Children, 1870–1930', *BC Studies* 144 (2004/2005): 61–89, Taylor, *Child Insanity*, 763.
[90] HGM 24, Grahamstown Lunatic Asylum Casebooks, 20.
[91] Chupik and Wright, 'Treating the "Idiot" Child', 87–88.
[92] HGM 24, Grahamstown Lunatic Asylum Casebooks, 26.
[93] Eva F. Kittay, 'Equality, Dignity and Disability', in *Perspectives on Equality: The Second Seamus Heaney Lectures*, ed. Mary Ann Lyons and Fionnuala Waldron (Dublin: Liffey Press, 2005), 113.
[94] Licia Carlson, *The Faces of Intellectual Disability: Philosophical Reflections* (Bloomington: Indiana University Press, 2010), 26.
[95] Wolf Wolfensberger, 'A Point of View: A Call to Wake up to the Beginning of a New Wave of "Euthanasia" of Severely Impaired People', *Education and Training of the Mentally Retarded* 15, no. 3 (1980): 171.
[96] Wolfensberger, 'A Point of View', 172.
[97] Jan Walmsley, 'Healthy Minds and Intellectual Disability', in *Healthy Minds in the Twentieth Century: In and beyond the Asylum*, ed. Steven J. Taylor and Alice Brumby (London: Palgrave Macmillan, 2020), 104.
[98] Malegapuru W. Makgoba, 'The Report into the "Circumstances surrounding the Deaths of Mentally Ill Patients: Gauteng Province": No Guns: 94+ Silent Deaths and Still Counting', Office of the Health Ombud', accessed 25 April 2017, http://ohsc.org.za/wp-content/uploads/2017/09/FINALREPORT.pdf
[99] Makgoba, 'The Report'.
[100] Charlotte Capri, Brian Watermeyer, Judith Mckenzie and Ockert Coetzee, 'Intellectual Disability in the Esidimeni Tragedy: Silent Deaths', *South African Medical Journal* 108, no. 3 (2018): 153–154.
[101] Wolf Wolfensberger, 'Normalization of Services for the Mentally Retarded: A Conversation with Wolf Wolfensberger', in *Leadership and Change in Human Services: Selected Readings from Wolf Wolfensberger*, ed. David G. Race (London: Routledge, 2003), 186.

REFERENCES

'Asylums'. *The Fort England Mirror* 5, no. 2 (1896): 8–11.
Bogdan, Robert. and Steven J. Taylor. 'Relationships with Severely Disabled People: The Social Construction of Humanness'. *Social Problems* 36, no. 2 (1989): 135–148.
Capri, Charlotte, Brian Watermeyer, Judith Mckenzie and Ockert Coetzee. 'Intellectual Disability in the Esidimeni Tragedy: Silent Deaths'. *South African Medical Journal* 108, no. 3 (2018): 153–154.
Carlson, Licia. *The Faces of Intellectual Disability: Philosophical Reflections*. Bloomington: Indiana University Press, 2010.
Chupik, Jessa and David Wright. 'Treating the "Idiot" Child in Early 20th-Century Ontario'. *Disability & Society* 21, no. 1 (2006): 77–90.
Clarke, Nic. 'Opening Closed Doors and Breaching High Walls: Some Approaches for Studying Intellectual Disability in Canadian History'. *Histoire Sociale/Social History* 39, no. 78 (2006): 467–485.

Clarke, Nic. 'Sacred Daemons: Exploring British Columbian Society's Perceptions of "Mentally Deficient" Children, 1870-1930'. *BC Studies* 144 (2004/2005): 61-89.
Craige, William A. 'The Pinboard in Practice: A Study of Method through the Case of US Telemedicine, 1945-1980'. PhD diss., Durham University, 2015.
Crawley, Alex. 'Method in His Madness: Enacting Male Normativity in Holloway Sanatorium for the Insane, 1880-1910'. PhD diss., University of Illinois at Chicago, 2018.
Du Plessis, Rory. 'The Life Stories and Experiences of the Children Admitted to the Institute for Imbecile Children from 1895 to 1913'. *African Journal of Disability* 9 (2020): 1-10.
Du Plessis, Rory. *Pathways of Patients at the Grahamstown Lunatic Asylum, 1890 to 1907*. Pretoria: Pretoria University Law Press, 2020.
Du Plessis, Rory. 'The Principles and Priorities of Dr T.D. Greenlees, Medical Superintendent of the Grahamstown Lunatic Asylum, 1890-1907'. *Historia* 60, no. 1 (2015): 22-46.
Du Plessis, Rory. 'Promoting and Popularising the Asylum: Photography and Asylum Image-Making at the Grahamstown Lunatic Asylum, 1890-1907'. *Image & Text* 22, no. 1 (2013): 99-132.
Eannace, M. 'Lunatic Literature: New York State's *The Opal* 1850-1860'. PhD diss., State University of New York, 2001.
Eastoe, Stef. 'Playing Cards, Cricket and Carpentry: Amusement, Recreation and Occupation in Caterham Imbecile Asylum'. *Journal of Victorian Culture* 24, no. 1 (2019): 72-87.
'Entertainment at the Asylum'. *The Grahamstown Journal*, 12 July 1892.
'Fort England Asylum'. *The Grahamstown Journal*, 13 December 1894.
Gillman, Maureen, John Swain and Bob Heyman. 'Life History or "Case" History: The Objectification of People with Learning Difficulties through the Tyranny of Professional Discourses'. *Disability & Society* 12, no. 5 (1997): 675-694.
Goffman, Erving. *Asylums: Essays on the Social Situation of Mental Patients and Other Inmates*. Harmondsworth: Penguin, 1968.
Greenlees, Thomas D. 'An Address on the Ethics of Insanity: An Address before the Norwood Division of the British Medical Association'. *British Medical Journal* 2, no. 2588 (1910): 301-303.
Greenlees, Thomas D. *The Brain: Its Development, Architecture, Functions, and Education*. Grahamstown: J. Slater Printers, 1892.
Greenlees, Thomas D. 'A Contribution to the Statistics of Insanity in Cape Colony'. *The American Journal of Psychiatry* 50, no. 4 (1894): 519-529.
Greenlees, Thomas D. 'The Etiology, Symptoms and Treatment of Idiocy and Imbecility'. *South African Medical Record* 5, no. 2 (1907): 17-21.
Greenlees, Thomas D. *Insanity: Past, Present, and Future*. Grahamstown: Grahamstown Asylum Press, 1903.
Greenlees, Thomas D. 'Medical, Social, and Legal Aspects of Insanity'. *South African Medical Record* 1, no. 8 (1903): 121-125.
Greenlees, Thomas D. *On the Threshold: Studies in Psychology*. A lecture delivered to the Eastern Province Literary and Scientific Society, Grahamstown. Grahamstown: Asylum Press, 1899.
Greenlees, Thomas D. 'Remarks on Lunacy Legislation in the Cape Colony'. *The Cape Law Journal* 14 (1897): 23-38.
Greenlees, Thomas D. 'Statistics of Insanity in Grahamstown Asylum'. *South African Medical Record* 3, no. 11 (1905): 217-224.
Grocott and Sherry's Album of Grahamstown. Grahamstown: Grocott and Sherry, 1898.

Hodes, Rebecca. 'Kink and the Colony: Sexual Deviance in the Medical History of South Africa, c.1893-1939'. *Journal of Southern African Studies* 41, no. 4 (2015): 715-733.

Hoole, Jean D. 'Idiots, Imbeciles, and the Asylum in the Early Twentieth Century: Bevan Lewis and the Boys of Stanley Hall'. PhD diss., University of Aberdeen, 2012.

'Ins and Outs of Asylum Life'. *The Fort England Mirror* 7, no. 3 (1898): 34.

Kittay, Eva F. 'Equality, Dignity and Disability'. In *Perspectives on Equality: The Second Seamus Heaney Lectures*, edited by Mary Ann Lyons and Fionnuala Waldron, 93-119. Dublin: Liffey Press, 2005.

Kittay, Eva F. *Love's Labor: Essays on Women, Equality, and Dependency*. New York: Routledge, 1999.

Klausen, Susanne. '"For the Sake of the Race": Eugenic Discourses of Feeblemindedness and Motherhood in the South African Medical Record, 1903-1926'. *Journal of Southern African Studies* 23, no. 1 (1997): 27-50.

Law, John. *Aircraft Stories: Decentering the Object in Technoscience*. Durham: Duke University Press, 2002.

Law, John. 'Pinboards and Books: Juxtaposing, Learning and Materiality'. 28 April 2006. Accessed 12 January 2017. http://www.heterogeneities.net/publications/Law2006PinboardsAndBooks.pdf

'Lecture on the Brain'. *The Grahamstown Journal*, 19 May 1892.

MacKinnon, Dolly. '"Amusements Are Provided": Asylum Entertainment and Recreation in Australia and New Zealand c.1860-c.1945'. In *Permeable Walls: Historical Perspectives on Hospital and Asylum Visiting*, edited by Graham Mooney and Jonathan Reinarz, 267-288. Amsterdam: Rodopi, 2009.

MacKinnon, Dolly. 'Divine Service, Music, Sport, and Recreation as Medicinal in Australian Asylums 1860s-1945'. *Health and History* 11, no. 1 (2009): 128-148.

MacKinnon, Dolly. '"The Trustworthy Agency of the Eyes": Reading Images of Music and Madness in Historical Context'. *Health and History* 5, no. 2 (2003): 123-149.

Makgoba, Malegapuru W. 'The Report into the "Circumstances surrounding the Deaths of Mentally Ill Patients: Gauteng Province": No Guns: 94+ Silent Deaths and Still Counting'. Office of the Health Ombud. Accessed 25 April 2017. http://ohsc.org.za/wp-content/uploads/2017/09/FINALREPORT.pdf

Miron, Janet. '"In View of the Knowledge to Be Acquired": Public Visits to New York's Asylums in the Nineteenth Century'. In *Permeable Walls: Historical Perspectives on Hospital and Asylum Visiting*, edited by Graham Mooney and Jonathan Reinarz, 243-266. Amsterdam: Rodopi, 2009.

Monk, Lee-Ann. 'Exploiting Patient Labour at Kew Cottages, Australia, 1887-1950'. *British Journal of Learning Disabilities* 38, no. 2 (2010): 86-94.

Mooney, Graham and Jonathan Reinarz. 'Hospital and Asylum Visiting in Historical Perspective: Themes and Issues'. In *Permeable Walls: Historical Perspectives on Hospital and Asylum Visiting*, edited by Graham Mooney and Jonathan Reinarz, 1-30. Amsterdam: Rodopi, 2009.

'Our Annual Ball'. *The Fort England Mirror* 6, no. 3 (1897): 50.

Parry-Jones, William L.I. *The Trade in Lunacy: A Study of Private Madhouses in England in the Eighteenth and Nineteenth Centuries*. London: Routledge, 1972.

Plug, C. 'Greenlees, Dr Thomas Duncan (Psychiatry)'. *S2A3 Biographical Database of Southern African Science*, 18 May 2020. Accessed 12 January 2017. http://www.s2a3.org.za/bio/print_action.php?sernum=1137&q_name=./includes/biofinal_query.inc&pf_name=./content/biofinal/biofinal_display.inc

Porter, Theodore M. *Genetics in the Madhouse: The Unknown History of Human Heredity*. Princeton: Princeton University Press, 2018.
Prior, Pauline and Gillian McClelland. 'Through the Lens of the Hospital Magazine: Downshire and Holywell Psychiatric Hospitals in the 1960s and 1970s'. *History of Psychiatry* 24, no. 4 (2013): 399–414.
Reaume, Geoffrey. *Remembrance of Patients Past: Patient Life at the Toronto Hospital for the Insane, 1870–1940*. Toronto: Oxford University Press, 2000.
'Red-Letter Day'. *The Grahamstown Journal*, 20 November 1894.
Reiss, Benjamin. 'Letters from Asylumia: *The Opal* and the Cultural Work of the Lunatic Asylum, 1851–1860'. *American Literary History* 16, no. 1 (2004): 1–28.
Swanson, Felicity. 'Colonial Madness: The Construction of Gender in the Grahamstown Lunatic Asylum, 1875–1905'. Honours thesis, University of Cape Town, 1994.
Taylor, Steven J. *Child Insanity in England, 1845–1907*. London: Palgrave Macmillan, 2017.
Topp, Leslie. 'The Modern Mental Hospital in the Late Nineteenth-Century Germany and Austria: Psychiatric Space and Images of Freedom and Control'. In *Madness, Architecture and the Built Environment: Psychiatric Spaces in Historical Context*, edited by Leslie Topp, James E. Moran and Jonathan Andrews, 241–262. London: Routledge, 2007.
Walmsley, Jan. 'Healthy Minds and Intellectual Disability'. In *Healthy Minds in the Twentieth Century: In and beyond the Asylum*, edited by Steven J. Taylor, and Alice Brumby, 95–111. London: Palgrave Macmillan, 2020.
Wolfensberger, Wolf. 'Normalization of Services for the Mentally Retarded: A Conversation with Wolf Wolfensberger'. In *Leadership and Change in Human Services: Selected Readings from Wolf Wolfensberger*, edited by David G. Race, 185–187. London: Routledge, 2003.
Wolfensberger, Wolf. 'A Point of View: A Call to Wake up to the Beginning of a New Wave of "Euthanasia" of Severely Impaired People'. *Education and Training of the Mentally Retarded* 15, no 3 (1980): 171–173.
Wright, David. *Mental Disability in Victorian England: The Earlswood Asylum, 1847–1901*. Oxford: Clarendon Press, 2001.
Wynter, Rebecca I. 2007. '"Diseased Vessels and Punished Bodies": A Study of Material Culture and Control in Staffordshire County Gaol and Lunatic Asylum, c.1793–1866'. PhD diss., University of Birmingham, 2007.

CONTRIBUTORS

Chris Broodryk is chair of Drama, School of the Arts, University of Pretoria, where he is a senior lecturer in Drama and Film Studies and also teaches screenwriting and non-fiction film-making. His research publications and papers are focused on Afrikaans and South African cinema and social media studies. He appears regularly on community radio and television to discuss film, television and popular culture.

Katlego Chale is pursuing a PhD in Drama at the University of Pretoria. His research explores the rich intellectual traditions in South African performance in the theatre, linking the idea of public intellectualism with activism and artivism. Katlego holds an MTech (*cum laude*) and a BTech (*cum laude*) from Tshwane University of Technology. His artistic practice includes screen and stage acting, playwriting and community engagement through a podcast titled 'A Theatre Maker in Mzansi'. He is current chair of The Writers' Lab, an non-profit organisation that provides a space for writers to sharpen their skills.

Lesley Cowling is an associate professor at the University of the Witwatersrand, where she runs the Master's and PhD programmes in the Department of Journalism and teaches media theory and creative writing. Her research focuses on the relationship of the media to South African public life, with a particular focus on journalism forms such as long-form reporting, opinion, analysis and debate. A related interest is in media histories in South Africa, including the legacies of literary journalism. She is an associate researcher at the Archive & Public Culture and Research Initiative at the University of Cape Town and co-editor of *Babel Unbound: Rage, Reason and Rethinking Public Life* (2020).

Luvuyo Mthimkhulu Dondolo holds a DLitt in History. He is the director and head of the Centre for Transdisciplinary Studies at the University of Fort Hare. His area of interest is nineteenth- and twentieth-century history of the then Cape Province.

His field of specialisation is public history with a specific focus on heritage studies, museology, pan-Africanism and Black Consciousness scholarship, racism and identity. Professor Dondolo was a Fulbright Scholar based at Cheyney University for the 2016/17 academic year. He is also a former Rockefeller Scholarship holder and spent a year studying at Emory University in Atlanta.

Rory du Plessis is a senior lecturer in Visual Studies at the School of the Arts, University of Pretoria. He obtained a PhD in Mental Health from the Centre for Ethics & Philosophy of Health Sciences at the University of Pretoria. He is the co-editor of the academic journal, *Image & Text* and author of *Pathways of Patients at the Grahamstown Lunatic Asylum, 1890 to 1907* (2020).

Carolyn Hamilton is the South African Research Chair in Archive & Public Culture at the University of Cape Town. She is the author of *Terrific Majesty* (1998), co-editor of the *Cambridge History of South Africa* (2012) and has edited or co-edited numerous collections of essays including *Babel Unbound: Rage, Reason and Rethinking Public Life* (2020); *Tribing and Untribing the Archive* (2016); *Uncertain Curature* (2014); *Refiguring the Archive* (2002) and *The Mfecane Aftermath* (1995). Her research interests range from the roles and forms of public deliberation in increasingly unsettled democracies to the operations of power in and through archives, and include the pre-industrial history of southern Africa.

Anna-Marié Jansen van Vuuren is a screenwriting lecturer in the film programme in the Department of Visual Communication at Tshwane University of Technology. She is a former post-doctorate research fellow in South African cinema at the University of Johannesburg. Her current research includes historical and contemporary South African cinema (especially Afrikaans cinema); the role of representation, ideology and identity in historical narratives; and the role of filmic landscape in identity construction (especially Afrikaner identity). She has published in journals such as *Journal of African Cinemas* and *Communicatio*. She is a film critic for https://www.bioskoop.co.

Pfunzo Sidogi is a lecturer in the Department of Fine and Applied Arts, Faculty of Arts and Design at the Tshwane University of Technology. His research interests are centred on art and design praxis in South Africa.

Keyan G. Tomaselli is Distinguished Professor at the University of Johannesburg. He was previously director of the Centre for Communication, Media and Society, University of KwaZulu-Natal. He is editor of *Critical Arts* and co-editor and founder of the *Journal of African Cinemas*. He was an active participant in the anti-apartheid movements discussed in his chapter.

INDEX

A

Abantu Abamnyama Lapa Bavela Ngakona 24, 35
Achebe, Chinua 55–56
ACTAG (Arts and Culture Task Group) Report 136
advertisements 129, 141–142, 145–146
aesthetic 77
affirmative cultural theory 136–137, 139, 147
African Centre for Migration and Society 181–182
African imagination 54
African Intellectuals in 19th and Early 20th Century South Africa 1–2
Africanism 55, 79, 98
African languages 55–57
African Leader 82n11
African literature 55
African National Congress (ANC)
  cultural policy 138, 142–144
  as government 14–15
  history of 24, 45, 57–58, 63, 90, 94, 97
  public intellectuals and 7
African nationalism 61, 63
African Presbyterian Church 65n39
African storytelling 27, 190
African values 46
Afrikaans films 112–118, 163, 167 *see also* Pretorius, William; Roets, Matthys Jacobus (Koos)
Afrikaans language 61, 115
Afrikaans-speaking audiences 114, 116–118, 170, 172

Afrikaans Studentebond 140
Afrikaner Broederbond 133–134, 140
Afrikaners 3, 96, 114, 130, 133–135, 145, 158–172
Age of Anger, The 2
Aladro-Vico, Eva 182
Album of Grahamstown 206
Alexander, Neville 57
Alidou, Ousseina 56
All Media and Product Survey 95
Althusser, Louis 132, 136
Always Another Country 6
amakholwa 24, 26, 34–35, 39n13, 89–90
amateurism 4–5, 10
Amathole District Municipality Heritage Unit 47
Amathole region 48
America *see* United States
ANC *see* African National Congress
Anglo-Zulu War 26
apartheid
  anti-apartheid struggle 6–7, 46, 86, 90, 130–133
  censorship under 170
  cultural policy and 140, 147
  intellectualism and 2, 3, 6–7
  National Party 80–81
  'open society' and 57
  trauma of 193–195
Apocalypse Now Redux (film) 118–119
Apocalypto (film) 119
Aquarius 133–134
Argus Printing and Publishing Company 82n10, 91–92, 94

Aronofsky, Darren 183
art
    crafts vs 78–79
    cultural policy and 134, 148
    in homes 75–76
    media and 72, 110
art criticism *see* black art criticism
'Art Criticism for Whom?' (article) 68
'Artists under the Sun' exhibitions 73
artivism
    definitions of 179–181
    examples of 181–184
    origins of term 180–181
    public intellectualism and 184–188, 195
Arts and Culture Task Group (ACTAG) Report 136
arts and humanities 8–10
Artslink 109, 116, 120
assimilation 56, 61
Association for Women's Rights in Development International Forum 181
asylum *see* Grahamstown Lunatic Asylum
Attwell, David 47–48
audiences 3, 112, 114, 116–118, 170, 172
Australian cultural studies 138–139

B
Babel (film) 119
'bad' films 117
Bailey, Olga 182
Baldwin, James 110–111
Bambatha Rebellion (1906) 31, 33
Banksy 182, 195
Bantu Crafts League 76
Bantu Dramatic Society 72
Bantu Press 70–71
Bantu Trade Development Exhibition (1934) 78–80
Bantu World, The
    black art criticism in 72–81
    history of 68, 70–71
Bantu World Trade Exhibition 73
Baran (film) 120
BEE *see* black economic empowerment
Beeld 108
Benda, Julien 185–186
Bennie, John 52

Bennie, William Govan 59
Bertelsen, Eve 131
Better Living through Criticism 111
Biko: Philosophy, Identity and Liberation 7
Biko, Stephen Bantu 6–7, 57, 69, 134
Bioskoop in Diens van die Volk, Die 135
Birth of a Nation, The (film) 111
Black Art & Communities at Heart (conversation series) 190, 193
black art criticism 68–85
    in *Bantu World, The* 68, 70–71, 72–81
    black intellectualism and 72–74
    context of 12, 68–72
    'serious' vs 'popular' 70, 74–77
    Western art criticism and 69, 81
Black Consciousness movement 6, 57, 86, 90, 91–95, 100, 132–134
black economic empowerment (BEE) 134, 135, 147
black film audiences 112
'Black Humanities' 11, 38
black journalists 71–73, 91–93
black newspapers 69, 70–72, 88, 90–93
black-on-black criticism 73–74
'black pain' 141
black women 75–76
Blueprint: How DNA Makes Us Who We Are 78
Boetie Gaan Border Toe! (film) 116
Bogdan, Robert 209, 210
Botha, Andries 144
Botha, Martin 113, 121, 163
Botha, P.W. 113, 141–142
Bowling for Columbine (film) 117
Brandwag 135
bricolage 24, 25, 35
Britain 3, 58, 112
British Documentary Film Movement 135
Broederbond *see* Afrikaner Broederbond
Broer Matie (film) 114–115, 162, 165
Broodryk, Chris 163, 166, 169, 170
Burger, Fabius (pseudonym) 113 *see also* Pretorius, William

C
Cape Colony 52, 56–57
Cape Town 188, 193
capitalism 8, 80, 134

CASA (Culture in Another South Africa) Conference 137
Castle Lager 129, 141–142
Castrol Motor Oil 141, 145
CCT *see* conservative cultural theory
censorship 2, 113, 117–119, 121, 162, 164, 166, 170, 172
Centre for Communication, Media and Society 137–138
Cetshwayo kaMpande, King 26–27, 36, 39n14
Chakrabarty, Dipesh 191
change 22, 25, 31, 32, 34–37, 110–111
Chapman, Michael 147–148
charity 201–202, 205, 206–207
Charney, Craig 92
Chatterjee, Partha 191
children 200–202, 208–212
Christian Express see *Isigidimi samaXhosa*
Christianity 24, 46, 48–56, 59–60, 168
Chronic Sick Hospital 200, 202, 208
Cinema of Apartheid, The 161
Cinemas of the Mind 120
Circles in the Forest (film) 114
City of God (film) 120
'civilising' enterprise 7–8, 47, 49–51, 56, 131
civil society 138–139
classes 15, 118–119, 136, 148, 171–172, 202, 204
Climate Conference in Paris (2015) 183, 195
Cobley, Alan 72
Codesa *see* Convention for a Democratic South Africa
Coertse, Francois 117
Coka, Jameson G. 73–74, 76
Collini, Stefan 9
colonialism
    Afrikaners and 3
    art and 73
    'civilising' enterprise 7–8, 47, 49–51, 56, 131
    decolonisation 15, 61, 89, 129, 147, 185
    eugenics 207–208
    'honest colonialism' 114, 115
    intellectualism and 2, 23–25, 36, 46–51, 54–57, 89

    oral traditions and 28–34
    post-colonialism 147–149, 185, 191–192
Colors (magazine) 117
'Colour Line in South Africa, The' (article) 6
columns 87–88, 90–91, 93–102, 116, 120
Comaroff, Jean 47
Comaroff, John 47
Combs, James 90–91
comedy 114–116, 118, 168–169, 172
    see also satire
commercial pressures 110, 114, 117–119, 121, 166
communities 94–95, 100, 204–205
Congress of South African Trade Unions (Cosatu) 134
Conservation of Culture Conference (1988) 139–144
conservatism 118, 139–141, 168, 170
conservative cultural theory (CCT) 130, 133–136, 137, 139–140, 141
Convention for a Democratic South Africa (Codesa) 137–138, 139, 148
COP21 *see* Climate Conference in Paris (2015)
Cosatu *see* Congress of South African Trade Unions
courts 27–28
Couzens, Tim 70
Covid-19 pandemic 15
crafts vs arts 78–79
Creary, Nicholas 89
cricket 204–205
Cringe, the Beloved Country 116
Critical Arts 15, 131
Cruising (film) 120
Cry, the Beloved Country (film) 116
cultural assimilation 56, 61
cultural boycott of South Africa 112–113, 137
cultural identity 48–50
cultural policy 129, 137–147, 148–149
Cultural Reconstruction and Development initiative 142
culture and power 135
Culture and Resistance Conference (1982) 135, 136–137

Culture in Another South Africa (CASA) Conference 137
culture wars 4–5

D
Dancyger, Ken 160
Davis, Bette 110
Dead Poets Society (film) 112
'death-making' 212–213
debate and dialogue 36, 45, 50, 54, 87–90, 143–145, 148–149, 184
decolonisation 15, 61, 89, 129, 147, 185
Defiant Ones, The (film) 111
dehumanisation 207–208, 212–213
De Jager, Sallas 164
democracy 2, 139
Department of Arts, Culture, Science and Technology 139
Desert Diners (film) 117
destigmatisation *see* stigma of asylums and mental illness
Devil Finds Work, The 110–111
De Villiers, Dirk 167
Dhlomo, Herbert I.E. 71
Dhlomo, Rolfes Robert R. 78–79
dialogue *see* debate and dialogue
differences 142–143
Dingane, King 22, 28–29, 35, 40n22
Dinuzulu, King 24, 25, 33
documentary films 119
Dodds, Dr 204–205
domestic workers 194–195
drag 167, 170, 171
Dube, John Langalibalele 23, 24–26, 33–37
Duff, Alistair 91
Duncan, Jane 10
Dutch Reformed Church 135, 166
Du Toit, Marie 161

E
Eagleton, Terry 109
Early African Intellectuals (documentary) 47
Earthquake (film) 119
education 45, 48–51, 54–56, 61, 75, 78–79, 210
Edwards, Iain 133, 139–140
Empire Exhibition (1936) 80

Engels, Friedrich 130
English language 50, 55–56, 61
'enlightenment' 47, 185
Equal Airtime project 181–182
Erfgenaam, Die (film) 160
escapism 114–116
Esterhuizen, Willie 166
ethnographic texts 37–38
eugenics 207–208
evaluation 111–112, 121
Exorcist, The (film) 111
experts 4, 10, 89

F
fake news 5
Fallism 129 *see also* Rhodes Must Fall movement
Fanon, Frantz 89
Federation of South African Trade Unions (Fosatu) 132, 134
#FeesMustFall protests 193–194
Felshin, Nina 180
film criticism 13, 108–113, 119–121
  see also Pretorius, William
film industry 12–13, 135, 167
Financial Mail 93
Fort England Mirror 200, 203, 205–207
Fosatu *see* Federation of South African Trade Unions
Foucault, Michel 3, 138, 191
Fourie, Pieter J. 113, 160
France 111, 182–183
Freddie's in Love (film) 160
Free Church of Scotland 44–45, 58, 61, 65n39
Freedom Charter 139–140
'FreeWheeling' column 116, 120
Fruit (play) 189
functionalism 132
Fuze, Magema Magwaza 23–26, 32–33, 35–37, 54

G
Gauteng Mental Marathon Project 213
Gavshon, Harriet 113
gay characters 170–171
General Intellects 5
George V, King, statue of 144

Ghent University, conference at 193–195
Giannetti, Louis 120
Gibson, Mel 119
Giliomee, Hermann 131
Glasgow Missionary Society 52
Godard, Jean-Luc 111
Gods Must Be Crazy, The (film) 118
Goosen, Jeanne 160, 171
Gorbachev, Mikhail 138
Gordimer, Nadine 136
Goris, Yannicke 182
Gouldner, Alvin 3
Gova, Mzi 47
Government of National Unity 137–138
governments 136, 138–139, 148, 186–188
Gqoba, William Wellington 47, 49, 50, 53
graffiti 181–182, 195
Grahamstown Journal, The 202
Grahamstown Lunatic Asylum 200–207, 212
Gramsci, Antonio 132, 134, 137, 184–186, 191
Grayling, A.C. 2
Greenlees, Thomas Duncan 200–221
    Chronic Sick Hospital 200, 202, 208
    'death-making' 212–213
    Fort England Mirror 200, 203, 205–207
    Grahamstown Lunatic Asylum 200–207, 212
    Institute for Imbecile Children 200, 202, 208–212
    Janus-faced nature of 14, 201–202, 212
    Law's pinboard approach 201, 212
    professional face of 200–202, 207–208, 212
    public face of 200–207, 212–213
    stigma of asylums and mental illness 201, 202–203, 205–207
Greig, Robert 113
Grensbasis 13 (film) 115
Griffith, D.W. 110–111
Groen Faktor, Die (film) 114–115, 159, 161–166
Guha, Ranajit 191–192
'gun to the pen' 46, 48–51, 90
Gwala, Harry (Mphephethwa) Themba 7–8

H
Hadland, Adrian 91
Hair (stage musical) 120–121
Haupt, Adam 5–6
Hayman, Graham 137, 147
Hiddlestone, Jane 191, 192
historical consciousness 25, 32, 35–38, 45–47, 191–192
historic significant events 62–63, 135
'histories' of art 69–70
history and the future 144–145
Hollander, Saskia 182
Holland, Francois 182
Holt, Alex 142
homelands 7–8
homes, art in 75–76
'honest colonialism' 114, 115
Hopkins, Pat 116
horror genre 119
Hough, Barrie 108
How to Read a Film 120
HSRC *see* Human Sciences Research Council
Hughes, Heather 24
Huisgenoot 135
humanities 8–10
Human Sciences Research Council (HSRC) 137–138
humour *see* comedy; satire
Humour and Irony in Dutch Post-War Fiction Film 168
Hunter, Ian 138
hypocrisy 162, 166, 168, 169

I
identity 2, 51, 55, 56, 170
Ikwezi 53
Ilanga lase Natal 24–25, 35, 68, 71, 89–90
imagination 54
imperialism 8, 207
Imvo Zabantsundu 53, 54, 57, 71
Indaba 53
independent intellectuals 187–188
Indian nationalism 191–192
indigenous churches 63
indigenous governance 29, 34
indigenous iconography 145–147

indigenous languages 11, 55–57, 60–61, 142
indigenous people 46–53, 61, 88, 192
individuality 211–212
inequality 70
Infecting the City Festival (2015) 190
Inkanyiso 24, 25, 54
Inkatha 144
Insila kaShaka 25, 35
Institute for Imbecile Children 200, 202, 208–212
Institute for the Creative Arts 193
institutional affiliation 187–188
Ipepa lo Hlanga 24
Isibuto Samavo 53
Isigidimi samaXhosa 52–55, 59
Isithunywa Senyanga 53
isiXhosa 49–54, 56–57, 59–60
isiZulu 23–28, 34, 36–38
Issit, John 158
I Write What I Like 6, 57
Izwi Labantu 53

J
Jabavu, John Tengo 47, 53, 54–55, 90
Jackson, Duncan 158
Jameson, Fredric 121
Jannie Totsiens (film) 160, 165
Jantshi kaNongila 31–32, 34, 37
Janus-faced nature of Dr Greenlees 201–202, 212
Jivkova-Semova, Dimitrina 182
Joe Dirt (film) 118
Jordan, Archibald Campbell 52, 56
journalism 11–12, 45, 52–53, 110
journalists 71–73, 87, 91–93
Joynt, Shaun 166
JR (French artist) 183
Judt, Tony 158
'Just for Today' column 93

K
Kaalgat tussen die Daisies (film) 159, 166–171
Kabali-Kagwa, Faye 189, 190–191, 193
Kaffir Express 52, 53
Kakutani, Michiko 4–5
Kandidaat, Die (film) 162, 165

Karvellas, Greg 188
KASI RC *see* Khayelitsha Art School & Rehabilitation Centre
Katrina (film) 159, 165
Kavanagh, Robert 131, 132–133
Keeble, Richard 88
Khayelitsha 179–180, 189–190
Khayelitsha Art School & Rehabilitation Centre (KASI RC) 180, 190, 195
Kies, Benjamin 7–8
Kirkwood, Mike 131
Klaaste, Aggrey 86–107
    columns of 87–88, 95–102
    death of 95
    detention of 92
    as editor of *Sowetan* 93–101
    legacy of 12, 102
    media and intellectuals 87–91
    nation-building 86–88, 91–102
Klocke, Astrid 165–166
Koloane, David Nthubu 68
Krauss, Rosalind 180
Kruger, Paul 141
KwaZulu-Natal region, intellectual thought in 21–43
    change 22, 25, 31, 32, 34–37
    Dube, John Langalibalele 23, 24–26, 33–37
    Fuze, Magema Magwaza 23–26, 32–33, 35–37, 54
    isiZulu 23–28, 34, 36–38
    Mhuyi kaThimuni 30–31, 34, 37
    Mokoena, Hlonipha 23–24, 32, 35–36, 39n13
    Ndlovu kaThimuni 28–37, 40n22
    Ndukwana kaMbengwana 29–32, 34, 40n21, 41n24
    newspapers 52–55, 59
    oral traditions 11, 21–23, 26–38
    reconciling past with present 22–24, 26–27, 30–31, 34–37
    writings of intellectuals 21–26, 34–38
kykNET 114

L
labour 209–210
land dispossession 47, 48

languages 3, 36–38, 52, 55–57, 60–61, 186–187
Latakgomo, Joe 92
Law, John, pinboard approach of 201, 212
Lawrence of Arabia (film) 111
laws 30, 71
Lead SA 179
Leon, Gabriella 180–181
Lesabe, Lilford 179
liberal politics 57, 139–140
Life Esidimeni 213
Lingenfelder, Charl-Johan 169–170
Lippard, Lucy 180
Lipstiek Dipstiek (film) 166
London Missionary Society (LMS) 49, 53
Longcast, W.K. 26
Long Night's Journey into Day (documentary) 119
Lovedale College 44–45, 53, 55, 58–59
Lovedale mission station 49, 52, 60
Lovedale Press 53
Lyk Lollery (film) 117

M

Mabe, Sam 93, 96
Mabutyana, Bulelani 189
Macfarlan Mission 58
Macmillan's Magazine 24, 26
Mail & Guardian 109, 113, 121
Maine, Sir Henry 50
Makgoba, Malegapuru 213
Makhanda *see* Grahamstown Lunatic Asylum
Makiwane, Elijah 44–67
  as Africanist scholar 55–57
  as architect of gender studies 51
  childhood of 44–45
  as church minister 44–45, 58–59
  'gun to the pen' 46, 48–51
  historical context 46–51
  legacy of 11, 45, 59–63
  as multidimensional figure 55, 62–63
  as newspaper editor 45, 52–55
  as politician 57–58
  as teacher 45, 58–59
  transculturation of 47–48
  as vernacular language proponent 55–57

Makukhanye Art Room 179–180, 189–191, 193
Makukhanye Entertainment Act Group 179
Malema, Julius 6, 11
Mamdani, Mahmood 50
Mamza (film) 115
Mancoba, Ernest 80
Mandela, Nelson 45, 60, 98, 139
Mandimila Casting Agency 195
Mantel der Liefde, De (film) 168
marginalised groups 2, 110, 181, 193–195
Mari and Kana (performance art installation and physical theatre) 190
Marikana massacre 14, 190
market values 110, 114, 117–119, 121, 166
Marxism 130, 132–133, 136, 137, 191
Maseko, Len 94
Mashilo, David 159
Masilela, Ntongela 54, 57, 60
Mass Democratic Movement (MDM) 131–132, 134–135, 138
Mazrui, Alamin 56
Mbonambi, Phakama 86, 92
MDM *see* Mass Democratic Movement
meaning construction 182
media 70–72, 87–91, 130, 132, 193–194
Media Workers Association of South Africa (Mwasa) 92–93
Medu Art Ensemble 137
memorials 48, 62–63 *see also* monuments
mental illness, stigma of 201, 202–203, 205–207
Merrifield, Andy 4–5, 9
Mesías-Lema, José María 179, 181
Meyer, Rudi 112
Mgwali Mission Station 51
Mhudi 7
Mhuyi kaThimuni 30–31, 34, 37
middle class 202, 204
Mills, Charles Wright 187–188
Mishra, Pankaj 2
missionaries 24, 47–54, 89–90
M-Net 114
modernity 26, 46–48, 50–53, 55, 60, 134
Mohl, John 73

Mokoena, Hlonipha 23–24, 32, 35–36, 39n13, 54, 89–90
Monaco, James 120
monuments 139–145 *see also* memorials
Moore, Kate-Lyn 193
More, Mabogo Percy 7
Moss, Glenn 133, 136
Mouffe, Chantal 132, 142
movie reviews *see* film criticism
Movies, Moguls, Mavericks 114, 115
Mqhayi, S.E.K. 47, 49, 50, 58, 60
Mr Bones (film) 118
Msimanga, Nondumiso 183–184
Msimang, Sisonke 6
Mudli kaNkwelo kaNdaba 28, 37
Muthien, Yvonne 7
Mwasa *see* Media Workers Association of South Africa
Mzimba, Pambani 44, 58, 65n39

N
Nando's 129, 141, 146, 148
Naremore, James 111
Nash, Andrew 143
Nasionale Pers 91
Nathan, Jeremy 112
nationalism 25, 56, 61, 63, 166, 169, 191–192
National Party (NP) 80, 162–164, 172
National Union of South African Students (Nusas) 133–134, 140
nation-building 12, 45, 86–88, 91–102
'Nation Building manifesto' 94, 100
Nation, The 6
Native Americans 145–147
Native Educational Association 55
nativism 50–51
Ndebele, Njabulo S. 2, 15, 131
Ndletyana, Mcebisi 1–2, 49
Ndlovu kaThimuni 28–37, 40n22
Ndukwana kaMbengwana 29–32, 34, 40n21, 41n24
New African Movement 57, 60, 63, 79, 82n16
New Nation 90
News24 116
newspapers 52–55, 59, 69
New York Times 8

NGOs *see* non-governmental organisations
Ngũgĩ wa Thiong'o 6–7, 46, 61, 89
Nicodemus, Everlyn 69
Nijenhuis, Jenny 183–184
Nimmo, Dan 90–91
Nofal, Emil 159, 161–162, 165, 166–167, 172
Noko, Paul 189
Nongila 32
non-governmental organisations (NGOs) 213
Not for Profit 9
NP *see* National Party
Nusas *see* National Union of South African Students
Nussbaum, Martha 9

O
Odendaal, André 45, 48, 53–54
Oh Schucks ... Here Comes UNTAG (film) 115
Olsen, Lance 165
'one man, one vote' 57–58
'On the Line' column 87–88, 93–102
'open society' 57
oral traditions 21–23, 26–38
organic intellectuals 184–185
Ortiz Fernández, Fernando 46
otherness 55, 136, 209–212
overproduction 9

P
Passion of the Christ, The (film) 119
pastoralism 134, 145
patient labour 209–210
patriarchy 116, 185
Pawpaw vir My Darling, 'n (film) 171–172
peaceful resistance 183
Pelem, Meshach 57, 62
perestroika 138
Perkins, V.F. 111–112, 117
Perskor 91
Peterson, Bhekizizwe 11, 38
Philander, Soli 169–170, 171
philanthropy *see* charity
pinboard approach, of John Law 201, 212
Plaatje, Solomon 7
Plomin, Robert 78

politics 4–6, 14–15, 22, 32–38, 57–58,
       114–115, 187–188
Poole, J. Ruscombe 26
'poor white' Afrikaners 171–172
popular culture 117–118, 131
'popular' vs 'serious' art criticism 70, 74–77
Posner, Richard 165, 171
Post 92, 93
post-colonialism 147–149, 185, 191–192
post-Marxism 130, 132–133, 142
postmodern satire 165–166
power and culture 135
Poyner, Jane 2–3
Pratt, Mary Louise 46
Presbyterian Church 58, 61
press *see* media
Pretexts 131
Pretoria City Council 140–141
Pretorius, William 108–128
    on Afrikaans films 112–118
    on American films 118–121
    on 'bad' films 117
    on censorship 113, 117–119, 121
    film criticism and 13, 108–113, 120–121
    as politically committed film critic
         109–110, 113, 121
    on popular culture 117–118
    writings of 108–109, 113
'primitive art' 78–79
printmaking 83n26
professionalism 4, 10
Proteus (film) 121
pseudonyms 71–72, 76
public debate 36, 45, 50, 54, 87–90,
       143–145, 148–149, 180, 184
public intellectualism
    definitions of 3–5
    kinds of 5–8, 195
public intellectuals, definitions of 10, 89,
       158–159
public sphere 21, 89
punditry 90–91

R
race relations 15, 54, 57–58, 69, 115,
       133–134, 136, 147, 164–165
Raeburn, Michael 172
rainbow nation 146

Raleigh, Paul 161, 162
Ramaphosa, Cyril 14
Ramgobin, Mewa 129–157
    career of 129–130
    Conservation of Culture Conference
         (1988) 139–144
    conservative cultural theory (CCT) 130,
         133–136, 137, 139–140, 141
    cultural policy and 13, 129, 137–147,
         148–149
    Culture and Resistance Conference
         (1982) 135, 136–137
    legacy of 129–130, 149
    monuments 139–145
    post-coloniality 147–149
    victimhood 131
Ramsden, Ché 181
rape 183–184
Rapport 108, 113
Rautenbach, Jans 158–162, 165, 172
reconciliation 144, 148–149
reconstruction 142–143
Regina Mundi Catholic Church 94,
       100–101
religion 166, 168
'Removing Apartheid' conference 193–195
'report back' tactic 97
representation 118, 136, 187
Representations of the Intellectual 3
Ressa, Maria 11
Rhodes Must Fall movement 129, 141, 143,
       147, 149, 193–194
Rhodes Trust 144–145
Robinson, Sir Hercules 26–27
Rodowick, David 163
Roets, Matthys Jacobus (Koos) 158–178
    Afrikaner community and 158–159,
         172
    career of 159–160
    censorship 162, 164, 166, 170, 172
    comedy 168–169, 172
    Groen Faktor, Die (film) 114–115, 159,
         161–166
    Kaalgat tussen die Daisies (film) 159,
         166–171
    legacy of 13, 158–159, 172
    Pawpaw vir My Darling, 'n (film)
         171–172

235

Roets, Matthys Jacobus (Koos) (*continued*)
   as public intellectual 158–159
   satire 164–171
Romare, Kristian 69
Rompel, Hans 135
Ronge, Barry 108, 113
Roodt, Darrell James 116
Rossouw, Cobus 160, 161
Rubusana, W.B.M. 47, 50, 53, 57–58
rugby 145
Rule, Peter 7
Runqu, Siphosethu 179
Ryklief, Shifaan 180

S
Sachs, Albie 131, 136–137, 147
SAFTTA Journal, The 115
Said, Edward 3–4, 87, 89, 90, 184–188, 195
Saint Helena 24, 33
Samuelson, R.C.A. 27
SANC *see* South African Natives Congress
Sandwith, Corinne 8
SA's Dirty Laundry (artivism campaign) 183–184
SASO *see* South African Student Organisation
satire 164–171 *see also* comedy
Schechter, Ruth 6
Schreiner, Olive 6
Schuster, Leon 115, 118
Scott, A.O. 110, 111, 121
Scott, John 164–165
screenplays 161
Sebidi, Lebamang 98
segregation 193–195
Seme, Pixley ka Isaka 49
Senzangakhona 31
'serious' vs 'popular' art criticism 70, 74–77
sex in cinema 118
sex workers 181–182
shack theatre, Makukhanye Art Room 179–180, 189–191, 193
Shaka, King 22, 25, 28–29, 31, 34–35, 37, 144
Sheikh, Simon 182
Shepherd, Robert 59
She Stoops to Conquer (play) 72
Showmax 115

Sindo, Mandisi 179–199
   as artivist 13–14, 179–181, 188–191
   career of 179–180, 195
   character of 188
   KASI RC 180, 190, 195
   in Khayelitsha 179–180, 189–190
   Makukhanye Art Room 179–180, 189–191, 193
   subalterns and 188, 191–195
Sipika 31
Sisonke Sex Worker Movement 181–182
S'ketch 131
Skota, Mweli 44, 58
Sobukwe, Robert Mangaliso 60, 98, 100
social classes *see* classes
social place for the Other 209–210
sociopolitical context 110–114, 119
Soga, T.B. 62–63
Soga, Tiyo 2, 47, 49, 51, 53
Sol Plaatje 7
Soudien, Crain 8
South African Associated Newspapers 91
South African Breweries 141–142
South African Medical Journal 200, 207
South African Natives Congress (SANC) 57–58
South African Student Organisation (SASO) 57, 133
South African Theatre Journal 131
South Africa's Dirty Laundry (artivism campaign) 183–184
Soviet Union 138, 143
Sowell, Thomas 4
Sowetan see also Klaaste, Aggrey
   circulation of 87–88, 94–95
   columns in 95–102
   history of 12, 86–88, 91–95
Soweto Uprising (1976) 92, 193
Speak 131
Speaking of Universities 9
specialised language 3, 186–187
Spivak, Gayatri 192–193
Spur 129, 143, 145–147, 148
Square, Die (film) 161
Staffrider 131
'Standing March, The' (video projection) 183
Star, The 72, 87, 93

statues 141, 143–144
Steadman, Ian 132
stereotypes 146, 187–188, 204–205
Ster Kinekor 167
Steyn, M.T., statue of 143–144
stigma of asylums and mental illness 201, 202–203, 205–207
Stopping the Spies 10
storytelling 27, 190, 201
structuralism 136
Stuart, James 28–36, 40n21, 41n24, 60
Stubbs, Aelred 57
Studentebond *see* Afrikaans Studentebond
subalterns 186–188, 191–195
Subaltern Studies Collective 181, 191–193
Suid-Afrikaan, Die 131
Sunday Star 95
Sunday Times 108
Sun, The 95
surveillance 10
Switzer, Donna 71
Switzer, Les 71
'symbolic goods' 158–160

T
talent 77–79
'Talk upon My Native Land, A' (pamphlet) 25
Taylor, Charles 89
Taylor, Steven J. 209, 210
television 114–116, 140–141
terrorist attacks, France 182–183
Theatre as Cultural Struggle 132–133
theatre sector 132, 188–190, 193
Thema, Selope 57, 60, 72, 82n10, 82n16
Thimuni kaMudli 28–29, 31–32, 37, 40n22
Thirteen Days (film) 120
Thloloe, Joe 94
Tissong, Mike 94
Titanic (film) 119
Tomaselli, Keyan G. 9, 88, 113, 161, 166, 172
Towards a People's Culture Arts Festival 137
townships 188–190, 193–194
tracking shots 120
traditional artists 136
traditional intellectuals 184–185
traditional satire 165–166
traditional societies 25, 60

transculturation 46–48, 51–52
trauma 193
Tredell, Nicolas 120
Triomf (film) 172
Trump, Donald 4–5, 6, 11
Turner, Rick 136, 139
TV *see* television

U
UBJ *see* Union of Black Journalists
ubuntu 97–98, 100
UCT *see* University of Cape Town
UDF *see* United Democratic Front
UFS *see* University of the Free State
Umshumayeli Wendaba 52–53
Umteteli wa Bantu 60, 68
Understanding Movies 120
Union of Black Journalists (UBJ) 92, 94
United Democratic Front (UDF) 93, 130, 131–132, 133–134, 142
United States 110, 112–113, 118–121, 180
unity 96
universities 8–10, 15, 131–133
University of Cape Town (UCT) 129, 143–144, 193
University of KwaZulu-Natal 137–138, 144
University of the Free State (UFS) 143–144
urbanisation 27, 134–135
US *see* United States
utopian thinking 136, 139

V
value 9, 147
values 46
Van der Kamp, Johannes 49
Van Nierop, Leon 108, 166
Van Rensburg, Manie 160, 161
Van Robbroeck, Lize 69–70
Vergunst, Nicolaas 140
vernacular languages 55–57, 60–61
Verstraten, Peter 168, 171
victimhood 131
victimology 144, 147–148
voting rights 57–58

W
war films 115, 116
Wark, McKenzie 5

Warner, Basil 159
Warner, Michael 88
wars 48–49, 80
Wasserman, Herman 110, 111
Wauchope, Isaac 46
Webb, Colin 26
Western art criticism 69, 81
Western world 1–2, 8, 46, 54–56, 77–79, 83n38
What Are Universities For? 9
white Afrikaans-speaking audiences 114, 116–118, 170, 172
White, Armond 120
white capital 70–72, 88, 91
white middle class 202, 204, 208
whiteness 57, 207
white supremacy 49, 56
Wild Season (film) 159
Willan, Brian 7
Williams, Donovan 51
Williams, John 147
Wolfensberger, Wolf 212–213
women 51, 75–76
World, The 12, 86, 90, 92
Worst of Both Worlds (play) 189
Wright, John 26
writings of early intellectuals 21–26, 34–38

X
Xhosa Express see *Isigidimi samaXhosa*
Xhosa language 49–54, 56–57, 59–60
Xhosa people 49, 55
Xulu, Philip 54

Y
YouTube 170–171

Z
Zabalaza Theatre Festival 189
Zulu language 23–28, 34, 36–38
Zulu people 24–34
Zulu Society 25
Zuma, Jacob 14, 148

www.ingramcontent.com/pod-product-compliance
Lightning Source LLC
Chambersburg PA
CBHW020904080526
44589CB00011B/434